South and Southwest

South and Southwest

Literary Essays and Reminiscences

by Jay B. Hubbell

Professor Emeritus of American Literature in Duke University

Chairman of the Board of Editors of AMERICAN LITERATURE, *1928-1954*

Duke University Press, Durham, North Carolina   1965

© 1965, Duke University Press. Library of Congress Catalogue Card number 65-26839. Printed in the United States of America by the Seeman Printery, Durham, N. C.

Acknowledgments

For permission to reprint certain materials in this book I make grateful acknowledgments to the following: Mr. Ashbel G. Brice, Editor and Director of the Duke University Press, for the chapter on Ralph Waldo Emerson and a few brief passages from *The South in American Literature, 1607-1900* (1954); Professor John H. Fisher, Secretary of the Modern Language Association, for "Vignette III," which appeared in *PMLA* in September, 1951; Professor Norman Foerster for "The Frontier in American Literature," first published in *The Reinterpretation of American Literature* (1928); Professor Clarence Gohdes, Chairman of the Board of Editors of *American Literature*, for "John Cotton: The Poet-Historian of Bacon's Rebellion," which was first published in that magazine in May, 1938, under the title "John and Ann Cotton of 'Queen's Creek,' Virginia"; Professor William B. Hamilton, Managing Editor of the *South Atlantic Quarterly*, for two essays: "Cavaliers and Indentured Servants in Virginia" and "Jesse Holmes the Fool-Killer," which appeared in the *Quarterly* in January, 1927, and October, 1937, under somewhat different titles: "Cavalier and Indentured Servants in Virginia Fiction" and "Charles Napoleon Bonaparte Evans: Creator of Jesse Holmes the Fool-Killer"; Miss Charlotte Kohler, Editor of the *Virginia Quarterly Review*, for "*The Virginians* of William Makepeace Thackeray," which appeared in the *Review* in January, 1927, under a different title, "Thackeray and Virginia"; President George M. Modlin of the University of Richmond for "The Southern Literary Renaissance," which under the title "Contemporary Southern Literature" first appeared in a booklet entitled *Addresses Commemorating the One Hundred Twenty-fifth Anniversary [of the] University of Richmond, 1830-1955* (1955); Mr. Robert L. Montgomery, Jr., Managing Editor of *Texas Studies in Literature and Language*, for "Edgar Allan Poe and the South," which was first published in that magazine in the Summer number, 1960, under the title "Edgar Allan Poe and the Southern Literary Tradition"; Mr. William M. E. Rachal, Editor of the *Virginia Magazine of History and Biography*, for "The Smith-Pocahontas Literary Legend," which appeared in that magazine in July, 1957; Mr. Decherd Turner, Jr., Editor of the *Southwest Review*, for "*Southwest Review*, 1924-1927," which was published in the Winter, 1965, number of the *Review*.

To

The Memory of

Reverend David Shelton Hubbell

Ruth Eller Hubbell

and

Judge William Jordan Joseph Smith

Ada Williams Smith

". . . *whatsoever things are true, whatsoever things are honest, whatsoever things are just, whatsoever things are pure, whatsoever things are lovely, whatsoever things are of good report. . . ."*

Philippians, iv. 8

There is
One great society alone on earth,
The noble Living and the noble Dead.

Wordsworth, *The Prelude,* xi, 394

Vignette III

[Vignette III was written by Lewis Leary, now head of the English and Comparative Literature Department at Columbia University, and William R. Parker, who in 1951 was Secretary of the Modern Language Association and Editor of *PMLA*. The Vignette appeared in the FMO ("For Members Only") section in *PMLA*, Vol, LXVI, No. 5 (September, 1951).]

Jay B. Hubbell of Duke, Vice President of the Association this year and member of the Executive Council 1946-49, has long been known as "the Judge" among younger colleagues who liked and admired him but did not dare use his first name. (Years ago, in Texas, he was judge of a series of scholastic poetry contests.) A Virginian who married a Texan, he is quiet spoken, almost shy, but with a ramrod up his back and dogged persistence when he sees something that needs to be done. A leader in the MLA American Literature Group, he was one of the founders of the quarterly, *American Literature*, which he has managed and left his imprint on for the last twenty-two years. His anthology, *American Life in Literature*, was chosen above others during the last war to be reprinted in armed services editions, and his magnum opus, a history of Southern literature, will soon be published. As a teacher he has been much beloved for his gentle enthusiasm; his undergraduate course in American literature is popularly known at Duke as "Hubbell's English," and it has grown so large that it has to be split into three big sections. He himself probably does not know how many doctoral dissertations he has directed, but he takes quiet pride in the continued productivity of his former students. Among his other pleasures are gardening, Poe, painting kitchen cabinets, telling foreigners about American literature (he taught at the University of Vienna in 1949 and 1950), and a granddaughter who is the apple of his eye. Last June he was made a Doctor of Letters by Southern Methodist University. A colleague recently said of him: "He knows more and carries his knowledge more gracefully than anyone else I know."

[This is the third in a series of word-portraits of members of the Council. For much of the above our thanks go to L. L.—ED.]

Vignette

Preface

In this volume I have brought together some unpublished pieces and a few of my many scattered articles that I wish to appear in book form. I have entitled the book *South and Southwest* because so many of the sixteen essays are in one way or another intimately connected with the two regions in which most of my life has been spent.

The first three essays and the fifteenth are to a large extent autobiographical. They concern my professional life as teacher, editor, and author; and they are based not so much upon my memory as upon letters and documents of various kinds that I have consulted in order to keep the record accurate. The nine essays in the second group are historical and literary studies which supplement the materials in my earlier books, *The South in American Literature* and *Southern Life in Fiction*. The two essays in the third group deal with life and literature in the West, a subject which has greatly interested me ever since I first saw the region in 1915. The two essays in the fourth group are concerned with two different kinds of teaching problems. The first of these records some of my experiences as a lecturer to students at the University of Vienna. The final essay deals with the difficult problem presented by the gifted undergraduate student who wants to be a writer and looks for guidance to the Department of English.

Those essays which have already appeared in print—most of them in periodicals where the reader of today is not likely to have seen them—have been revised, brought up to date, and in some instances enlarged by the inclusion of new materials. Although I have omitted nearly all of the numerous footnotes which those articles published in scholarly journals contained, my headnotes include some of the information contained in those footnotes. They also give place and date of publication so that any scholar who may wish fuller documentation will know where to look for it.

One essay which I had planned to include in this volume is now being expanded into a little book which I have tentatively entitled *Our Literary "Immortals": A Study of the Changing American Literary Canon*. Later I may publish more reminiscences of my professional life. At Harvard, Columbia, and other universities it was my good fortune to know some very able scholars and teachers. I have been fortunate enough also to know three of the best-known American poets: Vachel Lindsay, Carl Sandburg, and Robert Frost. The literary renaissance of the 1920's and 1930's in which these writers played an important part was accompanied by a remarkable upsurge of interest among scholars in the study and teaching of American literature. It was my good luck, as I have indicated in the first two essays in this book, to have a part in that movement.

I am indebted for many helpful suggestions to Mr. Ashbel G. Brice, Director of the Duke University Press, and to two fine scholars who read this book in manuscript: Floyd Stovall, Edgar Allan Poe Professor of English at the University of Virginia, and Richard Beale Davis, Alumni Distinguished Service Professor of American Literature in the University of Tennessee. I am also indebted to my wife, Lucinda S. Hubbell, and to my son, Jay B. Hubbell, Jr., who have given the book a critical reading in manuscript and galley proof.

I am indebted to the Duke University Research Council for clerical assistance and for a subsidy in aid of publication.

JAY B. HUBBELL

Duke University
Durham, North Carolina
March 7, 1965

Contents

I. Reminiscences

The power of writing one fine line transcends all the Able-Editor ability in the ably-edited Universe.

EDWARD FITZGERALD, *Letters*

SOUTHWEST REVIEW, 1924-1927

[In October, 1955, the *Southwest Review*, then edited by Allen Maxwell, published its 40th Anniversary number with reminiscences by Lon Tinkle, the late J. Frank Dobie, and Henry Nash Smith. Mr. Maxwell also reprinted editorial statements of policy by four of his predecessors, of whom I was one. The Anniversary number, covering four decades, gave only a sketchy account of the *Review* during the three years when I was one of its editors, and it did not tell the story of the transfer of the *Review* from Austin to Dallas in 1924.

When I read the Anniversary number, it seemed to me that some of the contributors did not realize how many of the continuing features of the *Review* were initiated during the three years when George Bond, Herbert Gambrell, and I were its editors. And yet as I look back now, I cannot always distinguish between ideas and policies that originated with me and those suggested by Mr. Bond, Mr. Gambrell, or Professor John H. McGinnis, who was primarily responsible for my coming to S.M.U. in 1915. For several years before 1924 McGinnis as literary editor of the Dallas *News* had done his best to cultivate in the Southwest an appreciation of its writers, and he cherished a hope that these would be followed by others of greater importance. In 1927, when I left for Duke University, he took over as the chief editor. He had the loyal support of some of our ablest students, notably John Chapman, Lon Tinkle, and Henry Nash Smith. We were a small group of friends and lovers of literature who shared with one another our ideas and our hopes; hence it is difficult to be sure who it was that suggested the two series of articles on Southwestern cities and on art in the Southwest. Furthermore, we were certainly influenced by some of the members of our Advisory Board, especially Witter Bynner and J. Frank Dobie.]

1

The *Texas Review* was founded in 1915 by Stark Young, who at that time was Professor of General Literature in the University of Texas. Young's ambition was to put out a literary magazine, not a critical review like the *Sewanee Review* or the *South Atlantic Quarterly*. What he particularly desired was excellent verse and light essays; he did not want learned articles by college professors. He was fortunate enough to get from England contributions from Maurice Hewlett, Edmund Gosse, and Gilbert Murray and in this country from Carl Van Doren, Madison Cawein, and Max Eastman. In the opening number the editor stated his policies in an informal essay entitled "On Reeking of the Soil," from which I quote:

> The *Texas Review* comes into the world with no mission, nothing so flamboyant or remonstrant or overt. It has in mind the law of thought and life and letters only; neither to upset nor convert the world, but only to speak with it in its finer and quieter moments. And this review does not dream—it cannot—of great popularity, with subscribers and revolutions, or of pleasing the general, for what begins on nothing but the wish to please the general, ends in being pleased by them.
>
> For the birth of such a venture no small amount of advice was asked, and sometimes taken: to include poetry in a respectable proportion to the other matter; to combine articles of varied interest; to eschew book reviews that are perfunctory and done on a formulary; to open on occasion the doors of our pages without the key of Phi Beta Kappa. The strongest advice, however, and the most assured, was to let your magazine reek of the soil.

The editor, however, had no intention of letting the *Texas Review* reek of the soil; he had, he said, no confidence in "the Burbank method applied to art." And so, he wrote, "The *Texas Review* asks of the critic and of some provincial citizens of the world, patience if we do not always reek." The passing of time and the emergence of new literary fashions were to have their influence upon the author of the as-yet-unwritten *So Red the Rose*. There is something very like "reeking of the soil" in "Not in Memoriam, but in Defense," the essay which Mr. Young in 1930 contributed to the symposium, *I'll Take My Stand*.

After publishing just two numbers of the *Texas Review*, Mr. Young was called to Amherst College. When he departed, his successor found in the editorial cupboard only scanty materials for future numbers. Apparently no one in the university faculty coveted the post of editor, and so a successor was drafted from the English department. This was the late Robert Adger Law, a Shakespearean scholar of some eminence, a fine teacher, and a man of excellent literary taste. Unfortunately for the *Review*, however, the new editor had a strong repugnance to soliciting contributions; and since he could not pay for articles, he soon found himself unable to keep the quality of the *Review* up to the standard set in the first two numbers. As time went on, the *Texas Review* became somewhat more like other university quarterlies. It published some excellent articles, chiefly by professors, and some admirable poems by Karle Wilson Baker.

Early in 1921 I sent to the *Texas Review* a brief article which I entitled "On 'Southern Literature.'" The editor promptly wrote me that he would print my article if the *Review* was not discontinued, as he thought it would be. It then naturally occurred to me that if the University of Texas was going to drop the *Review*, we should ask to have it transferred to Southern Methodist University. I discussed the matter with some of my English colleagues, and then with their approval I took the project to some member of the administration. He looked favorably upon it. We all felt that the *Texas Review* would bring prestige to a young university, which had first opened its doors in the very year the *Texas Review* was born. I compiled some data to show how little money the university would need to expend upon a literary quarterly. My estimate was much too low.

Meanwhile I had written to Dr. Law that if the *Review* was going to be discontinued, S.M.U. would be glad to take it over and continue it. Dr. Law in reply wrote to me that he had been much encouraged by our good opinion of the quarterly but that to his surprise the University of Texas authorities were not willing to let us have the *Review* and had decided to continue it. "On 'Southern Literature'" appeared in the October number.

Three years later Dr. Law wrote me that the University of Texas had definitely decided to discontinue the *Review* and that if we at S.M.U. still wanted it, we could have it. Dr. Law and I arranged the transfer in August, 1924, while I was teaching in the summer school in Austin. There were, as I remember, no formalities beyond his turning over to me a list of the *Review*'s continuing subscribers. There were disappointingly few of them, and I remember that it struck me as a little ominous that one of the sixteen unexpired subscriptions came from the Southwestern Insane Asylum. I remember also that while I was in Austin that summer the late Walter Prescott Webb, one of the best American historians of our time, told me that he had once suggested to Eugene Manlove Rhodes that he ought to send an article to the *Texas Review*. "Perhaps I will," Rhodes replied. "Send me a copy." After he had looked it over, Rhodes remarked: "This thing is an anachronism."

2

It was a very inexperienced editor who took over the *Texas Review* and somehow managed, in spite of a full teaching load and the various duties of a departmental chairman, to bring out the next number in October, 1924. I was extremely fortunate in securing two very able associates, both former students of mine and recent graduates of S.M.U. My associate editor was George Bond, whose fine group of poems, "Sketches of the Texas Prairie," had won considerable recognition and been republished in the *Texas Review*. Mr. Bond is now Professor of English at S.M.U. My managing editor was Herbert Gambrell, now Chairman of the History Department at his alma mater.

Mr. Bond and Mr. Gambrell agreed with me that we should alter the policy of the *Texas Review* and try for a wider circle of readers and contributors, and so we renamed it the *Southwest Review*. We had first thought of calling it the *Southwestern Review*, but that name too obviously suggested that the new sponsor of the quarterly was Southwestern University in Georgetown. In the early numbers the *Review* carried on its front cover a vignette of Dallas Hall, in the basement of which the *Review* at that time had its office. Ex-President Robert S. Hyer, who would not smoke in his physics laboratory, sometimes dropped in for a smoke and a friendly chat with us. By October, 1925, we had adopted a more appropriate symbol designed for us by Anne Toomey, a cowboy mounted on a mustang. This symbol went through several mutations over the years; it disappeared in 1944 when the magazine adopted a new format. We had no intention of suggesting anything radical when at the printer's suggestion we dressed our first number in a dark red cover which seemed to us beautiful as well as novel. We wanted the university's colors, red and blue, on the cover; but the printer was not able to find a suitable blue ink. It was somewhat later that *Harper's Magazine* appeared with a red cover.

Of the twelve members of our Advisory Board three—John H. McGinnis, John O. Beaty, and Frederick D. Smith—were from the university faculty. Two others who made their homes in Dallas were Hilton Ross Greer, poet and editorial writer on the Dallas *News*, and John William Rogers, literary editor of the Dallas *Times-Herald*, who had served on the editorial staff of Charles Scribner's Sons. From the University of Texas faculty I chose the retiring editor, Dr. Law. I added Mrs. Karle Wilson Baker of Nacogdoches because I rightfully considered her the best living Texas poet. To represent Oklahoma I chose J. Frank Dobie, who was at that time teaching at Oklahoma A. and M. College. He was already vigorously pioneering in the study of the literature and the folklore of the Southwest. It was not long before he returned to the University of Texas. To represent the *Review* in Arkansas, Colorado, and Louisiana, I chose three able professors of English who were friends of mine: Dr. Easley S. Jones, of Boulder, Colorado; John Clark Jordan, of the University of Arkansas; and Pierce Butler, Dean of Newcomb College at Tulane University. As it turned out, we had too many elderly professors on the Advisory Board, but at that time I knew of no important writers in those states. The *Review* was soon to uncover some able young writers in the various states of the Southwest. Mr. Bond and I looked over many of the current magazines hoping

7

to discover among the contributors promising young writers in our part of the country. Jordan and Butler, I remember, were somewhat shocked when they saw the red cover on our first number.

My happiest choice for a member of the Advisory Board was Witter Bynner, who had recently moved to New Mexico. He had lectured in Dallas, and I had met him when he visited the university the next day. He was not only a poet whose contributions—all too few—we valued, but also a man of letters with a wide acquaintance among authors, editors, and publishers. He had been on the staff of *McClure's Magazine,* and he had served as literary advisor to two publishing houses. We soon learned to value every one of the many suggestions that he sent us from Taos. We took his advice and kept as distinctive the red cover which had shocked the elderly professors on the Advisory Board. He secured for us a number of excellent contributions from writers whom he knew, and he told us how much —or rather, how little—we should pay them. It was he who sent us the essay "Pan in America," by D. H. Lawrence, then on an extended visit to Mexico and the Southwest. It appeared in the January, 1926, number.

I do not remember why we had no one on the Advisory Board to represent Arizona, but it may have been because I could think of no writer or professor of English in that state. California no doubt seemed too far off for us to claim it as part of the Southwest. In 1926, however, we got a letter and a poem from the Hawaiian Islands. Clifford Gessler, literary editor of the Honolulu *Star-Bulletin,* wrote somewhat plaintively that "Hawaii is away out here in the sea, more or less lost, as it were; but if we don't belong to the Southwest to what do we belong?" We printed his poem, ". . . Nor Any Man's," in the October, 1926, number.

Reproduced on facing page is the Table of Contents of our first number, which, I have been told, has long been a collector's item in Dallas.

Beginning with our first number we tried to secure a proper balance between articles written by Southwesterners, or articles about the Southwest, and articles from writers in other sections, preferably writers with something like a national reputation. I had asked Gamaliel Bradford to send me one of his admirable pen portraits of historical personages. He replied that after writing for many years

SOUTHWEST REVIEW

VOLUME TEN   OCTOBER, 1924   NUMBER ONE

CONTENTS

JAY B. HUBBELL, Editor

SOUTHWEST REVIEW *is a magazine of discussion. The printing of articles on controversial topics does not imply that either the Editor or the University endorses opinions expressed in these pages.*

Southwest Review, formerly The Texas Review, was founded by the University of Texas in June, 1915, and was transferred to Southern Methodist University in August, 1924. . . . Published quarterly in January, April, July and October. Subscription rate: 50 cents a copy, $2.00 a year. . . . All contributions should be addressed to The Editor of Southwest Review, Southern Methodist University, Dallas, Texas. . . . All business correspondence should be addressed to Herbert Gambrell, Southern Methodist University, Dallas, Texas. . . . Copyright, 1924, by Southwest Review. . . . Entered as second-class matter October 10, 1924, at the postoffice at Dallas, Texas, under the Act of March 3, 1879.

and being all that time paid little or nothing for what he had written, he had recently found himself commanding much higher prices than the *Review* could afford to pay. He did, however, send us some of his poems and also some admirable little dialogues of great Americans. These imaginary conversations he apparently thought had little market value, but the editor of the *Forum*, who saw them in the *Southwest Review*, promptly asked Bradford to send him something of the same kind.

It was John William Rogers' mother who introduced me to the poetry of John Hall Wheelock, who quickly became one of my favorite living poets. In the October, 1926, number of the *Review* I published "The Poetry of John Hall Wheelock," which is in great part based upon letters which Mr. Wheelock wrote in response to my inquiries about his aims and methods. Barrett H. Clark's article on Gerhart Hauptmann describes a visit to a German dramatist whose reputation was then much higher than it was after he became a Nazi.

We were lucky to have such excellent contributions from writers in New York and New England, but after all, we knew that the success of the *Review* would depend upon the quality of the materials we could get from writers in our own region. We gave first place to Rogers' play, "Judge Lynch." It was by a brilliant performance of this play in New York that the Dallas Little Theater had recently won the David Belasco Cup. The play had not yet appeared in book form. I remember that we paid Samuel French, who owned the copyright, $75 for it; and we hoped that we would more than make up for that amount in subscriptions from Dallasites who would want to read the play.

We wanted an article on Ex-Governor Jim Ferguson, who had been impeached and was not eligible for re-election. Not to be disposed of so easily, he was seeking to return to Austin with Mrs. Ferguson as governor. All Texans were excited about this unprecedented situation. Who, we wondered, could write the kind of article we wanted? I first asked Ted Dealey, who was at that time reporting the campaign for the Dallas *News*, but he was not willing to write the kind of article we wanted. The man who did write the article, Charles W. Ferguson (no relation of the ex-governor), was a recent graduate of S.M.U., where he had been both cheerleader and editor of the student newspaper. Mr. Bond and I, remembering the forceful editorials he had written for the *Campus*, thought he could write the article we wanted. Not long after the article appeared, Mr. Ferguson came over to Dallas from Fort Worth, where he was assistant pastor of a Methodist church, and told us that he wanted to be a writer and asked us for helpful suggestions. I remember that I suggested that he carefully compare his manuscript with the published article and see if he could see why Mr. Bond and I had made our various alterations in his phraseology. His article in the *Southwest Review* attracted the attention of H. L. Mencken, who promptly asked him to write an article on Texas politics for the recently founded *American Mercury*. "I think Charles Ferguson's future," he wrote me, "lies outside the Methodist pulpit." Mr. Ferguson is now a senior editor of the *Reader's Digest* and the author of several books, the most recent of which is that admirable biography of Cardinal Wolsey, *Naked to Mine Enemies*.

Two of the articles in our first number seem to me below our standard and perhaps not altogether appropriate to a literary magazine. In 1924 interest in Sigmund Freud and psychoanalysis was rapidly growing, and so I asked a Dallas psychiatrist, Dr. Gosline, to write an informative article on the subject. Until Mr. Gambrell reminded me of it, I had forgotten that, just in time to correct it, we discovered that the printer had set the running head on Dr. Gosline's article as "Psychoanalysis: Scientific or Fraudian." In 1924 there was much heated discussion concerning the abuses of intercollegiate athletics, and Dr. Penick, whom I asked to write the article, was an authority on the subject. Mr. Bond and I, however, had to recast and rewrite parts of the article to make it acceptable. Perhaps it was articles of this type that prompted Frances Newman to write that the *Southwest Review* was "not sophisticated enough."

We were pleased with the retiring editor's historical account of the *Texas Review*. It gave us—and I hope our readers as well—the feeling that we were continuing a worthy project. In his closing paragraph Dr. Law spoke hopefully of the *Review* under its new management and graciously attributed to the new editors qualities of "zeal and knowledge" that we were not sure we possessed.

Stanley E. Babb, whose "Train-Whistles at Midnight" appeared in our first number, was literary editor of the Galveston *News* and

11

an alumnus of the University of Texas. In the *News* he had uniformly high praise for the *Review*, which we of course liked; but he also again and again lambasted Dr. Law and the rest of the English department at Austin. I was embarrassed when Dr. Law, who was not insensitive to abuse, wrote to me more than once about the matter. He seemed somehow to feel that since we had published Babb's poem, we were responsible for him. In those years many another young writer seemed to regard his English professors as his natural enemies. The situation at S.M.U. was quite different. The members of our English staff were almost all young men and women who wanted to be writers, and our personal relations with those of our students who had literary ambitions were friendlier and more intimate than I have ever seen anywhere else.

"The New Southwest" is the editor's declaration of policy and a call for support from Southwestern readers. It was intended also to enlist the support of those promising young writers whom the editor did not know but felt sure were to be found in the cities and colleges of the Southwest. With them in mind he emphasized the rich unmined literary materials in the region. We were all Regionalists, I suppose, but we never, I think, used that word. As I reread my article, I feel that it betrays a certain irritation at the many erroneous notions of the Southwest—and especially of Texas—held in the North and East. In the early 1920's Southwesterners felt somewhat jealous as they noted that every region but their own had at one time or other figured prominently on the literary scene. In 1924 the South was beginning to have something like a literary renaissance, but there were only uneasy stirrings in the Southwest.

The editors planned to follow Carl Sandburg's advice and get into the pages of the *Southwest Review* "the five-gallon hat of the cowboy as well as the skyscrapers of Dallas and Denver." With Amy Lowell's permission I quoted the poem "Texas," which she had written in 1920 just after receiving an honorary degree from Baylor University. In Waco she had heard John A. Lomax sing some of the cowboy songs. In the poem she contrasted the Texas of the cotton farmer with the traditional cattle country and the rapidly developing urban and industrial Texas of the twentieth century. All of these, I felt, awaited the poets and novelists who would write something worthy of them. Gerald W. Johnson, somewhat amused by Miss Lowell's reference to Waco's lone skyscraper, suggested that this "totem pole among the Baptists" might serve the *Review* as a suitable emblem.

The editors were optimistic about the part the Southwest would play in the literary awakening of the twenties, but we spoke from faith rather than knowledge. We were, however, better prophets than we knew. There were young writers in the Southwest who would eventually make their mark. Poets who visited college campuses, like Carl Sandburg, Vachel Lindsay, Robert Frost, and Karle Wilson Baker, were revealing to young collegians the world of poetry. John A. Lomax and J. Frank Dobie talked convincingly about the richness of the Southwestern literary background. The Poetry Society of Texas had its headquarters in Dallas. In "The New Southwest" I quoted without naming him one of our advisory editors, Hilton Ross Greer, who had written to me: "For twenty years I wrote [poetry] with a feeling that no one in the entire Southwest cared anything about poetry; and now when I hear young people talking about poetry as a normal interest of the human race, I rub my eyes to see if I am awake." It was the heyday of the Little Magazine. There were, as I remember, no less than nine of them in Dallas at one time or another in the early 1920's. The quality magazines printed only a few short poems, mainly as fillers for white spaces that would otherwise have been blank; and their editors were as a rule not in sympathy with the aims and methods of the younger poets and writers of fiction. The Little Magazine played a significant part in the development of nearly every important poet and novelist of the 1920's and 1930's.

The first number of the *Southwest Review* brought us a number of favorable notices and congratulatory letters. Henry Goddard Leach, the editor of the *Forum*, wrote to me:

My congratulations on the make-up of the *Southwest Review*. Under your firm editorship I am convinced it is bound to succeed. As a fellow-editor I am, of course, a little jealous of your one-act play ["Judge Lynch"] and the historical dialogues by Gamaliel Bradford.

Donald Davidson wrote in the Nashville *Tennessean*:

With an assembly of local artists from which to draw, the *Southwest Review* has a real basis for existence and we heartily welcome it as a distinguished new force in Southern periodical literature. The first issue is thoroughly good.

Somewhat later Robert Graves pronounced the *Southwest Review* "A most alive journal, far in advance of our English monthlies for interest."

In a plea for support (written by Mr. Bond) addressed to the readers of the *Southwest Review* published in the July, 1926, issue the editors stated:

> With this number the *Southwest Review* closes its second year in Dallas. In the two years more than a thousand contributions—articles, short stories, plays, poems, and book reviews—have been published. Of these, thirty-three have been contributed by Texans, fourteen by writers of New Mexico, six by Oklahomans, six by natives of Colorado, nine by Californians. The Old South has been represented by DuBose Heyward, Lizette Woodworth Reese, Conrad Aiken, Paul Green, John Crowe Ransom; the East has been spoken for by Gamaliel Bradford, Marguerite Wilkinson, John Hall Wheelock, Barrett H. Clark; England, by John Drinkwater, D. H. Lawrence, Wilfrid Gibson; France, by J. Delcourt; Russia, by Maxim Gorky. The editors of the *Review* have tried to keep steadily before them their ideal: a magazine, definitely Southwestern in tone and content and yet never narrowly provincial.

It was Barrett H. Clark who got for us Maxim Gorky's "The Story of a Novel," which, as he wrote us, had not at that time been published either in the original Russian or in an English translation. Among the contributors to Volumes X and XI not named in Mr. Bond's appeal are Mary Austin, Edwin Björkman, Olive Tilford Dargan, John Gould Fletcher, Robert Graves, Harriet Monroe, David Morton, George Sterling, and George R. Stewart. Among the new names in Volume XII are those of Elizabeth J. Coatsworth, Sara Haardt (Mrs. H. L. Mencken), Ruth Manning-Sanders, and Eugene Manlove Rhodes.

On the whole, I think the verse we printed in the *Review* was better than the prose. The "New Poetry" movement may have been on the wane in the North and East but certainly not in the Southwest. Moreover, the editors had a special interest in poetry. Professor Beaty and I had in 1922 published *An Introduction to Poetry*, in which we included numerous selections from contemporary poets. We had at S.M.U. a very fine undergraduate poetry club, "The Makers." One of that group was Mr. Bond, who had written some of the best poems that had come out of the Southwest. He was an admirable judge of the quality of the verse submitted to the *Review*.

Early in 1925 we received in the mail a group of frontier ballads written by Walter Stanley Campbell, a member of the English department at the University of Oklahoma. Mr. Campbell wrote that if we accepted any of his ballads, he wished them to appear under the name "Stanley Vestal." Campbell, he said, was the name of his adopted parents; his father's name had been Vestal. In April, 1925, we printed his "Three Ballads of Kit Carson" and in October of the next year, "The Death of Satank." Mr. Campbell was grateful to us for publishing his ballads and with good reason. For soon after we printed the Kit Carson ballads, Harriet Monroe asked for more of the ballads for *Poetry* and H. L. Mencken at the same time wanted some of them for the *American Mercury*. Campbell's *Fandango: Ballads of the Old West* (1927) was followed by many historical and biographical works dealing mainly with the Southwest.

By the critical standards of the present day the best poem we published was probably John Crowe Ransom's "Antique Harvesters," which appeared in the April, 1925, issue along with the three frontier ballads of Stanley Vestal and John Gould Fletcher's "The Seven Cities of Cibola." In response to the puzzled editors' request for some clue to the meaning of his poem, Mr. Ransom wrote that the poem gives "the viewpoint of the local lean old veterans" and that it is "the appeal of the Old South to the young men to stand by the cause." Mr. Ransom thought so little of the poem—so Allen Tate told me in 1961—that but for the protests of his friends he would have left "Antique Harvesters" out of his next volume of poems. (At some time in the middle twenties I tried unsuccessfully to persuade Professor Ransom to leave Vanderbilt University and join the English staff at S.M.U.)

Some of the best short stories that we published were written by Paul Green. We knew of Mr. Green as the author of the one-act play *The No 'Count Boy*. It was by a notable performance of that play in New York that the Dallas Little Theater won the Belasco Cup for the third time. Mr. Green was for a brief and unhappy time the editor of the *Reviewer*, which had been moved from Richmond to Chapel Hill, North Carolina. When in 1925 his sponsor decided not to underwrite the magazine any longer, we took it over at Mr. Green's request and merged it with the *Southwest Review*.

In "The New Southwest" I opened the door to too many articles by professors when I wrote: "It [the *Southwest Review*] will now and then print articles that make a substantial contribution to scholarship even at the risk of occasionally boring a desultory reader; but it will not be a repository for professorial articles that no one wants to read." The majority of the writers whom I knew were professors of English. Most of them were not accustomed to being paid for what they wrote and were pleased to receive the small sums that the *Review* could afford to pay. At the time I was editing the *Southwest Review* I was also chairman of the American Literature Group in the Modern Language Association which was hoping to find a sponsor for a scholarly journal devoted exclusively to American literature. Such a journal was *American Literature,* which Duke University was to launch in 1929 after I had left S.M.U. Among the articles we printed in the *Southwest Review* there were a number that would have found more sympathetic readers if they had appeared in *American Literature*: among them Louise Pound's "Walt Whitman and the Classics" and my own "The Frontier in American Literature." On the other hand, Professor Stanley P. Chase's "The Scene of *The Everlasting Mercy*," which we published in January, 1926, was an illuminating discussion of a major work by John Masefield (now underrated and out of fashion) which the editor of the *Atlantic Monthly* might have accepted if it had been submitted to him. Mr. Bond and I had our reservations about Fred Lewis Pattee's "Recent Poetry and the *Ars Poetica*," which we published in the January, 1925, number. It was forceful and well written, but Professor Pattee's rating of the contemporary poets was much lower than ours. One conspicuous object of Pattee's derogatory comments was Carl Sandburg. He took the adverse criticism like the man he is; but on his next visit to Dallas, he remarked to me: "You must have had your fingers crossed when you published Pattee's article."

In July, 1925, we began an important series of articles on "Cities of the Southwest" with Willard Johnson's article on Santa Fe. Easley S. Jones's "Denver" followed in January, 1926. One of the best in the series, John McGinnis's "Taos," was written in the summer of 1927 while he and John Chapman were on a visit to New Mexico. Another new venture was Marion Murray's illustrated "Art in the Southwest" in July, 1926. It was followed by Frank Applegate's "Tourists and Art" in October of the same year. In July, 1925, we had printed Will James's story, "Filling in the Cracks," which he had illustrated with some fine pictures of horses and cowboys.

3

When I remember how great were our financial difficulties in 1926 and 1927, I wonder that we were able to get as many first-rate articles as we did. In the spring of 1925 we were informed that the university had decided to discontinue its financial support of the *Review*. Mr. Layton W. Bailey, the University Treasurer, was quoted as saying that we had already spent something like $3,000. To make matters worse, it was about this time that the Hargreaves Printing Company raised its rates on the *Review* and so we had to look for another printer unless we discontinued the magazine. This we were determined not to do, and the university was considerate enough to say that we might keep the money we had collected in subscriptions at $2 a year. Fortunately for us, the number of paying subscribers had increased, if my memory is accurate, from 16 to about 750.

The exact status of the *Southwest Review* had never been defined. Neither the administration nor the editors had had any experience with magazines. At that time S.M.U. had no university press which could have handled our financial affairs more efficiently. Some years after I had left Dallas, Henry Nash Smith wrote me that he would like to know if I could throw any light on the question: "Who owns the *Southwest Review*?" I replied that I thought it belonged to the university, but I remember signing a document giving to the university any rights that I might still have in the magazine.

In the July, 1926, issue appeared Mr. Bond's eloquent appeal to the readers of the *Review,* from which I quote again:

In the two years the *Review* has ... built up a circulation of more than a thousand copies. The three issues preceding this one have paid their own way, without subsidy or any financial assistance. The present number, however, is not paid for, and whether or not the magazine closes the year with a deficit depends upon the sale of this issue, the prompt renewal of expired subscriptions, and the securing of new subscribers.

. . . .

The *Review*, of course, is not a commercial enterprise; it pays no salaries to its staff; it does not expect to make profits. It owes its existence to the exertions of a group deeply interested in the development of this section; and if the magazine is to make the contribution to Southwestern life that it could, that group must be constantly enlarged. And the enlargement of the group can come about only by your efforts.

The financial crisis continued for another year or two. At one time I was so pessimistic about the future of the magazine that I wrote to Dr. Law to ask whether, if we had to discontinue the *Review*, the University of Texas would be willing to take it back and keep it going. After consulting the administrative authorities, Law wrote me that the University of Texas would be willing to take over the *Review*. He added, however, that in that event the new editor would be not himself but Professor L. L. Click, a younger member of the English staff. In the summer of 1927, not long before I left S.M.U., the university agreed to give us a subsidy of $1,000 for the next fiscal year.

Just here I may mention some of the other circumstances which at times troubled the inexperienced editors. We were all so ignorant of magazine format that we began our second number with page 1, instead of page 101 and thus had to page the other numbers of Volume X in like manner—to the disgust of librarians and index compilers. In the beginning we hoped that the Texas News Company would distribute the *Review* to newsstands all over the state. When we approached the Dallas manager, he asked: "How many copies of the widely known *Yale Review* do you suppose we take for the whole state of Texas?" We of course had no idea. "Five," he said. Mr. Gambrell remembers that every time he took a new number of the *Review* to the Terminal post office for mailing, Bruce Luna made so many difficulties about allowing us the rates we knew we were entitled to, that we thought of mailing the magazine from Vickery or some other Dallas suburb.

Our energetic managing editor got a few paying advertisements, but I remember best those we exchanged with the *Buccaneer,* the *Double Dealer,* the *Reviewer,* the *Sewanee Review,* and the *South Atlantic Quarterly.* I was always irritated by the *Double Dealer's* boast that it was "the only magazine in America which prints prose and verse on their own merits, ignoring the clamor of schools, smiling at the noisy advocates of new forms and steering through the welter of sentimentalists." That was advertising with a vengeance! But then, I remember, the *Double Dealer* did have the good fortune to print one of Ernest Hemingway's earliest short stories.

It is no wonder that Volumes XI and XII are slimmer than Volume X. The editors, with fewer pages at their disposal, discovered that they had accepted too many manuscripts. There were too many from college professors, and some accepted manuscripts were ceasing to be timely. Mr. Bond finally took the unpleasant but inevitable step of returning some manuscripts to their authors. He got some angry and a few gracious replies. At that time I did not know that when Walter Hines Page became editor of the *Atlantic Monthly,* he had promptly returned to their authors—one of them was no less a writer than Sarah Orne Jewett—manuscripts which he thought had little or no appeal to the wider circle of readers he knew the *Atlantic* must have if it was to survive.

Our financial difficulties go far toward explaining why a number of articles which the *Review* announced its intention of publishing never appeared. Most of them were no great loss, but I was sorry not to be able to print Mr. Rogers' "An Evening with Amy Lowell." Miss Lowell did not know that Rogers had any intention of writing about her, and when I asked her permission to print the article, she asked me to send it to her. She felt that Rogers had abused her hospitality, and since her life of Keats was about to appear, she wanted no unfavorable publicity regarding the number of Manilla cigars she smoked, for example. Miss Lowell noted a number of errors in the article—Rogers had mistaken her fine Adam furniture for Sheraton or Hepplewhite. She returned his manuscript with her own numerous revisions and a clean copy made by her secretary. Before we could print the article, however, Miss Lowell died in May, 1925, and Rogers withdrew his manuscript, which he thought now had a much greater financial value. What eventually became of it I do not know.

Meanwhile I have failed to note the various changes in the *Review*'s editorial staff that occurred before July, 1927, the last number in which I had a part. My various duties became so heavy that at the end of the first year I asked Mr. Bond to take over as editor while Henry Nash Smith and I served as associate editors. Each of the editors was carrying a full load of classes in addition to the many hours he spent on the *Review* each month. A year later when Mr. Bond left us to take an editorial position in New York City, I asked John McGinnis to join me as co-editor. John Chapman, who is now a distinguished Dallas physician, became assistant editor. In the July, 1927, number John Chapman and Henry Nash Smith (back at S.M.U. after a year at Harvard) are listed as associate editors. In April, 1927, Mr. Gambrell was succeeded as managing editor by Hemphill Hosford, who before he retired in July, 1962, was Vice-President and Provost of the university. Before Mr. Gambrell left the *Review*, he had been assisted for a short time by Mary Stone and Sarah Chokla. When I went to Duke University in 1927, Mr. McGinnis took over as editor. He was carrying a full teaching load and was still literary editor of the Dallas *News*, but he was nevertheless willing to take on the primary responsibility for the magazine. He was fortunate—and so was I—in having some very able associates. In the course of a long life as a teacher I have had many able undergraduate students, but I have had none more capable than George Bond, Herbert Gambrell, Henry Nash Smith, Ima H. Herron, and John Lee Brooks.

In spite of our financial difficulties and my other responsibilities, I thoroughly enjoyed my work on the *Southwest Review*. There was a deep satisfaction in being able to print a poem, an essay, or a story which I thought first-rate whether written by a veteran author like Gamaliel Bradford whom I had long admired, or by an unknown young writer like Stanley Vestal. I had the feeling that somehow I was having a part in the creation of an American literature. The feeling, I fear, was illusory. Literary magazines are of course a cultural necessity and not a luxury, but sometimes when I have heard complimentary remarks on my work as editor of the *Southwest Review* or *American Literature*, I remembered the passage from the *Letters* of Edward Fitzgerald that I have used as epigraph for this essay: "The power of writing one fine line transcends all the Able-Editor ability in the ably-edited Universe." In 1935 when Professor Bliss Perry of Harvard published his autobiography, *And Gladly Teach*, he printed Fitzgerald's sentence as epigraph for the chapter in which he told the story of the ten years in which he had been editor of the *Atlantic Monthly*. That sentence is enough to put any editor in his proper place.

Let America, then, prize and cherish her writers, yes, let her glorify them. They are not so many as to exhaust her good-will.

Herman Melville, "Hawthorne and His Mosses" (1850)

American Literature, 1928-1954

1

Sixty years ago there was in our universities little interest in the study and teaching of American literature. I went to Harvard for my graduate work because my English professor at Richmond College told me that Harvard had the finest English staff in the country. I had a notion that American literature was important, and it seemed to me that since so much of the best of it had been written in the Boston-Cambridge-Concord region, Harvard ought to be the ideal place in which to study Emerson, Hawthorne, Longfellow, Thoreau, and their contemporaries. In Cambridge, however, I discovered that Harvard, which had no less than four eminent Chaucer scholars, offered only a half-course in American literature; and that half-course was given only every other year. It was not offered in either of the two years.

I have singled out Harvard, but except at Columbia much the same situation prevailed in practically all our major American universities. To those of us who had a special interest in American literature it seemed that, as Vernon L. Parrington once phrased it in a letter to me, "There are too many Anglo-Saxon hounds guarding the sacred degree." As late as 1933, when the late Stanley T. Williams published his fine brief survey of American literature, he prefaced it with this expressive line from Emerson's "Uriel": "The stern old war-gods shook their heads." In December, 1935, Howard Mumford Jones read at a meeting of the Modern Language Association a paper entitled "American Scholarship and American Literature," in which he said:

The continuing tendency of this Association to ignore, patronize, or minimize the national literature is a weakness of the first order. I firmly believe that unless this organization sees the need of associating itself vitally with the cultural history of our common country, it will come in time to count for less and less in the intellectual life of the United States. Shall we leave the field to the social scientists, or shall we accept the challenge which the situation gives us?

It is clear to me now that some of us who were interested in American literature were suffering from feelings of inferiority. We were often reminded that, with rare exceptions, the few scholarly publications dealing with American authors were inferior to the work being done on Chaucer and the Elizabethans. Nevertheless, there were a number of young men who took the position—taken earlier by those able pioneers, William Peterfield Trent, Arthur Hobson Quinn, Fred Lewis Pattee, Killis Campbell, and the dean of them all, Moses Coit Tyler—that the literature of the United States was eminently worthy of serious study. When our critics reminded us that the United States had produced no writer who measures up to Shakespeare, Milton, or even Wordsworth and suggested that neither Emerson, Hawthorne, nor Poe was an important writer, we might have replied, as Sainte-Beuve did when his young friend Matthew Arnold remarked that he did not consider Lamartine an important poet: "He is important to *us*." Or perhaps better, we might have pointed to what the best of English and Continental critics had said in praise of Emerson, Hawthorne, and Poe.

With the active encouragement of Benjamin Sledd, my older colleague at Wake Forest College, I gave my first course in American literature in 1913-1914. In December, 1914, while a graduate student at Columbia University, I attended my first meeting of the Modern Language Association, which met at Columbia that year.

In those days the Association always met in a body whether to listen to the reading of papers, the transaction of business, or enjoying the "Smoke Talk" (now alas, no more), which was the feature of the annual dinner. At the 1914 meeting most of the members stood in the lobby of Earl Hall and talked with old or new friends unless someone was scheduled to read a paper that promised to be interesting. I remember that most of us tramped upstairs to hear John Erskine read a paper on the influence of Castiglione's *The Courtier* upon Spenser's *The Faerie Queene*. I recall only a single paper on an American topic. A young instructor from the Middle West, urged on by his department head, read an amateurish paper on the sources of Longfellow's *Evangeline*. I blushed for him when one of the "stern old war-gods" severely reproved him for not reckoning with Chateaubriand's glowing descriptions of the lower Mississippi River country, which Longfellow had never seen.

By 1920 the Association had grown too large and too unwieldy for any fruitful discussion of the widely varied interests of its more than 1,500 members. Obviously something had to be done if the Association was to function effectively. In his presidential address of that year Professor John M. Manly of the University of Chicago urged the Association to form its members into large Sections (English, Germanic, and Romance) and into smaller Discussion Groups in accordance with the special interests of the members. Professor Killis Campbell of the University of Texas—whose edition of Poe's poems was in 1920 probably the finest single example of scholarship in our field—noticed that Manly in his provisional list of Discussion Groups had made no place for those interested in American literature. He brought the matter to Manly's attention. When Manly asked whether there were enough interested members to justify the formation of an American Literature Group, Campbell assured him that there were; and Manly added English XII, American Literature, to his list. Campbell became the Group's first chairman. The second was Arthur Hobson Quinn of the University of Pennsylvania.

The first meeting of the American Literature Group that I attended—it was the Group's third annual meeting—took place at the University of Michigan in December, 1923. I had come to Ann Arbor to read a paper on "Thackeray and Virginia" before the

English Section. At the Group meeting only about twenty-five persons were present. At the meeting in New York in December, 1954 —the year in which I gave up my position as Chairman of the Board of Editors of *American Literature*—over seven hundred attended at least one of the two periods allotted to the Group. In 1923 only 467 members of the Association came to the annual meeting; in 1954 the total attendance was estimated at 4,200. That is less than half the number that attended the annual meeting in December, 1964.

The Group chairman, Professor Percy H. Boynton of the University of Chicago, did not attend the 1923 meeting of the Association. He had arranged for only a single paper, Fred Lewis Pattee's "American Literature in the College Curriculum," a historical study of the little that had been done in our field. After the paper had been read and briefly discussed, half of those present left the room. The ten or twelve of us who remained thought it was high time that the American Literature Group should do more than merely meet once a year to discuss a few papers. I quote from the report, published in *PMLA*, of the acting secretary of our Group, Robert E. Spiller of Swarthmore College:

> In reporting on Problems under Investigation Professor [Ernest E.] Leisy [of Illinois Wesleyan University] called attention to a list of articles to date in scholarly journals, to those theses now in progress, and to a number of possible subjects for investigation. Professor Pattee suggested rewriting official biographies because of their prejudiced matter; Professor Hubbell told of teaching literature by [geographical] backgrounds; Dr. [Thomas Ollive] Mabbott recommended biographical and bibliographical studies of local authors.
>
> A committee, consisting of Professors Hubbell, Mabbott, and Leisy (Chairman) is to report what theses are completed, what ones are under investigation, and what special collections are available for research in various libraries.

When the committee had completed its report, the Group had no journal of its own, but Professor James F. Royster of the University of North Carolina published our report in *Studies in Philology* for January, 1926. The report included: (1) a list of articles on American literature (no great number) which had appeared in the scholarly journals; (2) a list of doctoral dissertations completed and in progress (all too few); and (3) some much-needed information about "Americana in American Libraries," especially manuscript materials. Except for the bibliographies in *The Cam-*

25

bridge History of American Literature (1917-1921) there were few bibliographical sources to which the investigator could turn. There are today, thanks to members of the Group, many and better bibliographies available.

In the early 1920's the study of American literature was attracting more and more students, in Europe as well as in the United States. Our revised committee report, published in 1928 in *The Reinterpretation of American Literature*, listed as completed 56 dissertations and 77 as in progress. In January, 1933, Ernest Leisy and I published in *American Literature* a list that ran to a total of 406 titles. In 1948 Lewis Leary, then at Duke University, published a list which added 1,142 new titles. In 1957 the Duke University Press brought out James Woodress's *Dissertations in American Literature, 1891-1955*, which added 936 new titles, bringing the total to 2,484. In his 1962 edition Woodress added 959 new titles. In 1954 the Duke University Press brought out Lewis Leary's indispensable *Articles on American Literature, 1900-1950*, a revised and enlarged edition of a book which had covered only the years 1920-1945. As early as 1923 the American Literature Group had hoped somehow to compile and publish a guide to manuscript materials in American libraries. In the early 1930's a committee of the Group—Ralph L. Rusk, Kenneth B. Murdock, and Jay B. Hubbell (chairman)—met in Washington at the Library of Congress, under the auspices of the American Council of Learned Societies, with a similar committee from the American Historical Association. Professor Roulhac Hamilton of the University of North Carolina and I put into final form the plan we had sketched out in Washington. In those Depression days, however, the ACLS was not able to find any individual or foundation willing to provide the money needed to carry out the project. In 1960 it was carried to completion when the University of Texas Press published that invaluable guide, *American Literary Manuscripts*. What made it possible to bring out such a book was the generosity of the Lilly Endowment of Indianapolis, grants-in-aid from several universities, and the co-operation of numerous American librarians with Professor Joseph Jones and his editorial colleagues: Ernest Marchand, Dan Piper, Albert Robbins, and Herman Spivey.

The fourth annual Group meeting took place at Columbia University in December, 1924, with Professor Pattee as chairman and Ernest Leisy as secretary. At this meeting I read a paper on "The Frontier in American Literature," which in January of the following year I printed in the *Southwest Review*. At this meeting I was elected chairman and Leisy was re-elected secretary. We served as the Group's officers for the next three years, yielding place in December, 1927, to Kenneth B. Murdock of Harvard as chairman and Robert E. Spiller of Swarthmore as secretary.

2

I do not remember that any one at the 1923 Group meeting suggested that there ought to be a journal devoted exclusively to American literature, but the need was much on my mind in the three years, 1925-1927, when I was not only the Group chairman but also one of the editors of the *Southwest Review*. As I look over my file of the *Review*, I see now that I printed more than one article which would have been more appropriate in the as-yet-unfounded *American Literature* than in a Southwestern literary quarterly. A conspicuous example is Emory Holloway's "Whitman's Embryonic Verse," which appeared in the July, 1925, number. I doubt whether more than a dozen readers of the *Southwest Review* thought this Whitman notebook worth publishing anywhere, but for the few scholars then interested in the genesis of *Leaves of Grass* it was a document of the first importance. The *American Mercury* had published one Whitman notebook for Professor Holloway but, so he wrote me, Mencken had declined to publish any more.

Most of my American literature friends agreed with me that eventually there would probably be a journal devoted exclusively to that subject, but they always pointed to the great obstacle: "Who is going to pay the annual deficit? Scholarly journals don't pay their way." At the December, 1926, meeting in Cambridge Professor Louise Pound offered to try to persuade the University of Nebraska authorities, who were thinking of resurrecting a defunct quarterly, to make it the organ of the American Literature Group. Nothing came of her suggestion.

In the spring of 1927 I urged upon Ellis W. Shuler, Dean of the Graduate School at Southern Methodist University, the need of an

American literature journal. I argued that such a journal, if it succeeded, as I was sure it would, could add much to the prestige of a young university not well known outside the Southwest. Dr. Shuler did not share my enthusiasm. He did not say so, but he probably felt that the English staff had enough on its hands without launching a second quarterly. What Dean Shuler at that time wanted was a fund to publish a series of abstracts of our master's theses. I was discouraged, and so was a very able young instructor named Clarence Gohdes, who had gone with me to see Dr. Shuler. If the Dean of the Graduate School was not interested in my projected journal, we thought, certainly there was no use in taking the matter to any other member of the administration.

In the summer of 1927 I accepted a permanent position at Duke University. In my correspondence with the late Frank C. Brown, the head of the English department, I mentioned the desire of members of the Group for a journal devoted to American literature and our hope that some university would be willing to establish it. Dr. Brown took up the matter with President William P. Few, who had been for many years Professor of English in Trinity College. Dr. Few was quick to see that such a journal, if it were successful, would add prestige to a university which only three years earlier had been a small college; but he had of course many more pressing problems on his mind, and he was slow to come to any decision about the journal. The English department at Trinity College had devoted little attention to American literature. Soon after I came to Duke, Dr. Brown told me that there were some students who wanted to study American literature and that he and President Few had decided that I should offer every year one course in that subject, alternating an undergraduate with a graduate course. That, they thought, would be sufficient to satisfy the need for work in American literature. Fifteen years later there were in the English department three of us—Clarence Gohdes, Lewis Leary, and I—giving most of our time to courses in American literature. Charles R. Anderson had only recently left us to go to Johns Hopkins. The establishment of *American Literature* no doubt had something to do with the rapid increase in the number of our students in the Graduate School.

President Few, who had taken his doctor's degree at Harvard

with a dissertation on the *-ing* suffix in Middle English, doubted whether an American literature quarterly would be able to get enough acceptable articles to justify its establishment. To reassure him, I went through the current periodoicals in the library and reported that in 1927 the scholarly journals were publishing enough articles on American literature to fill the four numbers of at least three scholarly journals. Dr. Few's only comment was: "Well, won't these journals continue to publish articles on American literature?" "Yes," I replied, "but an American literature journal would get most of the best articles."

I wanted to be able to assure the administration that I was not alone in believing that there was a definite need for a scholarly journal devoted solely to American literature. And so in November, 1927, I wrote to several scholars who had done notable work in that field. The replies were on the whole quite favorable, but my correspondents all felt that unless the journal had a sponsor willing to pay the expected annual deficit, it would certainly fail. A majority of them believed that such a journal would get enough acceptable articles to justify its establishment. Percy H. Boynton of the University of Chicago wrote to me:

... it seems to me there is enough material. I should say, without question, that some of it of a very admirable sort, is coming from the best of my own graduate students. There are twelve of them now on the way toward their doctorates and they are doing very definite and valuable research.

Fred Lewis Pattee, who had retired from teaching at Pennsylvania State College only to begin teaching again at Rollins College, stressed the great increase in the number of college students who were studying American literature:

The field of American literature is growing with marvelous rapidity. Within the past two or three years at least three collections of American literature material for classes have been issued,—Foerster's, Shafer's, etc. and I hear that all of them are going strong; and yet my own *Century Readings in American Literature* had its biggest sale last year. ... I am heartily in favor of your magazine.

Even more encouraging was the letter I received from William B. Cairns of the University of Wisconsin:

Your idea of a journal of American literature is an interesting one, and one that I very much wish might be carried out. As for scholarly material to fill it, I think there can be little doubt that there would be an ample supply to choose from, from the first; and I believe that such a quarterly ... would take its place with any of the research journals in similar fields.

As a private business venture one might be afraid of lean years at first. But if Duke is willing to assume the financial responsibility—why, Good for Duke! Of course every man sees his own specialty big, but when one thinks that three or four big state universities are now looking for men in American literature, willing to give any reasonable salary and rank for the right man, and when he notes the graduate students that are already working in the subject it looks as if it might be one of the wisest things for a new institution to sponsor. I shall be glad if you can convince your President.

The administration finally gave me permission to inform the American Literature Group at its meeting in Louisville in December, 1927, that Duke University was willing to sponsor the projected journal if the two parties could agree on details of the arrangement. Meanwhile, I had received a letter from Dr. Theodore Zunder informing me that he had suggested to his colleagues at Brown University that Brown should establish a journal of American literature. And so when the Group met in Louisville, it had not one but two tentative offers to sponsor the desired journal. The new Group chairman, Kenneth Murdock, appointed a Committee on Publications to decide which of the two universities (if either) should be permitted to publish such a journal as the Group would be willing to make its official organ. The chairman of the committee was the new Group secretary, Robert E. Spiller. The other members were Professor Cairns, Ralph L. Rusk of Columbia, myself, and Murdock ex-officio.

The Committee on Publications met in New York City on February 17, 1928. Through the courtesy of Professor Rusk we held our meetings in a private room in the Columbia University Men's Faculty Club. Cairns and Murdock did not come to the meeting. The Brown University plan was presented by Professor Lindsay Todd Damon, an able and distinguished-looking gentleman, best known as co-author of a widely used treatise on rhetoric. He brought with him two of his younger colleagues whose names I do not remember. One of them was to be the editor-in-chief if the journal was published at Brown. Not one of the three had published anything of importance on American literature. There was no mention

of Theodore Zunder, who had recently completed at Yale a dissertation on Joel Barlow. Damon had persuaded the late Stanley T.
Williams to come along and support the Brown plan. This he did
but with little enthusiasm after the discussion got well under way,
or so it seemed to me.

The Duke University plan which I presented was in the form of
a letter addressed to the chairman of the Committee on Publications:

DUKE UNIVERSITY
DURHAM, NORTH CAROLINA
February 16, 1928

Dr. R. E. Spiller
Swarthmore College
Swarthmore, Pennsylvania

DEAR SIR:

Duke University will guarantee a sum of not to exceed $2000.00
annually for the period of five years to establish a Journal of American
Literature. This guarantee is made with the understanding that the
Journal is to be the property of the Duke University Press, and also that
the Editor-in-Chief is to be a member of the Faculty of Duke University
and appointed by the University.

We would be glad to have the American Literature Group of the
Modern Language Association make this Journal the official organ.

With the exception of the stipulations set forth above, we would leave
the other details to be worked out by your Committee.

This letter will be presented to you by Dr. Hubbell, who is greatly
interested in the establishment of the publication.

Very truly yours,

R. L. FLOWERS
Treasurer, Duke University

Dr. Flowers, who had been Professor of Mathematics and was a
graduate of the U. S. Naval Academy, had more faith in my projected
journal than any other member of the administration. When it
became necessary for me to take to New York the Duke plan—all
spelled out and made official—we could not find President Few.
Perhaps that was just as well, for he was still noncommittal in his
attitude toward my project. Then it was that Dr. Flowers made the
final decision. He turned to me and said: "Tell me just what you
want me to say in my letter to the Committee on Publications."

The plan which Damon brought from Brown University was
altogether different. He wanted a quarterly which had not less than

seven editors, all of whom were, as I remember, to be appointed by the authorities at Brown. At least three of the seven were to be members of the Brown University faculty. Harvard, Yale, and Columbia were each to have one editor. Later in the meeting Damon suggested that perhaps Brown University might be willing to add me as a representative of the Southern states. Nothing was said about the states west of the Appalachians. It quickly became obvious to the committee that the projected journal, if it went to Brown, would be too much of a New England affair to serve as the official organ of a Group operating within a national association of scholars from every section of the country. Under the Brown plan the American Literature Group would have no control over the magazine. What the Brown people wanted, it seemed, was a journal which too closely resembled the recently established *New England Quarterly*, which was then and is still one of the best of regional journals.

After a time the Brown delegation withdrew to permit the committee to discuss the rival plans. The burden of the decision fell upon Spiller and Rusk. They were firm in their determination not to recommend any plan unless the American Literature Group was empowered to elect a majority of the editors and control the policies of the journal. There was a second session with the gentlemen from Brown—Williams meanwhile had left—to allow Damon to present a slight modification of his original proposal. In the end this, too, failed to assure the Group the control which Rusk and Spiller considered indispensable.

After thirty-seven years my recollections are naturally somewhat dim. All day and well into the night we sat in what was literally a smoke-filled room. Poor Rusk, our host, did not smoke. I remember that the Brown representatives suggested that the Duke University Library did not have the resources which would permit an editor to check manuscripts submitted to the journal. I remember, too, my surprise at Damon's answer to the committee's question: "How large a magazine—how many pages in each issue—do you have in mind?" Damon replied that he thought that four numbers of sixteen pages each would contain all the first-class materials—both articles and book reviews—the journal would be able to get. When I was asked the same question, I replied that I had in mind four numbers of approximately one hundred pages each. (The four numbers of Volume I of *American Literature* ran to 470 pages).

My last recollection of that eventful February day is that the three of us were in Rusk's apartment not long before midnight drafting a letter to Damon, who had gone back to Providence, informing him that his latest plan would not, without still further modification, be acceptable to the American Literature Group. I remember that each of us in turn tried to type the letter without making any typographical errors. I cannot remember whether it was Rusk or Spiller who managed to achieve this difficult feat.

I returned to Durham tired and discouraged. I reported to Dr. Flowers that I did not think Duke would get the journal. A few days afterwards I wrote to Murdock that unless some decision was reached promptly, I feared that the Duke offer would be withdrawn. Soon after Murdock received my letter, he had a telephone call from Damon, who was still not willing to make his plan acceptable to the Group. Murdock then—so he wrote me later—told Damon that if he was unwilling to make his plan acceptable to the Group, he had better withdraw his offer. This he soon did, and the committee recommended that the Group accept the Duke offer.

3

On March 15, 1928, Robert Spiller mailed to members of the American Literature Group the report of the Committee on Publications. It summarized the provisions of the Duke plan and recommended its acceptance. The committee also provided for a Board of Editors, which was to consist of a managing editor (appointed by Duke University) who would serve as Chairman of the Board and four other editors to be elected by the American Literature Group and "chosen so that they will be as representative as possible of the country at large, of varying opinions with regard to the subject of American literature, and of large universities actively engaged in research in the field."

In order to facilitate the organization of the Board of Editors, the committee nominated Cairns to a two-year term and Murdock to a term of five years. Duke University had already named me as editor-in-chief.[1] The committee in its report recommended that we

[1] The Committee on Publications preferred the title managing editor, by which I

three choose the other two editors. We quickly selected Rusk for the four-year term; but before filling the remaining three-year term, we decided to ask for nominations from the members of the Group. The majority of these, as I had foreseen, named Fred Lewis Pattee, the best-known living teacher of American literature. He was, I believe, the first ever to be officially designated by any institution as Professor of American Literature.

The five editors were determined to hold the as-yet-unnamed journal up to the standard set in the committee's report:

> The editorial standards of the journal to be equal to those of the *P.M.L.A.* and the *American Historical Review,* and the field to be limited to the study of American literature of the past. The leading articles to be important contributions to the philological, biographical, bibliographical, critical, or historical knowledge of the field; unpublished manuscript sources to be printed occasionally. All scholarly books in the field to be reviewed by competent authorities as soon after their publication as possible. Other departments to be left to the active editorial board. Under no conditions should the journal be made "popular" at a sacrifice of scholarly standards.

The Committee on Publications stipulated that the Board of Editors should name at least ten scholars to serve as an Advisory Board. These were "to be chosen for their accomplishment and for their special qualifications in the field of American literature and related subjects. Historians, philosophers, custodians of collections of Americana, etc. to be considered for this Board, but the majority to be authorities in the field of American literature itself." The fifteen members of the 1929 Advisory Board were a distinguished group:

Percy H. Boynton	Bliss Perry
Killis Campbell	Louise Pound
Norman Foerster	Arthur Hobson Quinn
George Philip Krapp	Robert E. Spiller
Ernest E. Leisy	Frederick J. Turner
Thomas Ollive Mabbott	Stanley T. Williams
John Brooks Moore	Lawrence C. Wroth
Vernon Louis Parrington	

---

was known until 1932, when Clarence Gohdes became in effect associate editor. He was given the title managing editor, and I was designated thereafter as Chairman of the Board of Editors. The managing editor was elected annually by the American Literature Group.

The Committee on Publications had suggested that the new journal should be named *Studies in American Literature* with the descriptive subtitle: *A Quarterly Journal of American Literary History, Criticism, and Bibliography*; but it left the final choice to the Board of Editors. After considerable correspondence about various names that were suggested, the other editors finally accepted the title which Pattee and I had held out for, and so the official title became *American Literature: A Journal of Literary History, Criticism, and Bibliography*. Dr. Paull F. Baum was chiefly responsible for our selection of type face, paper, and color for the cover. The journal's format has changed little since 1929.

The editors had hoped to bring out the first number in January, 1929, but finally we decided to wait until March to make sure that we would get enough first-rate articles for our first volume. Meanwhile, the Duke University Press sent to members of the Modern Language Association and others a Preliminary Announcement in which the editors stated:

For several years the American Literature Group of the Modern Language Association of America has felt the need of a journal devoted exclusively to research in its field. The time has come for a greater degree of specialization than has been possible in the past, and our national literature has become sufficiently important to warrant the establishment of a quarterly devoted to this field alone.

· · · · · · · · · · · · · ·

AMERICAN LITERATURE is to be a coöperative enterprise. It will represent all those seriously interested in the study of American literature. It will serve not only as a clearing-house, an outlet, but also as a stimulus to further study. AMERICAN LITERATURE will not, however, be a pedagogical journal or a journal of contemporary letters; it will be a scholarly publication, not a popular magazine.

Some time in the winter of 1928-1929, Howard Mumford Jones, then at the University of North Carolina, told me that Professor James F. Royster, the editor of *Studies in Philology*, had said to him: "Hubbell won't get a hundred subscribers to his magazine." What Royster had actually said, so he told me later, was that *American Literature* would not get a hundred subscribers apart from libraries. Before our first number was published, I was able to tell Royster that we already had 125 subscriptions from individuals and had not yet asked the libraries to subscribe. "Why were you so pessimistic about the journal?" I asked. He then reminded me that he had recently devoted one issue of *Studies in Philology* to articles on American literature, and he had sent circulars announcing this special number to all members of the American Literature Group. "And how many of them do you suppose bought copies?" he asked. "I did for one," I said. "Yes," he replied, "you and just three others."

4

The March, 1929, number opened with a Foreword upon which I had bestowed much thought and labor. Before putting it in final form I received valuable suggestions from the other editors, especially Ralph Rusk, but the quotations from Emerson were my own idea.

FOREWORD

"If there be need of a new Journal, that need is its introduction: it wants no preface. It proceeds at once to its own ends, which it well knows, and answers now for the first time. That consummated fitness is a triumphant apology." Thus wrote Emerson in his journal in 1840, a few months before the appearance of *The Dial*.

The editors of *American Literature* make no apology for launching this new quarterly. The need for such a publication has for some time been evident to all serious students of our literature. In the century and more that has elapsed since Sydney Smith asked, "Who reads an American book?" our authors have produced a body of writing which, although it does not rival the great literatures of the Old World in artistic value, has an increasing importance. Until recent years our scholars were slow to study the national letters or their relation to European literatures and to American life and thought. American literature has been so continually overpraised in certain quarters and so neglected in others that we may well say of it—as Schopenhauer said of life—that it needs neither to be wept over nor to be laughed at but to be understood. Within the last few years American scholars have awakened to the fact that our literary history supplies a rich and comparatively unworked field. For those who wish to discuss the work of living authors, there are many periodicals available; but *American Literature* is the only scholarly journal devoted solely to research in the field as a whole. *American Literature* has been founded to fill a distinct need. Let us hope we may say of it—as Emerson said of *The Dial*—"It speaks to a public of its own, a newborn class long already waiting. They, least of all, need from it any letters of recommendation."

JAY B. HUBBELL.

And here is the Table of Contents of that first number:

American Literature

A Journal of Literary History, Criticism, and Bibliography

| Volume One | MARCH, 1929 | Number One |

CONTENTS

It was not so obvious in 1929 as it is in 1965 that the contributors to this first number represented a group of able and devoted scholars who possessed the energy, the ambition, the enthusiasm, and the intelligence needed to inaugurate a new era in American literary studies. In the three later numbers of Volume I there appeared other notable names: Harold Blodgett, Harry Hayden Clark, Merle Curti, Clarence H. Faust, Earl Leslie Griggs, Gregory Paine, Louise Pound, Archer Taylor, Stanley T. Williams, James Southall Wilson, and Napier Wilt.

"The Verdict of Sydney Smith," which Robert Spiller sent me from England, was the article that I decided to place first even though it dealt primarily with an English author. The article followed naturally upon the Foreword, and it served to suggest how rapidly American literature had developed since 1820, when Smith had asked the embarrassing question: "Who reads an American book?" The late Tremaine McDowell's article was an illuminating study of Bryant at a critical time when but for the encouragement of the *North American Review*, he might have given up poetry altogether. After McDowell had read the editors' comments on his manuscript, he wrote me that nothing he had ever written had been read with such scrupulously close and intelligent attention. Clarence Gohdes, who was to come to Duke University the next year, sent me from New York his Emerson article—a notable byproduct of his Columbia dissertation, *The Periodicals of American Transcendentalism*. The editors had hoped to have in our first number an article based upon, or embodying, unpublished manuscript materials. Aubrey Starke's three Lanier letters came at an appropriate time. In the first number also, remembering our subtitle, we hoped to have a good bibliographical article. Bowman's article, which Murdock secured for us, was, I believe, the only one we received.

The longest article in the March issue is the late George E. Hastings' "John Bull and His American Descendants," which runs to nearly thirty pages. The editors saw in the article a careful study of a subject of some historical importance, and we decided to publish it. (It was not until years later that I discovered that Hastings had overlooked President James Madison's brief allegory, "Jonathan Bull and Mary Bull.") The editors had suggested that Hastings' article could be improved by certain omissions and some condensation. The author, however, declined to make the changes we suggested; and yet when he received his galley proofs, he deleted two whole paragraphs and substituted for them a brief new paragraph. The result spelled trouble for the Seeman Printery and for me, and it delayed the appearance of the March number. After Hastings returned his proofs, the printers had to reset and renumber fifty or sixty footnotes and reset as many lines in the text. The published article contains 287 footnotes. An average of ten footnotes to a page is far too many, in my opinion; but in those early years the editors felt that it was best to err on the side of overdocumentation. American literature scholarship was still on trial.

The Notes and Queries section included one of the very few articles of an editorial nature ever to appear in the journal. In the beginning the editors had agreed for a time to read every manuscript submitted, no matter how bad; and a few of them were incredibly crude or naïve and sloppily written. In "To Our Contributors" we held up the high standard the journal was determined to maintain:

Of the manuscripts which we have felt compelled to decline, the majority fell short of our standard in two respects: they relied too exclusively upon secondary or readily accessible primary sources of information, and they showed a lack of thoroughness. It is too easy to rush into print with an article of some merit which does not go far enough or deep enough to have any permanent value. Such an article is hardly worth printing since in a year or two it will have to be done over.

Articles of particular value, we think, are those that bring to light new materials or new facts which might assist in the critical interpretation of an author or in fuller understanding of some aspect of our cultural history. Only less important are articles which, though based on old facts, present a new interpretation of some work or movement, made convincing by sound reasoning and the citation of adequate evidence.

Although we place the chief emphasis upon scholarship, we desire articles which are well written. Surely, however, it is not necessary, in a scholarly journal, to resort to superlatives and other journalistic devices in order to interest the reader.

Ernest Leisy's "Research in Progress" was in effect a continuation of the important project which, as I have indicated, the Group had undertaken at its 1923 meeting. There was in 1929 no such clearing-house for dissertation topics in English or in any of the modern languages. "Research in Progress" has saved many a graduate student from that feeling of embarrassment and frustration when he discovers that someone else is at work on his chosen subject.

The book review to which I gave first place calls for a word of explanation. *The Reinterpretation of American Literature* (1928, reissued in 1959) was sponsored by the same group of scholars who were launching the new journal. The book was, moreover, a challenge to scholarship in our field, and it set forth new and important methods and points of view. Such a book obviously ought to be reviewed at length and by a well-known scholar. I thought of Dr. Henry Seidel Canby, who had long been interested in American literature and was now editor of the influential weekly the *Saturday Review of Literature*. I asked Canby if he would be willing to review the book and to publish his review simultaneously in his magazine and in ours, in each case noting that the review was appearing in both magazines. It was easy enough for us in the *American Literature* office to send out our Preliminary Announcement to all the members of the Modern Language Association, but we had no other means of reaching the many non-academic readers of the *Saturday Review of Literature*. Canby's review served our purpose admirably, but I was vexed that while the review appeared in his magazine on March 2, the Seeman Printery did not deliver to the Duke University Press any copies of *American Literature* until March 25. I could not, however, have asked for a more favorable review. Canby's opening sentence was: "And now at last scholarship is ready for the long neglected problems of American literature." "The book . . . ," he continued, "is not perhaps for the general reader—his turn will come later—but it is of the greatest importance for all who take their native literature seriously, and especially for scholars, critics, and teachers."

I had hoped that the journal would get a considerable number of non-academic subscribers, but it never did. Yet if our first number did not interest the non-academic reader, it won for American literature scholarship the increasing respect of scholars working in English literature. I was particularly pleased by letters which came to me from two distinguished professors: Ashley H. Thorndike, under whom I had studied at Columbia, and James Holly Hanford, whom I had first known as a graduate student at Harvard. In almost identical language each of them predicted for the journal a very successful future.

One important feature of *American Literature* made its first appearance in November, 1929. "Articles on American Literature Appearing in Current Periodicals" was, I believe, the first checklist of its kind to appear in any scholarly journal; and possibly it is, as various persons have told me, the most valuable feature of the magazine. Such a checklist of course can never be absolutely complete, but even in 1929 it saved students and their professors many hours which might have been spent in a fruitless examination of the one hundred and sixty periodicals it included. In 1964 the checklist included more than twice that number. In the beginning the five editors planned to compile the checklist themselves, but it soon became apparent that the task was much too large for busy teachers who had to read manuscripts submitted to *American Literature*. The November checklist was compiled by the eighteen men whose names are listed on page 312. Several years later, after Clarence Gohdes became managing editor, the labor of compiling the checklist was turned over to the Group's Bibliographer and a committee representing the Group.

Early in April, 1929, there was a meeting of the Board of Editors in Durham. The university paid the travel expenses of the four editors who lived elsewhere, and they all came. My wife gave a tea so that many of our friends and colleagues might meet them, and the English staff gave in their honor a dinner to which we invited a number of professors of English from neighboring institutions. Murdock gave a public lecture on the poems of the Earl of Rochester. In between times the editors for three days put in many hours discussing the policies which hitherto we had been able to discuss only by correspondence, and I was deeply impressed with the professional competence of my editorial colleagues. Our March number had finally appeared, but by some oversight on the part of the Press, not one of the four editors had received the four copies which I had asked to be sent to each of them. Rusk in New York had seen a borrowed copy, but Pattee, Cairns, and Murdock had not seen the magazine when they came to Durham.

On the last day I gave a luncheon for the four editors so that they might have a chance to get better acquainted with President

41

Few, Dr. Flowers, and Mr. Ernest Seeman, the Manager of the Press. An hour or so before lunch the editors completed our discussion of policies, and the conversation turned to the probable future of Duke University. Someone asked me what I could hope for in the way of a special collection in the library. I said that I hoped that for one thing the library would build up a good collection in American literature with the emphasis upon the literature and the literary culture of the Southern states. The editors thought my idea was a good one, and when I suggested it, they agreed to mention it at lunch. This they did as perfectly as if they had rehearsed it. Rusk, I think it was, said to Pattee, who was now living in the South: "Dr. Pattee, what is the best place for one to study Southern literature?" Pattee replied: "I don't know of a first-rate collection in any American university library. The materials are scattered all over the country all the way from the Library of Congress in the East to the Huntington Library in California." Then it was that Cairns turned to President Few, who had not missed a word, and said: "Dr. Few, here is an opportunity for you. Build up a notable collection in Southern literature in the Duke Library and make it a place where specialists will have to come." "Yes," said Murdock, "Duke has come into the field too late to compete with Harvard and Yale in medieval or Elizabethan literature, but here is something worth while that you can do."

My editor friends had made a tremendous impression on Dr. Few and on Dr. Flowers, who was to succeed him as President. Within a week Dr. Few called me to his office and said: "There is a man by the name of Baskerville who owns a beautiful place in Southside Virginia named 'Waverley.' He is hard-pressed financially and is willing to sell some of his books and newspapers. Let's go up there and see what we can find." Years later when Percy Mackaye visited the Duke Library, I introduced him to Dr. Flowers, who repeated almost word for word what Murdock and Rusk and Cairns and Pattee had said to him about Southern literature and the Duke University Library.

5

I find in the office files of *American Literature* a detailed statement of our editorial policies which I put into final form soon after the meeting of the Board of Editors in Durham. Only in two or three particulars have the policies of the journal changed materially since 1929. The journal has printed very few bibliographical articles apart from those regular features: "Research in Progress" and "Articles on American Literature." In fact, nearly every bibliographical manuscript that I sent off to the other editors came back with the suggestion that the author be urged to send his manuscript to some other journal.

In 1929 it was generally taken for granted that contemporary literature was too close to us to permit objective investigation. I find this sentence in our 1929 statement of editorial policy: "In general, articles dealing with living authors will not be printed." Some scholars even in the late 1920's were beginning to study the literature of their own time. Nowadays of course there are many who devote their spare time to the study of contemporary classics written by Eliot, Frost, Faulkner, and Hemingway; and some of the best of their articles have appeared in *American Literature*. In the early 1930's, however, the editors rejected an article on the "cinquains" of Adelaide Crapsey, who had died in 1914. The article was written by some friend or student of Arthur Hobson Quinn, who sent it to me. Professor Quinn was disappointed—and so was I—that the other editors were unwilling to print it. They rejected the article, not because it seemed unworthy of publication but because they felt that we should save our space for articles dealing with the older writers.

In the early 1950's Howard Mumford Jones reported to me that some younger scholars whom he knew felt that the editorial policy of *American Literature* was unfriendly to those who had adopted the methods of the New Critics. I did not think our policy was unfriendly, but there had been much discussion and some controversy over the newer methods. There were young scholars who regarded their elderly opponents as old fogies, and there were conservative scholars of all ages who regarded the newer approaches as little better than unscientific guessing. I recalled a remark made by a distinguished professor from an Eastern university at a meeting of a Fulbright advisory committee of which we were members. "When we were graduate students," he said, "the great enemies of scholarship in our field were the philologists; now, damn it, it's the New Critics."

I did not want *American Literature* to suffer from the discord between rival schools of thought, and so I referred the whole matter to the other editors and the twelve members of our Advisory Board. They were in a position to find out what was in the minds of other professors and graduate students. Their almost unanimous opinion was that the journal had not been unfriendly to those who had adopted the methods of the New Critics. In the course of the next year or two *American Literature* printed an occasional article in which the newer methods were used, and I heard no more about the journal's hostility to the New Critics.

In the thirty-six years that have elapsed since the launching of *American Literature* there have come about some marked changes in methods and in emphasis on the part of those who study and teach our literature. Let me illustrate. At the 1923 meeting of the American Literature Group—I quote again from Robert Spiller's report—"The discussion that followed [the reading of Pattee's paper] favored presenting American Literature as an expression of national (historical) consciousness and not as an aesthetic offshoot of English literature." Nowadays scholars and teachers are little concerned with literary nationalism and have little interest in literary history. They are preoccupied with aesthetic theories, symbolism, and critical analysis. The emphasis is not upon the national but the international aspects of American literature. Among the most admired American writers there are two—Henry James and T. S. Eliot—who became British subjects and another, Ezra Pound, who during the Second World War broadcast propaganda for the dictator of a nation at war with the United States. Our creative writers of today owe much to these men and to others, like Yeats, Joyce, and Proust, who had little interest in democracy, American or any other.

Yet in spite of such radical changes I believe that *American Literature* has at all times remained fairly representative of the great body of scholars and teachers in our field. This would not be the case if the policies of the journal had been left in the hands of a single editor who as he grew older would have found himself unable to read sympathetically articles written by younger men using the newer methods of scholarship and criticism. The American

Literature Group has elected as editors men who on the whole have kept pace with the changing times. The changes to which I refer have come about so gradually that one is hardly conscious of them unless he has occasion to study our back files.

Nine-tenths of the articles we published underwent some revision and condensation before we printed them. In many instances the editors pointed to important materials which the author had not made use of, and they often made detailed suggestions for revision. The majority of our contributors were young instructors and graduate students, and some of them I rejoice to recognize as now among the elite in our profession. In rejecting manuscripts I never used a rejection slip, and I tried not to follow any particular form in my letters. Sometimes I tried to write something useful, often making use of the other editors' comments; but after a time I came to feel that in all too many cases there was no point in discussing with the author a manuscript which in all probability he could never make acceptable. One young instructor on receiving his rejected manuscript wrote to me that he did not believe the other editors had really read it. By way of reply I copied off the other editors' comments, without giving their names, and sent them to the author. The comments were quite devastating and I did not expect to hear again from the young instructor; but he wrote me after he had read them, "Well, I asked for it!"

Once, and I think once only, did I rewrite a manuscript to make it acceptable. A young Ph.D. whose name I shall not divulge—he died years ago—sent in a short article built around a letter by Timothy Dwight which threw light upon *The Conquest of Canaan*. The first editor who read the article commented to this effect: "The Dwight letter is important, and we ought to print it; but Dr. X's introduction is badly written and much too long." Editor No. 2 agreed with No. 1 and added: "If we print this, someone will have to rewrite Dr. X's introduction. I don't think he can do it to our satisfaction." Editor No. 3 endorsed the criticisms of the other editors and added: "Certainly the introduction will have to be rewritten. Let Hubbell do it." Editor No. 4 echoed: "Yes, let Hubbell do it." And so with some feeling of trepidation Hubbell undertook the task. I condensed to a single typewritten page Dr. X's wordy introduction and sent it to him with the suggestion that this was the kind of introduction which the editors thought appropriate. To my surprise, Dr. X accepted my version and, after making a few verbal changes, sent his manuscript back for publication.

For the first year or two I had very little clerical assistance, and I wrote on the office typewriter every letter addressed to editors, contributors, and publishers. Fortunately for me, when David K. Jackson was employed by the Duke University Press to do editorial work, he voluntarily took over for several years most of my clerical work. Mr. Jackson had been one of my ablest graduate students, and he has published important materials on Edgar Allan Poe, Philip Pendleton Cooke, and the *Southern Literary Messenger*. His expert help in editing copy and reading proof kept *American Literature* freer from errors of several kinds than it would otherwise have been. In January, 1933, *American Literature* brought out the lengthy list, "Doctoral Dissertations in American Literature," of which Ernest E. Leisy and Jay B. Hubbell were listed as compilers. As a matter of fact, Mr. Jackson and I did nearly all the work of revising and expanding Leisy's earlier list. When I suggested to Mr. Jackson that his name should be added as co-compiler, he modestly declined, saying that all he had done was only a part of the work for which he was employed by the Duke University Press.

I have quoted from Howard Mumford Jones's indictment of the Modern Language Association for its neglect of American literature. I must add, however, that as editor of *American Literature* I have every reason to be grateful to the officials of the Association and especially to those able and friendly secretaries, Percy W. Long and William Riley Parker. It was Long, as I remember, who on his own initiative suggested the financial arrangement by which for many years members of the Association were able to receive both *PMLA* and *American Literature* at a substantial reduction in cost.

6

My heavy burden as editor was greatly lightened in 1932 when Clarence Gohdes became managing editor. After a year or two of close collaboration, we decided that he would take the chief responsibility in the first half of the calendar year and I in the second half. The division of labor and responsibility made it possible for each of us to leave Durham while on sabbatical leave and to teach elsewhere than at Duke University in the summer. This arrangement, for example, made it possible for me to accept appointments at the universities of Vienna and Athens. On two occasions when Dr. Gohdes was away, his place was filled by Charles R. Anderson, now at Johns Hopkins, and Lewis Leary, now departmental chairman at Columbia University.

I do not mean to leave the reader with the impression that the editors made no mistakes. Years ago we published the letters that Lafcadio Hearn had written to his brother in Michigan without realizing that they had already been printed in—of all places—the *Atlantic Monthly*. On another occasion we printed a forgotten short story by Longfellow which had already been reprinted in the *Boston Transcript*. We had our troubles, too, with some of the authors of books which were reviewed in *American Literature*. I remember that it was Murdock who undertook to pacify one such author whose book had been reviewed in our very first number. Several authors whose books were reviewed in later numbers found it difficult to forgive either the reviewer or the editors who published reviews which they did not relish. Occasionally we were criticized for brief-mentioning a book instead of having it reviewed at length. On the whole, however, I feel that the relations among editors, contributors, and authors of books reviewed were not disturbed by the rivalries and antipathies which are only too common in academic circles.

I may note finally that although Duke University had agreed to pay an annual financial deficit up to $2,000 which the journal might incur, *American Literature* has not more than once or twice had any deficit. Many of the earlier years, however, might have shown a deficit if any part of my salary or Dr. Gohdes's had been charged to the journal. In 1929, when the journal was launched, I urged the Manager of the Duke University Press to set aside four hundred copies of each number. I felt sure that before many years the library demand for back files would make it profitable to store them. It was not long, however, before we ran out of copies of the November, 1929, number. As I look back now, I see that it would have paid the Press in 1929 to set aside a thousand copies of each number. All the earlier volumes have been reprinted elsewhere;

47

Volumes I-XXIX, 1929-1958, now cost $532.50 for a paperbound set, $592.50 for a clothbound set.

I used to say half seriously that I could never be wholly happy either with or without a magazine to edit, and I was an editor almost continuously from 1924 to 1954. But when the time came to send in my resignation, I had little regret and no cause for worry over the future of *American Literature*. Before I retired in August, 1954, I had already accepted a position as Visiting Professor at the University of Virginia. In the November number of the journal I published this brief valedictory:

> With my retirement from teaching at Duke University in August, 1954, it seemed best that I should resign my position as Chairman of the Board of Editors of *American Literature* which I have held since 1928. After serving more than a quarter of a century on the Board of Editors, I leave *American Literature* in the capable hands of my colleagues: Clarence Gohdes, whom Duke University has appointed as my successor, and Arlin Turner, whom the Executive Council of the Group has elected as Managing Editor.

In December of that year when the Modern Language Association met in New York, the American Literature Group celebrated the twenty-fifth anniversary of the founding of the journal. Howard Mumford Jones reviewed the history of *American Literature* and had some words of praise for the Founding Editor and the other editors and contributors. Ten years later the American Literature Group celebrated the "thirty-fifth birthday" of the journal. At the luncheon meeting Eric Larrabee delivered a fine address on the relations between history and journalism. On this occasion the Group chairman, Professor Lewis Leary, presented to the unsuspecting Founding Editor a beautiful silver medal. It is the first of a series of medals bearing my name to be awarded from time to time to scholars who have made important contributions to the study and interpretation of American literature.

The history of the South and its literature cannot profitably be divorced from the history and literature of the entire country....

W. P. TRENT (ed.), *Southern Writers* (1905), Preface, p. v

This book is a part of all that I have been and known....

WALTER PRESCOTT WEBB, *The Great Plains* (1931), Preface, p. vii

THE SOUTH IN AMERICAN LITERATURE

[This essay had its origin in a talk which, at the request of Professor Joseph T. McCullen, I gave at a joint meeting of his graduate seminar and the English staff at Texas Technological College in the spring of 1960. I have revised it in the hope that it may be of some use to young scholars who are interested in the literary history of the United States.]

1

In 1934, when I committed myself to writing a history of Southern literature, I was almost fifty years old; and if I had known that for the next twenty years it would absorb so large a portion of my time and energy, I might not have undertaken it. And yet as I look back, it was, I think, almost inevitable that I would eventually undertake such a book as *The South in American Literature*. My roots are in the South. My mother was a North Carolinian; my father, like myself, was a native of Virginia. Even more than most Virginians,

49

I have always been conscious of the long and eventful history of my state. Patrick Henry and John Randolph of Roanoke spent their last years in Charlotte County, where I lived from the time I was fourteen until I was twenty-five. Appomattox Court House, where Lee surrendered the Army of Northern Virginia, was only fifteen or eighteen miles from my home in those years. In Southside Virginia in my boyhood there were few farmers over fifty who had not been in the Confederate army. One of my mother's uncles was killed at Chancellorsville, and another who was wounded at Spotsylvania Court House carried a rifle bullet in his body until he died many years afterwards. One of my father's most vivid memories was of the day, in the last year of the Confederacy, when his father left home to rejoin the army, taking with him my father's older brother, a lad of sixteen or seventeen. The college I attended was situated in the Confederate capital. General Lee's old breastworks, or trenches as we call them now, were all round the outskirts of the city extending northward row on row for many miles. There were at that time hundreds of old soldiers in gray uniforms in the Richmond Home for Confederate Veterans. The ablest teacher in Richmond College was the history professor, Dr. Samuel Chiles Mitchell. It was, fittingly enough, one of his students, the late Douglas Southall Freeman, who wrote the great biographies of Lee and Washington.

The country people among whom I grew up had no bitter feelings about Northern soldiers. I do not recall hearing the phrase "damn-Yankee" until I went to college. Among my father's ancestors were several families from Massachusetts and Connecticut who settled in Southwest Virginia in the late eighteenth century. Until the Civil War came on, some of their neighbors called them "Yankees." For my mother, who grew up in northwestern North Carolina, the villains were not the Union soldiers but the bushwhackers. These scoundrels were deserters from the Confederate armies who became outlaws and terrorized the families of those loyal to the Confederate cause. They would have killed my grandfather but for a courageous and faithful slave who even when threatened with death refused to tell where his master was.

My two years in the Graduate School at Harvard had the unexpected effect of making me (and other Southern students) more consciously Southern than I had ever been. After teaching for a year in the University of North Carolina, I went to Columbia University, where I hoped to complete my graduate training working with William Peterfield Trent, a native of Virginia, who had published biographies of Lee and Simms, *A History of American Literature*, and an anthology of *Southern Writers*. Much as I delighted to read and to teach the great writers of England, I was not strongly attracted to any one of them as a subject of expanded research. It was a long time before I discovered a thoroughly congenial dissertation topic in "Virginia Life in Fiction." I found the subject absorbingly interesting. In writing it I learned to understand better the historical and cultural background of the region in which I purposed to spend the remainder of my life. My graduate work was interrupted by the First World War, and it was not until January, 1919, that, still in my army uniform, I returned to Columbia to complete my dissertation. I passed my final examination in September of that year and immediately returned to Southern Methodist University in Dallas to resume my teaching.

In October, 1921, irritated by certain inferior books on the literature of the South, I published in the *Texas Review* a short article entitled "On 'Southern Literature,'" in which I questioned whether, apart from the ante-bellum Southern humorists, there was anything *essentially Southern* in Southern writing before the time of Ellen Glasgow. In those days the Southern Methodist University Library lacked the materials I needed for research. Hence my writing for some years took the form of preparing textbooks (in collaboration with the late John O. Beaty) in the hope of supplementing my salary and of improving my own teaching. From 1924 to 1927 much of my time and thought was given to editing the *Southwest Review*. I was at that time keenly interested in contemporary poetry and in the literature and the history of the Southwest. I planned to write a book dealing with the influence of the frontier upon American literature. I did in fact write the essay on that subject reprinted in this volume, but when I came to Duke University in September, 1927, the literature of the South seemed for me a more appropriate field for research. In 1927 also appeared the first two volumes of Parrington's *Main Currents in American Thought*. His admirable discussion of certain writers of the Old South quickened my own interest in the subject. In 1929 at the request of the late Stanley T.

Williams I edited John Pendleton Kennedy's *Swallow Barn* for the American Authors Series published by Harcourt, Brace and Company. I had been teaching American literature since 1913, but it was not until nearly twenty years later that I was able to offer a course in Southern Literature and Culture.

Soon after the appearance in 1930 of that notable Southern Agrarian symposium *I'll Take My Stand*, Mr. William T. Couch, Director of the University of North Carolina Press, planned a larger symposium of a different kind which in 1934 was published under the title *Culture in the South*. At his request I wrote the essay on "Southern Magazines." Soon after the book appeared he wrote me urging me to write a history of Southern literature and added that he would be glad to publish it. There was no good book on the subject; in fact, no history of Southern literature had appeared since 1910, when Montrose J. Moses published *The Literature of the South*. Mr. Couch had in mind a book of from 350 to 400 pages, and he hoped that I would be able to bring him the completed manuscript in four or five years. For the next two years, however, most of my spare time had to be given to work on my *American Life in Literature* (1936). When *The South in American Literature* finally appeared on September 10, 1954, it contained nearly a thousand pages, and I had been for ten days Professor Emeritus. Twenty years is a long time.

2

Why in 1934 did it seem desirable that there should be yet another history of Southern literature? Sectional literary histories and anthologies, as some of my friends did not fail to remind me, were out of favor with scholars; and with few exceptions the Southern anthologies and literary histories were undoubtedly the most provincial and the least scholarly of the lot. Why should I spend my time on such an unpromising subject as ante-bellum Southern literature? If I must work on the literature of the South, why not study the literature of the twentieth-century South? Already by 1934 it was obvious that many of our best living writers were Southerners.

All this might be true, I realized, but before one could make a thorough study of contemporary Southern literature (if even then that were possible), one must know its background in the life and literature of the older South. I was troubled by the lack of interest among scholars in the background out of which the Southern Literary Renaissance had grown. Contemporary-minded critics failed to recognize the continuing strength of Southern traditions, literary and otherwise. No one, so far as I had observed, was aware of the strong resemblance between the ideas of the Southern Agrarians who in 1930 published *I'll Take My Stand* and the ideas of the proslavery writers of the Old South, who were also shrewd critics of the industrial civilization of the Northern states. There were still other instances. No one, it seemed to me, recognized the large indebtedness of Joel Chandler Harris and other local colorists of the New South to the humorists of the Old South, or the influence of the Southern local colorists upon the regionalists of the twentieth century.

For my graduate teaching I had examined such special literary and cultural studies as were available, and I was disturbed by the casual and superficial manner in which some Northern scholars treated the ante-bellum South. There were, for example, published studies of the American reception of Voltaire, Byron, and other European writers which neglected the South—and this at a time when half the people of the United States were living below the Mason-Dixon Line. There were two "standard" studies of Deism in America and another of the gentleman in American literature which paid scant attention to any Southern writer except Thomas Jefferson. What was the reason for this neglect? Was it that the Northern scholars thought it a matter of no importance what Southerners read or did not read, or was it not rather just too much trouble for these scholars to examine the dusty files of Southern newspapers and magazines and to look for essential materials in scattered manuscripts and rare books and pamphlets?

In 1934 most of our literary histories gave little space to a discussion of Southern writers, and their treatment of the subject was conventional and often unsympathetic. One of the least satisfactory of them all was the charmingly written *Literary History of America* by Professor Barrett Wendell, who in the 530 pages of his text gave only 15 pages to "The West" and only 20 to "Literature in the South." Wendell's treatment of William Gilmore Simms was typical. Simms was too important to be left out altogether, but Wendell's discussion was based mainly on Trent's life of Simms. I saw no indication that he had read any of Simms's numerous novels except *The Yemassee*. Fred Lewis Pattee, who was born and reared in the north-of-Boston country, once said that Wendell should have entitled his book *A Literary History of Harvard University, with Incidental Glimpses of the Minor Writers of America*.

Perhaps no one who knew that Wendell's book had been published as long ago as 1900 found its proportions surprising. The writers whom he stressed were much the same as those who had figured prominently in Lowell's *A Fable for Critics*, published in 1848. But when the three-volume *Literary History of the United States*—the work of fifty-five well-trained scholars—appeared in 1948, I was dismayed to find much the same disproportion in the space allotted to the Southern writers as I had noted in Wendell's *Literary History*. The inadequate treatment of the South was not, I knew, intentional. It was due partly to sheer ignorance and partly to the lack of such basic scholarly aids as were available for the writers of New England and New York but not for those of South Carolina, Georgia, and Virginia. Now more than ever, I felt, there was a need for a detailed and accurate history of Southern literature—one that future literary historians must reckon with.

By 1934 the best Northern and Southern historians had worked out a reinterpretation of the place of the South in American history which was generally accepted by American scholars. That, however, was not the case with the literature and literary culture of the South. The literature of the Old South still needed to be given its rightful place in the framework of the national literature. Parrington had included in the second volume of his *Main Currents* some admirable brief chapters on such ante-bellum Southern writers as William Alexander Caruthers and John Pendleton Kennedy, and at the University of Chicago Napier Wilt and Walter Blair were emphasizing the importance of the forgotten Southern humorists; but, it seemed to me, much more remained to be done—more in fact than I at that time realized.

The critical estimate of the literature of the Old South found in the literary histories and reference books of the 1930's had its basis in a tradition established by the Abolitionists and their sympathizers and confirmed in the Northern mind by the outcome of the Civil

War. The literary historians had accepted uncritically the view of Garrison, Phillips, Sumner, Lowell, and Emerson that the civilization of the Old South was semibarbarous and its literature of slight importance. Too many educated Southerners were accepting this tradition, which I believed to be false. If the Abolitionists had consulted the census reports of 1840 and 1850, they might have learned that the Southern states had a larger proportion of college-bred men than New York or New England—even if the Negro slaves were included in the total Southern population. Yet at a meeting of the National Teachers' Association at Harrisburg, Pennsylvania, in August, 1865, the war just ended was described as one of "education and patriotism against ignorance and barbarism."

The special interests of every scholar and teacher interested in American literature were suffering from the inadequate treatment of the Southern writers. Imagine—as I said in 1936 at a meeting of the Modern Language Association—a study of the American historical novel which omitted Simms, Kennedy, and Cooke; or a survey of the American short story which took no account of Cable, Harris, Allen, and Page; or a book on American humor which neglected the humorous tradition which lies back of Mark Twain; or a discussion of our political literature which made no mention of Jefferson, Madison, or Calhoun; or a study of Poe which attached no importance to his Southern background in Maryland, South Carolina, and Virginia. Even the scarcely imaginable student who had no interest in any single Southern writer, I felt, should be made to realize that he must know something about life in the South—if for no other reason—simply because so many Northern writers had written about it. For a hundred years and more the North had been disposed to see the South as a national problem, social, economic, political, cultural, and above all, moral. The North, when it has not sentimentalized over the South, as when it sings "My Old Kentucky Home" or reads *Gone with the Wind* or *So Red the Rose,* has wanted to reform it.

The literature which deals with the South represents two divergent and changing traditions, which in our time have become strangely intermingled and confused. Earlier literary historians of the South—who wished to exclude "Southern Yankees" like Moncure Daniel Conway and George W. Cable—had often wasted their energies in trying to determine what constitutes a "Southern" writer. I decided to include those writings concerned with the South that possessed literary merit no matter who wrote them. It seemed evident to me that no one could fully understand defenders of slavery like William J. Grayson and George Fitzhugh without devoting some attention to what Lowell, Emerson, and Mrs. Stowe had to say on the same subject. And again, the picture of the Reconstruction South found in Thomas Nelson Page's *Red Rock* needed to be supplemented by that in Albion W. Tourgée's *A Fool's Errand* and the novels and short stories of Constance Fenimore Woolson. As late as 1921 Ellen Glasgow could write:

There are two permissible fashions in which one may write of the negro in American fiction today—the fashion of the North which portrays him as a celestial victim in allegory, or the fashion of the South which presents him as the poetic figure of sentimental legend. The shadows of Uncle Tom and Uncle Remus are still falling across the American scene.

Most of the earlier Southern literary historians and anthologists had treated the literature of the South as though it had developed in a vacuum insulated from contact with the outside world. More than ever, as I proceeded with my investigation, I felt the truth of what my old teacher, Professor Trent, had written in his *Southern Writers* as long ago as 1905: "The history of the South and its literature cannot profitably be divorced from the history and the literature of the entire country. . . ." Intersectional literary relations seemed to me increasingly important, and yet except for the unfinished work of the late Max L. Griffin of Tulane University, I could find no scholarly studies of importance bearing on the subject. The literature of the South had not developed in a vacuum. In fact, most of the best books by Southern writers had been published in Northern cities, and important Southern materials had been printed in New York and Philadelphia literary magazines.

The literature of the South, I soon realized, cannot be understood and appraised if one neglects its many and complicated relations with the literature of the Northern states. Some of the Southern writers were of Northern birth and upbringing, like Margaret Junkin Preston; others who were born in the South had one or both parents from the North, like John R. Thompson; others, who were native to the South, were educated in Northern colleges, like Philip

Pendleton Cooke and Augustus Baldwin Longstreet. Paul Hamilton Hayne, a native of Charleston and educated at the College of Charleston, visited in the North, where he had influential friends among authors, editors, and publishers. Like many another Southern writer, he discovered that if what he wrote was to reach many readers, it would have to be through books published in Northern cities or through poems, stories, or essays printed in Northern magazines. The founders of the Southern historical societies were for the most part either Northern men who had come South or Southern men educated in the North. The Southern academies, colleges, and universities got many of their best teachers from New England.

Having decided to include Northern as well as Southern writers, I named my book *The South in American Literature*. When I had thus widened its scope, I found that I need no longer worry over the problem which so troubled my predecessors, namely, "What constitutes a Southern writer?" Yet in thus enlarging the field to be covered, I realized that I would once again have to defer the time when I would be able to complete my book.

If in 1934 I did not appreciate the magnitude of the task I had set for myself, I at least knew that I could look forward to little of that "academic leisure" which the layman imagines as the peculiar perquisite of the university professor. I had a full load of classes of both graduate and undergraduate students, and I was teaching in the summer school as well as in the regular session. I had many master's theses and doctor's dissertations to supervise, and for five years I served as Director of Graduate Studies. From 1928 until my retirement in 1954 I was Chairman of the Editorial Board of *American Literature*. The Second World War brought anxiety and distraction to me as to other fathers who had sons in the U. S. Army, and it gave me an extra class to teach for sailors and marines.

When Arthur Hobson Quinn asked me to join him as one of the four authors of *The Literature of the American People*, I hesitated. I finally declined regretfully partly because I did not want to defer for I did not know how many years the completion of my book and partly because the period Professor Quinn wished me to take was not the one I was best equipped to handle.

My progress was so slow that at one time I debated with myself whether or not to limit my book to the ante-bellum South. Yet it seemed to me highly desirable to point out the large but unrecognized debt which the literary New South owed to the Old, and it was not less important to supply the background needed by students interested primarily in the twentieth century. I finally brought my literary history down to the end of the nineteenth century. My section on the New South, however, includes detailed treatment of only seven authors. I would have liked to include at least as many more. In an Epilogue dealing with the twentieth century I discussed all too briefly O. Henry, Ellen Glasgow, James Branch Cabell, and one or two others; and I pointed out some of the historical factors which still have a large influence upon both Northern and Southern writing about the states that lie south of the Potomac and the Ohio.

Before the book was completed, I had laid it aside to spend two separate semesters at the University of Vienna and another at the University of Athens. This, however, I do not regard as altogether lost time, for the experience of lecturing to European students gave me a new perspective upon American literature and especially upon the South's contribution to it. As seen from the other side of the Atlantic many of our writers, Northern as well as Southern, seem much less important than they seem in an American university. Their importance is historical rather than intrinsic. They bulk much larger in the history of our literary culture than they do in any critical estimate of American letters.

I have demonstrated, I think, that there was more and rather better writing in the Old South than was generally supposed, but I make no claim to having discovered a neglected Southern literary genius. If I seem to write with undue enthusiasm about certain little-known authors, I have also reminded my readers that while the nineteenth-century South had many intelligent men and women who put pen to paper, some of whom are not even mentioned in my pages, it produced only two writers of the very first rank, Edgar Allan Poe and Mark Twain. These two writers have been so often described as "Southern only by courtesy" (as Barrett Wendell remarked of Poe) that I have been at some pains to point out the influence of their Southern upbringing and their relations with their Southern contemporaries.

3

I did not in the beginning realize how much spadework I should have to do if I were to discuss not only the numerous Southern writers for whom there were no dependable biographies but also the various aspects of literary culture for which no critical studies were available. The majority of the biographical sketches of Southern authors available to me in the 1930's had been written by amateurs, many of them prejudiced or incompetent or both. At that time there were comparatively few such guides to rare materials—books, magazines, newspapers, and manuscripts—as are now to be found in every large university library. In 1934 neither the Duke University Library nor other Southern libraries had the rich collections that some of them have now. Before I could complete my study of Southern literature, it was necessary for me to visit some of the great Northern and Western libraries.

In 1934 Southern literature was singularly poor in the apparatus of scholarship as compared with the literature of New York or New England. For example, my book must include a chapter on Henry Timrod, the most important Southern poet after Poe and Lanier. Yet in the 1930's there was no real biography of the poet, no complete edition of his poems, no collection of his essays or letters. We did not know the exact year of his birth and were not aware that his most famous poem—the Magnolia Cemetery "Ode"—had been written not in 1867 but in 1866 and that, unknown to scholars, there was in the yellowing pages of a Charleston newspaper a revised version of that poem not known to students of American literature. By the time *The South in American Literature* was published in 1954, however, important new materials on Timrod had been made available. These included Guy A. Cardwell's *Uncollected Poems of Henry Timrod* (1942), Edd Winfield Parks's *The Essays of Henry Timrod* (1942), and my own *The Last Years of Henry Timrod* (1941). I am happy to state that Professor Parks's *Henry Timrod* (1964) fills the need for a good biographical and critical study and to add that Professor and Mrs. Parks are soon to bring out a complete edition of Timrod's poems.

One of my first tasks was to compile a tentative list of Southern authors and their works. *The Library of Southern Literature* and other anthologies supplied many names and titles, but I consulted every other source that I could think of. I was surprised at the large amount of writing done in the Old South. That region was never the literary Sahara that the Abolitionists thought the slave-holding states must be. Yet in the end many of the writers on my list proved after some study not worthy of inclusion in even so large a book as *The South in American Literature.*

Many of the books, pamphlets, magazines, and newspapers containing the work of the Southern writers were rare and difficult to come by. The Union Lists in the Library of Congress and the University of Pennsylvania Library enabled me to locate some materials that otherwise I would never have seen. The Duke University Library purchased various books for me, obtained others on interlibrary loan, and brought me still others in the form of microfilms and photostats. There were many other materials, however, which I examined in the various libraries in which I was privileged to work. On week-ends I could visit the libraries in Raleigh and Chapel Hill, and during my winter and spring vacations I could manage to have a few days in Richmond, Charlottesville, Columbia, or Charleston. I made some use of the New York libraries while teaching in the Columbia University summer session; and while holding a similar position at the University of California at Los Angeles, I examined the Southern materials in the Huntington Library. I spent most of the summer of 1939 working in the Library of Congress, thanks to my sister, who turned over to me her house in Georgetown. Two sabbatical leaves of half a year each made it possible for me to examine many books, magazines, and manuscripts and to write large sections of the book.

In the literature of the Old South there were numerous anonymous and pseudonymous writings, and in many cases it was difficult or impossible to find out who wrote them. In another essay in this book I have described my difficulties with John Cotton, the author of "Bacon's Epitaph, Made by His Man." Nearly every essay and poem printed in our Colonial newspapers is anonymous, and so are most of the materials printed in the literary magazines of the Old South. I had frequent occasion to be grateful to my friend David K. Jackson for his *The Contributors and Contributions to "The*

Southern Literary Messenger." I was fortunate enough to find marked files of two important Charleston literary magazines: the first *Southern Review* and *Russell's Magazine*; but I could find nothing of the kind for the *Southern Quarterly Review.* The letters of some writers, especially Simms and Hayne, gave me clues to the authorship of certain articles and books; and sometimes I stumbled upon the name of a writer while going systematically through files of old magazines or newspapers. The *Southern Quarterly Review* in October, 1842, published an article on "Transcendentalism" which seemed to me important, and I wondered who in South Carolina had been reading the *Dial.* Several years later I learned who wrote the article while going through a file of the *Orion.* Its editor, W. C. Richards, who had recently returned to Athens, Georgia, from a visit to Charleston, stated that the article in question had been written by the editor of the *Quarterly,* Daniel K. Whitaker. Once again I was to identify an anonymous publication of this Massachusetts-born Yankee who came South and founded a number of Southern magazines both before and after the Civil War. I was in the Rare Book Room at the Library of Congress examining a rare pamphlet which had been attributed to Simms. A. S. Salley in the published catalogue of his fine collection of Simmsiana had stated that he did not know whether or not Simms had written *Sidney's Letters to William E. Channing . . .* (Charleston, 1837). I was glad to be able to write to Mr. Salley (who had shown me the manuscript records of Timrod's enlistment in the Confederate Army) that the Library of Congress copy of the pamphlet bore the inscription: "To Prof. Geo. Bush with the respects of the author D. K. Whitaker."

Some of the best Southern songs and ballads of the Civil War still appear as anonymous in the anthologies, most of them compiled by amateurs. Pseudonyms add to the confusion, especially when we find two different poets using the pen name of "Moïna." The stirring lyric which begins: "I give my soldier boy a blade" was actually written by the Irish poet, William Maginn. "The Good Old Rebel," which the late John A. Lomax took down from the singing of a Texas cowboy and printed in his *Cowboy Songs* in 1910, was written by Innes Randolph. There are two fine poems extolling

General Jackson written by John Williamson Palmer which often still appear as anonymous: "Stonewall Jackson's Way" and "In Martial Manner," beginning: "The Brigade Must not Know, Sir!" "The Picket-Guard," beginning: "All quiet along the Potomac," was claimed by more than one Confederate poet but was actually written by a Northern poet, Ethel Lynn Beers; it was printed in *Harper's Weekly* on September 30, 1861.

By the time I undertook to write my history of Southern literature, I had formed some conception of what such a literary history should include and how it ought to be written. As I proceeded with my investigation, however, it became evident that my book would be almost as much a study in literary culture as a literary history—even if that meant an increase in the size of the book. There were too many misconceptions and rash generalizations about Southern literature and life that must be corrected. There were also important aspects of Southern literary culture that no one knew much about. So I began gathering information about the books and magazines that Southerners read and the books that were in their libraries, public and private; about what was taught in Southern academies, denominational colleges, and state universities; about Southern booksellers, printers, and editors of newspapers and magazines; about the literary taste of Southern readers and their attitude toward those who wrote; and about literary relations with the Northern states. I found clues to some of the answers in the work of the modern Southern historians, whose intellectual interests are wider than those of some of our literary historians. I had no fixed formula for my literary history, but I tried to give an adequate account of each writer's literary career, his aims and technical methods, his relation to his contemporaries, and his representative quality as a writer. I made little use of certain approaches now in vogue, and I emphasized narrative and exposition rather than criticism. With the passing of time critical approaches and standards will change, but factual accounts such as I have provided will, I am sure, serve some of those critics who do not accept my critical estimates.

I was surprised, as I have noted, at the large amount of writing published by men and women in the Old South. This, too, in spite of the fact that, apart from newspapermen, the South had no professional authors except Simms and Poe—and Poe spent his later years in Philadelphia and New York. Who were the Southern authors? I asked myself. Not the gentlemen planters, surely, even though many of them were well educated and widely read. A planter might on occasion publish a political pamphlet or describe a hunting expedition for a Charleston newspaper; but if he published a novel, a play, or a poem over his own name, he was likely to be made to feel that he had done something not proper for a gentleman to do. The authors of the Old South lived not on the farms and plantations but in the towns and cities. So far as one can generalize, they were lawyers, journalists, doctors, clergymen, and teachers; or they were the wives or daughters of the members of these professions.

New literary impulses, originating in Europe, came to the South either directly from England or by way of New York, Philadelphia, and Boston. There was after about 1830 a cultural lag between South and North, and the literary taste of most Southern readers in the years 1830-1880 was somewhat old-fashioned. Southerners did not like to admit it, but in cultural matters the status of the South was best described as "colonial." The colonial status of the South continued in diminished form long after the Civil War had ended slavery and all hope of a separate nationality; and its colonial status had its influence upon Southern writing down to the end of the nineteenth century.

By 1934 I had read more of the older Southern literature than most scholars, but I did not make the mistake of beginning my book with a ready-made thesis to be imposed upon the literature and literary culture of the Southern states. I did not find it easy to see in proper perspective the crucial and controversial half-century 1830-1880, which included the movement toward a separate Southern nationality, the Civil War, the period of Reconstruction and reconciliation. In my Foreword to *The South in American Literature* I thus summarized my interpretation of these years:

The South has more than once been in and out of the main stream of national development. During the American Revolution and for many years afterwards the South was in the lead; and Washington, Jefferson, Madison, and other Southerners played a large part not only in building the framework of the nation but also in creating a notable political literature. All our early presidents came from either Virginia or Massa-

63

chusetts, and in those years Northern and Southern travelers found much to admire when they visited in Virginia or Massachusetts.

In the fourth decade of the nineteenth century this situation changed for the worse. The South, beginning now to defend slavery on principle, had finally turned its back upon the liberalism of Washington, Jefferson, and Madison. By this time New England, which had not felt the full force of Revolutionary liberalism, was sprouting all kinds of isms repugnant to the conservative South. The rapidly developing industrial North saw the slave-holding South in the ominous shape of an economic, political, and moral problem. The South was felt to be resisting the progress of industrialization and democracy, and so at all costs it must be made to fit into the "national" or "American" pattern. The South, on the other hand, felt that it was being exploited by Northern merchants and manufacturers and that its civilization was being attacked by fanatical reformers and unscrupulous politicians who knew nothing about Southern life. And so the South fought against what it regarded as the all-devouring state and ultimately left the Union to protect what it believed to be the rights of the states.

In the 1830's Southerners, who had been generally content to get their literature from England and the Northern states, were increasingly disturbed by the hostility to their section of the newer literature of the North, especially New England. They then began slowly and half consciously building up a rival literary tradition and creating a regional literature, which was often designed as a defense against Northern misrepresentation of Southern life.

The victorious North, after it had won the war and freed the slaves, repudiated the literature of the Old South on the dubious theory that no slave-holding people could possibly produce a literature of any intrinsic importance. The South, now chastened by defeat, accepted in good faith the end of slavery and secession and sought once again to find its place within the framework of the reunited nation. After the end of Reconstruction in 1877 a new era of intersectional good feeling developed. Constance Fenimore Woolson and other Northern writers rediscovered the charm of Southern life. A new generation of Southern writers created a notable body of local-color fiction, which was in part designed to correct the distorted picture of Southern life found in the writings of Harriet Beecher Stowe. Very slowly the South came to realize the tragic mistake it had made in abandoning the liberalism of Thomas Jefferson.

It should be continually borne in mind that for more than a century the Southern writer has always had to remember that if he wanted a market for his writings, he must reckon with literary fashion and the unpredictability of the changing Northern attitude toward the region in which he lives. The Northern writer who lived in the South sometimes found readers in his own section unwilling to accept his picture of Southern life. Albion W. Tourgée, who had lived in North Carolina in the Reconstruction period, was so irritated by Northern criticism of his novels that he wrote in the Preface to *A Royal Gentleman* in 1881: "The trouble is that the Northern man has made up a South for himself, and without the least hesitation, criticises any departure from the original of his own imagination as untrue to life." This situation goes far toward explaining the limitations of fiction as a full and accurate picture of Southern life; and it helps to explain why so many Northern visitors to the South fail to find what they have been led to expect to see. Southern mansions and poor-white cabins are not to be found at every bend in the road.

If I found no unknown literary masterpieces by Southern writers—and I had hardly expected to find any—I did find some important new materials on Poe, Timrod, George Tucker, and other writers. Some of these materials came to me from my graduate students and from friends on the Duke University Library staff. Others I found by systematically going through manuscript collections and files of old magazines. I found some new materials on Poe in a "Copperhead" magazine, the New York *Old Guard,* edited by his friend Charles Chauncey Burr. In a Richmond weekly, *Southern Opinion,* I found a new text of a juvenile poem which had been doubtfully attributed to Poe. As a result of the new evidence I was able to present, " 'O Tempora! O Mores!' " has been added to the Poe canon. I found so much new material on Henry Timrod— much of it in the Duke University Library—that I made a book of it. *The Last Years of Henry Timrod* includes Timrod's letters to his friend Paul Hamilton Hayne; letters about Timrod written by William Gilmore Simms, John R. Thompson, John Greenleaf Whittier, and others; four uncollected Timrod poems; and seven uncollected prose pieces.

Finding such new materials as these relieved the tedium of research in old newspapers, magazines, books, and pamphlets and in letters which, like those of Simms, were often difficult to decipher. One interesting and important find was the unpublished autobiography of George Tucker, now in the Alderman Library of the University of Virginia. In 1939 I was given permission to use a typewritten copy, which was all the library had at that time; but I was asked, for what I considered valid reasons, not to mention the autobiography or its whereabouts. I am hoping that the University of Virginia will eventually publish it. Quite unexpected was the discovery of some uncollected poems by Joseph Addison. Quite unexpected also was a discovery I made in the library of the Virginia Historical Society. In an album which once belonged to the

British novelist, G. P. R. James, I found no less than eleven un-published letters written to James by Walter Savage Landor.

4

When I left for Athens as Fulbright Professor of American Litera-ture and Civilization in January, 1953, I left my completed manu-script with Ashbel G. Brice, Director of the Duke University Press. After my return to Durham in July, I revised portions of the manu-script once more. James Brady Reece, now Professor of English in the Old Dominion College in Norfolk, checked hundreds of my quotations, footnotes, and bibliography; and Truman Frederick Keefer, now at the University of Cincinnati, helped me with the proofreading. The late Stanley T. Williams of Yale read my manu-script for the Duke University Research Council and recommended a subsidy in aid of publication. Norman D. Knox, now a member of the English staff at Hunter College, designed the format, which was rated by the Southern Books Committee of the Southeastern Library Association as one of the best printed books of the year. *The South in American Literature* was published on September 10, 1954, just as I was on the point of leaving for a year at the University of Virginia. The first printing was two thousand copies. There was a second printing of one thousand copies in February, 1959, and a third of eleven hundred copies in June, 1964.

I had no cause for disappointment in the reception the book re-ceived. It won for me in 1955 the Mayflower Award as the best non-fiction book written by a resident of North Carolina. It was favorably reviewed in many periodicals, including the *London Times Literary Supplement.* Among the reviewers were many of the finest scholars in the field of American literature: Lewis Ball, Roy P. Basler, Donald Davidson, Curtis Carroll Davis, Richard Beale Davis, Walter Harding, Ima H. Herron, Howard Mumford Jones, Lewis Leary, Ernest E. Leisy, D. M. McKeithan, Edd Winfield Parks, Louis Rubin, Randall Stewart, Floyd Stovall, John Donald Wade, James Southall Wilson, and Louis B. Wright. The most detailed review was that of Donald Davidson in the *Sewanee Review* which he reprinted in his *Still Rebels, Still Yankees* (1957) under the title "In Justice to So Fine a Country."

One of my reviewers, a well-known professor at one of the great New England universities, had high praise for my book; and yet something I had written apparently got under his skin and he lectured me on my antipathy to New England. Yet he had found so much to praise in the book that it seemed ungracious to call his attention to the following passage in my Foreword, in which I had warned against just such confusion of my personal attitude with that of many ante-bellum Southerners. With them and not with me New England was a "fighting word."

I have tried as well as I could to let the various writers, Northern and Southern, speak for themselves; and I am anxious that no casual reader shall confuse my own opinions with such sweeping pronouncements as Simms's "Charleston is worth all New England" or Emerson's "I do not see how a barbarous community and a civilized community can constitute one state."

Horace was perhaps wise to advise the poet to lay aside his poems for a decade before publishing them, but I have sometimes wondered if the advice applies as well to the work of the literary historian. *The South in American Literature* is no doubt a sounder book than it would have been if I had been able to complete it in the four or five years I at first planned to devote to it. A literary history of the older South would have seemed more timely in 1938 or 1939 than in 1954. Between 1934 and 1954 came the Second World War, the Cold War, the dawn of the Atomic Age, and the first of several notable pronouncements by the United States Supreme Court. The Old South and its literature had receded into the distant past. The twenty years in which I was working on my book brought changes in literary fashion that profoundly influenced scholarship and literary criticism. In 1954 many of the younger scholars, it seemed to me, had little if any interest in literary history. As I have noted, some of those who teach American history had a better appreciation of what I had done than many of those who were teaching American literature. The history professor by profession must concern himself with historical events—that is his business—but the English professor nowadays too often neglects the historical aspects of the subject he teaches. I sympathize with the teacher who wishes to make a thoroughgoing critical analysis of, for example, a novel by William Faulkner or Ellen Glasgow, but without some attention to its background in Southern history—political, social, and literary—one can never quite see a work of art as its creator saw it and fully comprehend his intention and his means of carrying it out. The emphasis in my book, as I explained in my Foreword, is upon narrative and exposition and not on literary criticism. My conception of the relation of the literary historian to the literary critic was admirably stated by one of the best of the New Critics, R. P. Blackmur, in *The Double Agent* (1935):

Upon scholarship all other forms of literary criticism depend, so long as they are criticism, in much the same way that architecture depends on engineering. . . . Scholarship, being bent on the collection, arrangement, and scrutiny of facts, has the positive advantage over other forms of criticism that it is a co-operative labor, and may be completed and corrected by subsequent scholars; and it has the negative advantage that it is not bound to investigate the mysteries of meaning or to connect literature with other departments of life—it has only to furnish the factual materials for such investigations and connections. . . . A last fact about scholarship is this, that so far as its conclusions are sound they are subject to use and digestion not debate by those outside the fold.

A few reviewers hailed my book as the "definitive" history of Southern literature. It is, as I knew only too well, no such thing. Two months after its publication I read a paper at a meeting of the South Atlantic Modern Language Association in Columbia, South Carolina, from which I quote:

No one, I hope will take *The South in American Literature* as the final word on the subject. It is rather a summary of what we now know about certain Southern writers and their cultural background. It is meant also to be a stimulus to further study—a point of departure. That is why I have included a Bibliography of nearly one hundred pages and thrown out many suggestions for further investigation. I shall be glad to see some of my chapters rendered out of date by any scholars who can add to what we now know about the writers whom I have discussed.

I am conscious of some of the limitations of my book. I have not included enough of the writers of the New South. I have not fully traced the development in the South of literary influences from England, the European continent, and the Northern states. I have not more than outlined the development of the Southern novel or of poetry in the Southern states, and I have given little attention to the theater and to Southern playwrights.

There are limits to what one can include even in so large a book as mine. Some readers, I know, would have liked more critical analysis of the poems of Timrod and Lanier and of the psychological novels of Simms. And there are doubtless some readers who will wonder why I have included so many minor writers. For the general reader, I might better have limited my book to a dozen authors, half of them from the twentieth century. Yet for the scholar who wishes to understand the literary history of his own country, many of the minor writers are significant. My book was written primarily for the student and the scholar. I shall be content if *The South in American Literature* enables future critics and literary historians better to understand and appreciate the Southern contribution to our American literature. It will also, I hope, induce them to discard the many conventional and inaccurate notions which one finds in even some of the best and latest of our literary histories.

In the ten years that have elapsed since I wrote these paragraphs I have been pleased to note fewer errors in the newer literary histories and reference books. I have noted also fewer of the traditional condescending remarks about the literature and the literary culture of the nineteenth-century South. I note with pleasure that the abler scholars and critics who have written about Wolfe, Faulkner, and the Fugitives now seem to appreciate better the long historical and cultural background against which these writers are best seen. Future literary historians will never again, I trust, give to the literature of the South such meager space and cursory treatment as I have pointed out in Barrett Wendell's *Literary History of America* and *The Literary History of the United States*.

There are no "definitive" literary histories. The individual historian cannot escape his own limitations. He is handicapped by his personal prejudices and prepossessions, by the defects in his training, by his shortcomings in literary taste and in his critical judgment. It is difficult for him to escape the limitations of the generation of scholars to which he belongs. He is handicapped also by the lack of time and by the difficulty of finding essential materials. The uses of the past are many and various, and each new generation of scholars has a different way of looking at those writers in whom it is interested. This is conspicuously true of Poe, Mark Twain, Lanier, and Cable. No doubt some of the less important Southern writers whom I have discussed will be rediscovered by younger scholars who find them interesting and important. The younger scholars may disagree with my critical estimates, but they will, I trust, find that the factual matter in my book is both accurate and useful.

II. The South

With the war of 1914-1918, the South re-entered the world—but it gave a backward glance as it stepped over the border: that backward glance gave us the Southern renaissance, a literature conscious of the past in the present.

ALLEN TATE in the *Virginia Quarterly Review*, Spring, 1945

Thou wert my guide, philosopher, and friend.

ALEXANDER POPE, *Essay on Man*

The Southern Literary Renaissance

[In November, 1955, the University of Richmond celebrated the one hundred and twenty-fifth anniversary of its founding and at the same time the dedication of the Boatwright Memorial Library. My address, originally entitled "Contemporary Southern Literature," was the first of the Frederic William Boatwright Fine Arts Lectures endowed by a donor who wished to be anonymous. It was first published in a booklet entitled *Addresses Commemorating the One Hundred Twenty-fifth Anniversary University of Richmond 1830-1955.*]

1

When I was growing up, it never occurred to me that when I went to college, I might go elsewhere than to Richmond College. My father had been a student here for a single year just after the Civil War when few Virginia fathers could afford to send their sons to college. He was an admirer of Dr. Boatwright and a friend of Dr.

Boatwright's father. He never thought of sending my brother Paul or me to any other college.

No one is prouder than I am of the growth of that small college into the University of Richmond or looks more hopefully to its future under its present faculty and administration. But the Richmond College I most vividly remember was on the old campus at Grace and Lombardy streets now far down within the city. It had, I think, less than three hundred students, including no more than a dozen young women. By the end of my first year I knew, by sight at least, every student and every member of the faculty.

Many of my classmates have attained distinction in widely different fields. I shall name only four: McIver Woody, in medicine; Clifton Howell, in engineering; Edward W. Hudgins, now Chief Justice of the Virginia Supreme Court; and another distinguished lawyer, John A. Cutchins, who is writing a history of the class of 1905. In the class just behind mine was Morris Sayre, who not long ago was President of the National Manufacturers Association; in the class of 1907 was the Junior U. S. Senator from Virginia, A. Willis Robertson; and in the class just ahead of me was Douglas Southall Freeman, one of the great American historians of our time.

I attribute no small part of the achievements of these men and of others whom I could name to the remarkable group of professors who then constituted the Richmond College faculty. In those days the lowly freshman studied under the ablest men in the faculty and not, as happens too often nowadays in all our colleges, under inexperienced young instructors. Of that small faculty the only one living is Dr. R. E. Gaines, an extraordinarily fine teacher of mathematics; but many of the alumni here will remember the lovable Dr. William A. Harris, who taught me Greek; Dr. William L. Foushee, under whose direction I read the Latin classics; and Dr. Samuel Chiles Mitchell, one of the finest history teachers any college ever had. In English I had Dr. Julian A. C. Chandler, who was later President of the College of William and Mary, and Dr. Frederick C. Woodward, who had been President of the University of South Carolina. I just missed studying under Dr. John Calvin Metcalf, who was afterwards Dean of the Graduate School in the University of Virginia. (I should like just here to assure President George Modlin, from what I have seen and heard on both sides of the lake, that the work of the English department is still in good hands.) Not all of the men under whom I studied held what is sometimes called the professor's union card, the Ph.D. degree; but they were competent scholars as well as fine teachers. Any college would have been—and would be now—lucky to have such men in its faculty.

I was fortunate to enter college when Dr. Boatwright was not only President but also Professor of Modern Languages. He was an admirable teacher, and he loved to teach. He gave me a lively sense of the quality of French culture and an appreciation of French poetry and drama. I remember my disappointment when in my last year he met his German class and rather sadly explained to us that his administrative duties had become so heavy that he must give up the class. Unlike some administrative officers whom I have known, Dr. Boatwright had no feeling that administrative work was any more worthy of honor than teaching. Teaching was the primary function of an institution of learning. Somebody, as he saw it, had to administer: to make it possible for the college to keep open its doors and to provide the indispensable facilities for the proper work of the college. Dr. Boatwright's distinguished successor, President Modlin, recently said of him:

When he became president in 1895 there were 183 students, a faculty of nine professors, campus property valued at $300,000, an endowment of $400,000, a total income of $30,000, and no debt. In his final Annual Report he reported an enrollment of 2,174 students, a faculty of 112 members, campus property valued at $2,706,606, an endowment of $7,188,181, income of $648,729, and no debt.

Frederic William Boatwright became President of Richmond College in 1895 and held that post until 1946; and he served as Chancellor until his death in 1951. He was the active head of this institution for more than fifty years; and, as I once heard Douglas Freeman say in introducing him to the Modern Language Association, the average duration of a college or university presidency is something less than three years. Before 1895 Richmond College, like the University of Virginia, had only a Chairman of the Faculty as its chief executive officer. Dr. Boatwright became President at the age of twenty-seven. He was young, energetic, full of ideas and enthusiasm for his work. Most of the professors had taught him; and a few of them, resenting his promotion over their heads, resigned their posts; and some of the alumni felt that the college trustees had made a grave mistake. The new President faced an extremely difficult situation. But it was not long before it was evident to students, faculty, and alumni that the college had entered a new era under its young President. In time he became one of the best-loved men in the faculty. With some students, however, the first impression was that the new President was a little haughty in his manner. He was in fact, as they slowly learned, somewhat shy. He had the carriage of a West Pointer, and he wore a beard, which he certainly needed to cover up his extreme youthfulness. I was at first a little afraid of him, but I quickly discovered that he was one of the kindest and most thoughtful of men. He had a sense of humor, too; and when he smiled, you knew that you were in the presence of a wise counselor and an understanding friend.

I am greatly honored in having the privilege of delivering the first Frederic William Boatwright Fine Arts lecture; and I am delighted to have the opportunity publicly to pay my tribute to a fine teacher, a great college president, a devout Christian, and a gentleman in the best Virginia tradition. No other man has had a larger share in the making of this institution, and it is eminently appropriate that the beautiful new library building should bear his name. "The library," Dr. Boatwright once said, "is the most vital building in a university." In his Dedication Address just four days ago Dr. Vernon B. Richardson said: "We dedicate this library gratefully, from wells of affection, to the memory of Frederic William Boatwright, whose name above its threshold will always bid us to the upward look and invite us to the quest of truth."

2

The particular topic I am to discuss brings to my mind a chapel talk in which Dr. Boatwright said that the South had not contributed to the nation its share of important writers and expressed the hope that some one of us Virginia boys might live to write a book of more than ephemeral importance. I do not know whether Douglas Freeman was in chapel that morning, but I am glad that Dr. Boatwright lived to see the publication of Freeman's great biography of Robert E. Lee. He lived long enough also to witness the rise of what is often called the Southern Literary Renaissance, which has brought to this part of the nation such literary recognition as it never before received.

Many a Northern writer has pointed to the South as the richest of all American literary backgrounds; but some of them, like George E. Woodberry, have held that the best novels of Southern life were written by outsiders like Thackeray and Mrs. Stowe. There are Northern critics who seem to think that the South had no important writers until about thirty years ago, and there are some Southerners who seem to know no better. They make me think of a two-line epigram written by one of the South's worst poets, J. Gordon Coogler:

> *Alas for the South! Her books have grown fewer;*
> *She was never much given to literature.*

As a matter of fact, the South has been producing important writers ever since the time of William Byrd, who was born nearly three centuries ago. Edgar Allan Poe, Sidney Lanier, and Mark Twain are by any standard among the better writers in American literature; and Jefferson, Madison, Calhoun, and Woodrow Wilson are among the ablest political writers this country has produced. There are other writers whose names will come to the mind of every student. The twentieth-century Southern writers have overshadowed their predecessors, but every literary movement has its roots in the past; and the Southern literature of our time has definite and important relations to the literature, the life, and the thought of that older South, the memory of which has grown dim.

In the writings of Lanier, Harris, Cable, and their contemporaries the New South produced a notable body of poetry and fiction which attracted wide attention in the North and helped to bring about a reconciliation between the two sections. By 1900, however, that movement had spent its force, and the next quarter of a century was to be a slack time in Southern writing. In the North by 1910 a new generation of poets and novelists was emerging, but for another ten or fifteen years the South seemed to have no part in the new movement. Yet in the early 1900's, in this city of Richmond, Ellen Glasgow and James Branch Cabell were writing their earlier novels and attacking certain traditional Southern attitudes.

Miss Glasgow severely criticized the outmoded education of Southern girls, and both she and Cabell suggested that Virginia gentlemen no longer lived up to the code of behavior they professed. Nor were Cabell and Miss Glasgow the first to attack Southern traditions. Walter Hines Page had condemned the backwardness of the South and blamed it upon "the Ghost of the Confederate Dead, the Ghost of Religious Orthodoxy, the Ghost of Negro Domination." Southerners, unlike the great Virginians of Jefferson's time, had no intellectual curiosity. Southern hospitality was genuine; but, he suggested, it did not extend to new ideas. Page said that when the South abandoned the liberalism of Washington and Jefferson to follow Calhoun and Davis into secession and war, it had committed "one of the most disastrous apostasies of history."

There was a strange dichotomy in the mind of the New South. It was an age of compromise. Many Southerners were living half in the present and half in the past. Reconstruction had come to an end with the Compromise of 1877, when President Hayes withdrew the last of the Union troops from the Southern states. The North was leaving the unsolved problem of the ex-slaves to the Southern whites. In those days Southerners were extremely sensitive, not to say intolerant, on the race question. George W. Cable of Louisiana was practically ostracized when he criticized the South's handling of the Negro problem. Yet the Southern people were now thoroughly loyal to the Union, and in 1898 Confederate veterans like Fitzhugh Lee and Joe Wheeler joined thousands of young Southerners in volunteering for the War with Spain.

At the same time the Southern people felt that they must somehow justify the tragic course their section had taken into secession and civil war. There were angry protests from the South when in 1884 Cable proclaimed the cause of the North a "just" one. Southerners had created a cult of old soldiers in gray jackets, and it was difficult in those days to elect to any office a man who had not worn the Confederate uniform. The New South did not want a really accurate history of the Civil War but, as someone phrased it, "an impartial history written from the *Southern* point of view." Some Confederate veteran was sure to denounce any historical textbook which did not tell the story as he remembered or imagined it. William E. Dodd, then teaching at Randolph-Macon College, found it so difficult to teach Southern history as he saw it that he went on to the University of Chicago. I recall my amazement when Dr. S. C. Mitchell, who never lacked the courage to speak his convictions, said to us in chapel one day: "Young gentlemen, there will never be an accurate and impartial history of the Civil War written until the last Confederate veteran is dead." I think he probably included the last Union veteran as well. Since that time a notable group of Southern scholars have rewritten the history of the South, and their writings are an important part of the achievement of the Southern Literary Renaissance.

Half a century ago the Civil War appeared in fiction as a romantic legend which included few of the actualities of warfare as we have come to know them since. Ellen Glasgow thus described the standardized pattern of Civil War romances: "A gallant Northern invader (though never of the rank and file) must rescue the person and protect the virtue of a spirited yet clinging Southern belle and beauty." Every Christmas in her girlhood Ellen Glasgow had received such a novel from a maiden aunt. "I could not believe," she says, "that the late invasion had been a conflict between handsome soldiers in blue uniforms and Southern ladies in crinolines." Later Southern novelists, like Clifford Dowdey and Margaret Mitchell, have given us a truer picture of the Civil War than that found in the romances prized by Ellen Glasgow's maiden aunt.

In the New South men and women often looked back upon the old regime as a kind of golden age. They had forgotten the unpleasant and sordid elements of that old life; and they did not realize how unhappy they would have been if by some miracle they could have set the clock back to the 1850's. The New South was seeing the Old South through the eyes of Thomas Nelson Page. On the great tobacco and cotton plantations they saw not the numerous field hands or the poor whites but gentlemen planters in white suits sipping mint juleps on their verandas and attended by contented house servants who had no embarrassing desire for emancipation. The four million hard-working yeomen farmers, who had few or no slaves, were ignored in the romantic legend of the Old South.

The great plantations had long ago been broken up into small farms, and the planters' sons were going to the towns and cities to seek their fortunes. The New South was building railroads and cotton mills, for the industrial revolution had crossed the Potomac on its way southward to Atlanta and Birmingham. For good or evil, the Southern way of life was fast coming to conform to that of the industrial North, and men and women could not go on indefinitely living in the past.

Hamlin Garland, who had grown up on the Middle Border, visited the South in 1919. It was, he found, "an unkempt, empty land, a land of tiny cabins with outside chimneys, and ugly, unpainted houses set in disorderly lawns." Like many a Northern visitor, he was surprised because he had expected to see the countryside "dotted with stately mansions and odorous with magnolia blooms." He concluded that the writers of the New South had conspired to maintain the fiction of a "sunny South" that never existed outside the pages of romance. He wrote in his diary: "Now . . . it is the duty of the men and women who see this land with present-day training to picture it as it really is, an unlovely time of sorry transition." And that is just what many of our later novelists have done. They have performed the task so well in fact that nowadays some Northern visitors are disappointed if they do not find at every bend in the road Jeeter Lester's cabin surrounded by degenerate poor whites gathering for a lynching party.

What we call the New South came to an end with the outbreak of the First World War. An age of wars and revolutions had begun; and peaceful, idealistic, isolated America had been drawn into the current of world affairs. It was to be an age of dictators, of conflicting ideologies, of mass insanities, of changing manners and morals, of anxiety, tragedy, and insecurity. It was also to be an age of extraordinary advancement in education and in pure and applied science, and it was to bring about a revolution in our thinking and our way of life. It was also to give a new direction to literature throughout the Western World. "Each generation," said Emerson, ". . . must write its own books; or rather, each generation for the next succeeding. The books of an older period will not fit this." After 1914 it was difficult for an American to share fully in the rather complacent optimism of Jefferson, Emerson, and Whitman, who had believed in the innate goodness of human nature. The new literature was to be pessimistic and realistic rather than opti-

　　　　　　　The Southern Literary Renaissance

mistic and romantic; and it was to be greatly concerned with primitive, often evil types of men and women.

The twentieth century brought with it tremendous forces making for change: a new science, new ideas, and a new way of living. It naturally followed that there would be a new literature to express them. In *Brave New World* Aldous Huxley forecast a future when men would no longer date historical events from the birth of Christ. A.D. would be superseded by A.F., which could be taken to mean either After Freud or After [Henry] Ford. Men who knew no physics or mathematics leaped to the conclusion that Einstein's theory of relativity proved that there were no absolute standards in morals. There were new economists, like Thorstein Veblen and Charles A. Beard; and belatedly the Young Intellectuals were discovering Karl Marx, who was all too often the only economist they knew anything about. There was a new psychology, too, and Sigmund Freud seemed to young novelists to have found the key to human behavior.

In literature the realism of Howells went out of fashion, and naturalism took its place. The old canon of the great English and American writers came under fire. Longfellow and Tennyson were condemned as "Victorians." Ezra Pound and T. S. Eliot in those years could not see Milton as a great poet. In 1922 thirty young Americans published their thoroughgoing indictment of our literature, art, and culture under the ironic title *Civilization in the United States*. For Willa Cather, who you may remember was born in Virginia, "The world broke in two in 1922 or thereabouts. . . ." In the same year Eliot published *The Waste Land* and James Joyce brought out his *Ulysses,* books which to young writers offered new and exciting literary techniques. Rebellious literary aspirants often fled to Greenwich Village or, if they could afford it, to London or Paris, where they were likely to brand their countrymen as Philistines and condemn American democracy as a failure. The Great Depression brought many of them home, but Eliot became a British subject and Ezra Pound, when the war broke out, broadcast propaganda for Mussolini and became a traitor to his own country. The naïve idealists who flirted with Russian Communism were finally disillusioned by the Nazi-Soviet Pact of 1939; but it remained for Pearl Harbor to convince some of them that American

81

democracy was something precious that a man must be willing to fight for. I must add that few American writers became Communists except Richard Wright, perhaps the most gifted of the Negro writers, and he was ultimately disillusioned.

The older men and women in my audience will well remember the 1920's when we were the younger generation and our parents and grandparents were troubled about our manners and our morals. College students who had gone off to war in a mood of high-minded idealism came home disillusioned and rebellious. In *A Farewell to Arms* and *Three Soldiers* Ernest Hemingway and John Dos Passos pictured the war as a horrible nightmare, not in the least like war as portrayed in the old romances of the Civil War. One of my former students at Wake Forest College, Laurence Stallings, who had lost a leg on a battlefield in France, collaborated with Maxwell Anderson to write the bitter disillusioned play *What Price Glory?*

In his autobiography, *Lanterns on the Levee,* William Alexander Percy, the Mississippi poet-planter-lawyer, described the "disintegration of that moral cohesion of the South which had given it its strength and its sons their singleness of purpose and simplicity":

> The old Southern way of life in which I had been reared existed no more and its values were ignored or derided. Negroes used to be servants, now they were problems; manners used to be a branch of morals, now they were merely bad; poverty used to be worn with style and dignity, now it was a stigma of failure; politics used to be the study of men proud and jealous of America's honor, now it was a game played by self-seekers which no man need bother his head about; where there had been an accepted plan of living, there was no pattern whatsoever.

I would agree with Percy that we have lost some of the values which marked the older South, but there are compensations. If I may judge from my experience with successive generations of college students, I see in the most recent no falling off in either character or intelligence. The young Virginians whom I taught in Charlottesville in 1954-1955 seem to me as fine a lot of young men and women as any I have ever taught.

The stronghold of Southern conservatism still seemed unshaken when in 1920 H. L. Mencken published "The Sahara of the Bozart." In this once-famous essay he said that the South had had a fine civilization but now it was "almost as sterile, artistically, intellectually, culturally, as the Sahara Desert. . . . If the whole of the late Con-

The Southern Literary Renaissance

federacy were to be engulfed by a tidal wave tomorrow, the effect upon the civilized minority of men would be but little greater than that of a flood on the Yangtse-Kiang." Cabell was "the only Southerner who could write." The modern South, said Mencken, had lost its "capacity for producing ideas" and was exhibiting only "the worst intolerance of ignorance and stupidity."

Mencken's diatribe brought a storm of denunciation from Southern congressmen and newspaper editors, but it set the Young Intellectuals to thinking. Four years later Mencken and Nathan launched the *American Mercury,* and soon all the bright boys and girls in Southern colleges were reading it. They began to write for it, too. At the end of the second year of the *American Mercury* Mencken noted with some pride, for he was a Marylander, that in the preceding two years Southern contributors had published in the *American Mercury* fifty-five articles; New England writers had published only forty-one. The Southern Literary Renaissance was under way at last, and from now on Mencken was saluting one new Southern writer after another.

In the middle twenties well-known Northern poets, like Robert Frost, Vachel Lindsay, and Carl Sandburg, were reading their poems to enthusiastic college audiences all over the South. Everywhere young writers in and outside the colleges were establishing little magazines to publish their own poems and stories. There were no less than nine of these in Dallas, where I was living then. I was at that time editing the *Southwest Review,* and I am pleased to remember that I had the good sense to publish in its pages some of the early work of Paul Green, DuBose Heyward, Conrad Aiken, John Gould Fletcher, and John Crowe Ransom.

The most notable group of Southern writers was at Vanderbilt University in Nashville, Tennessee. The English department had as its head Edwin Mims, the biographer of Sidney Lanier; and on its staff were two fine poets and critics, Donald Davidson and John Crowe Ransom. Among the younger writers who studied at Vanderbilt were Cleanth Brooks, Allen Tate, Jesse Stuart, Merrill Moore, and Robert Penn Warren. The group published its poems in a little magazine called the *Fugitive,* a name which suggested a flight from the Southern tradition; but in 1930 the Vanderbilt group, with some recruits from the outside, brought out the militant symposium *I'll Take My Stand*. This was a defense of the agrarian South and an attack upon Northern industrialism, which threatened to make of the South another North or a second Middle West. I am reminded of Ellen Glasgow, who wrote: "I had grown up in the yet lingering fragrance of the old South; and I loved its imperishable charm, even while I revolted from its stranglehold on the intellect. Like the new South, I had inherited the tragic conflict of types."

Just what caused the Southern Renaissance it is difficult to say. Allen Tate's explanation seems to me as good as any: "With the War of 1914-1918, the South re-entered the world, but it gave a backward glance as it stepped over the border: that backward glance gave us the Southern renaissance, a literature conscious of the past in the present." A somewhat similar view was expressed by Donald Davidson in an address entitled "Why the Modern South Has a Great Literature." Davidson noted the surprising fact that Stark Young, William Alexander Percy, Eudora Welty, and William Faulkner were born and reared—not in a wealthy Northern state with modern schools and cultural facilities like Massachusetts, which once produced so many notable writers—but in Mississippi, one of the most backward of Southern states with a low average income and a high rate of illiteracy. In the 1920's, as Davidson saw it, Mississippi and the other Southern states had "a traditional society which had arrived at a moment of self-consciousness favorable to the production of great literary works." The Southern way of life was being threatened by powerful forces making for change. Southerners were being urged to abolish the poll tax and the chain gang, to pass FEPC laws, to adopt the Northern way of life, and to abolish segregation in all its forms. It was officially proclaimed the nation's Number One Economic Problem. Now, said Davidson, "A traditional society can absorb modern improvements up to a certain point without losing its character. If modernism enters to the point where the society is thrown a little off balance but not yet completely off balance, the moment of self-consciousness arrives." And so, he concluded, William Faulkner awoke "to realize what he and his people are in comparison with what they are being urged to become." The conflict between the new and the traditional is found in nearly every book that has come out of the Southern Renaissance.

The Southern writers of our time have often been highly critical of Southern traditions, but few of them have been willing to throw overboard all of our rich inheritance.

DuBose Heyward's *Porgy* and Stark Young's *So Red the Rose* presented no great difficulty to Southern readers who were familiar with Harris's *Nights with Uncle Remus* and Page's *In Ole Virginia*, but there were new books which either puzzled the Southern reader, like the poems of John Crowe Ransom, or angered him, like Erskine Caldwell's *Tobacco Road*. Caldwell, like George W. Cable before him, was accused of libeling his own people to please Northern readers. A former Texas student of mine, George Thomas, now Professor of Religion at Princeton, who saw *Tobacco Road* on the New York stage, wondered what could possibly explain the enormous vogue of such a distorted picture of Southern poor whites. So during the intermissions he listened for comments by the spectators. He thought he found a clue when he heard a young Northern woman say to her escort: "And these Southerners think they are so much better than we are!"

Much Southern writing is, as Jonathan Daniels once explained in an article entitled "F.O.B. Dixie," produced for the export trade. The publishers, the magazine editors, and the great majority of the readers are in the North; and if a Southern author wishes his books to be published and to sell, he must consult their wishes or, if you like, their prejudices. Thomas Nelson Page told Edwin Mims that the city of Boston bought more of his books than the entire state of Virginia. But no publisher would today accept a novel modeled on Page's *Red Rock*. You might have a chance if you took as your model *Tobacco Road* or Faulkner's *Sanctuary*. Such books as the last two shocked even Ellen Glasgow. She wrote in *A Certain Measure*:

One may admit that the Southern States have more than an equal share of degeneracy and deterioration; but the multitude of half-wits, and whole idiots, and nymphomaniacs, and paranoiacs, and rakehells in general, that populate the modern literary South could flourish nowhere but in the weird pages of melodrama. There is no harm in the fashion, one surmises, until it poses as realism. It may be magnificent, indeed, but it is not realism, and it is not peculiarly Southern.

I have nothing to say in defense of Erskine Caldwell, but I do not think Miss Glasgow was quite fair to Faulkner. We must not expect the serious writer to flatter our vanity by picturing Southern life in a fashion to please our chambers of commerce. Until the twentieth century the South has had too few such critics of American life as Fenimore Cooper, Emerson, Melville, and Thoreau. When the serious Southern writer deals with degenerates and perverts, poor whites and illiterate Negroes, he says to us in effect: "Here are people living in the South whose very existence you do not like to admit. Here they are, and you ought to do something about them." If you have ever served on a jury in criminal cases, you may have had, like myself, the rather shocking experience of seeing in your own home town degenerate whites and blacks who might have supplied models for some of the characters of Faulkner and Caldwell.

I have not found it easy to appreciate some of Faulkner's novels. His Mississippi, for me, does not have the reality which I feel in Ellen Glasgow's "social history" of Virginia. It resembles rather the nightmare world of Thomas Hardy's later novels. I have no doubt that you could find in the state of Mississippi many persons who might have posed as models for Faulkner's characters; but there is a great deal that is characteristic of Mississippi that rarely appears in his Yoknapatawpha cycle. Soon after Faulkner received the Nobel Prize for Literature, Carl Sandburg remarked to me that Faulkner's address to the Swedish Academy was a noble and moving piece of writing. "But," he added, "you can't find a word of it in his novels." It is there, nevertheless, and if you look long enough, you will find it. In Faulkner's short story "The Bear," a father, recalling Keats's "Beauty is truth, truth beauty . . . ," says to his young son: "He [Keats] was talking about truth. Truth doesn't change. Truth is one thing. It covers all things which touch the heart—honor and pride and pity and justice and courage and love." Faulkner's artistic imagination is haunted by the violence and cruelty in life which we are so disposed to ignore, in the South as elsewhere; but his view of the function of the serious writer is similar to that held by Dante, Milton, Goethe, Emerson, Whitman, and Lanier: "The poet's voice need not merely be the record of man, it can be one of the props, the pillars to help him endure and prevail."

The best work of the new Southern writers was done before the end of the Second World War. Some of them, like Ellen Glasgow, Thomas Wolfe, William Faulkner, Elizabeth Madox Roberts, and DuBose Heyward, are no longer living. Some of them no longer live in the South. There are of course promising writers of a still younger generation, but few of them have yet made their mark. I have no doubt that some of the writers of the Southern Renaissance are now overrated and will in the course of time be overshadowed by the younger writers of tomorrow. But the Southern Renaissance has given us a few books which we shall not, I trust, willingly let die. Its writers have pictured vividly various aspects of Southern life which Simms and Harris and Page and Cable overlooked; and they have helped to bring us into closer touch with the great world outside the South.

The Southern Renaissance has given us some very beautiful poems. Unfortunately too many of our English and American poets seem to write mainly for the sophisticated few who understand the symbolic language which they employ. Many of our contemporary poets have practically lost the audience their predecessors had and seem to be talking only to themselves. Nevertheless, I am sorry for the lover of poetry who does not know Allen Tate's "Ode to the Confederate Dead" or Donald Davidson's "Lee in the Mountains." When we turn to other literary types, we must not forget the work of such Southern historians as Ulrich B. Phillips, William E. Dodd, and Douglas Freeman. Memorable also are Paul Green's pageants, *The Lost Colony* and *The Common Glory*, which are intended to remind us of great events and great characters in Southern history.

It is in fiction, however, that one finds the best work of the twentieth-century Southern writers. Let me remind you of a few of the best of their novels: Stark Young's *So Red the Rose*; Thomas Wolfe's *Look Homeward, Angel* and *Of Time and the River*; Elizabeth Madox Roberts' *The Great Meadow* and *The Time of Man*; Faulkner's *The Sound and the Fury* and *As I Lay Dying*; Eudora Welty's *Delta Wedding*; and DuBose Heyward's *Porgy*. The romances of James Branch Cabell are now out of fashion, but they are still read by those who care for style and expert craftsmanship. There are many fine short stories, too; and some of the best were written by Faulkner and Katherine Anne Porter, who is greatly admired by other writers of fiction.

My own favorite and perhaps yours is Ellen Glasgow. The Negro has no very prominent role in her novels, but otherwise she gives us a more complete and a more accurate account of Southern life in the past as well as the present than one can find anywhere else in Southern fiction. Most of our writers—Northern as well as Southern—neglect the great middle class, which supplies the bulk of those who read fiction. Somehow we prefer to read about the doings of Page's Virginia planters or Faulkner's primitive Negroes and illiterate poor whites rather than about the class to which we ourselves belong. Miss Glasgow portrays the poor whites and the "good families" of Virginia, but, unlike most other novelists, she has much to say about the "good people" who in Virginia must be carefully distinguished from the "good families." In *Barren Ground* (1925) she thus distinguished the two classes:

. . . "Good people," a comprehensive term . . . implies, to discriminating Virginians, the exact opposite of the phrase "a good family." The good families of the state have preserved, among other things, custom, history, tradition, romantic fiction, and the Episcopal Church. The good people, according to the records of clergymen, which are the only surviving records, have preserved nothing except themselves. Ignored alike by history and fiction, they have their inconspicuous place in the social strata midway between the lower gentility and the upper class of "poor white," a position which encourages the useful rather than the ornamental public virtues.

In her novels we have a memorable history of the changes which have come over this state between 1850 and 1939. No writer since 1879, the year in which appeared Ibsen's *A Doll's House* and Meredith's *The Egoist*, has satirized so effectively the egotism and the vanity of husbands and lovers in their treatment of women. Through all her novels runs the theme which her friend James Branch Cabell has called "The Tragedy of Everywoman, As It Was Lately Enacted in the Commonwealth of Virginia." Unlike so many of her contemporaries, Miss Glasgow had no prejudices against good birth or good breeding. She put much of her own philosophy of life into a Virginia gentleman, General Archbald of *The Sheltered Life*, whom she described as "a lover of wisdom, a humane and civilized soul, oppressed by the burden of tragic remembrance. . . . He represents the tragedy, wherever it appears, of the civilized man in a world that is not civilized." Ellen Glasgow complained with some justice that even in the South her readers did not understand her aims and preferred to her fine novels popular romances of no literary importance. Recognition came to her late. I am glad to note that in 1938, seven years before her death, she received honorary degrees from Duke University and the University of Richmond. Recognition came late also to William Faulkner and other Southern writers, including Edgar Allan Poe, Henry Timrod, and Sidney Lanier. Let us hope that when their peers publish their books in the second half of the twentieth century, they will more quickly find in the South and elsewhere understanding and appreciative readers, readers who possess something like the just and discriminating literary taste of the man in whose honor the Boatwright Fine Arts Lectures were established. For my closing word I give you the Dedication which we of the Class of 1905 have chosen to appear in our class history next year:

This Book Is Dedicated with Gratitude and Affection
to the Memory of
FREDERIC WILLIAM BOATWRIGHT

Nothing really matters but to preserve, at whatever cost, one's own sense of artistic integrity.

To LEWIS GANNETT, May 25, 1933, *Letters of Ellen Glasgow* (1958), p. 135.

My comprehension of Virginian life and manners was a knowledge of the blood, as well as the brain, and instinct warned me that here alone could I break through the surface of appearances and strike some vein of fundamental humanity.

ELLEN GLASGOW, *A Certain Measure* (1943), p. 153

Ellen Glasgow: Artist and Social Historian

1

I cannot remember when or where I first read one of Ellen Glasgow's novels, but it was several years before May, 1915, when in a bookstore in New York I bought a copy of her first novel, *The Descendant* (1897), even at that time long out of print. At ten cents that was quite a bargain. Fifteen or twenty years later the Duke University Library paid ten dollars for its copy.

In my doctor's dissertation at Columbia University, "Virginia Life in Fiction," I discussed the books she had published before 1919. Going systematically through her novels after reading much inferior fiction, I was filled with admiration for *The Battle-Ground, The Voice of the People, The Deliverance,* and *Virginia.* Elmer Davis, whom I met in 1919, was singing the praises of James Branch Cabell every time I saw him; but Ellen Glasgow seemed to me then and now a more significant literary figure—even though none of the novels she regarded as her best had yet been written. Her Virginia was the Virginia I knew, and the vividness and accuracy of her picture of it gave me great pleasure and a desire to see more of her work.

Soon after my return to Dallas in the fall of 1919 I wrote at the request of my colleague John H. McGinnis an article entitled "Ellen Glasgow as a Literary Pioneer," which appeared in a Special Book Section of the *Dallas Morning News* on November 23, 1919. "The last two decades," I wrote, "have witnessed a little noticed change in the literature of the South which is really so pronounced as to be described only by the term 'revolutionary.' So far as this change is due to any one person, it is due to Miss Glasgow." She was, it seemed to me, the first modern Southern novelist. In the abstract of my dissertation, privately printed in 1922, I said:

In choosing as the hero of her first novel an illegitimate poor white who leaves Virginia to escape the odium attached to his birth and class, Miss Glasgow deliberately violated a long literary tradition. She chose to write of the present rather than of the romantic past; and later when she portrayed the old Virginia gentleman, she took off his halo and pictured him as a human being. She was the first to see that certain social classes had been almost entirely ignored by her predecessors. She was, in short, the first Virginian novelist to attain a genuinely national outlook upon the life of her state, the first Virginia novelist with a democratic attitude toward life.

In an article entitled "On 'Southern Literature,' " which I published in the *Texas Review* in October, 1921, I referred to her priority in the portrayal of modern Southern life: "She was the first to treat the old soldiers not as demigods but as human beings. She was the first to escape the tyrannical spell of the past, and the first to draw her heroes from the despised 'po' white trash.' "

In one of his last books, *As I Remember It* (1955), Cabell said that when Doubleday arranged to publish the Old Dominion Edition of her *Works* (1929-1933), he asked Ellen Glasgow why she did not play up her novels as "a social history of Virginia . . . since the War Between the States"; and he added that he helped her select and group the best of her novels "so as to make them conform as nearly as might be with this resonant notion of social history. . . ." He maintained that Miss Glasgow finally convinced herself that ever since 1899 she had been consciously writing a "social history" of Virginia.

I do not think Cabell's memory on these points is accurate. Her letters indicate that though she did not employ the term "social history," Ellen Glasgow was quite aware of what she was doing. On December 2, 1899, she wrote to Walter Hines Page that if *The Voice of the People,* on which she was at work, "should chance to find a wide reading public, I should probably work upon a series of Virginia novels as true as I believe this one to be." Later in the same month she wrote to her literary agent, James B. Colvert: "It [*The Voice of the People*] is not historical in the conventional sense, & it is not romantically exciting, but it is a good, sound, solid, true-to-life kind of novel." By "not historical in the conventional sense" she meant undoubtedly that she was not using the pattern set by Sir Walter Scott and had no intention of introducing historical personages or describing historical incidents or episodes. She was not interested in the historical pageantry then in fashion, and had no intention of trying to rival Mary Johnston or Winston Churchill. I feel certain that long before the Old Dominion Edition was thought of, she knew that the best of her early novels might legitimately be described as "a series of novels which composes, in the more freely interpretative form of fiction, a social history of Virginia from the decade before the Confederacy." In fact, she told Professor Blair Rouse that she had consciously planned to write such a group of novels, and he adds that it was while writing *The Battle-Ground* (1902) and *The Deliverance* (1904) that she had come to see what she might accomplish in her "social history." Cabell, it should be noted, forgot that *The Battle-Ground* was included in her social history and thus overlooked the fact that the series began with the old regime and included the Civil War which destroyed it.

Neither Cabell nor the scholars who have discussed the "social history" have called attention to the phrase which in *A Certain Measure* (1943) she more than once applied to it: "my history of Virginian manners." Ellen Glasgow no doubt knew that neither phrase was an exact description of what she was trying to accomplish, but what other terms could she have employed that are any better? From the point of view of the historian and the sociologist her novels—in spite of their historical framework—are not quite "social history."

The term "history of Virginian manners" is suggestive, but one must interpret the word "manners" in the wide sense applied to comedies of manners on the stage. *The Romantic Comedians* and *They Stooped to Folly* are better examples of the novel as comedy of manners than any one of her earlier novels.

In her "social history" Miss Glasgow planned, she says, to treat "the static customs of the country," "the changing provincial fashions of the small towns and cities," and "to portray the different social orders." The "dominant theme" was to be "the rise of the middle class as the dominant force in Southern democracy." A related theme is well stated in a notebook in which she indicated the theme of *Virginia* (1913): "The struggle between idealism and materialism in the South of the last thirty years. The transition from an aristocratic to a commercial civilization." A minor theme which in *Virginia* and the later novels becomes a major theme is, in the words of Cabell, "The Tragedy of Everywoman, As It Was Lately Enacted in the Commonwealth of Virginia."

In *The Battle-Ground* she dealt with both the old regime and the epic years of the Civil War. In *The Voice of the People* and *The Deliverance* she dealt chiefly with the Reconstruction period; and in *Virginia* and *Life and Gabriella* she attacked the cherished ideals of the Southern "lady." These two novels are largely concerned with the years immediately preceding the First World War. In my discussion of her novels I never used the term "social history," but I did point out various aspects of the changing social and economic life of the state which she had treated in these early novels. It is likely enough that Cabell suggested the phrase "social history of Virginia," but she knew well enough what she had been doing, and so did some of those who reviewed her early novels long before she adopted the term "social history."

In that "social history" her urban characters seem to me somewhat better than the country people; and certainly she portrayed the gentry—the class to which she belonged—more successfully than any other class. She was less successful with her businessmen, and her picture of Virginia life would be more nearly complete if some of her more memorable Negro characters had played a more important part. And yet no other state has been so faithfully reflected in a series of novels. Her "social history" is a more accurate account of the life of a state than Faulkner's fabulous Yoknapatawpha cycle of novels and short stories.

I do not know whether Miss Glasgow ever saw the two articles I have mentioned, but she did read the printed abstract of my dissertation. She wrote to me on March 12, 1925: "What I have tried to do (and you are one of the few critics in the South who appear to grasp this) is to break away from the sentimental tradition in Southern literature. In my new book *Barren Ground* I have gone much farther in this direction."

Some of Miss Glasgow's early novels had sold rather widely, but she had not received the critical recognition which she knew she deserved. She was to quote with approval Stuart P. Sherman's remark: "Northern critics have never known how to take her." Until 1936, when Harper & Brothers published my *American Life in Literature,* none of her work had been included in an anthology designed for college students of American literature. I felt strongly that she ought to be in my book, and I wrote to her for suggestions as to what I should include. I have no copy of my letter, but I remember mentioning my admiration for certain scenes in *The Deliverance.* Here is Miss Glasgow's reply to my letter:

VENTNOR, NEW JERSEY   October 10.
                                                             1935

DEAR MR. HUBBELL:

Oh, no, if you please, Not *The Deliverance!* I do not wish to be remembered by my earlier works. Why do you not select a passage from *Barren Ground* or *The Romantic Comedians* or *The Sheltered Life* or *Vein of Iron?*

From *Barren Ground,* you might take the chapter in which Dorinda watches from the woods while her lover drives by with his bride. Better still would be a passage from the *Deep Past* section in *The Sheltered Life*—Or the pages that describe the breadline from *Vein of Iron.* I can think of a hundred passages that represent my prose style better than anything in *The Deliverance*—for example, the first chapter of *The Romantic Comedians* has always been a favorite with me. But I think I should choose the latter pages of *The Deep Past* in *The Sheltered Life.* Yet, even as I write this, I wonder if the final dramatic scene in that book would not be the best choice.

I am away on my first vacation in four years, and this note has to be dashed off, without reflection, before I start again on my way.

I remember an interesting essay you once sent me on *The Novel in the South*. It would be a pleasure to see more of your critical work.

Sincerely yours,

ELLEN GLASGOW

The passage that I reprinted in *American Life in Literature* came from "The Deep Past" section of *The Sheltered Life*. (More than one anthologist has since used the same passage.) Even before I read her discussion of this novel in *A Certain Measure*, I felt that she had put much of her "ultimate feeling about life" into the "lonely spirit" of old General Archbald. In 1944 she wrote to Signe Toksvig: "... I think the middle section called 'The Deep Past' contains the writing I should wish to be remembered by in the future."

2

In December, 1936, Ellen Glasgow gave a reception for some of the members of the Modern Language Association, then meeting in Richmond; and I was fortunate enough to receive an invitation. I arrived late at 1 West Main Street to find the house full of people. There were a few Richmond writers—I remember Emily Clark and James Branch Cabell—and many professors. Miss Glasgow was an admirable hostess, very much the gracious Virginia lady. She seemed to me the kind of person that no one could help liking immediately, but it was not easy to talk to her, especially in a crowd of people. The hearing aid which she used resembled a small model of a cheerleader's megaphone; and when she placed the larger end to my mouth, it was so disconcerting that I forgot what I wanted to say. Her deafness was perhaps the greatest tragedy of her life. She had too little of that "vein of iron" which sustains many of her finest characters in times of trial and suffering.

I saw Ellen Glasgow again in June, 1938, when she came to Duke University for an honorary degree. She did not wish to be photographed, and I think she had been promised that the press photographers would not be permitted to take her picture. Yet when the doctor's hood was being raised over her head, I saw her turn her back on the photographers who were about to take her picture. My wife and I saw her once more at the home of Miss Alice Baldwin, Dean of the Woman's College. Only a few of us were there, and it was easier to talk to her. I remember that she told us that she had written her autobiography but that she did not know whether or when it would be published. In *The Woman Within* (opposite page 69) there is a photograph, taken in the year she came to Duke University, which seems to me an excellent likeness. Hers was a refined, sensitive face, the face of one who was (as she wrote of General Archbald) "a lover of wisdom, a humane and civilized soul, oppressed by the burden of tragic remembrance."

3

Ellen Glasgow died in November, 1945. Ten years afterwards I was in Richmond at the invitation of the Richmond Area University Center lecturing at the eleven colleges and universities affiliated with it. The University Center in Virginia (as it is now called) had its headquarters in the Glasgow House. By November, 1955, the neighborhood had greatly deteriorated, and the Glasgow House seemed very bare, for few of the original furnishings were there. In the hall, however, I noticed first one and then a second Duke University diploma. They were, I found, identical except that while one diploma conferred on Ellen Glasgow the Litt.D. degree, the other made her an honorary LL.D. I then recalled a University faculty meeting at which Dean William H. Glasson had informed us that Miss Glasgow had complained that she had not been given the degree which she wanted and which she thought she had come to Durham to receive, the LL.D. degree. Dean Glasson explained that of course the University had sent her the diploma she wanted. She had received a Litt.D. degree from the University of North Carolina in 1930; and, as a matter of fact, she had received an LL.D. degree from the University of Richmond only two months before she came to Duke University for another. She was to receive still another LL.D. from the College of William and Mary in 1939. It is strange that writers, like Ellen Glasgow and Hamlin Garland, who were not college-bred, held such an exaggerated notion of the importance of honorary degrees. Still, I must confess I have been greatly pleased to see Duke University honor itself by conferring honorary degrees upon Ellen Glasgow and Robert Frost.

At the request of the Director of the University Center, Colonel

Herbert W. K. Fitzroy, I lectured on the early novels of Ellen Glasgow in Glasgow House to an audience composed chiefly of professors of English from the various colleges and universities affiliated with the Center. Several Richmond women were there, and some of them had known Ellen Glasgow far better than I had. I had read *The Woman Within*, which had been withheld from publication until 1954; but I had not realized what a sensation it had produced in Richmond. One of the women who heard my lecture remarked to me afterwards that she really didn't know what Richmond society would have had to talk about if it hadn't been for *The Woman Within*. At least one of my listeners suggested that she thought it was a mistake for Miss Glasgow's literary executors (Irita Van Doren and Frank Morley) to permit the publication of the book. Another woman said that Ellen Glasgow seemed interested in almost nothing except her writing and that her sister, Mrs. Cary McCormack, was much better liked in Richmond.

Shortly before my lecture I had noticed in a window at the Miller & Rhoads department store (Richmond's largest) the typed manuscript of James Branch Cabell's *As I Remember It*. It was open at the first page of the chapter entitled "Speaks with Candor of a Great Lady." There I first read Cabell's verdict that *The Woman Within*—"that beautiful and wise volume"—"contains a large deal of her very best fiction."

Many persons outside of Richmond who had read *The Woman Within* were wondering just who was the man that Miss Glasgow referred to as "Harold S——" and to whom she had been at one time engaged to be married. In the months that followed the First World War "Harold" was in the Balkans as head of the American Red Cross. There he indulged in a flirtation with the beautiful Queen Marie of Romania—something that Ellen Glasgow could not quite forgive. She wrote in *The Woman Within*: "Afterwards, when I read, in the 'life Story' of a Balkan Queen, that, as she said farewell to a Southern Colonel, he had fallen on his knees before her and kissed the hem of her skirt, I recognized the last act of chivalry. So Harold had parted from me when he sailed for the Balkans." Before I lectured at the Glasgow House, one of my University of Virginia colleagues had told me—what all Richmond knew by now—that "Harold" was Colonel Henry Watkins Anderson, a prominent Richmond lawyer. In the library of the Virginia Historical Society I saw his portrait and the numerous medals and decorations which he had bequeathed to the Society.

It was not until after Colonel Anderson's death that Ellen Glasgow's literary executors permitted the publication of her autobiography. In the spring of 1955 they turned over her manuscripts and miscellaneous papers to the Alderman Library of the University of Virginia. Ellen Glasgow had finally decided that in spite of the University's failure to admit women students (there were many in my classes there in 1954-1955), her manuscripts should go to "Mr. Jefferson's College." The manuscripts came to Charlottesville in the late spring of 1955, and there I examined them hastily in the little time I could spare. Among the letters addressed to Ellen Glasgow I noted some seven hundred and fifty letters, notes, and telegrams from Colonel Anderson. In one of the few that I read he admitted that he was a sinner but pleaded with her to forgive him. In Richmond in November, 1955, I was told that a niece of Colonel Anderson, whose name I do not recall, was boasting that she had destroyed eight hundred letters from Ellen Glasgow addressed to her uncle.

There is a passage in *The Romantic Comedians* (1926) which, I think, was written with "Harold's" Balkan adventures in mind. The speaker is Judge Honeywell's twin sister, Mrs. Edmonia Bredalbane, who might easily have been modeled upon Chaucer's Wife of Bath, who at the church door had wedded five husbands "Withouten other companye in youthe":

"As provincial as you are in America, it is hopeless to try to make you understand that behaviour as much as beauty is a question of geography, and that my respectability increases with every mile of the distance I travel from Queenborough. In France, my reputation is above reproach, by the time I reach Vienna, I have become a bit of a prude; and contrasted with the Balkan temperament, I am little more than a tombstone to female virtue."

The Woman Within leaves the reader with the feeling that Ellen Glasgow was a very unhappy woman. As early as 1906 she had written to Mary Johnston: "I was born with a terrible burden of melancholy —of too much introspection—but for a whole year, for the first time in my life, I have not known a single instant of the old depression." This was written while she was in love with the man whom in *The*

Woman Within she calls "Gerald B——" and who died not long afterwards. (Even Miss Glasgow's secretary, the late Anne Virginia Bennett, could not tell me who "Gerald" was.) After the death of her mother, whom she idolized, Ellen Glasgow's home life was not a happy one. Her father had little sympathy with her literary ambitions, and he was shocked by her unorthodox religious views. A favorite brother is believed to have taken his own life.

Perhaps, however, Ellen Glasgow was not so unhappy as she thought she was. In the Alderman Library I found a few brief bits which she had jotted down on her typewriter and labeled "Miscellaneous Pungencies." One of them reads: "I have had as much love and more romance than most women, and I have not had to stroke some man the right way to win my bread or the wrong way to win my freedom." As a member of a well-to-do family Ellen Glasgow did not have the formidable handicap of poverty. She was under no compulsion to write the kind of popular fiction that she despised. If she suffered from lack of understanding and appreciation in her earlier years, she did finally win the admiration of competent critics who could agree with her own estimate that her later novels represented "some of the best work that has been done in American fiction."

Edgar Allan Poe and the South

[This essay, which was read at a meeting of the South Atlantic Modern Language Association in Atlanta in November, 1959, was published in the University of Texas *Studies in Literature and Language*, II, 151-171 (Summer, 1960) under the title "Edgar Allan Poe and the Southern Literary Tradition."]

1

In an essay entitled "Our Cousin, Mr. Poe" Allen Tate said of him: "A gentleman and a Southerner, he was not quite, perhaps, a Southern gentleman." Just how Southern was Poe? He was certainly much more of a Southerner than is implied in Barrett Wendell's phrase, "Southern only by courtesy"; but perhaps he was, as W. J. Cash suggested in *The Mind of the South*, "only half a Southerner."

In March, 1837, when Poe left Richmond for the North, he was twenty-eight years old. Except for his five years as a boy in the British Isles and a few months at West Point, practically all his life had been spent in Virginia, South Carolina, and Maryland. It was in the South, too, that he won his first recognition as a writer and made his first literary friends. He was still calling himself a Virginian in June, 1841, when he wrote to Frederick W. Thomas: "I am a Virginian—at least I call myself one, for I have resided all my life, until within the last few years, in Richmond."

Poe was a Southerner, but he was by no means so representative a Southerner as William Gilmore Simms, who is the central figure in the literature of the ante-bellum South, or Robert E. Lee, who was just two years old on the very day that Poe was born—and of all improbable places for a Virginian—in Boston, Massachusetts. Poe's literary friends—John Pendleton Kennedy, Beverley Tucker, Philip Pendleton Cooke, and Thomas Holley Chivers—all belonged to good Southern families. Poe's father displeased his family by going on the stage. Poe's mother and her mother were both English-born actresses at a time when the social standing of the profession was extremely low. Simms in 1836 married a planter's daughter; Poe married a penniless cousin. Poe had spent five impressionable years in England and Scotland. His foster father was a Scot, and he grew to manhood in the circle of Scotch merchants in Richmond. That little world no doubt bore some resemblance to the larger world of Scotch religion, Scotch manners, and Scotch drink which seemed to Matthew Arnold to offer so little to a poet like Burns. At the University of Virginia Poe's professors were all foreign-born. Is it any wonder that his literary aims and standards seem cosmopolitan rather than national or regional?

Except on the comparatively rare occasions when he was intoxicated, Poe impressed those he met—especially Northern women—as a well-bred Southern gentleman—a type not always understood or appreciated by men in the Northern cities where he lived. But Poe was an urban, not a rural type. His slight connection with the plantation tradition—and he made nothing of it in his writings—came through Frances Valentine Allan and her sister Nancy, daughters of a small Virginia planter. Most of the students at the University of Virginia when Poe was there in 1826 came from good Southern families, and presumably they found the well-bred youth from Richmond socially acceptable, all the more readily now that he was the putative heir of John Allan, who had recently inherited a fortune from old William Galt. But when Allan refused to pay his debts of honor and practically disowned him, Poe (whose status as the child of actors had always been precarious) must have felt that he had completely lost caste. He failed to better his social standing when he enlisted as a private in the United States Army or later when he got himself dismissed from the U. S. Military Academy, or when at last he became a poorly paid professional magazinist.

In the South as in the North Poe was a lonely and gifted professional writer among mediocre amateurs, and his subject matter was of no especial interest to Southern readers. Unlike Kennedy, Tucker, and the Cooke brothers, he had no part in the upbuilding of the plantation literary tradition. Unlike Simms and the younger Cooke, he wrote no Southern local-color stories or historical romances, and he wrote no poems glorifying the Cotton Kingdom or any one of the Southern states in which he had lived. He did not expend his energies in defending the institution of slavery, nor was he, like Thomas Cooper, a champion of nullification and secession. He was quick to perceive the merits of Longstreet's *Georgia Scenes,* so different from anything he himself was ever to write; and he defended Southern writers when he thought they were underrated in the North, but he had no interest in what Henry Timrod called "Southernism in literature." I would not, however, go so far as James Branch Cabell did when he wrote in *Ladies and Gentlemen* (1934):

> In brief, America has produced just one literary genius whose existence the world recognizes; and once only during the exercise of his genius did he fully recognize the existence of America. That—I regret to say—was when he remarked, "As a literary people, we are one vast perambulating humbug."

Killis Campbell has listed in *The Mind of Poe* those stories which have American backgrounds, some of them Southern; but they are so lacking in realistic details that it is hardly worth while to discuss them. The best-known of them, "The Gold Bug," won a prize in which an American setting was stipulated. Simms was disturbed because Poe had been "so grievously regardless of the geographical peculiarities of the *locale*" as to place "rocks and highlands in and about Sullivan's Island."

Poe was quick to resent British attacks upon American writers whom he esteemed, and he often took Northern critics to task for failing to recognize the merits of Southern poets and novelists; but his view of what we may call the American literature problem was not calculated to please many persons in either South or North. He saw the New England writers as trying to impose upon the whole country what was really not a national but a provincial literature. In the course of the so-called "Longfellow War" he tried unsuccessfully to rally the West and the South in behalf of a genuinely national literature. His primary interest, however, was not in the subject matter of that literature but in its artistic quality. He wrote in "Marginalia":

That an American should confine himself to American themes, or even prefer them, is rather a political than a literary idea—and at best is a questionable point. . . . *Ceteris paribus*, a foreign theme is, in a strictly literary sense, to be preferred. After all, the world at large is the only legitimate stage for the autorial *histrio*.

"But," Poe went on, "of the need of *that* nationality which defends our own literature, sustains our own men of letters, upholds our own dignity, and depends upon our own resources, there cannot be the shadow of a doubt." Poe, I think, would have agreed with Goethe, who in the year that *Tamerlane* appeared in Boston told Eckermann that he thought the phrase "national literature" a "rather unmeaning term; the epoch of World-literature is at hand . . . ," he said; "and if we really want a pattern, we must always return to the Greeks. . . ."

If there is anything Southern about Poe's poems and tales, it is something more elusive than a Virginia or South Carolina local coloring. During the Civil War Timrod wrote an editorial on "Nationality in Literature," in which he said: "It would be quite possible for a Southern poet to write a hundred odes to the Confederate flag, or for a Southern novelist to fill his book with descriptions of Southern scenes, and yet to be un-Southern in every respect." "There is," Timrod concluded, "but one way to be a truly national writer, and that is by being a truly original writer. No one who does not speak from himself can speak for his country. . . ." If you ask me to define that elusive Southern quality which I feel in Poe's poems and tales, I can do no better than to quote from Ellen Glasgow's *A Certain Measure*. She is commenting upon John Esten Cooke's statement: "This great and sombre genius was rather a cosmopolite than a citizen of any particular state." She continues:

This fact is certainly evident; but it seems to us nowadays that it should be only a way of measuring the wide and high quality of Poe's art. It does not deny the Southern essence in his genius, and Poe is, to a large extent, a distillation of the Southern. The formalism of his tone, the classical element in his poetry and in many of his stories, the drift toward rhetoric, the aloof and elusive intensity,—all these qualities are Southern. And in his more serious faults of overwriting, sentimental exaggeration, and lapses, now and then, into a pompous or florid style, he belongs to his epoch and even more to his South.

Ellen Glasgow was perhaps too much the feminist to care to note that there is something Southern about Poe's attitude toward women. In him this goes beyond the Southern glorification of the lady and is nearly akin to what that admirable Renaissance scholar, the late Jefferson B. Fletcher, designated in the title of his book as *The Religion of Beauty in Woman* (1911). Aside from Poe, among Southern writers the nearest approximation to the attitude of Dante or Petrarch is to be found in the poems of Richard Henry Wilde, but there is something akin to it in the poems of Edward Coote Pinkney, Philip Pendleton Cooke, Albert Pike, James M. Legaré, Mirabeau B. Lamar, Henry Timrod, Paul Hamilton Hayne, and Sidney Lanier. Something not unlike it appears also in the novels and short stories of Thomas Nelson Page, Joel Chandler Harris, James Lane Allen, and Mark Twain, notably in his *Joan of Arc*.

The British poets who meant most to the youthful Poe were Byron, Moore, Coleridge, and Milton. If we substitute Scott for Coleridge, we have here the names of the most popular poets in the South in the 1820's. Poe, as he wrote to Lowell, had "no faith in human perfectibility"; and, like other Southerners, he had little use for the various reforms with which some New Englanders were trying to make the world over. For him poetry was "the rhythmical creation of Beauty."

It is remarkable that so many of our Southern poets have striven for verbal melody. In addition to Poe, Chivers, and Lanier, I should mention Pinkney, Cooke, Wilde, Hayne, Pike, Legaré, Lamar, Theodore O'Hara, Father Ryan, and John Henry Boner. One might well include two later admirers of Poe: Conrad Aiken, born in Savannah of Northern parents, and Vachel Lindsay, an Illinoian of Southern parentage. Verbal melody is an important characteristic of some of Simms's poems, as Poe was quick to note. Chivers had

Edgar Allan Poe and the South

high praise for the rhythms of Negro folksongs, which Hervey Allen thought had some influence on Poe's poetry. Be this as it may, I feel sure that Negro ghost stories are in the background of such tales of terror as "Berenice" and "The Black Cat." Poe was particularly fond of just those British poets who excelled in word music: Milton, Coleridge, Shelley, Keats, and Tennyson. In turn his own poems have drawn high praise from those British masters of verbal melody: Tennyson, Swinburne, and Yeats. It was Yeats who in 1909 pronounced Poe "one who is so certainly the greatest of American poets, and always and for all lands a great lyric poet." Basil L. Gildersleeve, who heard Poe read his poems in Richmond in 1849, felt that the poet "emphasized the rhythm unduly—a failing common, I believe, to poets endowed with a keen sense of the music of their own verse." Is it a failing? One afternoon in 1920 I heard that most musical of modern poets, William Butler Yeats, give a reading of his poems in Dallas, Texas. He prefaced his reading by stating that he had been accused of chanting his poems. In his own defense, he said, he wished to say that as nearly as he could ascertain, all poets from Homer down to Kipling have chanted their poems. Yeats remarked also that he could not carry a tune, but no listener could fail to feel the music in his poetry—even though from time to time his reading was punctuated by the horrible sound of steel riveting going on in a building under construction just across the street. In a review of Longfellow's *Ballads and Other Poems* Poe expressed his "firm conviction, that music (in its modifications of rhythm and rhyme) is of so vast a moment to Poesy, as *never* to be neglected by him who is truly poetical—it is of so mighty a force in furthering the great aim intended [the creation of supernal beauty] that he is mad who rejects its assistance. . . ." I am not unaware that there are critics nowadays who have no taste for lyric poems with a singing quality like many of those of Shelley, for instance. They are welcome to the gnarled and knobby verses which excite their admiration; but I make bold to say that those who prefer the rugged verses of Donne and Hopkins to the magnificent music of Milton or Keats are not the best judges of the poetic art. Said Coleridge in his *Biographia Literaria*: "The man that hath not music in his soul can indeed never be a genuine poet."

In his lecture on Poe, John R. Thompson said of him: "He was the Beethoven of language. . . ." Poe of course is no Beethoven, but he did have in greater measure than other American poets what, according to Leonard Bernstein, makes Beethoven the greatest of composers: *"the inexplicable ability to know what the next note has to be*. . . . in the 'Funeral March' of the *Eroica*—he produced an entity that always seems to me to have been previously written in Heaven, and then merely dictated to him. . . . When you get the feeling that whatever note succeeds the last is the only possible note that can rightly happen at that instant, in that context, then chances are you're listening to Beethoven."

In Poe's poetry at its best one finds the perfect conjunction of meaning and form which Rudyard Kipling found so rare. In a short story entitled "Wireless" he wrote: "Remember that in all the millions permitted there are no more than five—five little lines—of which one can say: 'These are the pure Magic. These are the clear Vision. The rest is only poetry.'" The five magical lines which for Kipling represented "the high-watermark [that] but two of the sons of Adam have reached" are the familiar lines from Coleridge's "Kubla Khan" and Keats's "Ode to a Nightingale":

> A savage place! as holy and enchanted
> As e'er beneath a waning moon was haunted
> By woman wailing for her demon-lover!

> Charmed magic casements, opening on the foam
> Of perilous seas, in faery lands forlorn.

By a kind of witching musical incantation these lines affect the reader like some powerful charm or spell of enchantment. Free verse and prose poetry are hardly the proper medium for "the pure Magic" or "the clear Vision." There are of course many more than five such lines in English, but they are few enough especially in our American poetry. Rare in any country are the poets of whom one can say that they have drunk of "the true, the blushful Hippocrene, / With beaded bubbles winking at the brim" or who "on Honey-dew [have] fed, / And drunk the milk of Paradise."

I think there are more than five lines of pure magic in Poe's poems. The earliest appear in Nesace's song in "Al Aaraaf," published when the poet was only twenty years old. I quote a few lines:

Edgar Allan Poe and the South

> Ligeia! wherever
>   Thy image may be,
> No magic shall sever
>   Thy music from thee.
> Thou hast bound many eyes
>   In a dreamy sleep
> But the strains still arise
>   Which *thy* vigilance keep. . . .

No man or woman now living ever heard Poe read these lines, but among my cherished memories is hearing Colonel Thomas Wentworth Higginson, the friend of Emily Dickinson, describe the effect upon himself of Poe's reading of this poem in Boston in 1845. I quote, however, not from memory but from the published account in the Higginson-Boynton *Reader's History of American Literature* (1903):

. . . his voice seemed attenuated to the faintest golden thread; the audience became hushed, and, as it were, breathless; there seemed no life in the hall but his; and every syllable was accentuated with such delicacy, and sustained with such sweetness as I never heard equaled by other lips. When the lyric ended, it was like the ceasing of the gypsy's chant in Browning's *Flight of the Duchess*; and I remember nothing more, except that in walking back to Cambridge my comrades and I felt that we had been under the spell of some wizard. Indeed, I feel much the same in the retrospect, to this day.

"When he [Poe] read Poetry," wrote Chivers, "his voice rolled over the rhythm of the verse like Silver notes over golden sands—rather monotonously and flute-like—so that, it may be said here, that he rather *cantilated* than read."

The first recognition of Poe's literary talents came from Southern writers: Kennedy, Beverley Tucker, and Philip Pendleton Cooke. As a youthful contributor to the *Southern Literary Messenger* Cooke wrote to its proprietor in 1835: ". . . he [Poe] is the first genius, in his line, in Virginia. And when I say this, how many other States are included—certainly all South of us." In the *Messenger* circle, however, Thomas W. White, James E. Heath, and Lucian Minor saw in Poe little more than a competent magazinist who had a perverse delight in unpleasant subjects for his stories. Southern literary taste was already a little old-fashioned. William Wirt missed his chance when he tried to read "Al Aaraaf" in manuscript. He could make nothing of even the beautiful song to Ligeia.

In looking through the numerous newspaper notices of the *Messenger* which at one time White and Poe reprinted in the magazine, I found much more praise for Poe's critical notices than for his poems or his stories. The Natchez *Christian Herald*, which failed to mention "To Helen," even in its earlier form an extraordinarily fine poem, said: "The poetic writers for the Messenger, as a whole, are not the favorites of the Muses. . . ." The Baltimore *Patriot* pronounced the poem "a pretty little gem," and the Norfolk *Herald* referred to it as "a sonnet [*sic*] full of grace." The *National Intelligencer* pronounced "The Valley Nis" (which we know as "The Valley of Unrest") "characteristically wild, yet sweetly smooth in measure as in mood." The Richmond *Compiler*, on the other hand, said: ". . . there is a deep poetical inspiration about Mr. Poe's 'Valley Nis,' which would be more attractive if his verses were smoother, and his subject matter less obscure and unintelligible."

The younger Virginia writers of the *Messenger* circle—John R. Thompson, John Esten Cooke, and John Moncure Daniel—who probably saw Poe only on his last visits to Richmond in 1848 and 1849, recognized in him a man of considerable talent but hardly a writer of genius. Both Thompson and Cooke were on friendly terms with Rufus W. Griswold, and they regarded the notorious "Memoir" as a fairly accurate portrait of the man they had known. That biased and synthetic portrait was long destined to color Poe's reputation as a writer and as a man in the South as well as in the North and overseas.

2

Poe died in Baltimore on October 7, 1849, under distressing circumstances which seemed to confirm the notion that he was a man of very low character indeed. Chivers was one of the few Southerners who made any effort to defend him, but no publisher seemed to want the kind of book that Chivers had in mind. Poe was simply not the sort of writer that the South wanted in the mid-nineteenth century. Neither was Chivers, for that matter. Simms, who finally arrived at a better understanding of Poe's greatness than most of his contemporaries, wrote to Chivers on April 5, 1852, to stop imitating Poe: "Give him up as a model and as a guide. He was a man of curious genius, wild and erratic, but his genius was rather curious than valuable—bizarre, rather than great or truthful." You may recall Chivers' indignant reply: "I am the Southern man who taught Mr. Poe all these things."

After the publication of *Uncle Tom's Cabin* in 1852 anti-Northern feeling rose to a new pitch, and the demand for a great defensive Southern literature became louder and more insistent. New England Abolitionists were denouncing the Southern states as barbarous and, it was said, were asking sarcastically: "Who reads a Southern book?" Southern magazinists now played up Poe as a Southern writer shamefully neglected by Northern critics and anthologists, especially Griswold. Once in a while one of Poe's poems was reprinted in the poets' corner of a Southern newspaper. Even in the midst of war the Southern magazinists occasionally remembered that Poe was a Southern writer. For example, on October 31, 1863, the *Southern Punch* referred to him as "the brilliantest literary genius that America has produced." Two years after Poe's death a contributor to the *Quarterly Review* of the Methodist Episcopal Church, South, then published in Richmond, wrote: ". . . an eminent writer of our time has declared 'that a long poem does not exist.' This writer is equally well known in the departments of criticism and poetry, and has done much to build up American literature. We allude to the lamented Edgar A. Poe, whose poems, to use the expressive language of another, are 'enough to sweeten a whole continent.' " The writer, who may have been the editor of the quarterly, D. S. Doggett, D.D., added on a later page of the same number: ". . . and Poe's 'Raven,' a work not exceeding one hundred lines, has achieved more for the reputation of American poetry than a dozen Thalabas or Madocs would have done." In February, 1858, a writer in *De Bow's Review* in discussing "American Literature—Northern and Southern" wrote: "Poe, if not the very first of American poets—in our opinion *facile princeps*—cannot be denied by any just and discriminating Northern man, full equality, at least, with the best of them."

The later nineteenth century saw Poe's name finally cleared of most of the slanders for which his longer-lived enemies were mainly responsible; but the part that Southerners had in his vindication was surprisingly small. Much more vocal and effective were Poe's

Northern friends: George R. Graham, N. P. Willis, Charles Chauncey Burr, Annie Richmond, and Sarah Helen Whitman. Even in Virginia there were few defenders. On May 2, 1868, Henry Rives Pollard, the editor of the Richmond weekly, *Southern Opinion*, did write in response to an anonymous "Inquirer":

> Gross injustice has been done poor Edgar Poe by the report you mentioned.—He was not an habitual drunkard. On the contrary, for months he would lead as pure and abstemious a life as that of some high-caste Brahmin. Then a fit of desperation would seize him; he lost all self-control, and became a vagabond and a maniack. It was during one of these unfortunate "seizures" that he lost his life in the streets of Baltimore.

Poe's stoutest champion was not a Southerner or even an American. Our countrymen left it to an Englishman, John H. Ingram, to produce the first real biography of the poet. In this book and in a better edition of Poe's writings than Griswold's, Ingram provided effective refutation of the notorious "Memoir." The man who contributed most to Poe's world reputation was a Frenchman, Charles Baudelaire.

In the postwar years some Southerners looked back and lamented that their section had neglected the living Poe. One is reminded of Thomas Carlyle and other Scots grieving over the failure of their countrymen to care for the living Robert Burns. For example, in December, 1869, A. W. Dillard wrote in the Charleston *XIX Century*:

> We have always felt a pride in the genius of Poe, because he was a Southern man by birth [*sic*], and education, yet with this feeling is mingled a profound regret that no Southern man stepped forward to rescue him from the destitution and annoyances that crushed him to the earth. . . .
> Had the experiment been tried the South would at least have escaped the reproach of indifference to the sufferings of genius, with which it now stands chargeable.

Nowadays the visitor in Charlottesville who looks at the classic buildings and grounds designed by Thomas Jefferson will hardly fail to visit No. 13 West Range and pause to read the memorable inscription, *"Domus parva magni poetae."* It was nearly twenty years after Poe's death, however, before any one took the trouble to look up his excellent academic record and announce that there was nothing to his discredit in the University's books. On the fiftieth anniversary of the poet's death Zolnay's bust of Poe was unveiled in the University library with appropriate ceremonies. Poe's room was finally set aside as a memorial.[1] In 1909 the University made much of the centenary of Poe's birth, and sixty years after the poet's death it created the Edgar Allan Poe Chair of English. The first Poe Professor was the late C. Alphonso Smith. He was succeeded by James Southall Wilson. No unworthy successor of these scholars is the present distinguished Poe Professor of English, Floyd Stovall. Notable work on Poe has been done by others connected with the University of Virginia as students or teachers or both: Charles W. Kent, James A. Harrison, W. M. Forrest, and John Ward Ostrom. The finest of all Poe scholars was another Virginian and a graduate of the College of William and Mary, the late Killis Campbell, who was for many years Professor of English in the University of Texas.

In the Northern states Poe's reputation rose very slowly. In 1893 the New York weekly, the *Critic*, took a poll of its readers to select the ten greatest books by American authors. First place went to Emerson's *Essays* with 512 votes and second to *The Scarlet Letter* with 493, but nothing by Poe got as much as twenty votes. Edmund Gosse immediately wrote from England that the exclusion of Poe seemed to him "extraordinary and sinister." "If I were an American," he added, "I should be inclined to call it disastrous." In 1901 William Dean Howells wrote: "The great New Englanders would none of him [Poe]." There were, however, two lesser natives of New England who did much to promote a better understanding of Poe. George E. Woodberry wrote one of the best biographies of the poet, and he and Edmund Clarence Stedman edited what was for that time an excellent edition of Poe's writings. In important essays Brander Matthews, who though he was born in New Orleans regarded himself as a New Yorker, resurrected Poe's doctrine of the single effect and discussed his cosmopolitan fame. It is surprising to find that conscious and laborious artist in prose fiction, Henry James, referring to Poe's "very valueless verses," later changing his phrase to "very superficial verses."

The literary aims and the subject matter of the writers of the

[1] The last student to live in that room was my uncle, the late Dr. J. Edgar Hubble.

New South were for the most part quite distinct from those of Poe, and yet there were important Southern writers who were indebted to him. George W. Cable in a well-known letter to Fred Lewis Pattee mentioned Poe among writers who had influenced him. Thomas Nelson Page considered Poe the greatest of American writers, and the Poe influence is, I think, discernible in some of his stories, notably in "Elsket" and " 'No Haid Pawn.' " Mark Twain, who had read Poe in his youth, remarked that he could read Poe on a salary but not Jane Austen. Nevertheless, I doubt if Mark Twain would ever have written "The Facts Concerning the Recent Carnival of Crime in Connecticut" if he had never read "William Wilson."

The writers of the New South, I think, owed more to Poe's poetry than to his short stories. Few of them, however, had any praise for his critical writings. A North Carolina poet, John Henry Boner, wrote "The Poe Cottage at Fordham," a better poem than others on the same subject by Father Tabb and Judge Walter Malone. It was the music of Poe's poetry that fascinated Boner and Father Ryan, but their poems are often reminiscent not only of Poe but also of another admirer of Poe, Algernon Charles Swinburne.

Paul Hamilton Hayne probably did more to promote Poe's reputation than any other Southern writer of his generation. As early as October 9, 1852, the *Southern Literary Gazette*, of which Hayne had recently become assistant editor, pronounced "The Raven" "(with two or three exceptions only) the most *purely original* poem in the English language. . . ." As editor of *Russell's Magazine* in the late 1850's he lost no opportunity to praise Poe. On June 27, 1863, he published in the *Southern Illustrated News* his long poem, "The Southern Lyre," in which he hailed Poe as the first among Southern poets.

> That mystic Bard whose "Raven" broods,
> Broods sternly, o'er his solemn moods,
> His weird, funereal solitudes;—
>
> Whose genius lives in realms of Blight,
> Yet oft towards the Infinite
> Essays to rise on wings, of might;—
>
> Who sought the nether gulfs profound,
> Deep as Thought's daring plummets sound—
> A lurid spirit, wildly crowned,

With bays of supernatural bloom—
Yet, flashing from his wizard tomb
An Angel's glory, thro' the gloom!

In the summer of 1874, as he said on August 11 in a letter to
Oliver Johnson, Hayne saw Poe's grave in Baltimore "a perfectly
barren mound of earth, the rank weeds growing all over, and around
it; and not a sign to tell what passionate heart, and fertile brain
mouldered underneath!" It was not until the next year that a monument was erected over Poe's grave. Hayne's experience prompted
him to write a sonnet, which he sent to Johnson, who was on the
editorial staff of the *Christian Union*. Hayne was justifiably indignant when Johnson rejected his poem, apparently on the ground
that a religious magazine would be risking the loss of its reputation
if it printed a poem in praise of a man of Poe's low character. That
was in 1874. On October 28 of that year in his "Literary Chitchat"
column in the Louisville *Argus* Hayne recalled a dinner at the
Albion House in Boston which he had attended just twenty years
earlier. It was a gathering of New England literati, and one of the
topics discussed was the relative merits of Poe and a New England
poet whose name Hayne did not give. At first only a stray New
Yorker who happened to be present expressed the opinion that Poe
was the better poet of the two. Finally, Hayne, who as a young man
of twenty-four had kept discreetly silent, was pressed for his opinion.
When he expressed his conviction that Poe was the most original
American literary genius, he remembered ". . . the very air appeared
to grow thick with a demurrer of argument, sarcasm, and invective."
After twenty years he wrote more confidently: "I *was* right!"

Many poets have been fascinated in early life by the music of
Poe's poems—Robert Frost was one of them, as I have heard him say—
but later found other poets who seemed to them better models. This
was apparently the case with Sidney Lanier. Poe was, with the possible exception of Tennyson, the poet who most influenced Lanier
during his early years, as indeed one might have inferred from the
preoccupation of the three poets with verbal melody and the theory
of versification. Lanier was familiar with *Eureka* and "The Rationale
of Verse," which are read less often than any of the poems or tales.
In later years he was greatly impressed by Emerson, whose concep-

tion of the poet's mission is so close to his own. Nevertheless what impresses most readers of Lanier's poems is not the poet's "message" but the haunting melodies and the marvelous pictures found in the poems which deal with the Marshes of Glynn. In more than one poem, it seems to me, Lanier attained "the pure Magic" and "the clear Vision" which seemed to Kipling so rare in English poetry.

John Banister Tabb was a friend of Lanier, whom he had first known in the Federal prison at Point Lookout, and he was an admirer of both Lanier and Poe. Poe's argument that there is strictly speaking no such thing as a long poem convinced him, and he early made up his mind to cultivate only the brief lyric. In a poem now entitled "To a Songster" but first entitled "Ambition" he wrote:

> O little bird, I'd be
> A poet like to thee,
> Singing my native song—
> Brief to the ear, but long
> To love and memory.

In Father Tabb's collected poems I find no less than seven poems about Poe. One of these was occasioned by the failure of the judges to admit Poe to the Hall of Fame, probably in 1900. It is entitled "Excluded":

> Into the charnel hall of fame
> The dead alone should go.
> Then write not there the living name
> Of Edgar Allan Poe.

The Hall of Fame—that shrewd private venture of New York University—had its first election in 1900; but Poe was not among the fifty Americans elected. Among those chosen were Emerson, Hawthorne, Jonathan Edwards, Longfellow, and Irving. In 1905 Lowell and Whittier got in, but not Poe. When he was finally admitted in 1910, Walter Hines Page was moved to write: "Edgar Allan Poe might be described as the man who made the Hall of Fame famous. He made it famous for ten years by being kept out of it, and he has now given it a renewed lease of fame by being tardily admitted to it." It was doubtless the almost universal praise of Poe in the centennial year of 1909 that made it evident to the judges that Poe belonged in the Hall of Fame.

3

The evidence to which I have pointed seems to me to prove that Poe belongs among our Southern writers. The Southern people, however, have never loved him as they loved Lanier. After Poe's death in 1849 a few of them defended him against unfriendly Northern critics, but too often they displayed no real understanding of either the man or his writings. It was Poe's Northern friends and his English biographer who finally cleared his name of the libels of his enemies. Poe's greatest vogue has been in France, where he had an important influence upon three great poets: Baudelaire, Mallarmé, and Valéry. He also—and partly through them—influenced Rainer Maria Rilke, William Butler Yeats, and T. S. Eliot.

If there is a living Southern literary tradition, we should be able to point to Poe's continuing influence upon important Southern writers of the last half-century. Most of the American writers esteemed as great in 1910, when Poe was admitted to the Hall of Fame, have since been consigned to the literary limbo which holds so many forgotten Victorians. For William Faulkner and Ernest Hemingway, our literature began with *Huckleberry Finn*, which first appeared a quarter of a century after Poe's death. Of Poe, Hemingway wrote in *The Green Hills of Africa* (1935): "Poe is a skillful writer. It is skillful, marvellously constructed, and it is dead." When Malcolm Cowley reviewed Hervey Allen's *Israfel* for the *Dial* in August, 1927, he noted how greatly fashion in fiction had changed since 1833 when Kennedy and the other judges in the Baltimore *Saturday Visiter* contest had praised Poe's tales because they possessed "a wild, vigorous and poetical imagination, a rich style, a fertile invention, and varied and curious learning." "To win a prize in 1927," said Cowley, "a story should possess none of these qualities; instead it must be 'vivid, penetrating, profound in its psychology,' and perhaps even 'photographically exact.' " We want something else again in 1965; and the wonder is that in a man born a century and a half ago we find today a pioneer explorer in fiction not only into the world of outer space but also into the workings of the tortured human mind. Whether or not we can fit Poe into a Southern—or even an American —literary tradition, there is today as for more than a century in the past a passionate minority among readers of books who keep his name alive. They at least are sure that Poe belongs in the canon of the Great American Writers.

Nevertheless, even those who admire him, like Van Wyck Brooks, sometimes find that they cannot fit him into any American literary tradition. Mr. Brooks wrote in *The World of Washington Irving* (1944):

The Transcendentalists and their heirs won the day in American letters because the main stream of American feeling ran through them, and Poe was outside of this main stream that reached full flood in Whitman and left him in an eddy of his own. . . . Poe himself had never shared the developing mood of the American tradition, which his fellow-Virginian at Monticello had done so much to shape, and as he never shared it he could not guide it. So American literature flowed past Poe, without dislodging him indeed, but without even being diverted or seriously affected by his presence. . . . He was even outside the main stream of the human tradition.

Until about the time of the First World War the South was in political and other respects still a Solid South. You could tell a Southerner not only by his speech but by his opinions on crucial subjects. Then indeed we had a Southern tradition. That time is past, I fear, even in the Deep South. The industrialization of large parts of the South has notably increased the average Southerner's income, but the South as we have known it is rapidly disintegrating under the pressure of forces from the outside. How could it be otherwise when daily and nightly we are bombarded by voices from north of the Potomac and from west of the Rockies on radio and television and in motion picture theaters—not to mention the reading matter which, like our advertisements, contains "hidden persuaders" enticing us to "buy" what will alienate us more and more from our Southern traditions?

Like Americans in other sections, we have in large measure lost our sense of the past. No longer does the Southerner know the history of his own state and section. Except as a very small part of the requirements in high school and college we do not read any Southern literature that was written before the First World War. Does any one today read Simms? Is there more than a single one of his eighty-odd books in print at the present time? We still remember vaguely a few of the Uncle Remus tales, a few poems by Lanier, one or two of Mark Twain's books dealing with life in the Old South, and a few

Edgar Allan Poe and the South

poems and tales by Poe. Are those sufficient to carry on a Southern literary tradition? I fear not.

And yet there is the Southern Renaissance, that remarkable movement which blossomed in Mencken's "Sahara of the Bozart." In fact, a large proportion of the best contemporary American writers are Southerners—and that paradoxically has happened at the very time when the South was losing most of what has hitherto distinguished its way of life from that of less fortunate regions. And so I wonder if the literature of the Southern Renaissance is not in reality a swan song—the last literary achievement of a generation of provincials at last becoming "Americanized."

Some of our twentieth-century Southern writers have owed something to Poe, but probably not many. Perhaps his writings meant a good deal to DuBose Heyward, who wrote a notable poetic tribute to Poe. Heyward's one-time collaborator, Hervey Allen, planned a novel that finally took the form of a biography of Poe in which he stressed the importance of Poe's Southern background. John Gould Fletcher in his autobiography said that he had to go to London to learn that Whitman was a great American poet and that for many years he regarded Lanier as "largely a vague sentimentalist," but Poe had been "an early idol." One of Fletcher's better poems—"In the City of Night"—is dedicated "To the Memory of Edgar Allan Poe." Two other poets who greatly admired Poe are only in part Southern, Conrad Aiken and Vachel Lindsay. At the age of thirteen Aiken, like Stephen Crane before him, carried in his pocket a volume of Poe; and as Henry W. Wells has pointed out, "Repeatedly his own works reflect this unceasing devotion." In the prefatory essay in his *Collected Poems* Lindsay tells us that before he was fourteen he had read Poe's "complete works, criticism and all" and that in the Springfield High School he was "a kind of literary outcast, because [he] championed Poe and his view." "The Wizard in the Street," one of the finest of all poetic tributes to Poe, appeared first in Lindsay's *Village Magazine*. Here it attracted the attention of Hamlin Garland, who when he visited Springfield said to the youthful poet's father and mother: ". . . any youth who can write such a poem as that which your son has written on Edgar Allan Poe is certain of recognition. I know of no other tribute to Poe of equal grace and power. . . . Your son is a genius. Be patient with him a little longer."

Among Southern writers no one has praised Poe more often

or more highly than James Branch Cabell. For him Poe was the "one true literary genius" that this country has produced, and all of our earlier literature that mattered was "A sufficing amount of Poe; and a tiny fraction of Mark Twain." Poe would undoubtedly have been willing to endorse Cabell's statement that "books are best insured against oblivion through practise of the auctorial virtues of distinction and clarity, of beauty and symmetry, of tenderness and truth and urbanity."

With the exception of Allen Tate the scholarly poets and critics who belonged to the Fugitive and Agrarian groups have not had much to say about Poe that has come to my attention. I do not think Poe would have had much sympathy with the position taken by the authors of *I'll Take My Stand*. Cleanth Brooks and Robert Penn Warren in their anthologies, *Understanding Poetry* and *Understanding Fiction*, have analyzed "Ulalume" and "The Fall of the House of Usher" without displaying much sympathy for Poe's methods and aims. Nevertheless, as Robert D. Jacobs and George Snell have pointed out, there is up to a certain point a strong resemblance between Poe's critical methods and those of the New Critics.

Allen Tate included in *The Forlorn Demon* (1953) two important essays: "The Angelic Imagination: Poe as God" and "Our Cousin, Mr. Poe." Taking his cue from D. H. Lawrence's *Studies in Classic American Literature*, he suggested that "Poe is the transitional figure in modern literature because he discovered our great subject, the disintegration of the modern personality, but kept it in a language that had developed in a tradition of unity and order." Yet Mr. Tate would not, I think, admit that Poe's style and technique have had an important influence on his own writing. In the summer of 1939 he took part in a symposium conducted by the *Partisan Review* on "The Situation in American Writing." In response to the question: "Are you conscious, in your own writing, of the existence of a 'usable past'? Is this mostly American?" he said in part:

. . . the literary past that interests me is highly eclectic, and is more European than American. . . . For example, until the time of Pound and Eliot, there are no American poets whose styles have been useful in working towards a style that is suitable to my own kind of American experience—more useful in fact than the New England poets or the poets of the Old South (including Poe) have been.

Edgar Allan Poe and the South

4

I do not know of any successful attempt to define the Southern literary tradition or the larger American tradition which presumably includes it. There have been, however, several suggestive attempts to characterize English literature, although none that I shall mention takes into account the literature of the twentieth century. The two who in my opinion best succeeded were Matthew Arnold and Ashley H. Thorndike. I shall assume that American and English literature are not yet essentially different; they certainly were not in Poe's time. With that assumption, then, let us ask ourselves how well Poe fits into this Anglo-American tradition, always remembering that every definition of a literary tradition is only a kind of majority report.

Arnold maintained that the English writers were characterized by energy and honesty. In comparing them with the writers of France he lamented "the want of a quick flexible intelligence, and of the strict standard which such an intelligence tends to impose. . . ." Professor Thorndike saw English literature as marked by energy, variety, novelty, individuality, and great fertility in the creation of new art forms. The greatest faults of the English writers were, he thought, overemphasis upon moral purpose and lack of form. He may have been thinking of Poe when he said: "The Moral, indeed, has been too much with us."

As Thorndike noted, much criticism of English literature has been concerned with pointing out how much better things are ordered across the English Channel. In the concluding chapter of his *Landmarks of French Literature* Lytton Strachey said: "The one high principle which, through so many generations, has guided like a star the writers of France is the principle of deliberation, of intention, and of a conscious search for ordered beauty; an unswerving, an indomitable pursuit of the endless glories of art." Is it any wonder that for a century Poe's reputation has been higher in France than in either England or the United States? That shrewd critic and historian of English literature, H. A. Taine, found the English writers lacking in moderation, regularity, and urbanity—qualities which come from the acceptance of some established authority or standard of excellence. My feeling is that American literature has, and in greater degree than the English, the faults commonly attributed to the English writers; and these artistic short-comings are in the main identical with those that Poe so often criticized in his reviews. Of the many great writers who have used the English language, how many are there—apart from Milton, Keats, Henry James, and Poe—who have been consistently fine artists? The French and the Latin-Americans have had no great difficulty in fitting Poe into their literary traditions. Indeed, in Baudelaire's prose and Mallarmé's verse his tales and poems may be artistically superior to the originals in English. Is Poe, then, an un-English or un-American "sport" or "mutation" that cannot be fitted into an English or an American or a Southern literary tradition? Or does his present vogue justify us in redefining our traditions so as to include him? T. S. Eliot, who cannot find a place for Poe in the English literary tradition, refers to him as "a kind of displaced European."

5

When Matthew Arnold and after him Ashley Thorndike defined the English literary tradition, they did not of course reckon with the as-yet-unwritten literature of the twentieth century. They did not foresee the coming revolt against the literary ideals and practices of many of the older English writers. Latterday critics have argued that the genuine tradition does not run through Milton, whose stock has gone down, but through Donne, who for two centuries was considered only a rather eccentric minor poet. Romantic poets like Shelley and Tennyson have found little favor with twentieth-century critics. On our side of the Atlantic there occurred a similar shift in literary taste and critical standards, and the result was a new canon of the Great American Writers which includes such new names as those of Melville, Thoreau, and Emily Dickinson. In the 1920's the New England poets—Bryant, Longfellow, Whittier, Lowell, and Holmes—became for many the symbols of what was bad in craftsmanship and literary taste.

In the South, too, there was a revolt against the literary ideals of romantic local colorists like Thomas Nelson Page and James Lane Allen, who had idealized and sentimentalized the Old South. Indeed, so far have our later Southern writers departed from the older literary tradition of the South that, since the First World War, they have created what we may be justified in calling a new Southern literary tradition.[2] The qualities most conspicuous in the work of Ellen Glasgow, Thomas Wolfe, William Faulkner, Robert Penn Warren, Allen Tate, Katherine Anne Porter, William Styron, and other Southern writers of fiction are a high level of craftsmanship, an acute consciousness of evil in human nature and in society, a pessimistic outlook on life, a sense of the past which is often also a tragic sense, and a consciousness of the regional background which is not like that of the Southern local colorists. They are realists and naturalists rather than romancers. In reading their books one is reminded of the frustration and defeat which for over a century the South has experienced as other regions have not. As a result Southerners have found it difficult to share in the characteristic American faith in unlimited progress and in the excessively high valuation placed upon status and material possessions as compared with personal qualities.

Most of the literary characteristics that I have mentioned can be found in a few older Southern writers, notably in the poems and short stories of Poe, in the psychological novels of Simms, and in Mark Twain's stories of the Old South, *Huckleberry Finn* and *Pudd'nhead Wilson*.

I do not know what William Faulkner thought of Poe. Perhaps Harry Levin was right when he wrote in *The Power of Blackness* (1958): "Much that seems forced, in William Faulkner's work, becomes second nature when we think of him as Poe's inheritor. We think of Caddy and Quentin, those two doomed siblings of the house of Compson, or of Emily Grierson, that old maid who clings to the corpse of her lover." Whether or not Faulkner, Warren, and other Southern novelists have been directly influenced by Poe, they are certainly like him in their preoccupation with violence, disease, death, and morbid minds in distress. Most of our modern Southern writers of fiction are better craftsmen than any of their Southern predecessors except Poe. They have set a high standard for writers who come after them.

If Poe is still influential in the South, that, I believe, is due only in part to the fact that he was a Southerner. It is rather

[2] See C. Hugh Holman's "Ellen Glasgow and the Southern Literary Tradition" in *Virginia in History and Tradition*, ed. R. C. Simonini, Jr. (Farmville, Va., 1958), pp. 85-105.

owing to the fact that he is an important figure in world literature. He was our only nineteenth-century American writer who made an important contribution to aesthetic theory. Poe's high standing in his own country in this century is due in part to the fact that since the First World War our literature has probably owed more to the literature of France than to that of the British Isles.

Finally, if there is a Southern literary tradition and if Poe is a part of it, may we not say that he has done more to keep that tradition alive than it has done to preserve his memory and to induce Southerners to read his poems and tales? I do not mean to be cynical, for there *is* something Southern about his writings. He is still, in Allen Tate's phrase, "Our Cousin, Mr. Poe." Shall we call him our French cousin or perhaps our second cousin once removed who was unfortunately born in Boston and is more at home in Paris than in New York, Philadelphia, Baltimore, or Richmond?

But after all the place for a man who is complete in all his powers is in the fight. The professor, the man of letters, gives up one-half of life that his protected talent may grow and flower in peace. But to make up your mind at your peril upon a living question, for purposes of action, calls upon your whole nature.

JUSTICE OLIVER WENDELL HOLMES, *Collected Legal Papers* (1921), p. 224

Ralph Waldo Emerson and the South

[Emerson is one of three or four American writers—Poe is another—whose writings have given me the greatest pleasure in teaching. In the Old South there were few who read Emerson's writings and fewer still who understood them, but I have found my Southern students quite as appreciative of the best in Emerson as students from New England or the West. In Vienna I discovered that Emerson's writings made a strong appeal to Austrian students. I remember a young priest who registered for my seminar and told me that he would like to write a paper on Emerson. I wondered what it was that attracted an orthodox Catholic to so thorough a nonconformist as Emerson. When I asked how he had become interested in Emerson, he told me that he had discovered Emerson while in a prisoner-of-war camp in Tennessee. During certain hours, he said, the POW's had access to the library of an American officers' club, and it was there that he had first read Emerson's *Essays.* When I read the priest's term paper, I found that it was the semimystical aspect of Emerson's thought that most deeply appealed to him. Emerson's Over-Soul was one manifestation of the God he worshiped.

This essay is a revised and much enlarged version of the chapter on Emerson in *The South in American Literature*. It embodies some new materials and something additional in the way of interpretation.

As I said in the earlier version of this essay, I hope that no admirer of Emerson will think me lacking in appreciation for a great American writer because I chose him to illustrate the extent to which sectional controversy prevented the New England writers from understanding the ante-bellum South. In a recent study, *The South in Northern Eyes 1831 to 1861* (1958), Howard R. Floan has demonstrated that apart from the question of slavery the New England writers "had almost no awareness of the South and apparently no desire to learn more about it to understand it better." "The image of the South assembled from the numerous and often scattered comments of Whittier, Lowell, Longfellow, Emerson, and Thoreau is," he found, "essentially the same image of evil which was portrayed by Garrison and Phillips in their fight against slavery." "Garrison's hatred of slavery," he says, "became hatred of the slave-holder"; and the Southern slaveholder was "a whip-bearing villain, the Negro an earthbound angel." This fictionalized picture of the South still colors the attitude of some Northerners toward the South even in the twentieth century.]

1

Soon after his graduation from Harvard in 1821 Emerson wrote to a friend in Baltimore: "You know our idea of an accomplished Southerner; to wit, as ignorant as a bear, as irascible and nettled as any porcupine, as polite as a troubadour, and a very John Randolph in character and address." Emerson's notion of the Southern character shows plainly some marks of the traditional New England conception, but it was based in part on an acquaintance with Southern students at Harvard. For a brief time he shared a room with a Charlestonian, John Gourdin, whom Dr. Holmes described as showy and fascinating. The recognized leader of Emerson's class was another South Carolinian, Robert Woodward Barnwell, whom President Josiah Quincy remembered as the "first scholar of the class . . . a noble specimen of the Southerner, high-spirited, interesting, and a leader of men." We shall hear of Barnwell again.

Health-seekers from New England often went South to avoid the cold Northern winter. It was thus that Emerson, recently ordained as a minister, spent the winter of 1826-1827 in Charleston and St. Augustine. This journey into what he felt was a foreign country had no such determining influence as his European visit six years later. The verses he wrote and the entries in his *Journals* indicate that he thought of himself as an exile. Nevertheless Emerson was impressed with the superiority of the manners of Charlestonians white and black; and he liked St. Augustine well enough to write a poem which included the line: "Farewell; & fair befall thee, gentle town!" The Catholic priests and the Methodist ministers whom he heard, or heard of, confirmed his low opinion of the state of religion in the South. He felt, however, no deep repulsion from slavery as yet. That, as with Dr. Channing, was to come some years after he had left the South. He did, however, note a certain incongruity between slavery and Christianity. In St. Augustine he wrote in the *Journals* that he had attended a meeting of a Bible society, of which the treasurer was the district marshal. By "a somewhat unfortunate arrangement" the treasurer had called a meeting of the society in the government house while a slave auction was being conducted just outside. "One ear therefore heard the glad tidings of great joy, whilst the other was regaled with 'Going, gentlemen, going!' And almost without changing our position we might aid in sending the Scriptures into Africa, or bid for 'four children without the mother' who had been kidnapped therefrom."

The most memorable event of Emerson's winter in the South was his meeting with Prince Achille Murat, a nephew of Napoleon, now married to a distant relative of George Washington and living on a plantation near Tallahassee. Emerson and Murat boarded at the same place in St. Augustine while waiting for the ship that was to take them northward, but they did not become much acquainted until the sloop *William* put to sea. The voyage to Charleston took nine days, and the two talked incessantly. Emerson wrote: "He is a philosopher, a scholar, a man of the world very sceptical but very candid & an ardent lover of truth. I blessed my stars for my fine companion. . . ." Never had Emerson met anyone like Murat. In Charleston he wrote:

I have connected myself by friendship to a man who with as ardent a love of truth as that which animates me, with a mind surpassing mine in the variety of its research, and sharpened and strengthened to an energy for *action* to which I have no pretension, by advantages of birth and practical connection with mankind beyond almost all men in the world,—is, yet, that which I had ever supposed only a creature of the imagination—a consistent Atheist,—and a disbeliever in the existence, and, of course, in the immortality of the soul. My faith in these points is strong and I trust, as I live, indestructible. Meanwhile I love and honour this intrepid doubter. His soul is noble, and his virtue, as the virtue of a Sadducee must always be, is sublime.

After his encounter with Emerson, Murat excepted the Unitarians from his harsh criticism of American religious sects. In September, 1827, he wrote to Emerson urging him to come to Tallahassee and by his preaching "substitute reason, learning and morality for nonsense, ignorance and fanaticism." Murat's influence undoubtedly did something to shake the young minister's provincial notions and to widen his outlook upon life. Many, many years later Emerson was to remember his friend when he wrote in *Society and Solitude* (1870): "If we recall the rare hours when we encountered the best persons, we there found ourselves, and then first society seemed to exist. That was society, though in the transom of a brig or on the Florida keys."

Emerson's winter in the South brought him improved health, a better knowledge of his own country, and friendship with a man who had forced him into questioning some of his cherished beliefs. It should be remembered, however, that in Achille Murat, Emerson saw not a highly intelligent Southern planter but a European intellectual whom chance had brought to America. A few years later, when he visited Europe, Emerson was to meet other thinkers —Landor, Wordsworth, Coleridge, and Carlyle—who would contribute still further to his intellectual development; but it was Murat who first brought Emerson out of the narrow little world of Unitarian New England.

For nearly a decade after his return from the South one finds in Emerson's writings few comments on the South or slavery. By October, 1837, however, he had come to view the Southern collegian much more critically:

The young Southerner comes here a spoiled child, with graceful manners, excellent self-command, very good to be spoiled more, but good for nothing else,—a mere parader. . . . Treat them with great deference, as we often do, and they accept it all as their due without misgiving. Give them an inch and they take a mile. They are mere bladders of conceit. Each snipper-snapper of them all undertakes to speak for the entire Southern States. "At the South; the reputation of Cambridge," etc., etc., which being interpreted, is, In my negro village of Tuscaloosa, or Cheraw, or St. Mark's, I supposed so and so. "We at the South," forsooth. They are more civilized than the Seminoles, however, in my opinion; a little more. Their question respecting any man is like a Seminole's,—How can he fight? In this country [New England], we ask, What can he do? His pugnacity is all they prize in man, dog, or turkey. The proper way of treating them is not deference, but to say as Mr. [Samuel] Ripley does, "Fiddle faddle," in answer to each solemn remark about "The South." "It must be confessed," said the young man, "that in Alabama, we are dead to everything, as respects politics." "Very true," replied Mr. Ripley, "leaving out the last clause."

Emerson's conscience did not deeply trouble him about slavery until the antislavery controversy became acute. It was so also with William Ellery Channing and Bronson Alcott, who had both spent more time in the South than Emerson. As time went on, men who, as Lowell once pointed out, owed much of their culture to slave-holding Rome, Greece, and Palestine began to denounce Southern slaveholders as representatives of a semibarbarous civilization. Emerson resisted the tendency longer than most of the Transcendentalists, but eventually he was swept along by the tide like lesser men. In the New England of his day, however, no one would remind him that in "The American Scholar" he had said:

Is it not the chief disgrace in the world, not to be an unit . . . but to be reckoned in the gross, in the hundred, or the thousand, of the party, the section, to which we belong, and our opinion predicted geographically, as the north, or the south?

Barrett Wendell, a New Englander of the New Englanders, wrote in *Stelligeri* in 1893:

It is hiding the truth that, for all their noble enthusiasm, the Abolitionists, after the good old British fashion, directed their reforming energies not against the evils prevalent in the actual society of which they formed a part, but against those that prevailed in a rival society which they knew chiefly by hearsay.

As late as 1841, when he published his essay, "Self-Reliance," Emerson could write:

If an angry bigot assumes this bountiful cause of Abolition, and comes to me with his last news from Barbadoes, why should I not say to him, "Go love thy infant; love thy wood-chopper; be good-natured and modest; have that grace; and never varnish your hard, uncharitable ambition with this incredible, tenderness for black folk a thousand miles off. Thy love afar is spite at home." Rough and graceless would be such greeting, but truth is handsomer than the affectation of love.

A year earlier Emerson had written in his *Journals*:

Does he not do more to abolish slavery who works all day steadily in his own garden than he who goes to the abolition-meeting and makes a speech? He who does his own work frees a slave. He who does not his own work is a slave-holder.

Much that Emerson wrote about the South and slavery was at odds with some of his most characteristic ideas. This inconsistency did not disturb the Concord sage, but it may disturb some of his admirers. He once referred to Abolitionists and other professional reformers as "an altogether odious set of people, whom one would shun as the worst of bores and canters." The only way to make the world better, he thought, was to make better the individuals in it, and he was echoing Jefferson when he said that "the less government we have the better,—the fewer laws, and the less confided power." It was useless to try to reform society by attacking a single abuse. In "New England Reformers" he said in 1844:

Do not be so vain of your one objection [to society]. Do you think there is only one? Alas! my good friend, there is no part of society or of life better than any other part. All our things are right and wrong together. The wave of evil washes all our institutions alike. Do you complain of our marriage? Our marriage is no worse than our education, our diet, our trade, our social customs.

Might he not logically have added: ". . . than African slavery on Southern plantations or industrial servitude in New England mills and factories?"

I have noted the changing attitude toward the South and slavery that came over Emerson and many another Northerner. The change that came over the South is no less striking, but it is much more difficult for the modern American to understand and sympathize with it. Writing in the *Southern Literary Messenger* for February, 1861, a Louisiana doctor with a sense of history, William H. Holcombe, thus summed up the changed attitudes of North and South:

It has not been more than twenty-five years since Garrison was dragged through the streets of Boston with a rope around his neck, for uttering Abolition sentiments; and not thirty years since, the abolition of slavery was seriously debated in the Legislature of Virginia. Now, on the contrary, the radical opinions of Sumner, Emerson and Parker, and the assassination schemes of John Brown, are applauded in Fanueil Hall, and the whole Southern mind with an unparalleled unanimity regards the institution of slavery as righteous and just, ordained of God, and to be perpetuated by man.

The South, Dr. Holcombe concluded, must choose between "a separate nationality" and "the Africanization of the South."

The fatal "mistake that was made by the Southern defenders of slavery," said Lucius Q. C. Lamar in 1888 in an oration on Calhoun, "was in regarding it as a permanent form of society instead of a process of emergence and transition from barbarism to freedom." Those who defended slavery, he pointed out, failed to see that

Every benefit which slavery conferred upon those subject to it; all the ameliorating and humanizing tendencies it introduced into the life of the African; all the elevating agencies which lifted him higher in the scale of rational and moral being, were the elements of the future and inevitable destruction of the system.

Lamar continued: "The existing industrial relations of capital and labor, had there been no secession, no war, would of themselves have brought about the death of slavery." Why, one wonders, had Calhoun and his Southern contemporaries failed to see this? Emerson had written in his *Journals* on December 31, 1843:

We rail at trade, but the historian of the world will see that it was the principle of liberty; that it settled America, and destroyed feudalism, and made peace and keeps peace; that it will abolish slavery.

2

By 1850, when he published *Representative Men*, Emerson had given to the world his "selectest thoughts" embodied in the finest prose and verse he was ever to write. Of course we could ill afford to lose *English Traits*, some of the later poems, and many entries in the *Journals*; but in his earlier writings he had given us the best that was in him as poet, essayist, and philosopher. Up almost to the middle of the century he had been able to think and write in comparative seclusion without being unduly disturbed by political events.

By 1850, however, "Things [were] in the saddle," and Emerson could no longer honestly and honorably refrain from publicly avowing his abhorrence of slavery and his deep dissatisfaction with leading politicians. As long ago as 1837 he had written in the *Journals*: "Right-minded men have recently been called to decide for Abolition." In the same year he had said to the Phi Beta Kappa Society: "Action is with the scholar subordinate, but it is essential. Without it he is not yet man." Emerson, however, was not optimistic enough to believe that he could speak or write anything that would change the current of events. As late as 1854 he would say: "I do not often speak to public questions;—they are odious and hurtful, and it seems like meddling or leaving your work."

The annexation of Texas seemed to Emerson, as to many another New Englander, a great calamity; and the War with Mexico, which soon followed, a war for the extension of slavery. Emerson did not refuse to pay his taxes and go to jail, like Thoreau; nor was he as yet, like the extreme Abolitionists, willing to break up the Union. He had, however, come to accept the Abolitionist legend of a barbarous South. In his "Second West Indies Emancipation Address" on August 1, 1845, he said:

Elevate, enlighten, civilize the semi-barbarous nations of South Carolina, Georgia, Alabama—take away from their debauched society the Bowie-knife, the rum-bowl, the dice-box, and the stews—take out the brute, and infuse a crop of civility and generosity, and you touch those selfish lords with thought and gentleness.

The "Ode Inscribed to W. H. Channing" throws light upon Emerson's thinking in 1846, the year the War with Mexico began. Channing, a nephew of the great Unitarian divine and an Abolitionist as well as a Transcendentalist, had implored Emerson to take to the platform as an outspoken opponent of slavery. This Emerson was not yet ready to do. Much as he abhorred slavery, he had, he said, "quite other slaves to free than those negroes, to wit, imprisoned spirits, imprisoned thoughts." The poem begins:

> If I refuse
> My study for their politique,
> Which at the best is trick,
> The angry Muse
> Puts confusion in my brain.

Much as Emerson sympathized with Channing, he was not yet willing to disrupt the Union to get rid of the stain of slavery.

> What boots thy zeal,
> O glowing friend,
> That would indignant rend
> The northland from the south?
> Wherefore? to what good end?
> Boston Bay and Bunker Hill
> Would serve things still. . . .

Eventually, as the poet assured his friend, "The over-god / Who marries Right to Might" would free the slaves.

But it was not alone thoughts of the slaves and slaveholders that troubled Emerson's mind. In the mountains of New England he had seen "The jackals of the negro-holder," slave-traders and overseers like Mrs. Stowe's Simon Legree, who was a New England Yankee. The New Hampshire that Robert Frost was to celebrate in a notable poem had given birth to Daniel Webster, whom Emerson had come to distrust, and Franklin Pierce, now a soldier in Mexico.

> The God who made New Hampshire
> Taunted the lofty land
> With little men. . . .

When Emerson in 1863 received his copy of Hawthorne's *Our Old Home*, he cut out the page in which the novelist had dedicated the book to his old college friend Ex-President Pierce.

In the great "Ode," as in many other passages in Emerson's writings, one finds him expressing opinions that seem to contradict earlier utterances.

> He who exterminates
> Races by stronger races,
> Black by white faces. . . .

These lines in remarkable fashion seem to anticipate Darwin's theory of the survival of the fittest, but it is almost shocking to discover that Emerson—like so many Americans, especially in the South —apparently subscribed to some theory of racial inequality.

Emerson was no unqualified admirer of American democracy. The following sentences from *The Conduct of Life* sound more like Carlyle than Emerson: "Leave this prating about the masses. Masses are rude, lame, unmade, pernicious in their demands and influence, and need not to be flattered, but to be schooled." And this: "The mass are animal, in state of pupilage, and nearer the chimpanzee. . . ." That sentiment is not unlike that expressed in a once-notorious passage written by Senator James H. Hammond of South Carolina, who insisted that there must always be "a class to do the menial duties, to perform the drudgery of life. That is, a class requiring but a low order of intellect and but little skill. . . . It constitutes the very mudsill of society and of political government. . . ."

The end of the War with Mexico brought on a new political crisis. The United States deprived Mexico of a vast territory which the New Englanders felt sure would permit the extension of slavery all the way to the Pacific Ocean. In the greatly enlarged area of the nation, little New England seemed destined to lose what political power and influence it still had. The outmoded Missouri Compromise could no longer be depended on to keep slavery out of the Northwest. Finally, through the efforts of Henry Clay, Stephen A. Douglas, and—to Emerson's disgust—Daniel Webster, a new compromise was adopted which averted civil war until the North was strong enough to win. But the Compromise of 1850, in order to placate Southern extremists who were so unwise as to demand it, included a new and much more stringent Fugitive Slave Law, which shocked and angered many humane men and women in the North. Emerson wrote in his *Journals*: "This filthy enactment was made in the nineteenth century by people who could read and write. I will not obey it, by God." Did he remember that in the essay on "Politics" (1844) he had written: "But the wise know that foolish legislation is a rope of sand which perishes in the twisting; that the State must follow and not lead the character and progress of the citizen. . ."?

Emerson placed the chief blame for this iniquitous act, not upon Southern politicians but upon the statesman whom he had long idolized. He held Daniel Webster personally responsible for the new Fugitive Slave Law, for though the Senator was not its original proponent, Emerson knew that it could not have been enacted without his powerful support. In the Emerson home the anniversary of Webster's Seventh-of-March Speech was observed as a day of infamy. He wrote:

> Why did all manly gifts in Webster fail?
> He wrote on Nature's grandest brow, For Sale.

Emerson, like Whittier, Lowell, Parker, Sumner, and Garrison, failed to see that the Seventh-of-March Speech was probably the most courageous act of the great Senator's political life. After talking with Clay and other Southern leaders, Webster had concluded that "the inevitable consequences of leaving the existing controversies unadjusted would be Civil War." He knew that the speech would cost him the support of many of his constituents and friends, but it was more important to preserve the Union than to placate the impractical Abolitionists. And so, as another distinguished Senator from Massachusetts—the late President of the United States—wrote in *Profiles in Courage* (1956):

Summoning for the last time that spell-binding oratorical ability, he abandoned his previous opposition to slavery in the territories, abandoned his constituents' abhorrence of the Fugitive Slave Law, abandoned his own place in the history and hearts of his countrymen and abandoned his last chance for the goal that had eluded him for over twenty years— the Presidency. Daniel Webster preferred to risk his career and his reputation rather than risk the Union.

It was a great speech and it earned for him, in President Kennedy's words, "a condemnation unsurpassed in the annals of political history."

In that speech Webster proved himself a better economist than his opponents when he maintained that beyond Missouri and eastern Texas there was no place for slavery to go, for the high and dry plains and the Rocky Mountains blocked the westward extension of the slave plantation. He saw, as the late Charles W. Ramsdell was to point out in 1929, that slavery "had reached its limits in both profits and lands" and that "The free farmers in the North who dreaded its further spread had nothing to fear."

In the middle fifties Emerson came to feel that the nation's bulwarks which had hitherto prevented the extension of slavery had all failed: the Federal Constitution, the Missouri Compromise, the U. S. Supreme Court, even state sovereignty; and now the Kansas-Nebraska bill was opening the way for slavery in the territories. In January, 1856, he wrote to his brother William: "If the Free States do not obtain the government next fall, which our experience does not entitle us to hope, nothing seems left, but to form at once a Northern Union, & break the old." Speaking in Concord in 1851 he had said: "Under the Union I suppose the fact to be that there are really two nations, the North and the South."

On May 19, 1856, Emerson's friend Charles Sumner delivered in the United States Senate a vitriolic tirade entitled "The Crime against Kansas," in which he shamefully abused Senator Andrew P. Butler of South Carolina. Butler's young kinsman Preston S. Brooks, a member of the House of Representatives, retaliated by striking Sumner to the floor with his cane. Many but by no means all Southerners defended Brooks, but in New England Sumner was regarded as a martyr. Emerson said in a Concord address:

I do not see how a barbarous community and a civilized community can constitute one state. I think we must get rid of slavery, or we must get rid of freedom. Life has not parity of value in the free state and in the slave state. In one, it is adorned with education, with skilful labor, with arts, with long prospective interests, with sacred family ties, with honor and justice. In the other, life is a fever; man is an animal, given to pleasure, frivolous, irritable, spending his days in hunting and practising with deadly weapons to defend himself against his slaves and against his companions brought up in the same idle and dangerous way. Such people live for the moment, they have properly no future, and readily risk on every passion a life which is of small value to themselves or to others.

Emerson had come to accept the Abolitionist legend of a barbarous South. He had forgotten his friend Barnwell when he added: "The whole state of South Carolina does not now offer one or any number of persons who are to be weighed in the scale with such a person as the meanest of them all has now struck down." This is even more ungenerous than a passage in a letter written by William Gilmore Simms on the last day of 1860: "Charleston is worth all New England."

In November, 1859, Emerson referred to John Brown, then under sentence of death, as "that new saint, than whom none purer or more brave was ever led by love of men into conflict and death,— the new saint awaiting his martyrdom, and who, if he shall suffer, will make the gallows glorious like the cross." A truer estimate of Brown is found in a passage that Hawthorne, no lover of reformers, wrote with Emerson in mind: ". . . nor did I expect ever to shrink so unutterably from any apothegm of a sage, whose happy lips have uttered a hundred golden sentences, as that saying . . . that the death of this blood-stained fanatic has 'made the Gallows as venerable as the Cross!' Nobody was ever more justly hanged."

While the Southern states were seceding one by one, Emerson took the same position as Hawthorne and Whittier that the North was well rid of them and no compromise should be made to bring them back. The attack on Fort Sumter, however, affected Emerson and millions of other Northerners as the Japanese attack on Pearl Harbor affected a later generation. Now the secessionists must be punished and the Southern states forcibly brought back into a Union which they hated.

Emerson was not the first nor the last philosopher who in wartime found himself expressing opinions at variance with his fundamental convictions. In an address on "War" he had said in 1838: "Nothing is plainer than that the sympathy with war is a juvenile and temporary state." In the same year he had written in the *Journals*: "I do not like to see a sword at a man's side. If it threaten man, it threatens me. A company of soldiers is an offensive spectacle." This is a far cry from the Emerson who at the Charlestown Navy Yard was to say: "Ah! sometimes gunpowder smells good."

Two years after the end of the Civil War Emerson could write: "The armies mustered in the North were as much missionaries to the mind of the country as they were carriers of material force, and had the vast advantage of carrying whither they marched a higher civilization." Did Emerson not know about the devastation which Sherman had left behind him in Georgia and the Carolinas and Sheridan in the Shenandoah Valley? In a saner mood, however, Emerson in his *Journals* would quote Cicero (in Latin) to the effect that: "Everything about a civil war is lamentable . . . but nothing more so than victory itself." Northerners and Southerners alike had not heeded the memorable warning in Edmund Burke's "Speech on Conciliation with America": "I do not know the method of drawing up an indictment against an whole people."

Before the outbreak of war Emerson had insisted that when the slaves were freed, the owners should be compensated. He wrote in 1855 one of his most eloquent passages:

'Tis said it will cost two thousand millions of dollars. Was there ever any contribution that was so enthusiastically paid as this will be? We will have a chimney-tax. We will give up our coaches, and wine, and watches. The churches will melt their plate. The father of his country shall wait, well pleased, a little longer for his monument; Franklin for his, the Pilgrim Fathers for theirs, and the patient Columbus for his. The mechanics will give, the needle-women will give; the children will have cent-societies. Every man in the land will give a week's work to dig away this accursed mountain of sorrow once and forever out of the world.

That was in 1855. On January 1, 1863, the poet read his "Boston Hymn," in which he said:

> Pay ransom to the owner
> And fill the bag to the brim.
> Who is the owner? The slave is owner
> And ever was. Pay him.

On this poem Professor Ralph Rusk's comment seems just:

It was a fine burst of moral indignation. So far as the slave was concerned, it was just; but it added to the general feeling of bitterness toward the white Southerners, bitterness that later begot the madness of the reconstruction era and disgraced the conquering North.

As the war came to an end, Emerson felt that the terms which General Grant offered to Lee looked "a little too easy." For his part he was glad that "the rebels have been pounded instead of negociated into a peace. They must remember it, and their inveterate brag will be humbled, if not cured." Emerson regarded Andrew Johnson, who was trying to carry out Lincoln's humane Reconstruction policies, as a tool of the Southern planters and a traitor to the cause of liberty. "If we let the Southern States into Congress," he said, "the Northern Democrats will join them in thwarting the will of the Government. And the obvious remedy is to give the negro his vote."

I do not think that Emerson ever realized how mistaken the Reconstruction policy of Thaddeus Stevens and Charles Sumner was, but he did express a certain disillusionment about the war. In November, 1865, he wrote in the *Journals*:

We hoped that in the peace, after such a war, a great expansion would follow in the mind of the Country; grand views in every direction,—true freedom in politics, in religion, in social science, in thought. But the energy of the nation seems to have expended itself in the war, and every interest is found as sectional and timorous as before. . . .

3

By 1850, as we have seen, Emerson had come to feel that he must testify publicly to his abhorrence of human slavery. In that manner he proved himself a loyal citizen of Massachusetts and won the esteem of many who would otherwise have regarded him as an impractical philosopher. But in speaking to partisan audiences highly charged with emotion he had had to give up his carefully chosen position as a philosophical observer and thinker. In 1856 he said in a "Speech on Affairs in Kansas": "There is this peculiarity about the case of Kansas, that all the right is on one side." Alas, the right never is all on one side in such critical times; and Emerson had no notion how completely South and North had come to misunderstand each other. Rather sadly, Professor Rusk summed up his feeling about Emerson's plight at the end of the war:

For him, an idealist, the war had been a disease in his own system as well as in the body politic. He found it hard to get the poison of hate out of his blood. At the end of the conflict he could not refrain from writing down privately a list of the atrocities charged against the South. His thinking did not thrive so well as before. . . . For him the idea of liberty had become too much constricted in the symbol of the manumitted slave. It was hard even for so puissant a liberal as Emerson to free himself from the narrowing boundaries of his postwar world.

Two years after the war Emerson could say: "Of course, there are noble men everywhere, and there are such in the South. . . ." He had to add, however: "But the common people, rich and poor, were the narrowest and most conceited of mankind. . . ." A year earlier he had remembered his South Carolina friend Barnwell and on July 6, 1866, had written to him urging him to come to Cambridge for a reunion of the class of 1821:

But I wish you to know that distance, politics, war, even, at last, have not been able to efface in any manner the high affectionate regard in which I, in common I believe with all your old contemporaries of 1817-21, have firmly held you as our avowed chief, in days when boys, as we then were, give a tender & romantic value to that distinction, which they cannot later give again.

In the spring of 1876 the two literary societies of the University of Virginia asked Emerson to deliver an address in Charlottesville as a part of the commencement program. Emerson, now seventy-three years old and in failing health, had practically given up speaking in public; but he accepted the invitation, "thinking it of happy omen that they should send to Massachusetts for their orator." Here is the account as given in J. E. Cabot's official biography, published in 1887:

The visitors [Emerson and his daughter Ellen] were treated with every attention in the society of the place, there was no intentional discourtesy, but the Southern self-respect appeared to demand that they should be constantly reminded that they were in an oppressed and abused country. And the next day, at Emerson's address, the audience in general—mostly young women with their admirers, but also children, as well as older persons—seemed to regard the occasion chiefly as one for social entertainment, and there was so much noise that he could not make himself heard.

Emerson felt hurt. He thought that if the audience had remained quiet, he could have made himself heard; but his daughter thought otherwise. In later life she, too, came to feel that part of the trouble was a determined hostility on the part of the Southern audience, but the letters she wrote home in 1876 tell quite a different story.

The uproar of people coming in late and hunting seats continued some ten minutes into the address and I saw with dismay that Father's voice seldom rose clear above it, and all the young & gay perceived the same thing, and like the audience at Mr Adams's oration at the Dedication of the Memorial Hall, concluded they couldn't hear very well and had better enjoy themselves, so the noise rather grew than decreased.

It seems obvious that finding themselves unable to hear, the youngsters talked, as others were to do six years later when a Southern writer, George W. Cable, delivered a commencement address at the University of Mississippi. Ellen Emerson summed up her own sane reaction: "If the oration had been my first thought in the visit, I should be disappointed, but as I regard the expedition principally as a right hand of fellowship, I am contented." In Washington on the way home she wrote of

the fun . . . of seeing all the world burn incense to Father [which] was never so great as now, just because it is the South. . . . To see people come & stand before him in the aisle of the cars & gaze at him, and bring their children & ask him to shake hands with them. People from Tennessee, Alabama, Texas [on their way to the Centennial Exhibition in Philadelphia].

In 1876 Reconstruction was coming to an end, and the South, which had not been hospitable to many New England writers, was at last beginning to accept Emerson as a contemporary classic. It had taken a long time. Southern readers, as we shall see, found it much easier to understand and appreciate Hawthorne, Longfellow, and Holmes than Thoreau or Emerson.

4

Emerson's writings, which were often misunderstood even in his native Massachusetts, held peculiar difficulties for ante-bellum Southern readers. In the Southern states, which were largely rural, there were few cities and fewer towns than in the North. Bookstores were not plentiful; and for various reasons to be pointed out, Emerson's books were rarely stocked in the bookstores and were often not reviewed in Southern magazines and newspapers. In the North and the Middle West Emerson was able by his lectures to win many new readers for his books, but Southerners had no such opportunity to see and hear him. Few of the Southerners who tried reading his *Essays* had any real understanding of the Unitarian-Transcendentalist background out of which his thought had developed. He seemed to them to speak a foreign language. In the Revolutionary period many educated Southerners had been Deists, but in the nineteenth century the South had become the "Bible-belt" of evangelical orthodoxy. Unitarians were now regarded as heretics almost as obnoxious as atheists, and the Transcendentalists were considered visionaries or wild-eyed radicals. One exasperated Southern reviewer wrote: ". . . Mr. Emerson writes in a language which even his own children cannot understand." In our own time Emerson's poetic, oracular, semiclerical language sometimes misleads the unwary reader. Then, too, Emerson had, as I have shown, his provincial side; and the Southern reader, who had his own provincialisms, was often repelled. Lowell thought Emerson the most American of our writers; few Southerners would have agreed with him.

For orthodox Southerners Emerson was an exponent of heretical doctrines that were dangerous. By 1850 the Southern churches had broken with the Northern, which they regarded as tainted with rationalism and fanatical on the slavery question. In January, 1852, John Custis Darby of Lexington, Kentucky, published an article on "Ralph Waldo Emerson" in the *Quarterly Review* of the Southern branch of the Methodist Church. "Mr. Emerson," he said, "is the representative of the New England infidelity; at the head of which form of doctrines, stands Strauss of Germany." For Emerson, as for Strauss, he thought, biblical history had only a symbolic value. "Strauss receives the truth, but denies the record as genuine, authentic history. . . . There is no God; it is all a myth."

It is a favorite doctrine with him [Emerson] to praise and admire the doctrines and excellencies of all religions except Christianity; and if he name the latter, to disparage it by a comparison with the doctrines of Vishnu and the philosophy of Plato. Among his representative men, the only Christian he has chosen to introduce, is the good and the learned, but the deranged Swedenborg.

A curious example of the Southern religious objection to Emerson is found in the second novel of Augusta Jane Evans, *Beulah* (1859). Its popularity suggests that in other sections there were many readers who regarded Emerson as an infidel. Beulah, a studious orphan girl, "with a slowly dying faith," is reading books one would not expect a Southern girl to read—although Miss Evans herself had evidently read them:

It was no longer study for the sake of erudition; these riddles involved all that she prized in Time and Eternity, and she grasped books of every description with the eagerness of a famishing nature. What dire chance threw into her hands such works as Emerson's, Carlyle's, and Goethe's? Like the waves of the clear, sunny sea, they only increased her thirst to madness. Her burning lips were ever at these fountains; and, in her reckless eagerness, she plunged into the gulf of German speculation.

Somewhat later Beulah has a long conversation with her friend Cornelia Graham, a widely traveled young woman who is rapidly becoming an invalid. Cornelia has absorbed the "grim Emersonian fatalism" completely, but Beulah has come to the conclusion that "of all Pyrrhonists he is the prince."

Beulah took up one of the volumes, and turned the pages carelessly.
  "But all this would shock a Christian."
  "And deservedly; for Emerson's works, collectively and individually, are aimed at the doctrines of Christianity. There is a grim, terrible fatalism scowling on his pages which might well frighten the reader who clasped the Bible to his heart."
  "Yet you accept his 'compensation.' Are you prepared to receive his deistic system?" Cornelia leaned forward and spoke eagerly. Beulah smiled.
  "Why strive to cloak the truth? I should not term his fragmentary

system 'deistic.' He knows not yet what he believes. There are singular antagonisms existing among even his pet theories."

When Cornelia replies, "I have not found any," Beulah points them out and adds: "His writings are, to me, like heaps of broken glass, beautiful in the individual crystal, sparkling, and often dazzling, but gather them up, and try to fit them into a whole, and the jagged edges refuse to unite."

Cornelia on her deathbed says:

Oh, the so-called philosophers of this century and the last are crowned-heads of humbugry [sic]! . . . . They mock earnest, inquiring minds with their refined infinitesimal, homeopathic 'developments' of deity; metaphysical wolves in Socratic cloaks. Oh, they have much to answer for!

She admits that she has finally lost faith in Emerson and Theodore Parker:

Emerson's atheistic fatalism is enough to unhinge human reason; he is a great, and I believe an honest thinker, and of his genius I have the profoundest admiration. An intellectual Titan, he wages war with received creeds, and rising on the ruins of systems, struggles to scale the battlements of truth. As for Parker, a careful perusal of his works was enough to disgust me.

In the end Cornelia dies without recovering her faith. Beulah is more fortunate, for her faith returns and so does her lover, who had vanished somewhere in China.

Until the middle of the nineteenth century Emerson's reputation developed slowly outside New England largely because until about 1850 his books were not easily obtainable elsewhere. As William Charvat has pointed out, the early Boston publishers were primarily retailers, and were not skilled in the distribution of their wares. Emerson's publisher, James Munroe, was not one of the best, and Emerson himself was unwilling to allow his publisher as large a discount as was customary elsewhere. Hawthorne, who had discovered that New York and Philadelphia publishers could sell more of his books, wrote in 1845 to Evert Duyckinck in New York: "His [Emerson's] reputation is still, I think, provincial, and almost local partly owing to the defects of the New England system of publication." Emerson finally gave his books to Ticknor & Fields, who sold many more than Munroe had been able to sell. By 1850 the railroads had penetrated beyond the Alleghenies, and Emerson's new publishers made his books available in the Middle West, where many New Englanders had settled and where Emerson now found it profitable to lecture.

In the South, however, railroad facilities were poor, even after 1850. Books shipped from Richmond to Savannah had to change trains half a dozen times. Many of the small Southern towns had no bookstores, and the planter who wanted a copy of Emerson's *Essays* had to order it or wait until he was able to visit a bookstore in some Southern city or town. Bookstores in the coastal cities, like Charleston, were better able to secure the new books than inland cities like Nashville and Raleigh.

Before 1840 the South had been a major outlet for New York and Philadelphia publishers. By 1850, however, Northern publishers had found the South increasingly hostile to books and magazines which were outspoken in condemnation of slavery. One Northern publisher declined to publish *Uncle Tom's Cabin* because he thought it would alienate Southern readers. The unprecedented sales of that famous novel convinced Northern publishers that there was a large market in the North and the West for books which might antagonize the South. Ticknor & Fields, who had been trying hard to sell their books in the South, in 1849 stopped sending review copies to the *Southern Literary Messenger*. By that time Southern booksellers had discovered that their customers were being urged on all sides not to buy books and magazines hostile to the South. Many Southerners of course had always preferred English books and magazines to American, often even to those published in the Southern states.

Educated New Englanders who lived in the South were more likely to hear of Emerson's books, but they, too, had their difficulties with his writings. One of them was Dr. Samuel Gilman, pastor of the Unitarian Church in Charleston and a Harvard graduate. After reading Emerson's "Divinity School Address," he wrote in his wife's magazine, the *Southern Rose*, on November 24, 1838: "A new comet, or rather meteor, is shooting athwart the literary sky of old Massachusetts, in the form of Ralph Waldo Emerson." Gilman, whose favorite New England author was Hawthorne, thought that Emerson's admirers overrated this "profound admirer, student, and imitator of Thomas Carlyle. . . ."

Joseph Holt Ingraham, a native of Maine and the prolific author of subliterary novels, was in later life a minister in Mississippi. In

Ralph Waldo Emerson and the South

1860 he published *The Sunny South,* hoping to bring about a better understanding between North and South. He put into the mouth of his New England governess his own admiration of Emerson's *Nature* and *Representative Men.* Ingraham, however, like many another Southern reader, lamented the absence, in Emerson's writings, of "the humble faith of the New Testament." "How so great a mind," he said, "can approach so near the Cross and not see it, is to me a cause of the profoundest marvel."

The fairest and ablest discussion of Emerson that I have found in the ante-bellum Southern magazines is Daniel K. Whitaker's "Transcendentalism," published in the *Southern Quarterly Review* in October, 1842. It is a review of the first two volumes of the *Dial.* Whitaker had grown up in Massachusetts and, though he did not like it, he had some understanding of what Transcendentalism was. "The Transcendentalists," he wrote, "are the enemies of antiquity, and equally hostile to existing institutions, and prevaling [*sic*] systems in morals, in philosophy, and religion. They are the champions of change and reform in all things." Thus they endangered the entire social and economic order. The Transcendentalists had no philosophic system and were, as Whitaker perceived, united only "by sympathy of spirit." Their heresies were only "opinions that were prevalent previous to the time of Locke, and which appear to us to have been fully met, and triumphantly refuted, by that illustrious metaphysician." Whitaker indulged in no denunciation, but he mildly ridiculed a passage in one of Emerson's essays.

In April, 1846, Whitaker somewhat belatedly reviewed the Second Series of Emerson's *Essays* (1844). He found "many bright and bold thoughts in these essays, and not a few strange ones." "Still," he added,

Mr. Emerson often thinks justly and beautifully. His genius sometimes fires, and sometimes cheers us, and if he would use his mother tongue without affectation and speak in pure Addisonian English, we might well be content to read his books and listen to his lectures. He may call himself an American, but the copyist of a copyist of a bad model [Carlyle] belongs to no nation or tribe or kindred of scholars who deserve the name.

In the South abler men than Ingraham, Gilman, or Whitaker had their difficulties with Emerson. The Swedish novelist Fredrika

Bremer records her experience with Joel R. Poinsett in the late forties:

I wished to make him a little acquainted with my friends the Transcendentalists and Idealists of the North, and I have read to him portions of Emerson's Essays. But they shoot over the head of the old statesman; he says it is all "unpractical," and he often criticizes it unjustly, and we quarrel. . . . Mr. Poinsett is, nevertheless, struck with Emerson's brilliant aphorisms, and says that he will buy his works. It is remarkable how very little, or not at all, the authors of the Northern States, even the best of them, are known in the South. They are afraid of admitting their liberal opinions into the Slave States.

One could hardly expect Edgar Allan Poe to be a great admirer of Emerson, who in a conversation with William Dean Howells was in 1860 to refer to him as "the jingle man." Their literary aims were poles apart, and Poe had no sympathy with the radical ideas of the Abolitionists and Transcendentalists. He was no admirer of Emerson's friend Carlyle. In one of his "Autography" papers he wrote in *Graham's Magazine* for January, 1842:

Mr. Ralph Waldo Emerson belongs to a class of gentlemen with whom we have no patience whatever—the mystics for mysticism's sake. . . .
His love of the obscure does not prevent him, nevertheless, from the composition of occasional poems in which beauty is apparent *by flashes.*

Poe singled out for praise "The Sphinx," "The Problem," "The Snow Storm," and "some fine old-fashioned verses entitled 'Oh fair and stately maid whose eye.' " Emerson, it must be noted, had not yet published a volume of his poems. On December 20, 1845, Poe reprinted Emerson's poem "A Fable" in the *Broadway Journal* and noted: "Here is something exceedingly *piquant* and *naïve.*" In the same month he wrote in an instalment of "Marginalia" which appeared in *Graham's Magazine*: "When I consider the true talent—the real force of Mr. Emerson, I am lost in amazement at finding in him little more than a respectful imitation of Carlyle."

Poe's friend Chivers, who had lived in New England, was an admirer of Emerson's poems. "All *true* poetry," he said, "is certainly transcendental." In 1850 he referred to Emerson as a "Literary Ganymede—or in other words, an Ambrosial Eclecticist"—whatever that means!

The notion that Emerson was only an imitator of Carlyle appears over and over in Southern notices of Emerson's writings. As late as

February, 1876, a writer in the *New Orleans Monthly Magazine* wrote:

He [Emerson] long ago adopted the vicious style of Carlyle, and endeavored to conceal poverty of thought under oddity of speech. This Mr. Emerson has done, and the whole host of literary fungi of our modern Athens have followed in his wake, until the English tongue, under the manipulations of those transcendental dreamers has lost its primitive beauty and simplicity.

The reviewer, however, was an admirer of Carlyle, who had expressed a strong sympathy with Southern slaveholders. In July, 1850, the *Southern Quarterly Review*, then edited by William Gilmore Simms, had urged Southern newspaper editors to read Carlyle's *Latter-Day Pamphlets* and stop repeating Yankee denunciations of "one of their best friends and champions."

In November, 1845, Simms, who had been a subscriber to the *Dial*, wrote in *Simms's Magazine*:

Of Emerson, we frankly confess, our expectations are very high in spite of his Carlyleisms. We are not disposed to underrate Carlyle, but we loathe this readiness, which is so American (in our literature at least) of being this or that Englishman's man. Emerson's essays declare a mind of his own, which can only be sure of itself and of future justice, by breaking loose, as soon as possible, from the leading strings of the European model.

Simms went on to name Emerson as one of a dozen American writers "equal in real genius to the writings of almost any that we import. . . ." Simms thought Emerson's prose writings were inferior to his poems, which he found "at once fresh, felicitous, and true."

As Emerson began to speak out on public questions, Simms's enthusiasm cooled. He was greatly irritated by Lowell's *A Fable for Critics*, which omitted all Southern writers except Poe. "This critic, for example," he wrote in the *Southern Quarterly Review* for October, 1849, "expends all his praise upon the children of the East. He finds no others in the country, or, if he does, he dismisses them with a scornful complacency. . . ."

Hear our satirist discourse on Emerson, whom he styles a "Greek head on Yankee shoulders," and you fancy him one of the most marvellous men that the world has produced. A parallel is run between him and Carlyle, greatly to the discredit of the latter. None less than Plato will content him for a comparison. . . . And all this said of a man who is really half-witted, and whose chief excellence consists in mystifying the simple and disguising commonplaces in allegory. One Mr. Alcott follows, of whom we know nothing. . . .

In July, 1850, writing in the same periodical nine months later, Simms wrote in a calmer mood:

Emerson is an able essayist, of a school too much on stilts, too ambitious of the mystical, to be always secure of the sensible and true. He is decidedly popular with the *Transcendentalists*, if we may recognize, by a term so dignified, a rather inflated race, who presume somewhat upon the fact that their place of birth is a few degrees nearer the rising sun than ours. Emerson aims to be a reformer, after the fashion of Carlyle; and no doubt has large merits, which might be available to common and beneficial use if they were less clouded and embarrassed with his affectations of the Delphic.

English Traits seems to have pleased Southern readers better than any of Emerson's other books. Paul Hamilton Hayne wrote in *Russell's Magazine* for January, 1858:

. . . we happened upon the last published book of Mr. Emerson, which was issued in 1856, under the concise and expressive title of "English Traits." This is a remarkable work, as full of views at once clear and profound, acutely sensible, yet broadly philosophical, that we would advise its perusal to those of our readers who may be interested in the topics of which it treats.

Yet Hayne, who had met Emerson and admired some of his poems, wrote to a New England friend, Mrs. Julia Dorr, on May 16, 1882, that he wished Emerson's

Essays were *some* of them *clearer*, and informed by a loftier spirit of Faith, instead of that vague species of half-Pantheistic philosophy, which, after all, is pre-eminently unoriginal, a mere *elaborated echo* of the "Neo-Platonism" of Alexandria in the 4th and 5th centuries.

In 1859 Hayne had praised "Threnody" as refuting the charge that Emerson's poems were "cold." In 1880 he addressed a poem to Emerson on the occasion of his seventy-seventh birthday.

Emerson's Southern critics too often confused him with other Transcendentalists and attributed to him the faults which they observed in the *Dial*. For example, John R. Thompson, the editor of the *Southern Literary Messenger*, in 1850 wrote in a notice of the death of Margaret Fuller: "At one time she was associated with EMERSON in the editorial conduct of the 'Dial,' a journal of great authority with a certain new-light school of philosophy, but affording only penumbral indications of the day-beam of intellect." In 1856, however, when Thompson was reviewing *English Traits*, he expressed his pleasure at discovering something written by Emerson that he could read "with even a moderate assurance that [he could] comprehend it. . . strange to say, the cloudy oracle of the Transcendentalists no sooner sets foot upon the foggy isle of Albion than straightway he becomes wonderfully transparent and comprehensible."

A Charlestonian, Professor Frederick A. Porcher, writing in *Russell's Magazine* for December, 1858, lamented that the fine old city of Boston had abandoned "the old Puritan dogmas" and adopted instead "the Delphic utterances of the Dial." He was pleased to note that "this sublimated nonsense" was not in Hawthorne, Longfellow, Lowell, Prescott, or Bancroft; but he thought that Emerson, Parker, and Margaret Fuller were full of it. "Now," he continued, "it may be very fine. It may be sublime. But to us it is unintelligible." Porcher, nevertheless, could say: "As a prose writer, Mr. Emerson commands our highest respect. It is impossible not to reverence him as a thinker of the first order; but we regard his thoughts as far too refined to be popular." Porcher had not seen the *Poems* which Emerson had published in 1847: ". . . but if we may judge of them from the samples which are to be found interspersed among his essays, we must say that a people must have an intense yearning after poetry who will run after such verses; and they are generally fantastic and frequently unintelligible."

It was unfortunately not Southerners alone who had difficulty in understanding Emerson's poems. The able Philadelphia historian, Henry Charles Lea, wrote in the *Southern Literary Messenger* in May, 1847: "But it is only in his prose that Mr. Emerson is a poet; this volume of professed poetry contains the most prosaic and unintelligible stuff that it has ever been our fortune to encounter."

In Mrs. Sophia Bledsoe Herrick the South had one of its most perceptive critics of Emerson. Her father, the Reverend Albert Taylor Bledsoe, the editor of the ultra-conservative *Southern Review*, had not cared for Emerson. In January, 1868, he published in the *Review* an article entitled "Quackery in American [i.e., Yankee] Literature," in which he ridiculed Emerson's claim that "the poet alone knows astronomy, vegetation, and animation." When this unreconciled defender of the South died in December, 1877, his daughter took over the editorship and kept the quarterly going for two years. Not long afterward she became a valued member of the editorial staff of the *Century Magazine* and a friend of James Russell Lowell, Thomas Nelson Page, and other well-known writers. In July, 1878, she published in the *Southern Review* a long review of Emerson's *Letters and Social Aims* (1876), in which she said: "Among American essayists Emerson is as conspicuous for style as for original thinking." In spite of an occasional "unadvised mannerism," his style was "an individual style, admirable of its kind." "Emerson's style," she continued, "is of that class which contains melody rather than rhythm, where the music is found rather in the vibrating word or resonant image than in the luxurious flow of periods."

5

In Moncure Daniel Conway Emerson had his most notable (I had almost said *his only*) Southern disciple,[1] but it is significant that the Emerson influence helped to bring to this Virginian alienation from his family, his friends, and his church and made it necessary for him to make his home outside the South. After graduation from Dickinson College Conway began the study of law in Warrenton, Virginia, but he was much more interested in literature than in the law. In April, 1850, while he was ill and going through an obscure spiritual crisis, he returned to his home in Falmouth for a few weeks. One morning he went off to spend the day in the country, taking with him a copy of *Blackwood's Magazine* for December, 1847. The title of the leading article was "Emerson," a name new to Conway. The first passage quoted—it was from Emerson's essay on "History"—"fixed itself in me like an arrow."[2] New England Transcendentalism had reached Conway by way of Britain through a magazine over two years old. At the bookstore in Fredericksburg Conway found a copy of "Emerson's Arithmetick" but none of Emerson's *Essays*. The obliging bookseller ordered the desired volume; and while Conway was reading it, he discovered that

---

[1] I have not been able to learn anything more of the Southern admirer of whom Longfellow wrote to Emerson on May 26, 1852:
"There is a gentleman here from Alabama who is very eager to see you, and has, I believe a letter of introduction for you. It is Mr. Lipscombe: a great reader of your writings. I said to him 'You will go to Concord to see Emerson.' 'Yes; if I have to walk' was his reply. And so you will be sure to have a visit, from a thoughtful man, and an ardent admirer."
[2] In April, 1852, the *Southern Literary Messenger* printed an article entitled "Ralph Waldo Emerson—History," in which J. H. B. [The Rev. J. H. Bocock?] did his best to refute Emerson's "idealist scheme of interpreting history."

his cousin, John Moncure Daniel, had been writing about Emerson in the Richmond *Examiner*. In an article on Poe which Daniel published in the *Southern Literary Messenger* in March, 1850, he had singled out Emerson's "The Humble Bee" as the only American poem comparable in merit to "The Raven."

Emerson's influence had something to do with Conway's decision to become a Methodist minister. While riding the circuit in Maryland, he became acquainted with some Hicksite Quakers, whose hostility to slavery influenced him. On November 4, 1851, he wrote to Emerson and mentioned his debt to the master's writings: "I have shed many burning tears over them; because you gain my consent to Laws which, when I see how they would act on the affairs of life, I have not the courage to practice." In his reply Emerson wrote: "A true soul will disdain to be moved except by what natively commands it, though it should go sad and solitary in search of its master a thousand years." Conway finally enrolled himself in the Divinity School at Harvard. On May 23, 1853, he wrote in his diary: "The most memorable day of my life: spent with Ralph Waldo Emerson." In the summer of 1853 Conway stayed for some time in Concord, where he talked with Emerson, browsed in his library, came to know Thoreau, and read in the sacred literature of the East.

In September, 1854, Conway became pastor of the Unitarian church in Washington. His heretical religious views and his antislavery stand had shocked his family and his Virginia friends; and when he returned to Falmouth on a visit, the young men there practically ordered him out of town. From now on he was to feel himself a martyr and an exile. In November, 1856, Conway became pastor of a Unitarian church in Cincinnati, where he once more saw something of Emerson on a lecture tour. In 1860 he edited the second Transcendentalist magazine to be named the *Dial*, and Emerson contributed to it some quatrains and miscellaneous pieces.

In 1862 Conway was back in New England editing an antislavery magazine. In April of the next year he went to England to speak and write in behalf of the Union cause. On April 9 of that year Emerson wrote to Matilde Ashurst Biggs:

Will you let me make you acquainted with Mr Moncure D. Conway, a gentleman of great worth & ability, who goes to London on the invitation of some friends of Freedom & of America there. . . . Mr Conway is a native of Virginia, & thoroughly knows the South Country, &, for the last ten years, has been a resident in the North; which is his true home. He is a very accomplished person, & has eminent ability as a public speaker, as well as an intelligent companion.

In England Conway rashly entered into correspondence with another Virginian, John M. Mason, a Confederate agent; and with no authority whatever for making such a promise, wrote that if the Confederate States would emancipate their slaves, the anti-slavery leaders of the North would immediately oppose further prosecution of the war. When Mason published the correspondence in the London *Times*, Conway found himself outmaneuvered. If he returned to America, he would stand alone. By this time Emerson's warlike speeches and writings had deeply disturbed Conway. And so when he was offered the pastorate of the unorthodox South Place Chapel, he decided to accept it and remain in England, where he lived for most of his remaining years.

Shortly after Emerson's death in 1882, Conway published his hastily written *Emerson at Home and Abroad*, made up largely of sermons and articles of varying merit already published. Conway also managed to discover certain missing letters which Emerson had written to Carlyle, copied them, and sent them to Charles Eliot Norton, who was preparing the Carlyle-Emerson correspondence for publication.

In his later years Conway was hardly to be described as a Transcendentalist. As his biographer, Mary Elizabeth Burtis, remarks, "He had never gone the whole way because he always distrusted all mystical raptures and vague ecstacies—all that he later dubbed the 'fog-bank of neo-Platonism.'"

Conway's most notable literary achievement—apart from his two-volume *Autobiography* (1904)—was a life of Thomas Paine and a collected edition of his writings. Conway had himself progressed along the road from orthodox Methodism to Unitarianism, Transcendentalism, and finally to rationalism and skepticism. It was not until late in life that he began to see himself as a throwback to an earlier and more liberal generation of Virginians, many of whom were Deists like Paine. Conway's paternal grandfather had been shocked when his son was converted to the Methodist faith, which he regarded as a form of vulgar fanaticism. The same grandfather once took into his own home a New England peddler who had been bundled out of the inn in the village because he took a walk on Sunday instead of going to church. The peddler, Conway discovered, was none other than the New England Transcendentalist philosopher and friend of Emerson, Bronson Alcott.

6

The one important Southern writer upon whom Emerson's writings exerted a notable influence was Sidney Lanier, who had grown up in a Presbyterian home in Macon, Georgia. Lanier seems first to have discovered Emerson in the winter of 1876-1877 while convalescing in Florida. On May 25, 1877, he wrote to his new friend Bayard Taylor that he would like to discuss with him:

Emerson, whom I have been reading all winter, and who gives me immeasurable delight because he does not propound to me disagreeable systems and hideous creeds but simply walks along high and bright ways where one loves to go with him—then I am ready to praise God for the circumstance that if corn were a dollar a bushel I could not with my present finances buy a lunch for a pony.

Lanier's earlier poems had been written largely under the influence of Tennyson and Poe, both poets notable for their verbal music. The influence of Emerson did not affect Lanier's technique so much as his conception of the role of the poet. Charles R. Anderson, the General Editor of the Centennial Edition of Lanier's *Works*, has said:

And in discovering Emerson, he found himself as a poet. His true vein lay, not in social protest nor in celebrating the national spirit nor even, except subordinately, in the marriage of music to words—it lay in his religious interpretation of nature. This was the best thing that happened to him in Florida, though it was another year before he realized it in a memorable poem ["The Marshes of Glynn"] and one worthy of his great discovery.

No other writer of the New South, so far as I know, cared much for Emerson. On April 15, 1895, Joel Chandler Harris wrote in reply to William Malone Baskervill's inquiry about his favorite authors that the book which had first attracted his attention and held it longest was *The Vicar of Wakefield*:

Apart from this, all good books have me interested more or less. But the queer self-consciousness of Emerson has never appealed to me as strongly as it has to some of my friends. This is not Emerson's fault, but mine. You cannot expect an uncultured Georgia cracker to follow patiently the convolute diagrams of the Over-Soul. I find Sir Thomas

Browne far more stimulating (I hope I am not treading on your corns here. Confidentially, Emerson's attitude as the New England Bigod—if I may use so crude an expression—has amused me no little.) You see I am perfectly frank in this, presenting the appearance of feeling as proud of my lack of taste and culture as a little girl is of her rag doll. It may give you a cue.

Perhaps it was just as well that the fiction writers of the New South were not greatly influenced by Emerson. So at least thought Robert Underwood Johnson, who as one of the editors of the *Century Magazine* had had a large share in publishing the stories of many Southern writers. I quote from Johnson's *Remembered Yesterdays* (1923):

These [Southern] writers and their successors have excelled in the direct narrative style. I account for this by the fact that the South was not affected by the subtleties of Emerson or Lowell or by the other transcendental influences of New England literature. These did not come into its ken for those influences were related for the most part to the Abolition movement. Rather, the writers of the South derived their style from Thackeray, Macaulay, Addison, and the other essayists of the Spectator type. This made them, first of all, good storytellers and as a tendency, if not as a school, they are worthy the attention of the historian of literary America.

By 1895 Southerners had come somewhat reluctantly to accept, as a part of the new order, the Northern rating of Emerson and other New England writers. Simms and Whitaker in the forties and fifties were not ashamed to admit a failure to see in Emerson a great writer. In 1895 Harris was.

That was well enough, but one Southern scholar at least was disturbed because, as it seemed to him, Southerners were accepting also the low Northern estimate of the writers of the Old South. In 1899 Professor Charles W. Kent, of the University of Virginia, said in a commencement address at the University of Tennessee: "I venture the assertion that our Southern youth to-day are as familiar with the writers of the New England school as are the boys of Boston or of Concord, but the New England boys—alas! it is true of our Southern youth as well—are lamentably ignorant of the literature of the South."[3]

[3] *The Revival of Interest in Southern Letters* (Richmond, 1900), p. 7. Kent charged that Northern anthologists were still neglecting the Southern writers. He might have noted that in *Parnassus* (1874), which displeased Whitman's followers because none of the Good Gray Poet's poems were included, Emerson found a place for only two Southern poems: Randall's "Maryland, My Maryland" and Timrod's Magnolia Cemetery "Ode."

. . . and he [Thackeray] had always looked upon Virginians as resembling more closely his own people in England than the Americans of other states.

JOHN ESTEN COOKE, "An Hour with Thackeray," *Appletons' Journal*, N.S. VII, 252 (September, 1879)

I have found many thousand more readers than I ever looked for. I have no right to say to these, You shall not find fault with my art, or fall asleep over my pages; but I ask you to believe that this person writing strives to tell the truth. If there is not that, there is nothing.

THACKERAY, Preface to *Pendennis* (1850)

THE VIRGINIANS *of* William Makepeace Thackeray

[In my Columbia University dissertation I included a detailed discussion of *The Virginians*. In December, 1923, I read a revised version of it before the English Section of the Modern Language Association. Later I reworked it and sent it to Carleton Brown, Secretary of the Association, for publication in *PMLA*. Professor Brown, always kindly and thoughtful of others, wrote me that he would be glad to print it, but he thought it might interest many readers who would never see *PMLA*. He suggested my submitting it to a literary magazine which would pay me something for it. The article appeared in the *Virginia Quarterly Review* in January, 1927. Since 1927 much new and important Thackeray material has appeared, especially in Gordon N. Ray's biography and his edition of Thackeray's letters. The later biographies of John Pendleton Kennedy by Edward M. Gwathmey and Charles H. Bohner and an unpublished Columbia University dissertation by Professor William

S. Osborne have thrown new light upon Kennedy's relations with Thackeray.]

Early in the nineteenth century British writers made the important discovery that although they could not copyright their books in this country, they could with profit visit the United States and give lectures or readings from their books to the many Americans who were eager to see and hear them. Charles Dickens came to America in 1842 and met with a tumultuous welcome, but he offended many Americans by his tactlessness and bad manners and he later alienated many more by the publication of *American Notes* and *Martin Chuzzlewit*.

Ten years after Dickens's first visit Thackeray came to America hoping by his lectures on "The English Humorists" to make money needed to provide security for his two daughters. He had been in this country little more than a month when he wrote to Frederick Pratt Barlow: "Merely about my books it would have been worth my while to visit America. Appleton Harper & others all give or offer me money. I shall be able to add something like 40 per Cent to the value of my future books." He returned to America in 1855 with a second series of lectures, "The Four Georges." In 1859 he estimated that by his two series of lectures he had made fifty thousand dollars, two-thirds of this amount coming from his American audiences.

With Dickens's unfortunate experience in mind, Thackeray decided not to write a travel book about the United States; and in 1852, when Mrs. Stowe's recently published novel was creating a sensation in England as well as in America, he would not read *Uncle Tom's Cabin* until after he had visited the Southern states and seen Negro slaves with his own eyes. Dickens had seen so little of the South that he had borrowed much of his material (unacknowledged) from Theodore Weld's *American Slavery as It Is*, which was compiled in New York libraries, chiefly from materials in Southern newspapers.

1

Just before he sailed from Liverpool on October 30, 1852, Thackeray was handed a copy of *Henry Esmond*, just off the press. In the closing pages of this, his favorite novel and perhaps his best, he had sent Henry Esmond and his bride, Lady Castlewood, to the hereditary Esmond estates in Virginia, the gift of King Charles I to a Cavalier ancestor. There "on the beautiful banks of the Potomac" the Esmonds would build a new Castlewood, where they hoped to live out the happy and serene Indian summer of their lives.

The long Preface to *Henry Esmond*, which bore the title "The Esmonds of Virginia," purported to be the work of Henry Esmond's daughter; and it was dated from "Castlewood, Virginia, November 3, 1778." For this Preface Thackeray had created three new characters in Madam Esmond-Warrington and her two sons, George and Harry; and American readers correctly inferred that the novelist was thinking of writing an American sequel.

As yet, however, Thackeray's plans for *The Virginians* were quite vague. He would give the leading roles to Henry Esmond's twin grandsons, and they would fight on opposite sides in the Revolutionary War. Their friend and neighbor, George Washington, would also play an important part in the novel. Yet when *The Virginians* began to appear in instalments in November, 1857, attentive readers noticed a marked change in Madam Esmond-Warrington. In the Preface to *Esmond* she had spoken of "our lamentable but glorious War of Independence" and "our friend Mr. Washington"; in the novel, however, she turned out to be a thoroughgoing Tory, and she and her son George had little use for General Washington.

In Boston, New York, Philadelphia, and Washington Thackeray's lectures on "The English Humorists" were a great success, and he made many new friends among writers and other cultivated people. On February 26, 1853, he wrote from Washington to his New York friend, Lucy Baxter: "Tomorrow I shall pass down the Potomac on w^h. M^{rs}. Esmond-Warrington used to sail with her 2 sons when they went to visit their friend M^r. Washington. I wonder will anything ever come out of that preface [to *Henry Esmond*], and will that story ever be born?" The novelist's friend and secretary, Eyre Crowe, wrote in his *With Thackeray in America*: "I sketched the distant outline of Washington's home, and we tried to spot the new 'Castlewood,' which was raised on the beautiful banks of the Potomac." On April 3, back in New York after his first visit to the Southern states, Thackeray wrote to Mrs. Bayne: "Then I went away into Virginia crossing the pretty Rappahanna [sic] (where you know the Esmond family had their large estates). It gave me a queer sensation to see the place, and I fancied the story was actually true for a minute or two—and that one might ride over yonder hills and come upon the old Mansion House, where the little Colonel lived with his jealous wife."

From Richmond on March 3 Thackeray had written to Mrs. Baxter that he was

delighted with the comfortable friendly cheery little town—the *picturesquest* he has seen in America—that the negroes instead of horrifying me I am sorry to say amuse me with their never ending grotesqueness and please me with their air of happiness and that in all respects but one I am having a good time—pleasant people, good audience—quiet handsome cheap comfortable hotel everything in fact but a letter from [the Baxters]. . . .

On the same day Thackeray wrote in the same strain to Mrs. Elliot and Kate Perry but added that Crowe had "just come out from what might have been and yet may be a dreadful scrape. He went into a slave market and began sketching; and the people rushed on him savagely and obliged him to quit. Fancy such a piece of imprudence." Richmonders, as Thackeray must have known, had not forgotten Dickens's chapter on slavery and his unsympathetic account of their city. On March 12 Thackeray wrote to Mrs. Baxter from Charleston that he expected to return to New York via Richmond: ". . . I am sure of a great welcome at the pretty little cheery place—such a welcome as is better than dollars,—much pleasanter than the dreary acquiescence of the audiences here."

After his return to England in the spring of 1853, Thackeray was still not ready to write *The Virginians*—his next novel was *The Newcomes*—and *The Virginians* was still unwritten when he made his second visit to the United States in 1855 to lecture on "The Four Georges." Thackeray was no longer a well man. He had not fully recovered from the malaria which he had contracted in Rome in 1853. The winter of 1855-1856 was an exceptionally severe one, even in the Southern states. The novelist found traveling and lecturing tedious and tiring, and he was irritated by abusive articles in some newspapers. British-American relations had deteriorated, and Thackeray was pained and depressed by talk of war between the two countries; and he felt that the British minister in Washington, Crampton, for whom he had a high regard, was being made a scapegoat.

On his earlier visit Thackeray had gone no further south than Savannah, but this time he decided to go overland to New Orleans and up the Mississippi. He wished afterwards that he had gone to New Orleans by way of Havana, for the journey through Georgia, Alabama, and Mississippi proved not only extremely tedious but comparatively unprofitable and he found the landscape dreary and depressing. After his return to England he wrote to Mrs. Baxter: "I fear I'm not near so good an American as I was after my first visit. . . ." Still there was compensation in the reflection that his lectures had brought him £3,000.

In January, 1856, Thackeray spent at least ten days in Richmond and lectured there five times. He admired the Houdon statue of George Washington, and he saw something of his friend the novelist G. P. R. James, who held the post of British consul in Richmond. Perhaps before writing *The Virginians* he would read James's *The Old Dominion; or, A Tale of Virginia* (1856), which contains an excellent account of social life in Virginia. Among the Richmonders who entertained Thackeray, James Grant Wilson listed in his *Thackeray in the United States* John M. Daniel, the city's brilliant journalist; Col. Henry C. Cabell; and Robert Craig Stanard, Poe's boyhood friend, whose mother was the "Helen" of a famous poem. (Wilson also mentioned among Thackeray's hosts "John Allan, who adopted Edgar Allan Poe," not realizing that Allan had been dead for twenty years.) After Robert Stanard's death in 1857 Thackeray wrote to another Richmond friend, John R. Thompson, asking him "to tell Mrs. Stanard and her boy how very warmly and gratefully I think of Robert Stanards kindness to me, and how heartily I liked and respected him." In Stanard, Thackeray had met a fine specimen of the Southern gentlemen whom he once described as "the most generous and kind people." "How hospitable they were, those Southern men!" he wrote in "A Mississippi Bubble" during the Civil War.

A friend of Mrs. Stanard, whom Wilson refers to as "Mrs. A.," wrote of Thackeray's lectures in Richmond: ". . . his audience of Richmond's best people, the same set meeting every evening to hear him: his beautiful reading—simple and full of expression: his lovely voice full of pathos, and generally in the minor key, especially in reading poetry or passages in [on?] the closing years of George the Third."

It was John R. Thompson, editor of the *Southern Literary Messenger*, who made the arrangements for Thackeray's Richmond lectures in 1853. The grateful novelist bought a new rocking chair to replace the dilapidated one he had seen in the editor's office. In that office one morning Thackeray wrote what is perhaps his best known poem, "The Sorrows of Werther," which Thompson published in the *Messenger* in November, 1856.

Thompson was also librarian of the Virginia State Library, which, so Dickens stated in his *American Notes,* contained "some ten thousand volumes." Mrs. Burton Harrison, a Virginia novelist who knew Thompson in his later years, wrote: "Thackeray was at this time occupied in overhauling the library for material for 'The Virginians': and to Thompson he owed many suggestions of value for that delightful book." It may be doubted whether, in the few days he had in Richmond, Thackeray found time for many hours in the library, but Thompson was well qualified to supply suggestions for a novel dealing with life in Virginia.

It was Thompson who in 1853 introduced to Thackeray the youthful Virginia novelist, John Esten Cooke, whose first novel was not to be published until the following year. Cooke, then only twenty-three years old, was practicing law but wishing he could devote all his time to writing. Thackeray said to him: "If I were you I would go on writing. Some day you will make a fortune. Becky Sharp made mine. I married early and wrote for bread." Cooke was thoughtful enough to make some notes of his talk with Thackeray, and in September, 1879, he published in *Appletons' Journal* an article entitled "An Hour with Thackeray." Cooke found the English novelist "a most excellent genial gentleman and companion."

Richmond was an attractive place to him, he declared—he had been received with the utmost kindness and attention—and he had always looked upon the Virginians as resembling more closely his own people in England than the Americans of other states. They seemed "more homely," I think was his phrase—which I recall, from the curious employment of the word "homely" in the sense of "home-like."

Thackeray told Cooke that he was going to write an American novel to be called "The Two Virginians." "I shall lay the scene glish side in the war, and the other the American, and they will both be in love with the same girl." (In the published novel George and Harry Warrington are not in love with the same girl.) Thackeray added: "It will take me at least two years to collect my materials, and become acquainted with the subject. I can't write upon a subject I know nothing of. I am obliged to read up upon it, and get my ideas."

Still other American friends supplied Thackeray with hints or materials for *The Virginians*. It was in Boston in the study of William H. Prescott, the historian, that Thackeray saw the two crossed swords which suggested the felicitous opening paragraph of *The Virginians*. "The one sword was gallantly drawn in the service of the king, the other was the weapon of a brave and honoured republican soldier." Prescott's grandfather had fought in the American army; his wife's grandfather, in the British army.

Another helpful friend was William Bradford Reed of Philadelphia. Soon after beginning his American novel Thackeray wrote to Reed: "How I wish I had you here that I might keep out of blunders in THE VIRGINIANS! wʰ. is to be D. V. the name of the New Story." He added that Reed's little book, *The Life of Esther De Berdt* (1853), would be "very serviceable" to him. This English girl had married Reed's grandfather, Joseph Reed, who served as Washington's "military secretary" at Cambridge. From this admirable brief biography Thackeray took at least a suggestion for the character of Theo Lambert. There are in fact a number of resemblances between the De Berdts and the Lamberts and there is a certain similarity between Joseph Reed's love for Esther and George Warrington's love for Theo Lambert. In his published tribute to Thackeray, *Haud Immemor*, Reed wrote in 1864:

It was during this [second] visit to the United States that, as he told me, the idea of his American novel, "The Virginians," was conceived; and I have reason to think that some of the details in the story were due as well to Mr. Prescott's "Crossed Swords" as to conversations with me at a time when my mind was full of historical associations and suggestions, and when to think of my country's story was matter of pride and pleasure.

During the Civil War Reed's sympathies, like Thackeray's, were with the Confederate States.

Thackeray's indebtedness to Reed was greater than one would guess from *Haud Immemor*. Mrs. Burton Harrison (née Constance Cary) wrote after a visit to Thackeray's daughter Anne (Lady Ritchie) that until she met Reed she had felt that somehow Thackeray must have read some of the unpublished letters and papers of her Fairfax and Cary ancestors.

This gentleman, an accomplished historiographer and littérateur . . . was thoroughly imbued with the romantic and picturesque aspects of relations some Virginian families long bore to England before and after our Revolutionary War. He mentioned the Fairfaxes as conspicuous examples. . . . He spoke particularly of the return to England in 1775, to take possession of patrimonial acres in Yorkshire, of young George William Fairfax, who married Sally Cary, of Virginia, where George Washington was his comrade in an intimacy not interrupted even by the war itself; and he recalled various bits of Fairfax and Cary family history and of old-time gossip that lend colour to Thackeray's romance.
Of these, with many other details of American life in Colonial and Revolutionary times; Mr. Reed said he had repeatedly talked with Thackeray, as they sat over their wine on occasions during the latter's visit to the United States when *The Virginians* was conceived.

Mrs. Harrison's suggestion was no casual one. In 1895, when she published her article in the *Bookman*, she was writing her own novel of the Revolution, *A Son of the Old Dominion* (1897), in which she is known to have drawn upon her family letters and traditions. The resemblances between her novel and the American part of *The Virginians* are unmistakable, but not all of the similarities are due to the influence of Thackeray, who was perhaps the chief literary passion of her life. There are passages in *The Virginians* which seem like echoes of such family history as Reed and other American friends gave the English novelist. Something perhaps of Madam Esmond-Warrington's scorn for Washington as a "provincial surveyor" is to be traced to the tradition that when Washington requested permission to pay his addresses to one of the Cary girls, the incensed father replied: "If that is your mission here, sir, you may as well order your horse. My daughter has been accustomed to her coach and six." The woodcock pie which Madam Esmond-Warrington served to General Braddock recalls a humorous letter from Washington to Sally Cary, now Mrs. Fairfax, in which he tells her that the General's fondness for potted woodcocks explains why he likes Mrs. Wardrope better than Mrs. Fairfax.
One of the best friends that Thackeray made in America was

the Baltimore novelist and lawyer, John Pendleton Kennedy. At the time of Thackeray's first visit to Washington Kennedy was Secretary of the Navy, and he noted in his diary his pleasure at being able to take Thackeray and Washington Irving with him on the trial run of Captain John Ericsson's "caloric" ship. In his diary Kennedy wrote that in Thackeray he had found "A noble specimen of a real, fresh, true thinking and true speaking gentleman, whom I think honest fellows everywhere ought to love." It would seem that Kennedy, like other Americans, had feared to find in Thackeray—I am quoting George William Curtis—"a severe satirist who concealed scalpels in his sleeves and carried probes in his waistcoat pockets; a wearer of masks; a scoffer and a sneerer, and general infidel of all high aims and noble character. . . ."

On his second visit Thackeray saw more of Kennedy, who was now back at home in Baltimore. On January 11, 1856, in a letter to Mrs. Baxter, Thackeray mentioned "M^r. J. P. Kennedy exceedingly pleasant and good-natured. . . ." Apparently, however, Thackeray did not care for some of Kennedy's Baltimore friends, for he added: ". . . and he has introduced me to a Club—O Gods such a dreary Club! such a desperate dinner! such a stupid man that would talk!" A week earlier in Kennedy's study Thackeray had explained his plan for the Virginia novel and asked for helpful information. Kennedy lent him some books which he thought might be useful. He also took Thackeray on a visit to the home of his brother Andrew Kennedy in the Shenandoah Valley near Charles Town (now in West Virginia) so that he might see Virginia life for himself.

The books which Kennedy lent to Thackeray were "Graydon's Memoirs of the Revolution," "Heath's Memoirs," and "Garden's Anecdotes." It was from Alexander Graydon's *Memoirs of His Own Time* (1848) that Thackeray got the notion of marrying Lady Maria to the Irish actor Hagan. Graydon tells the story of Lady Strangeways, who outraged her family's sense of propriety by marrying the Irish actor O'Brien, and was promptly packed off to America in the same way as Lady Maria and her husband. Gordon Ray notes that Thackeray made use of Bancroft's *History of the United States*, Chastellux's *Travels*, and Robert Beverley's *History and Present State of Virginia*. Beverley's book is mentioned in Chapter XVI of Volume I of *The Virginians*. The catalogue of Thackeray's library, which was sold in 1864 by Christie, Manson, and Woods, lists among

161

other American titles: the 1855 edition of Beverley's book, "Light Horse Harry" Lee's *Memoirs of the War in the Southern Department of the United States,* the *Memoirs* of General Charles Lee, the *American Annals* of Abiel Holmes, the *Complete Works* of Benjamin Franklin, Mrs. Grant's *Memoirs of an American Lady,* the *Virginian Historical Register* for the years 1848 and 1851, and Chastellux's *Travels* "with the autograph of George Washington." The two volumes of the *Register* contain notices of other books which might have interested Thackeray and a sketch of William Byrd with selections from his writings. I have noted Thackeray's use of Reed's *Life of Esther De Berdt.* I would like to know whether or not he ever read G. P. R. James's *The Old Dominion* and Kennedy's *Swallow Barn* and *Horse-Shoe Robinson,* both of which had been reprinted in the early 1850's. *Horse-Shoe Robinson* is one of the best American novels of the Revolution, and *Swallow Barn* gives what is the best account in fiction of Virginia plantation life in the early nineteenth century.

2

It was not until May, 1857, that Thackeray began writing *The Virginians.* He completed the last instalment on September 7, 1859. The novel appeared in book form later in the same year. Thackeray's popularity as a lecturer had induced his publishers to offer him £6,000, which was a larger sum than any of his earlier books had brought him. In addition Harper & Brothers paid him £500 for the right to print the novel serially in their magazine.

The Virginians is not Thackeray's best novel, but it is, in the words of his editor and biographer, Gordon N. Ray, "a rich book, if a chaotic one." It contains one of the finest character portraits he ever drew in Madam Bernstein, the old woman who had been the beautiful young Beatrix of *Henry Esmond.* The proportions of the novel are not what they should be and are not what the novelist had planned. At one point in the story, so Thackeray wrote on March 29, 1859, he "was so ill and dawdled between Nos. V and X that the American part w^h. was to have been in 12 numbers now has dwindled to 6. . . ." Indeed, much of what was to have been the main action was crowded into Number XII. Thackeray was not able to carry out his original intention to bring in Goldsmith, Garrick, Johnson, Wilkes, and other notable eighteenth-century historical personages. On April 23, 1858, he wrote to Mrs. Baxter:

The book's clever but stupid thats the fact. I hate storymaking incidents, surprises, love-making, &c more and more every day: and here is a third of a great story done equal to two thirds of an ordinary novel —and nothing actually has happened, except that a young gentleman has come from America to England. . . .

A part of Thackeray's difficulties in *The Virginians* was the result of trying to keep going simultaneously the stories of two brothers who much of the time are separated by the Atlantic Ocean. History and fiction are not so skilfully blended as in *Henry Esmond,* and each of the two volumes has a different hero. Thackeray's readers, he discovered, liked Harry Warrington better than his brother George, who takes the lead in the second volume. He was disappointed to find that his American friends and admirers were almost unanimous in their dislike of his portrait of the young George Washington.

The fear of making fatal historical errors had something to do with his "dawdling" in the earlier portions of the novel. In the winter of 1858 he wrote to William Duer Robinson:

Where the deuce was George Warrington carried after he was knocked down at Braddock's defeat? Was he taken by Indians into a French fort? I want him to be away for a year and a half, or until the siege of Quebec. If you see Fred. Cozzens or George Curtis, ask them to manage this job for me, and send me a little line stating what has really happened to the eldest of the Virginians.

It was Kennedy who several months later worked out for Thackeray the best way to get George Warrington from Fort Duquesne to the coast. Both Kennedy and Thackeray were in Paris when the former wrote in his journal on September 26, 1858:

Thackeray calls to see me and sits an hour or two. He is not looking well. He tells me he has need of my assistance with his Virginians—and says Heaven has sent me to his aid. He wants me to get his hero from Fort Duquesne where he is confined a prisoner after Braddock's defeat and to bring him to the coast to embark for England. "Now you know all that ground," he says to me "and I want you to write a chapter for me to describe how he got off and what travel he made." He insists that I shall do it. I give him a doubtful promise to do it if I can find time in the thousand engagements that now press upon me on the eve of our leaving Paris. I would be glad to do it if circumstances would allow.

Kennedy's first biographer, Henry T. Tuckerman, printed this passage but carelessly overlooked other passages in Kennedy's journal that throw light upon what he actually wrote. After Kennedy's death his old friend John H. B. Latrobe stated in his sketch of Kennedy in *Appleton's Cyclopaedia of American Biography* that Kennedy had told him that he had written the fourth chapter of the second volume of *The Virginians*. In the years that followed there was some controversy over what if anything Kennedy had written. Lady Ritchie pointed out that the manuscript of the novel was entirely in her father's handwriting, and she ridiculed the idea that anybody could have written a chapter in one of her father's books. Others were not so sure.

That was the state of the matter when I began my study of *The Virginians*. I noted that the episode in question covered not only the fourth chapter but also a portion of the third. A single sentence, that describing the Will's Creek neighborhood in western Maryland, seemed to me to contain the only definite descriptive touch that Thackeray must have owed to Kennedy. And in the same paragraph I found the curious blunder (which no one had noticed) of referring the making of maple sugar to the fall of the year. Kennedy could hardly have committed that error.

Kennedy's later biographers—Edward M. Gwathmey in 1931 and Charles H. Bohner in 1961—found in Kennedy's journal other passages dealing with *The Virginians*. On September 30 Thackeray went to see Kennedy again. At that time Kennedy gave him in conversation "a few hints for the description he wishes" and promised "to repeat it in some notes which I shall prepare for him." On October 3 Kennedy noted: "I write nearly all the morning in preparing notes for Thackeray—an outline of the chapter he wants— and in making a rough map of illustration."

On January 17, 1864, Kennedy referred to Thackeray's death on Christmas Eve, 1863, as "the extinguishment of the brightest light in the present literature of England." He continued: "When I last saw him, it was at the Bristol Hotel in Paris, where he was sick in bed, and got me to write him a sketch for a chapter in the 'Virginians'—which I did and he afterwards partially incorporated it in the book."

3

When Henry Esmond came to the New World, it was in West-moreland County, Virginia, that he chose to build the New Castle-wood. Thackeray in thus making the Esmonds neighbors of George Washington had indicated his intention of giving Washington an important role in his projected novel. That was a bold venture, particularly for a writer who was not an American. Cooper in *The Spy* had been almost the only American writer who had given Washington an important role in a work of fiction, and he had been criticized for so doing. Thackeray was not fully aware of the extent to which the Washington legend made Americans hyper-sensitive to anything that looked like criticism of the national hero. He should have taken warning when his American readers took offense at a passage in *The Newcomes,* in which he had meant only to suggest the typical British attitude toward Washington at the time of the Revolution: ". . . when Mr. Washington was heading the American rebels with a courage, it must be confessed, worthy of a better cause. . . ." Thackeray felt obliged to explain his real intention in a letter to the London *Times* in which he said: "I think the cause for which Washington fought entirely just and right, and the Champion the very noblest, purest, bravest, best, of God's men."

Thackeray's portrait of Washington in *The Virginians* was the first attempt in fiction to paint what Paul Leicester Ford was to call "the true George Washington," but it was too unconventional, too realistic to please Thackeray's American contemporaries and yet too conventional to please the modern historian. In the mind of the average American in the mid-nineteenth century Washington was a legend, a symbol rather than a real person, a demigod and a national hero in whom no fault must be found. Thackeray tried hard to get at the man behind the legend. In addition to various books, he read the as-yet-unpublished correspondence between Washington and his Tory neighbor, Jonathan Boucher, thanks to Boucher's grandson, the poet Locker-Lampson. While still in Virginia, with Judge Eustace Conway as his guide, Thackeray had visited "Washington's farm [Mount Vernon?] and other localities associated with the illustrious patriot. . . ."

Thackeray also consulted his American friends as to Washington's character and personality. When Kennedy gave him the traditional account, Thackeray is said to have interrupted him "somewhat testily, saying: 'No, no, Kennedy, that's not what I want. Tell me, was he a fussy old gentleman in a wig? Did he take snuff and spill it down his shirt front?' " When Thackeray showed to the Baxter family his copy of one of Gilbert Stuart's portraits of Washington, he said: "Look at him. Does he not look as if he had just said a good, stupid thing?" If Thackeray ever realized the character of Washington to his own satisfaction, he apparently never came to love him. "Hang him!" exclaims George Warrington, the twin brother who fights for the King. "He has no faults, and that's why I dislike him. When he marries that widow—ah me! what a dreary life she will have of it."

In *The Virginians* it is chiefly the youthful Washington that we see. He is a superb horseman and a gallant soldier who, Mrs. Mountain complains, has never sown any wild oats.

[The Warrington twins] had looked up to their neighbour of Mount Vernon as their guide, director, friend—as, indeed, almost everybody seemed to do who came in contact with the simple and upright young man. Himself of the most scrupulous gravity and good-breeding, in his communication with other folks he appeared to exact, or, at any rate, to occasion, the same behaviour. His nature was above levity and jokes: they seemed out of place when addressed to him. He was slow of comprehending them: and they slunk as it were abashed out of his society.

This is not the young Washington portrayed in Douglas Southall Freeman's monumental biography. When he completed his study of the youthful Washington, Freeman was surprised to find him a much more complex character than Robert E. Lee had been.

. . . a rapidly developed young man of complicated character—moral, just, patient, amiable and able to win the affection of his Captains and Lieutenants, but at the same time humorless, ambitious, persistent to positive obstinacy, acquisitive, suspicious of rivals and extraordinarily sensitive. Within this fundamental antithesis of qualities, there were conflicts, gradations and contradictions. Scarcely a doubt can remain that he was in love with [Sally Fairfax] the wife of a neighbor and friend. . . . He was, in a word, an immensely vital and definitely emotional young man.

Freeman thus characterized the young Washington of the legend:

Apparently there have been two orthodox approaches to the youth of Washington—one forward through [Mason Locke] Weems and the other backward from Gilbert Stuart and John Marshall. If Weems were followed, Washington was a cross between a prig and a paragon. When seen through the eyes of the Chief Justice or those of the Rhode Island painter, he was so awesome and reserved a figure that he never could be credited with a youth.

It would seem that Thackeray finally decided that the traditional conception of the youthful Washington was not far from the truth; and so he concluded that the best way to make the priggish young soldier behave like a human being was to place him in a situation where, by the standards of the time, he must fight a duel to maintain his honor as an officer and a gentleman. Thackeray was right in seeing that Washington had a naturally strong temper which, as Thomas Jefferson phrased it, if ever "it broke its bonds, he was most tremendous in his wrath." Mrs. Mountain leads the Warrington boys to believe that Colonel Washington is planning to marry their mother. In the tavern scene, aided and abetted by half-drunk British officers in Braddock's army, they challenge Washington to a duel. In this scene Washington, badgered beyond endurance, finally loses his temper.

"Is this some infernal conspiracy in which you are all leagued against me?" shouted the Colonel. "It would seem as if I was drunk, and not you, as you all are. I withdraw nothing. By heavens! I will meet one or half-a-dozen of you in your turn, young or old, drunk or sober."

The duel does not take place, but the scene, so George William Curtis wrote to Thackeray, raised "the most tempestuous teapot you ever heard." Among Thackeray's American friends who protested was John R. Thompson, who in the *Southern Literary Messenger* for February, 1858, condemned:

the liberty taken by Mr. Thackeray in hurrying Washington into a couple of duels with a pair of drunken youths, which, though arrested before an actual exchange of shots with either party, place our venerated hero in a somewhat ridiculous position. Mr. Thackeray should never have ventured upon bringing Washington into his story farther than to permit him to cross the stage and be seen no more.

A few Americans, it would seem, were not displeased to see Washington made "like other men"; but Cornelius C. Felton, who taught the ancient classics at Harvard, wrote in the *North American Review* in October, 1860: "Why, this is the very essence of the falsehood. Washington was not like other men; and to bring his lofty character down to the level of the vulgar passions of common life, is to give the lie to the grandest chapter in the uninspired annals of the human race."

Thackeray was the first writer of importance to picture Washington as the product of his Virginian environment. The process by which Washington had been transformed into the great American symbol had almost deprived him of his connection with his native state. Few of the many published eulogies that followed his death in 1799 even mentioned the fact that he was a native of Virginia. Thackeray's Washington is a Virginian of the planter class in his stately dignity, his elaborate courtesy, and in his love of horses and hunting. "Up to the last," writes George Warrington,

our Virginian gentry were a grave, aristocratic folk, with the strongest sense of their own dignity and station. . . . Amongst the great folks of our Old World I have never seen a gentleman standing more on his dignity and maintaining it better than Mr. Washington: no—not the King against whom he took arms.

And, George continues, "in the eyes of all the gentry of the French Court" who fought in the American war, "the great American chief always appeared as *anax andrōn,* and they allowed that his better could not be seen in Versailles itself."

Washington's role in *The Virginians* is largely limited to the opening chapters. In the closing chapters, however, Thackeray put into the mouths of the Warrington brothers some of the finest tributes to the great general ever written. In the very last chapter Harry after the war talks to his brother about his old chief, particularly during "the awful winter of '77" at Valley Forge when General Gates was regarded as "the only genius fit to conduct the war" and Congress was promoting Conway of the infamous Cabal. It was at such an inauspicious time that Harry Warrington, now a colonel and without his knowledge being recommended by Washington for promotion, aired his jealousy of Lafayette: "a boy of twenty made a major-general over us, because he is a Marquis, and because he can't speak the English language." Harry in a huff offers his resignation but withdraws it when he sees that his chief and old friend is deeply hurt. This time, however, Washington keeps his naturally high temper under control.

Somewhat later the two friends in talking of old times laugh over the duel that never took place.

"Ah! [says Washington] an open enemy I can face readily enough. 'Tis the secret foe who causes the doubt and anguish! We have sat with more than one at my table to-day to whom I am obliged to show a face of civility, whose hands I must take when they are offered, though I know they are stabbing my reputation, and are eager to pull me down from my place. . . . What humiliation is yours compared to mine, who have to play the farce of welcome to these traitors; who live to bear the neglect of Congress, and see men who have insulted me promoted in my own army? If I consulted my own feelings as a man, would I continue in this command? You know whether my temper is naturally warm or not, and whether as a private gentleman I should be likely to suffer such slights and outrages as are put upon me daily; but in the advancement of the sacred cause in which we are engaged, we have to endure not only hardship and danger, but calumny and wrong, and may God give us strength to do our duty!"

"And then," Harry continues, "the General showed me the papers regarding the affair of that fellow Conway, whom Congress promoted in spite of the intrigue, and down whose black throat John Cadwalader sent the best ball he ever fired in his life."

After hearing Harry's story, George, who had never liked Washington, joined in praise of the great patriot:

"We talked but now of Wolfe. . . . Here, indeed, is a greater than Wolfe. To endure is greater than to dare; to tire out hostile fortune; to be daunted by no difficulty; to keep heart when all have lost it; to go through intrigue spotless; and to forego even ambition when the end is gained. Who can say this is not greatness, or show the other Englishman who has achieved so much?"

". . . here indeed," as George had said earlier, "is a character to admire and revere; a life without a stain, a fame without a flaw. *Quando invenies parem?*"

4

Thackeray was interested in Virginia not only as the home of Washington but also as a part of that eighteenth-century England which he knew and loved so well. "The whole usages of Virginia, indeed," he wrote, "were fondly modelled after the English customs." Englishmen who settled in Virginia tried as best they could to duplicate the way of life of the English country gentleman, whom George Warrington praised as "that noblest specimen of the human race, the bepraised of songs and men, the good old English country gentleman." The aristocratic Virginia planter and the English country gentleman held much the same ideals; each was in his own way "a fine gentleman." Indeed, Madam Esmond-Warrington's portrait of her father in the Preface to *Esmond* might pass with little alteration for a portrait of such an old-school Virginia gentleman as Thomas Dabney or Washington himself. One main purpose of *The Virginians,* as Gordon Ray has pointed out, was to uphold the ideals of the gentleman at a time when they were fast fading. Thackeray's friend Tennyson wrote of Arthur Hallam in *In Memoriam*:

> And thus he bore without abuse
> The grand old name of gentleman,
> Defamed by every charlatan,
> And soil'd with all ignoble use.

"What is it to be a gentleman?" Thackeray had written in *The Book of Snobs* (1848). "It is to be honest, to be gentle, to be generous, to be brave, to be wise, and, possessing all these qualities, to exercise them in the most graceful outward manner."

Thackeray was not unaware of wide differences between Virginia and England. In fact, he continually used Virginia life as a foil to the corrupt life of the idle upper classes in England. This is simply, in a new form, the old contrast of the virtues of the country with the vices of the city, as old as the time of the *De Coverley Papers* or, for that matter, as old as the pastorals of Theocritus. There is less of this in the second volume, for George Warrington is from the beginning more English and less Virginian than Harry. Even George, however, cannot be made to understand why his English kinsmen have allowed Harry to remain in jail. And those kinsmen know that but for the quixotic generosity of Henry Esmond, George and Harry would be the proprietors of the English Castlewood estate. "Our Virginia was dull," George writes to Harry; "but let us thank Heaven we were bred there. We were made little slaves [to their mother], but not slaves to wickedness, gambling, bad male and female company. It was not till he left home that my poor Harry fell among thieves."

The first volume, in which Harry takes a leading role, is the story of the reaction to English society life of a young, generous, and high-spirited but unsophisticated Virginian. The disillusioned youth becomes a sadder and wiser man. The theme is as modern as what we find in the boy stories of Hemingway, Faulkner, and Mark Twain; and I doubt whether any one of these novelists handled his theme more convincingly than Thackeray.

One by one Harry's illusions are dispelled. At the outset he finds his kinsmen inhospitable. "Had any of them ridden up to his home in Virginia, whether the master were present or absent, the guests would have been made welcome, and, in sight of his ancestors' hall, he had to go and ask for a dish of bacon and eggs at a country ale-house!" So unsophisticated is Harry that even "old Maria" has no difficulty in making him her slave. Even when he finds out that he is not in love with her, he swears, like a true Virginian, that he will keep his promise to marry her. He blushes like a girl at the indecent talk of his English associates. "Even Aunt Bernstein's conversation and jokes astounded the young Virginian, so that the worldly old woman would call him Joseph, or simpleton." Harry has "no victories over the sex to boast of," and is shocked when he learns that Catterina is regarded as his conquest. "It isn't the custom of our country, Sampson," he says, "to ruin girls, or frequent the society of low women. We Virginian gentlemen honor women. . . ." Until the very last Harry cannot believe that his kinsman, Lord Castlewood, means to cheat him out of every penny he has. Only the bailiff and the jailer can bring him to his senses and make him see how inferior the idle upper class is to the simple people of his native colony.

The picture of life in Virginia which Thackeray draws is on the whole quite accurate. A few blunders were to be expected. He seems not quite certain of the spelling of the name of the widow whom Washington married; sometimes it is "Custis" and sometimes it is "Curtis." He has General Braddock riding from Williamsburg to Castlewood on the Potomac in a single day, an impossible distance.

Thackeray's picture of Virginia, however, is less touched with legend than that to be found in the romances of John Esten Cooke. In spite of his close association with Virginians, Thackeray was too shrewd a realist to fall under the spell of the romantic Virginia tradition. He saw what many others have failed to see, that a homespun simplicity was the most striking characteristic of Virginia life. He never describes the planters as feudal barons, but, like most other novelists, he does practically ignore the lower classes of whites. The most serious criticism to be made of his picture is that he has merely described Virginia life when he should have presented it as a living complex social organism. Aside from Washington and the Esmond-Warrington family there are practically no Virginians in the book. Nevertheless, Thackeray's picture of Virginia life was good enough to move his American friend Cozzens to write: "Your 'Virginians' have surprised and pleased all your intimate friends. We all think your pictures of Virginia life are perfect and wonder how you are able to do it."

The Virginia planter's life as Thackeray describes it is like that of the English country gentleman modified by the presence of Negro slaves and tobacco and the proximity of the frontier.

A hundred years back there were scarce any towns in Virginia; the establishments of the gentry were little villages in which they and their vassals dwelt. Rachel Esmond ruled like a little queen in Castlewood; the princes, her neighbours, governed their estates round about. Many of these were rather needy potentates, living plentifully but in the roughest fashion, having numerous domestics whose liveries were often ragged; keeping open houses, and turning away no stranger from their gates; proud, idle, fond of all sorts of field sports as became gentlemen of good lineage.

"The Virginian Squire," Thackeray adds, "had often a barefooted valet, and a cobbled saddle; but there was plenty of corn for the horses and abundance of drink and venison for the master within the tumble-down fences, and behind the cracked windows of the hall." This is the Virginia which Thackeray had seen for himself and not that of the romantic Virginia novelists.

The Negro slaves, as we know from Thackeray's letters, interested him very much. In *The Virginians* he notes:

The question of Slavery was not born at the time of which we write. To be the proprietor of black servants shocked the feelings of no Virginian gentleman; nor, in truth, was the despotism exercised over the negro race generally a savage one. The food was plenty; the poor black people lazy and not unhappy.

Thackeray saw the value in fiction of the Negro's grotesqueness and humor as clearly as the dialect writers of the New South, but he rarely attempted the Negro dialect and never with complete success. In *The Virginians* the Negroes appear only in vaguely defined groups with the exception of Gumbo and Sady. In Gumbo we have a striking portrait of a lazy Negro valet, who though a great liar in harmless fashion, is absolutely faithful to his master when everybody else seems to have deserted him. The Gumbo illustrations which Thackeray drew for *The Virginians* (the last book he illustrated) are among the best in the book.

The erroneous notions of Virginia which Thackeray's English

characters hold are worthy of mention. Sir Miles Warrington thinks that Virginia is an island. Harry Warrington's Esmond relatives expect to find him a man of "uncouth manners" and "coarse provincial habits." Lady Castlewood asks her daughter Fanny: "You don't want to marry a creature like that, and be a squaw in a wigwam?" The servant Molly when for the first time she sees the grandson of Henry Esmond, exclaims: "Lord, your honour! Why, your honour's skin's as white as mine." Had she expected to find it red or black? I wonder. Thackeray undoubtedly had read how Robert Beverley, "in Justice to so fine a Country," had written his book

because it [Virginia] has been so misrepresented to the common People of *England*, as to make them believe, that the Servants in *Virginia* are made to draw in Cart and Plow, as Horses and Oxen do in *England*, and that the Country turns all People black, who go to live there, with other such prodigious Phantasms.

Toward the close of *The Virginians* George Warrington, who now lives in England, gives us his conception of his brother's way of life after the Revolution. Harry had served with distinction in two wars, but now he has settled down to the leisurely life of a country gentleman.

My brother Hal, when settled on his plantation in Virginia was perfectly satisfied with the sports and occupations he found there. The company of the country neighbours sufficed him; he never tired of looking after his crops and people, taking his fish, shooting his ducks, hunting in his woods, or enjoying his rubber, and his supper. Happy Hal, in his great barn of a house, under his roomy porches, his dogs lying round his feet: his friends, the Virginian Will Wimbles, at free quarters in his mansion; his negroes fat, lazy, and ragged; his shrewd little wife ruling over them and her husband, who always obeyed her implicitly when living, and who was pretty speedily consoled when she died! I say happy, though his lot would have been intolerable to me; wife and friends, and plantation, and town life at Richmond. . . . How happy he whose foot fits the shoe which fortune gives him!

Harry Warington's way of life would have bored his brother, and it would seem empty and tedious to most Americans of our city-bred generation. Today we find it difficult to credit Washington and Jefferson when they express a marked preference for life on their plantations to life in any city in the world. Thackeray probably did not realize how different Harry Warrington's way of life was from that which went on at Mount Vernon, Monticello, Montpelier,

Stratford, and Gunston Hall. Jefferson once noted the choice which at Shadwell confronted him in his boyhood:

. . . I was often thrown into the society of horse racers, card players, fox hunters, scientific & professional men, and of dignified men; and many a time have I asked myself, in the enthusiastic moment of the death of a fox, the victory of a favorite horse, the issue of a question eloquently argued at the bar, or in the great council of the nation, well, which of these kinds of reputation should I prefer? That of a horse jockey? a fox hunter? an orator? or the honest advocate of my country's rights?

Did Thackeray, I wonder, ever ask himself just what it was in the Virginia way of life that enabled the colony to give to the nation the most distinguished group of great men that the nation has ever had? But we may well ask ourselves: Has any other writer, novelist or historian, given us a complete explanation of that phenomenon? I think not. Thackeray, however, has given us—and this is no mean achievement—what is probably still the best of the many novels that have their scenes in Virginia. *The Virginians* is also one of the first and best of Anglo-American international novels, and for a century and more it has been an influence making for friendship and mutual understanding among Englishmen and Americans.

You brave Heroique minds,
Worthy your Countries Name;
That Honour still pursue,
Goe, and subdue,
Whilst loyt'ring Hinds
Lurke here at home, with shame.

MICHAEL DRAYTON, "To the Virginian Voyage"

Pocahontas' body, lovely as a poplar, sweet as a
red haw in November or a pawpaw in May,
did she wonder? does she remember? . . .
in the dust, in the cool tombs?

CARL SANDBURG, "Cool Tombs"

The Smith-Pocahontas Literary Legend

[This essay, which was printed in the July, 1957, issue of the *Virginia Magazine of History and Biography*, was written at the request of its editor, Mr. William M. E. Rachal, for an issue given over largely to celebrating the 350th anniversary of the founding of Jamestown. My interest in the subject goes back beyond 1919, when I completed my Columbia University dissertation on "Virginia Life in Fiction." This essay, however, includes much that has been published since 1919.

I have indicated various ways in which Smith and Pocahontas have been used as symbols, but I have preferred not to indulge in the kind of speculation about symbols and myths popular with scholars and critics in recent years. Since revising this essay I have read an article in the *Kenyon Review* (XXIV, 391-415, Summer, 1962) entitled "The Mother of Us All: Pocahontas Reconsidered," by Philip Young, who concludes:

... Americans must see the Indian girl in one last way: as progenitress of all the "Dark Ladies" of our culture—all the erotic and joyous temptresses, the sensual, brunette heroines, whom our civilization (particularly our literature: Hawthorne, Cooper, Melville, and many others) has summoned up only to repress. . . . Pocahontas is the archetypal sacrifice to respectability in America—a victim of what has been from the beginning our overwhelming anxiety to housebreak all things in nature, until wilderness and wildness be reduced to a few state parks and a few wild oats.

That may be what Pocahontas represents for Professor Young, but it is not what she represented for any one of the numerous writers whom I have discussed.]

1

Until after the American Revolution the founding of the Jamestown colony in 1607 seemed an event of no great historical importance except perhaps to Virginians; and in Colonial times even Virginians rarely remembered the beginnings of the "Ancient Dominion." The land was, in the words of Robert Frost, "still unstoried, artless, unenhanced." The early eighteenth-century historian, William Stith, expressed surprise and mortification that Virginia gentlemen "seemed to be much alarmed, and to grudge, that a complete History of their own Country would run to more than one Volume, and cost them above half a Pistole."

After the Revolution, however, Americans pointed with increasing pride to the founders of all the thirteen colonies, which as sovereign states had united to form a new and proud nation. Political orators, historians, and men of letters alike began to find in Captain John Smith heroic traits which seemed to them characteristically American: indomitable courage, self-reliance, resourcefulness, and faith in the future of the new land. Virginia writers in particular saw in Smith not only the founder of the oldest and largest state in the Union and a worthy forerunner of Washington and Jefferson but also a chivalrous knight errant, the first of the Cavaliers, and the prototype of the Virginia gentlemen of the old regime. And Pocahontas, whose name in history and legend is now inseparable from Smith's, was both the guardian angel of the infant colony and the ancestress of distinguished Virginia families. In *The Hero in America: A Chronicle of Hero-Worship* (1941) Dixon Wecter rightly began with a chapter on "Captain John Smith and the Indians." Pocahontas and Smith, he noted, "have gone hand in hand to immortality."

By 1803, when William Wirt's *The Letters of the British Spy* was published in Richmond, Smith and Pocahontas were already becoming national figures and the demand for a native literature was running high. By that time also east of the Appalachians few families had anything to fear from the tomahawk and the scalping knife; and, along the Atlantic seaboard at least, Americans were willing to admit that the Indians had been greatly wronged and misunderstood. By 1803 the European image of the Indian as a romantic and uniquely American figure had begun to make its impression on our native writers. Wirt included in his book two chapters (Letters IV and VI) in which he mentioned visits to the ruins of Jamestown and to Powhatan's deserted village near the falls of the James. "Where," asked the Spy, "is Smith, that pink of gallantry, that flower of chivalry?" He had high praise for Pocahontas as "the patron deity" of the Jamestown colony, and he wondered why the Virginians had "instituted no festival or order in honour of her memory."

Even before 1820, when Sydney Smith in the *Edinburgh Review* was scornfully asking: "Who reads an American book?" Americans were made to feel that their claim to national greatness must be justified by the production of an important national literature. The vogue of Scott's *Waverley* (1814) and its successors set some of our writers to exploring the nation's brief but rather unromantic past. Fenimore Cooper, though not our earliest novelist, set the pattern for his successors; and the American Revolution, the frontier, and the period of colonization became the three "matters of American romance." Europeans might regard the American past as plebeian and commonplace, but they could not deny that the frontiersman and the Indian were attractive figures without any close European parallel. Inevitably, the Smith-Pocahontas story with its romantic and tragic incidents attracted the attention of our poets, playwrights, and novelists.

There is an epic quality about the story of the founding of Jamestown which helps to explain its fascination for American writers. The historian of seventeenth-century Virginia, Philip Alexander Bruce, went so far as to write:

The remote past of the oldest part of the Southern States offers the most splendid theme to be found in the entire range of modern events for an epic comparable with the *Iliad* and the *Odyssey*; this is the ever memorable embarkation from London for Virginia in 1606 of the little band of Englishmen, their long sail across the lonely ocean, their first view of the scented shores of the Chesapeake, and all the heroic and terrible episodes that soon followed, including the idyllic romance of Pocahontas.

(Bruce himself wrote no epic, but he did celebrate Pocahontas in a book of sonnets.) American poets and romancers saw in Captain John Smith a hero not unlike Vergil's Aeneas, the bearer of an old civilization to a new and better land. The love story of Pocahontas and Smith recalled a famous episode in the *Aeneid*; and the Indian princess was often portrayed as the Dido of disappointed love and sometimes as Lavinia, the Italian bride of Aeneas.

Yet the reader who looks for a great American epic poem among the numerous treatments of Pocahontas must remain content with Stephen Vincent Benét's posthumous and unfinished *Western Star* or Hart Crane's difficult poem *The Bridge*. The epic poem, like the pastoral, is almost an extinct literary genre. In verse and prose hundreds of men and women have written about Smith and Pocahontas, but we may still say, as William Gilmore Simms said in 1845, that the subject has been treated "unhappily, in most cases, by very feeble hands." There is no classic treatment of the subject comparable to Longfellow's *The Courtship of Miles Standish*, which made the story of the founding of the Plymouth colony familiar to every literate American.

In the nineteenth century the poets and writers of fiction were—from the historian's point of view—unduly fascinated by the story of Pocahontas's rescue of Smith from death at the hands of Powhatan's executioners. Alexander Brown complained with some cause that romantic and ill-informed writers had neglected other important historical figures of the Jamestown colony. For close to a century some historians have either doubted the truth of the rescue story or regarded it as a matter of slight historical importance. True or not, it has become a part of our American folklore. The story is one of our finest literary "myths"—which does not necessarily mean that the rescue did not take place. In *Let Me Lie* (1947) James Branch Cabell, who did not believe the story of the rescue, noted parallel situations in folk tales and myths:

The Smith-Pocahontas Literary Legend

Everywhere in folklore does one find this story, of a young man in the power of a ruthless foreign captor, whose daughter falls in love with and releases the prisoner from the cruelty of her father—with the father appearing, variously, as a gaoler, an emperor, a fiend, a sultan, a god, a giant, or a sorcerer—and, with varying sequels. . . . The true point is not at all that Smith plagiarized his story, but the fact that in our Virginian mythology Pocahontas has her fit place, and that, howsoever she became enshrined there, the event was praiseworthy.

Americans are perhaps as much given to myth-making as other peoples; but our early history is better documented than that of older nations, and the disposition to idealize the past has been held in check by literary debunkers, historians, and teachers of history in school and college. Most of the great literary legends of the world developed, like the greatest of them all, the story of Troy, in those credulous dark ages when there were no printing presses and no historians except the poets.

Here one is tempted to speculate just how the Smith-Pocahontas story might have developed if Virginia had been settled in the "dark backward and abysm of time" when the great Arthurian cycle of stories was taking form. In that event we might now have the fully developed national legend of a gallant knight and explorer who married an Indian princess and became the ancestor of the great Virginian soldiers and statesmen of the Revolution. Indeed, Mark Twain, whose father was born in Virginia, suggested something of the kind in *Pudd'nhead Wilson*. In that novel the illiterate slave Roxana berates her cowardly son, Tom Driscoll, who has been brought up in Missouri as the white son of a Virginia gentleman:

"My great-great-great-gran'father en yo' great-great-great-great-gran'father was Ole Cap'n John Smith, de highest blood dat Old Virginny ever turned out, en *his* great-great-gran'mother or somers along back dah, was Pocahontas de Injun queen, en her husbun' was a nigger king outen Africa—en yit here you is, a-slinkin' outen a duel en disgracin' our whole line like a ornery low-down hound!"

Tom has disgraced the family, for "De Smith-Pocahontases ain't 'fraid o' nothin', let alone bullets."

2

Captain John Smith was not only one of the dominant figures in the Jamestown colony; he was also its most important contemporary historian. Hence it is necessary briefly to consider him in his role of historian, for the Pocahontas story comes largely from him and he is our sole authority for the rescue scene. In modern times Smith's reliability as a historian has often been called in question, but so far as we know no one publicly questioned it during his lifetime. About thirty years after his death, however, Thomas Fuller in *The Worthies of England* (1662) described as incredible Smith's account of his exploits in the Balkans. Of Smith's Virginia adventures Fuller remarked: ". . . such his perils, preservations, dangers, deliverances, they seem to most men above belief, to some beyond truth. Yet," Fuller added sarcastically, "have we two witnesses to attest them, the prose and the pictures, both in his own book; and it soundeth much to the diminution of his deeds that he alone is the herald to publish and proclaim them." The skeptical Fuller chose to ignore the evidence of some thirty poems contributed to Smith's *The Generall Historie of Virginia* (1624) by friendly English poets, including George Wither, John Davies of Hereford, and John Donne, the Dean of St. Paul's, who once hoped to be made Secretary of the Virginia colony. In 1624 the great Dean contributed to Smith's *The Generall Historie of Virginia* a poem—not yet included in any edition of Donne's poems—"To His Friend Captaine John Smith, and His Worke," which begins:

> I know not how Desert more great can rise,
> Then out of Danger t'ane for good mens Good;
> Nor who doth better winne th' Olympian prize,
> Than he whose Countryes Honor stirres his bloud;
>   Private respects have private expectation,
>   Publicke designes, should publish reputation.

> This Gentleman whose Volume heere is stoard
> With strange discoveries of GODS strangest Creatures,
> Gives us full view, how he hath Sayl'd, and Oar'd
> And Marcht, full many myles, whose rough defeatures,
>   Hath beene as bold, as puissant, up to binde
>   Their barbarous Strength's, to follow him dog-linde.

In the early nineteenth century New Englanders were much more inclined to glorify the Pilgrim Fathers than the men who had founded the Jamestown colony thirteen years earlier, but their writers did not wholly neglect Virginia. In *The Little Reader's Assistant* (1791) Noah Webster painted Captain Smith as a hero worthy of admiration by the young. In 1829 Samuel G. Goodrich, author and publisher of the widely used "Peter Parley" school-books, published in Hartford his *Stories about Captain John Smith, of Virginia, for the Instruction and Amusement of Children.* The book opens with what would seem to have been the quite unnecessary question: "Little boy! have you ever heard of such a state, as *Virginia?*" Like so many children's books of the time, this one now seems insufferably moralistic and condescending. The young John Smith is portrayed as an unrepentant prodigal son, and the biographer moralizes: "How much more useful, and honorable, and happy would he have been, had he stayed at home—had he been sober and industrious; and, especially, had he assisted his mother!" But from the time he set sail for Virginia Smith is portrayed as a useful man, although Goodrich felt compelled to add: "I do not mean to say that he was a pious man." Goodrich had higher praise for Pocahontas: "What a worthy girl was this! She was a savage, but her deed was noble! She [unlike Smith] had never been taught to love her enemies; but she shewed a benevolent disposition. . . . The name of Pocahontas, and her generous deed, ought to be remembered, and will be remembered while America lasts."

In 1860 and again in 1866 a Massachusetts scholar, Charles Deane, expressed grave doubts about Smith's reliability as a historian and in particular his account of the rescue. In those years of sectional ill feeling Southerners resented the New Englander's attack upon one of their heroes. One Southern newspaper, as Deane remembered in 1885, went so far as to ask: "Is it not enough that the ruthless Yankee has devastated our fields and ruined our homes and slain our children? Must he also despoil the tomb? Will he not rest until he has rifled our very history of our choicest traditions, and stolen the highest jewels of our romance?"

Deane's motives were above reproach, but that is rather more than can be said for the motives of the eminent New England historian, Henry Adams, whose earliest venture into historical criticism appeared in January, 1867, under the caption, "Myth of Pocahontas Exploded." In *The Education of Henry Adams* he tells us that it was an older New England historian, John G. Palfrey, who "suggested to Adams, who wanted to make a position for himself, that an article in the *North American Review* on Captain John Smith's relations with Pocahontas would attract as much attention, and probably break as much glass, as any other stone that could be thrown by a beginner. . . . The task seemed likely to be amusing." In his article Adams represented Smith as an incompetent official, an unreliable historian, and an incurably vain man. When Adams republished the article in his *Historical Essays* in 1891, he ignored his Southern critics. He would in fact have found it quite difficult to refute some of the shrewd criticism which William Wirt Henry had made in an address to the Virginia Historical Society in 1882.

Later historians have expressed divergent estimates of Smith's reliability, but they no longer divide on sectional lines. Three notable Northern historians, John Fiske, Charles M. Andrews, and James Truslow Adams (not related to Henry Adams), have held that, as Adams phrased it, "There is nothing inherently improbable in the [rescue] story." John Spencer Bassett, a North Carolinian, had written: "By every canon of good criticism we must reject the story." The most persistent critic of Smith's veracity was a Virginian and a Confederate veteran, Alexander Brown, who devoted his later years to a study of the first years of the Jamestown colony. Brown would certainly have agreed with the Harvard historian Albert Bushnell Hart, who numbered Smith among the "American historical liars." Another Harvard historian, Samuel Eliot Morison, has pointed out that New England, which has not cherished Smith's memory, owes almost as much as Virginia to Smith for his explorations, maps, and various writings.

A thoroughgoing study of Smith as a historian came from a young Assistant Professor of History at Brown University, Jarvis M. Morse, who in May, 1935, published in the *Journal of Southern History* an article entitled "John Smith and His Critics: A Chapter in Colonial Historiography." Morse re-examined the evidence with great care and skill and reached the conclusion that "Captain John Smith ranks as one of the few great [American] historians of the seventeenth century. His only American rivals, Edward Johnson, Nathaniel Morton, William Hubbard and Increase Mather, occasionally surpassed him in accuracy of detail but never equalled him in breadth of interest or comprehension." In his *American Beginnings* (1952) Morse reaffirmed his earlier estimate and added: "With considerable justification can Captain John Smith lay claim to the title 'Father of Anglo-American History'. . . ."

A scholar who in our time has contributed much to the rehabilitation of Captain John Smith is, appropriately enough, yet another

Smith—Bradford Smith, the biographer of William Bradford, the great leader of the Plymouth colony. In 1953 Bradford Smith published the best of the many biographies, *Captain John Smith: His Life and Legend*. The biographer confessed that when he began his research, he was a skeptic but noted that before he completed it, he was convinced that Captain John Smith was one of the authentic American heroes.

Bradford Smith was fortunate enough to be able to enlist the services of an able collaborator, the Hungarian-American scholar, Mrs. Laura Polanyi Striker. It had long been felt that Captain Smith's *True Travels* was his least credible book, especially after an earlier Hungarian writer, Lewis Kropf, in 1890 had maintained that the *True Travels* was so filled with errors that he did not believe Captain Smith was ever in the Balkans. Those familiar with Kropf's arguments felt that if one could not accept Smith's accounts of earlier rescues by the "beauteous Lady Tragabigzanda" and "the charitable Lady Callamata," there was certainly little reason for believing that the "blessed Pokahontas, the great Kings Daughter of *Virginia*" ever saved his life. But now that Dr. Striker has shown that the *True Travels* is authentic autobiography and not a romantic novel, it is much easier to believe that Smith really experienced the Virginian adventures which are narrated in his other works.[1] In the latest and best history of Colonial Virginia Richard L. Morton finds Smith's "account of his two years in Virginia essentially true." The rescue seems to him "the most reasonable explanation of Powhatan's treatment of Smith and later friendship for the English, which brought peace as long as Smith remained in Virginia." During Smith's presidency conditions in Virginia steadily improved, but "The savages, upon Smith's departure, began a general series of attacks on the colonists."

In yet another excellent biography, *The Three Worlds of Captain John Smith* (1964), Philip L. Barbour has unearthed new evidence that confirms Smith's account of his adventures in the Balkans and his achievements in Virginia. In an eloquent concluding paragraph Mr. Barbour writes that "more and more evidence of John Smith's basic honesty has been dug out of obscure and widely scattered rec-

[1] In November, 1962, Mrs. Striker and Mr. Smith published in the *Journal of Southern History* (XXVIII, 474-481) an article entitled "The Rehabilitation of Captain John Smith."

ords. . . . Let it only be said that nothing John Smith wrote has yet been found to be a lie."

Bradford Smith, who has done much to rehabilitate Smith as a historian, is fully aware of the literary value of the Smith-Pocahontas story. He writes: "We owe as much to John Smith as a legend, a symbol, as we owe to the actual man. And it is very hard to separate them—a sure sign of durability." He sees in Smith "our Odysseus, our Siegfried, our Aeneas." He adds:

> The popular myth of Plymouth or Jamestown is neither fiction nor fact. It is history interpreted through the emotions of those who receive it, it is history somewhat simplified but essentially true. It is our good fortune to possess a folk myth which corresponds with the facts, to be able to believe a story which not only should have been, but was.

The chief circumstance which has led historians and biographers to question the truth of the rescue story is that in *A True Relation* (1608), Smith's first published account of his captivity among the Indians, either he failed to mention it or else his London printer omitted the passage. Pocahontas had been dead for seven years when Smith's fullest account of the incident appeared in *The Generall Historie of Virginia* in 1624. Yet in that book he published what he claimed was an "abstract" of a letter that he had addressed to the Queen in 1616, when Pocahontas and her husband were in London. By 1624 Pocahontas and John Rolfe were dead, but the Queen was still living; and Smith with enemies in London would hardly have dared to claim that in 1616 he had written to her: "After some six weeks fatting amongst those Salvage Courtiers, at the minute of my execution, she hazarded the beating out of her owne braines to save mine; and not onely that, but so prevaild with her father, that I was safely conducted to *James* towne. . ." and again: ". . . she next under God, was still the instrument to preserve this Colonie from death, famine and utter confusion. . . ."

If Smith invented the story of the rescue, it is very strange that in his final and fullest account of this extraordinary scene he gave the rescue only part of one long and formless sentence in a folio volume of 248 pages:

> . . . having feasted him after their best barbarous manner they could, a long consultation was held, but the conclusion was, two great stones were brought before *Powhatan*: then as many as could layd hands on him, dragged him to them, and thereon laid his head, and being ready

with their clubs, to beate out his braines, *Pocahontas* the Kings dearest daughter, when no intreaty could prevaile, got his head in her armes, and laid her owne upon his to save him from death: whereat the Emperour was contented he should live to make him hatchets, and her bells, beads, and copper. . . .

If the Captain had expected this incident to be better remembered than any other of his many substantial achievements and thrilling adventures, surely he would have expanded and embroidered this bare outline of a great romantic episode.

In one of the better biographies, *John Smith—Also Pocahontas* (1928), the Southern poet, John Gould Fletcher, asserted: "It was the universal practice among Indian tribes to grant the life of a captive, white or red, only at the instance of some favourite squaw; and Pocahontas was notoriously Powhatan's favourite daughter." To illustrate this supposed Indian custom, Fletcher retold a parallel story which is found in the narrative of the Portuguese Gentleman of Elvas, who accompanied De Soto on his disastrous expedition. De Soto's guide was Juan Ortiz, a Spaniard who had been captured by Florida Indians twelve years earlier. At that time the Indian chieftain, Ucita, had condemned Ortiz to be burned alive; but his daughter interceded, "telling him, that it was more for his honour to keepe him as a Captive"; and so Ortiz was released and given "the charge of the keeping of the temple." (Richard Henry Wilde's once popular poem, "My Life Is Like the Summer Rose," was inspired by the story of Ortiz's captivity and is more properly entitled "The Captive's Lament.")

The Ortiz story, however, can be used to discredit Smith's own account of the rescue, and it is so used in James Branch Cabell's *Let Me Lie* (1947). In his *Ladies and Gentlemen* (1934) Cabell had already treated the rescue story as a "myth," possibly derived from the Miranda-Ferdinand episode in Shakespeare's *The Tempest*. An English translation of the narrative of the Gentleman of Elvas, as Cabell notes, was published in London in 1609. There was a second edition in 1611. Smith was living in London and he may very well have read the narrative, as Cabell assumes that he did. In *Let Me Lie* Cabell's spokesman, Alonzo Juan Hernandez (Professor A. J. Hanna) says:

. . . we can imagine the chagrin with which John Smith, in reading his friend's [Hakluyt's] spirited translation, observed with what ease the fine episode of this rescue by an Indian princess could have been adjusted to some one or other of the many daughters of Powhatan; but, alas, Smith's own book [*A True Relation*] had been printed a few months earlier; and he was thus compelled to wait, for fifteen years, until the death of Pocahontas in England, as a figure of some casual notoriety, had afforded to him a chance to reprint selected portions of the story of Ortiz as being his own story. He did not pretend to any intimacy with Pocahontas until after she had become celebrated and was safely dead.

Later biographers and historians are somewhat less skeptical than Cabell. Bradford Smith does not find the story of the rescue improbable. The accuracy of the rescue story is of vital importance to the serious poet, dramatist, or novelist who wishes to give it literary form; but the historians usually regard the story as relatively unimportant. Jarvis M. Morse relegated to a long footnote his own conclusion: "Whatever mental reservations one may have as to the probability of the incident, by no sound application of the laws of historical testimony can it be disproved, save by the appearance of contrary evidence yet undiscovered."

3

Although Smith nowhere states that Pocahontas was in love with him or he with her—she was apparently a child of ten or twelve at the time of the rescue—he or one of his collaborators in *The Generall Historie* does state that he might have married her if he had wished, that he had in fact been accused of planning to marry her and make himself King of Virginia, and, finally, that she married Rolfe believing that Smith was dead. Romantic love as the explanation of her friendship for the whites is a natural inference. The anonymous English writer who published in the *London Magazine* in 1755 *A Short Account of the British Plantations in America* concluded:

Pocahontas easily prevailed with her father and her countrymen to allow her to indulge her passion for the captain, by often visiting the fort, and always accompanying her visits with a fresh supply of provisions; therefore it may justly be said, that the success of our first settlement in America, was chiefly owing to the love this young girl had conceived for Capt. Smith, and consequently in this instance, as well as in many others,

Love does all that's great below!

Attractive as the Smith-Pocahontas story seems at first glance, it presents difficulties to those who would treat it in drama or fiction.

The Smith-Pocahontas Literary Legend

The big scene, the rescue, comes in the first act, so to speak; and the rest of the story is anticlimactic. One of the first writers to call attention to the epic aspects of the story, the Irish-American historian of Virginia John Daly Burk, expressed a fear that his readers would "vent their spleen against the historian, for impairing the interest of his plot, by marrying the princess of Powhatan to a Mr. Rolfe, of whom nothing had previously been said, in defiance of all the expectations raised by the foregoing parts of the fable."

The first writer of any importance to exploit the story of Smith and Pocahontas in fiction was not an American but the English traveler and novelist John Davis, who spent more than fifteen years (1798-1802, 1805-1817) in this country, most of them in Virginia. Davis, when he aspired to a literary career, was shrewd enough to see that there were rich and as yet unexploited materials in the New World. The earliest of his four versions of the Pocahontas story was, awkwardly enough, introduced into his novelette *The Farmer of New Jersey* (1800). An improved version appeared in his *Travels* (1803). Here Davis introduced his short story by describing his meeting with a group of friendly Indians at Occoquan in northern Virginia. In the group he saw a charming girl of seventeen who "appeared such another object as the mind images *Pocahontas* to have been." Davis's Captain Smith has "every quality of a hero," but he does not respond to Pocahontas, who falls in love with him at first sight. There is an extraordinary scene in which Rolfe woos and wins the Indian princess beside the imaginary grave of Captain Smith, which she has come to bedeck with flowers. "The breast of woman," explains Davis, "is, perhaps, never more susceptible of a new passion than when it is agitated by the remains of a former one." Rolfe's wooing is not so convincingly presented as the somewhat similar wooing of Shakespeare's Richard III. In 1805 Davis, now back in this country for his second and longest stay, published in Philadelphia his novelette *Captain Smith and Princess Pocahontas*; and in New York later in the same year he brought out a full-length novel, *The First Settlers of Virginia*. The short story in the *Travels* is in some ways better than the longer versions, for in them the love story is almost buried under more or less irrelevant historical materials. In these later versions Davis borrowed heavily and without acknowledgment from the historians William Robertson and Jeremy Belknap, often merely substituting the first person for the third. The best that can be said for Davis's various versions of the story is that his Pocahontas comes nearer to being a real Indian woman than most of those found in later novels, poems, and plays.

The first native American playwright to dramatize the Smith-Pocahontas story was a Philadelphian, James Nelson Barker, who was at one time Comptroller of the United States Treasury. The theme of *The Indian Princess,* which was produced in 1808, was apparently suggested by Davis's novelette. Barker's name appears in the printed list of subscribers to *Captain Smith and Princess Pocahontas,* and he borrowed from that work certain details which he could have found nowhere else. A better play than Barker's is the *Pocahontas* (1830) of George Washington Parke Custis, the grandson of Martha Washington and father of Mrs. Robert E. Lee. When the play was produced, his wife took a leading part. (Her daughter, Charlotte Barnes Conner, published another Pocahontas play, *The Forest Princess,* in 1840.) Custis showed some ingenuity in making the rescue scene the climax of his play. In order to achieve this effect, however, he had to make a Christian of Pocahontas before her time, and he represented her as theatrically announcing her conversion just before she rescues her Christian friend. Custis made Cavaliers not only of Smith and his followers but also of Rolfe, who may have been a Puritan.

There were many other plays about Pocahontas, including some operettas, but few of them are of any importance now. In Robert Dale Owen's *Pocahontas* (1837) the author's feminist sympathies seem out of place in the mouth of the Indian princess. Among the later plays Mary Virginia Wall's *The Daughter of Virginia Dare* (1908) is remarkable only for the author's attempt to connect Jamestown with the Lost Colony of Roanoke by making Pocahontas the daughter of the first English child born in this country. In view of the dates it would be easier to believe that Pocahontas was Virginia Dare herself.

In 1846 James Rees was writing that plays about Indians had become *"a perfect nuisance."* About a fourth of them deal with the Pocahontas story. Readers and playgoers were weary of imitations of the Leather-Stocking Tales and, by 1855, of the much-parodied *Song of Hiawatha.* The time was right for a burlesque of the Smith-Pocahontas story. On Christmas Eve, 1855, the English actor-playwright, John Brougham, produced in New York his *Po-ca-hon-tas; or, The Gentle Savage,* an operetta in two acts with Brougham himself in the role of Powhatan. On the title page this operetta is described as "An original aboriginal erratic operatic semi-civilized and demi-savage extravaganza, being a per-version of ye trewe and wonderrefulle hystorie of ye rennownned princesse. . . ." In the published play we are informed that the story is based upon *"an entire epic poem"* found "in the vest pocket of the man in armor, dug up near Cape Cod . . . written by a Danish Poet, the Chevalier Viking, *Long Fellow* of the Norwegian Academy of Music." Brougham turns topsy-turvy both history and traditional romance. His Indians speak not Cooper's eloquent periods but the latest American slang. The pious Rolfe has become a Dutchman (Rolff) who sings:

> I wish from mein soul all de rocks round about,
> Would to sausages turn and the trees to sourcrout,
> The ocean, a vast bowl into *lager* bier roll,
> And I was an earthquake to swallow the whole.

Powhatan presides over a council obviously intended as a caricature of the American Congress. Pocahontas is a product of the Jamestown Finishing School, and she wishes to perform:

> Some deed of desperation nice and new,
> Something would startle all the world with fright,
> That is, provided it *left* me all *right!*

In the rescue scene she rushes in "heroineically distressed and dishevelled" and cries out: "Husband! for thee *I scream!*" *Lemon* or *Vanilla?*" coolly asks the brave Captain. When the rescued Smith gratefully proposes to marry her, she cries:

> Stop! One doubt within my heart arises!
> A great historian before us stands,
> *Bancroft* himself, you know, forbids the *banns!*

The resourceful Smith, however, cites precedent for the violation of historical fact; and the Anti-marry-folks-against-their-will Society urges the match on Powhatan, who favors Rolfe. The rivals finally settle the princess's fate by a game of cards. Smith wins and marries her in spite of George Bancroft and the whole tribe of historians.

4

The nineteenth-century poets who wrote about Pocahontas were more numerous than the playwrights, but their portraits of her are no more lifelike. She practically ceased to be an Indian, and except for the color of her skin she might have passed for the conventional romantic heroine. One of the first poets to celebrate her was Joel Barlow, the "Connecticut Wit," who in the fifth book of *The Columbiad* (1807) represented her as a benevolent Medea who helped Jason (Smith) and the other Argonauts to outwit her royal father. In *Letters from Virginia, Translated from the French* (1816) George Tucker, a better essayist and economist than poet, included "The Indian Maid," a ballad in which he retold the story of Pocahontas's night journey to Jamestown to warn Smith that her father was planning to massacre the settlers. Washington Irving's one-time collaborator, James Kirke Paulding, who visited Virginia in 1816, wrote an "Ode to Jamestown."

In 1841 two New England poets paid tribute to the Indian princess. In her *Pocahontas* Mrs. Lydia Huntley Sigourney, "the Sweet Singer of Hartford," described Pocahontas as "the saviour of the Saxon vine" and at the same time a model of mid-Victorian "modesty, simpleness, and grace." Seba Smith, whose "Jack Downing" letters in the Maine dialect are an important early example of American humor, glorified the noble savage in *Powhatan: A Metrical Romance*, which is remembered only because it occasioned one of Edgar Allan Poe's severest reviews. "The simple truth is," Poe said, "Mr. Downing never committed a greater mistake than when he fancied himself a poet, even in the ninety-ninth degree." Seba Smith, like many another writer who retold the familiar story, prided himself upon his fidelity to historical fact. This, said Poe, was not its principal merit but its "leading fault." "The truth is," he said, "Mr. Downing has never dreamed of any *artistic* arrangement of his facts."

Poe, the greatest of the Virginia poets, wrote no poem about either Smith or Pocahontas, but there were a number of Virginians who did. Their view of Smith was, as John Moncure Daniel put it in prose: "He is the Roland of our early history, and the future Achilles of the Virginian Homer. . . ." The name of his hero troubled John Robertson, who in *Virginia: or, The Fatal Patent* (1825) wrote:

> JOHN SMITH, a name not deem'd, as I opine,
> Fit to be measured in a Poet's song:
> What tho' it soundeth low along the line,
> Yet does a hero's fame to it belong.

St. Leger Landon Carter in *The Land of Powhatan* (1821), dedicated to "the people of Virginia," frequently referred to this yeoman's son as "Knight" or "Baron." "Sir John" is more euphonious than plain "Captain Smith." In *Pocahontas, Princess of Virginia* (1841) William Watson Waldron went so far as to rechristen both Smith and Rolfe; they appear respectively as Alcanzor and Rodolph.

The truth is that our romantic poets and novelists, in trying to make of this lower-middle-class Englishman a knight from Camelot, missed the opportunity to glorify Captain John Smith as our pioneer example of that figure so dear to American readers, the self-made man. Smith was a worthy forerunner of Franklin and Lincoln. Our American writers also might have made more of Smith as a frontier fighter and explorer whose exploits antedated those of Daniel Boone and David Crockett.

The *Pocahontas* (1840) of Mrs. Mary Webster Mosby, herself a descendant of the Indian princess, is a smooth, pious, and sentimental romance in which in pseudo-epic fashion the poetess introduces a sibyl who predicts for Pocahontas a happy marriage and a long line of illustrious descendants among the First Families of Virginia. Mrs. Mosby also gives Pocahontas some distinguished ancestors in the Norse Vikings and the Lost Ten Tribes of Israel. James Barron Hope, journalist, orator, and poet, wrote sonnets on Smith, Pocahontas, and Raleigh; and he praised them again in his ode, "A Poem Recited at the Two Hundred and Fiftieth Anniversary of the Settlement at Jamestown." In the last of these poems Hope saw in Captain John Smith:

> An image half of Border chivalry,
> And half presented to our eager eyes,
> The brilliant type of modern enterprise.

Mrs. Margaret Junkin Preston, a Virginian by adoption, wrote one of the best ballads, "The Last Meeting of Pocahontas and the Great Captain," which may have been suggested by a reading of John Esten Cooke's *My Lady Pokahontas* (1885).

In 1847 William Gilmore Simms, the most prolific of Southern writers, published a readable life of Smith. Two years earlier he had published a long article entitled "Pocahontas; A Subject for the Historical Painter." In *Southward Ho!* (1854) he described Smith as "the embodiment of the best characteristics of chivalry." In that book he reprinted from his *The Book of My Lady* (1833) "Pocahontas; A Legend of Virginia," which is not one of Simms's better poems. The rescue scene is romantically described, but the name

191

"Smith" does not appear in the poem. "It is difficult," commented Simms, "to believe in the heroism of a man named Smith."

One of the best of the shorter poems is Thackeray's ballad, "Pocahontas," but the British novelist should have known better than to represent Smith as about to be burned at the stake rather than clubbed to death. The poem first appeared in *The Virginians* (1857-1859). In that novel George Warrington, a Virginia grandson of Henry Esmond, is represented as writing the ballad in order to arouse interest in his forthcoming London play on Pocahontas. Thackeray's summary of George Warrington's plot is likely to be read when other dramatic versions of the story have been forgotten:

An Indian king; a loving princess, and her attendant, in love with the British captain's servant; a traitor in the English fort; a brave Indian warrior, himself entertaining an unhappy passion for Pocahontas; a medicine-man and priest of the Indians . . . capable of every treason, stratagem, and crime . . . these, with the accidents of the wilderness, the war dances and cries . . . and the arrival of the English fleet, with allusions to the late glorious victories in Canada, and the determination of Britons ever to rule and conquer in America. . . .

Virginia's first important historical romancer, Dr. William Alexander Caruthers, wrote no novel dealing with the settlement of Jamestown; but in *The Cavaliers of Virginia* (1835) he included a striking scene which, as the novelist's biographer, Curtis Carroll Davis, has pointed out, was certainly borrowed from the Smith-Pocahontas story. The Chickahominy Indians have captured Nathaniel Bacon, condemned him to death, tied him to the stake, and begun to torture him. "At this moment a piercing scream rent the air, and all tongues were mute, all hands suspended." An "Indian female of exquisite proportions"—she is Wyanokee, daughter of the dead chieftain—rushes to the scene, throws herself "between the half immolated victim and his bloodthirsty tormentors," and cries: "Strike your tomahawks here, into the daughter of your chief, of him who led you on to battles and to victory, but harm not the defenceless stranger." The braves are reluctant to free the prisoner but finally consent when Wyanokee cries: "I will be his wife!" The marriage, however, turns out to be not a real marriage but a legal device to free Bacon.

One of the best of the many fictional treatments of the Smith-Pocahontas story is John Esten Cooke's *My Lady Pokahontas* (1885). This novelette, however, is not Cooke's first but his final treatment of the subject. In "A Dream of the Cavaliers," which appeared in *Harper's Magazine* in January, 1861, he had described Smith and Pocahontas as respectively:

> The founder of Virginia,
> And the pride of the Southern land!

Cooke retold the familiar story in greater detail in *Stories of the Old Dominion* (1879) and again in *Virginia: A History of the People* (1883). In *My Lady Pokahontas* he gives his style somewhat the flavor of a Colonial voyager's "true relation" by putting the narrative in the mouth of Anas Todkill, one of the Captain's "Old Soldiers." This device unfortunately necessitates our getting the story of the rescue at second-hand, and it makes of Todkill so persistent a worshiper of Pocahontas that one wonders that it never occurs to My Lady to ask: "Why don't you speak for yourself, Anas?" With one exception Cooke follows closely Smith's own account of events. Since he has chosen to represent Smith and Pocahontas as in love with one another, he has found it necessary to alter the character of Rolfe, who is here the villain who separates the lovers. Cooke's Rolfe is a most unlovable Puritan hypocrite, tormented by scruples about marrying a heathen but nevertheless eagerly spreading the false report that Smith is dead. Pocahontas is the very feminine type of Mrs. Sigourney's poem but much more lachrymose. There is nothing of the Indian in her character and personality. Even in his history of Virginia Cooke had written that her "kind heart and brave spirit belong to no clime or race."

The imaginary love scenes are woven into the texture of historical events with great skill. The last meeting of Smith and Pocahontas in London is an excellent example. Merely by putting the following sentence into the mouth of Smith: "The child forgot one who loved her," Cooke has turned the last meeting of two friends into the final parting of two hopeless lovers. The meeting takes place in the Globe Theatre, to which Pocahontas has been invited by the Queen. The play is *The Tempest*, by Captain Smith's good friend, Master William Shakespeare.

Is yonder truly the Princess Pokahontas? he [Shakespeare] asks. His friend Captain Smith hath told him how she once saved him, and he hath figured her in his *Miranda*, that is, *One to be wondered at*; as see where Miranda cries, "Beseech you, father! Sir, have pity; I'll be his surety!" when *Prospero* would smite down *Ferdinand* as Powhatan would

193

smite Smith. This *Ferdinand* is Smith, he says laughing, though a king's son; and *Caliban* is a deformed Indian, one Rawhunt, whereof Smith hath oft told him; which *Caliban* saith in the play that *Duke Prospero* calleth *Miranda* his "Nonpareil," which is what Captain Smith calleth the Lady Pokahontas.

Cooke has here anticipated the eminent Shakespeare scholar, Sir Sidney Lee, who saw Caliban as in some sort an Indian. In *The Tempest* there are echoes of what Shakespeare had heard or read of the wreck in the Bermudas of the *Sea Venture* while on her way to Virginia; but Shakespeare was, I fear, too much the "little Englander" to wish to celebrate Captain Smith's adventures in Virginia. American writers have always been tempted to bring into their stories of Colonial Virginia the glamorous figures of Elizabethan England: Shakespeare, Raleigh, and the great Queen herself.

The Jamestown Tercentenary of 1907 occasioned a number of plays, poems, and novels; but Vaughan Kester's *John o' Jamestown* (1907) is the only one which can be read with pleasure half a century later. I had hoped that the 350th anniversary of the notable event would bring forth something really worthy of the subject, but with the exception of Paul Green's *The Founders* I know of nothing of intrinsic importance.

The most interesting of the later novels is *Pocahontas or The Nonparell of Virginia* (1933), by the English novelist, David Garnett, who claims to have read the important historical documents and to have visited the Virginia scenes which he describes. He states in his preface that he has tried both "to draw an accurate historical picture and to make it a work of art." In so doing, he concedes, he has imprisoned his imagination in a "straight-waistcoat" and set it "the narrow, yet impossible, task of calling [his] characters from their graves and making them live, act, feel and think, though not speak, as once they did." Later in the book Garnett notes the writer's great difficulty in effacing from his mind the conventional historical picture so that he may substitute for it something better. In his best-known novel, *Lady into Fox* (1922), Garnett had not hampered his imagination with historical facts.

Pocahontas, whom Garnett tries to portray as a very real Indian woman, is almost the only admirable character in the book. The white settlers are for the most part dirty, unscrupulous, scheming and yet gullible. His conception of the Indian character, which is not unlike that of Fenimore Cooper, is that: "they knew no half-measures in feeling and behaviour. They could be cruel, treacherous, savage and inhumanly bloodthirsty; but within a few hours of having barbarously slaughtered his [Smith's] companions, they greeted him with song and laughter, with proffered fruits and gay glances."

Captain John Smith is "intensely pugnacious," always sure he is right, "violent in speech and more violent still in deeds." He seems on the point of betraying the settlers when he leaves Jamestown for England, "I would like a last look at the damned place," he remarks just before his ship sails down the James.

At the time of the rescue Pocahontas is still a child.

The stone tomahawks wavered for a moment, the throng slackened, but no one spoke or interrupted the child as she cried out with pathetic, tiger-cat defiance: "He is mine: my man. I take him." Then, a little less certainly, she added: "I am old enough. I want him. He can make me beads and coper bells."

Powhatan considered for a moment silently. Pocahontas was very young; it was absurd for her to claim to adopt this prisoner as a right, but he was very fond of her, and it would be difficult to have the man killed without making her furiously angry. The white man would be useful, no doubt, if he were one of the tribe, if he could really be trusted.

After Smith's departure for England Pocahontas is captured and brought to Jamestown. There she develops with incredible rapidity. This is how she impressed two of the ablest of the colonists:

Gates and Strachey had been used to meeting fine ladies of higher rank in England, and the girl beside them dominated them by her dress and her dignity. She was no savage child whom they had kidnapped in order to blackmail her doting father, but a princess of a royal house whom it was necessary to treat with chivalry and deference.

There is, however, still enough of the Indian in Pocahontas to make it sometimes extremely difficult for her husband, Rolfe, to understand her.

In England, which she has long dreamed of visiting, Pocahontas conducts herself admirably. In London we are introduced to Raleigh, now old and disillusioned, and to Ben Jonson, who is disgustingly drunk, and in London of course she meets Smith again. But this is not the Captain Smith whom Pocahontas had known in Virginia.

The Smith she had known was dead, and in his place was this fatter, thickened, middle-aged man. The fire had gone out of him, the air of authority had degenerated into a pitiful bluster. When that stopped, he looked quite empty.

At thirty-seven he was a failure. Something had snapped in him, and from being the hero of a hundred legendary exploits he had become an imposter. He knew, and every one else knew, that he was impersonating Captain Smith, the man he had been and was no longer.

When read as fiction, this scene and many others in Garnett's novel are impressive, but I do not believe that the novelist has given us the real Captain John Smith. Nor do I find the real Smith in the vain, uninhibited, and libidinous hero of Edison Marshall's *Great Smith* (1935). Marshall, Garnett, and other writers have relied too exclusively upon the debunking biographers. For my part I prefer the memorable tribute written by one of Smith's comrades-in-arms which is found in his *Map of Virginia* (1612) and appears again in *The Generall Historie of Virginia* (1624):

> What shall I say? but thus we lost him that, in all his proceedings, made Justice his first guide, and experience his second; ever hating basenesse, sloth, pride, and indignitie more then [than] any dangers; that never allowed more for himselfe then his souldiers with him; that upon no danger, would send them where he would not lead them himselfe; that would never see us want what he either had, or could by any meanes get us; that would rather want then borrow, or starve then not pay; that loved actions more than wordes, and hated falshood and covetousnesse worse then death; whose adventures were our lives, and whose losse our deaths.

5

In the earlier years of the present century, when the debunking of the traditional American heroes was fashionable, some of the more striking treatments of the Smith-Pocahontas story took the form of burlesque. The Pocahontas of Philip Moeller's *Pokey; or, The Beautiful Legend of the Amorous Indian* (1918) is the antithesis of the traditional modest lady of poetry and fiction. When the play opens, she is seen violently kissing Rolfe, who protests: "You mustn't kiss me to death. There's no such death on record." She threatens to throw him over the cliff unless he instantly promises to marry her. Just in the nick of time Captain John Smith comes to the rescue remarking: "When in danger, I remember the heroes"; and seizing Rolfe in his arms, he leaps over the cliff to safety. In the second scene we are introduced to Pocahontas's mother, a modernist, and to her grandmother, who holds fast by the old traditions. Pocahontas rescues Smith because she wants a husband. When the Captain learns that he is to be spared on condition that he marry her, he exclaims: "No. No. Kill me. Rather a thousand deaths than one anxious female." Fortunately, Rolfe reappears. Smith immediately demands that Rolfe fulfil the promise he had made when Smith rescued him from the like predicament. Rolfe finally agrees to marry Pocahontas, but he cannot help reminding Smith that the price of honor is high. Mrs. Powhatan says to her daughter: "Come here, darling, don't be timid. Marriage is one third imagination and two thirds keeping your eyes shut." Smith concludes: "You know, in a few centuries the whole thing may seem awfully jolly."

In the title poem of *Noah an' Jonah an' Cap'n John Smith* (1921) Don Marquis, a popular humorist and author of some excellent light verse, thus pictured:

> Noah an' Jonah an' Cap'n John Smith,
> Mariners, travelers, magazines of myth,
> Settin' up in Heaven, chewin' an' a-chawin'
> Eatin' their tobaccy, talkin' and' a-jawin'. . . .

In a dubious dialect resembling that of James Whitcomb Riley, they spin tall tales of their exploits as fishermen. Noah brags of the fish he caught while sailing in the Ark; Smith goes him one better when he recounts his adventures while fishing for "the perilousest varmints. . . the bloody octopuses"; but neither fisherman can match the exploits of Jonah, who catches the biggest fish of all, a whale. At the end of the contest we leave the yarn-spinners:

> Strummin' golden harps, narreratin' myth!
> Settin' by the shallows forever an' forever,
> Swappin' yarns an' fishin' in a little river!

A third burlesque is Christopher Ward's *The Saga of Cap'n John Smith* (1928). In a manner reminiscent of Gilbert and Sullivan the poet goodnaturedly satirizes the English, the Indians, the Boston Irish, and the Turks. Only the second of the three books deals with Smith's adventures in Virginia. When Powhatan is about to have Smith put to death, the cry is heard: "She comes! She comes!" and Pocahontas appears on the scene.

> She was a girl of sweet sixteen,
> The kind in movies often seen.
> All golden was her golden hair,
> Her cheeks like Georgia peaches,
> And on her legs she wore a pair
> Of English riding breeches.

A stetson hat was on her head.
Her eyes were blue as bluing.
Her nose was white, her lips were red,
But needed some renewing.
Her manner, people might be led
To think, was autocratic,
For "Stick 'em up!" was all she said,
And waved an automatic.

When she had procured Smith's release,

She blushed and softly murmured, "Now,
Please introduce him."

Pocahontas demands that Powhatan explain the mystery that surrounds her birth. She displays a handkerchief, which had belonged to her dead mother, embroidered with a lion, a unicorn, and the letter E; and she produces some letters addressed to Powhatan by "Your loving friend and playmate, Lizzie." The chieftain reluctantly explains that he is an English nobleman who had secretly married the youthful Princess Elizabeth but was dismissed when she became Queen of England. Although their daughter Pocahontas cannot prove her claim to the British throne, still—now that she is revealed as the daughter of the Earl of Upper Tooting—she obviously cannot marry plain Captain Smith. In a long speech Powhatan proposes an Anglo-American union while Pocahontas goes to sleep and Smith disappears to turn up next in Boston. Unlike other parodists, Ward concludes his book with a handsome "Apologia" to the shade of Captain Smith:

I know you, sir, for what you were,
Intrepid caballero,
A stout and brave adventurer,
A man of men, a hero.
And, though I think for chaff like this
You do not care a tinker's dam, sir,
If, perchance, it seems amiss
I'm sorry, Captain Smith, I am, sir,
And tender to you humbly these,
My most sincere apologies.

In *Young Love* (1936), a book of short stories, John Erskine continued to exploit the vein he had discovered eleven years earlier in *The Private Life of Helen of Troy*. In the ninth story he treats in flippant fashion the story of John Alden, Miles Standish, and Priscilla Mullins. Pocahontas is the central figure in the story entitled "Variation XIII." In the opening scene, which is by much the most effective, we are introduced to Pocahontas soon after the rescue. Smith has gone back to Jamestown. Powhatan is sitting in state under an elm, but the princess is standing "not because there wasn't a seat, but because she looked better standing." Powhatan is speaking: "Daughter, it was an error of judgment. You should have let me knock out his brains." He philosophizes: "Men hunt for two things— for food and for women. I gave him corn, but he wasn't satisfied. I then thought it must be women, and tried him out by letting you carry on communications with him, but he wasn't interested." Pocahontas insists that Captain Smith will return and marry her. Powhatan is not convinced: "You claimed him for a husband—and the tribe accepted him. Do you really believe he will forsake his people and remove the hair from his face and become one of us?" After Smith returns to England, she marries Rolfe when she discovers that her own people do not care to have her return to them.

6

In the period of disillusionment and rebellion that followed the First World War too few of our creative writers had any serious interest in the American past. Some of the younger writers, believing that their own country was dominated by Philistines, fled to London or Paris. Those influential expatriates, Ezra Pound, Gertrude Stein, and T. S. Eliot, saw little vitality in the American literary tradition and found little to interest them in their country's history.

There were notable exceptions of course; and conspicuous among them was Stephen Vincent Benét, whose best-known work is *John Brown's Body*, a romantic epic of the Civil War. At his death in 1943 Benét left unfinished a long poem dealing with the settlement of America and the westward movement across the continent. The completed portion of the poem was posthumously published in 1943 under the title *Western Star*. Benét undertook to commemorate the thousands of nameless pioneers rather than the traditional heroes, but he did introduce a few of the leading figures of Plymouth and Jamestown. He was somewhat kinder to Smith than Garnett and the writers of burlesques.

This bushy-bearded, high-foreheaded, trusting man
Who could turn his hand to anything at a pinch,
Bragging, canny, impatient, durable
And fallen in love with the country at first sight. . . .
        You can see the difference in Percy,
Who is always the Englishman among the natives
And never sheds his skin or his English ways,
A good man, an excellent colonial-governor
But not this skin-changing stepchild of Ulysses,
On fire, yes, fed or fasting, to see new things,
Explore, map out, taste, venture, enjoy, astound
And look, look, look with a fly's remembering eye,
A child's delight in marvels, a liar's gorgeousness,
And the patient, accurate pen that mapped two great coasts.

Pocahontas first appears as:

        A wild child-princess, bursting out of the woods,
Her train of girls behind her, shouting and screaming,
With deerhorns set on their foreheads—a Bacchant rout,
Led by the nonpareil, and daring child,
Who was to die a Christian and a lady
And leave her slight bones in the English earth
And her son's sons to know Virginia still,
Such being the fate.
        And they were to meet again,
Years later, in England, the lady Rebecca Rolfe
And Captain Smith—a strange meeting—strange and sad,
The Indian princess in her fine English clothes
And the bearded, baldish Ulysses, both nine years older
And one very soon to die as caged things will
Just when they seem acclimated to the cage.

The debunking biographers and historians have treated Pocahontas more kindly than Smith, and she has fared far better than he
at the hands of the twentieth-century poets. Two of them indeed
have seen in her a beautiful and fitting symbol of the American spirit.
In 1916 Carl Sandburg published "Cool Tombs," which contains the
memorable lines:

        Pocahontas' body, lovely as a poplar, sweet as a red haw
            in November or a pawpaw in May, did she wonder? does
            she remember? . . . in the dust, in the cool tombs?

These lines serve as epigraph for Vachel Lindsay's "Our Mother
Pocahontas," which was written in the following year. Lindsay's
parents were Southerners, and there was a special tenderness in his
feeling for Virginia. He wrote his poem "Virginia" when he was

asked to visit a London bank to see a gold model of the *Mayflower*. In 1917, when the United States declared war against Germany, patriotic feeling was intense; and Pocahontas seemed to Lindsay an appropriate symbol of the American spirit. The same natural forces that made her, he felt, had transformed European immigrants into the new race of Americans. We are the children of Pocahontas, the great American Earth Mother.

> Her skin was rosy copper-red.
> And high she held her beauteous head.
> Her step was like a rustling leaf:
> Her heart a nest, untouched of grief.
> She dreamed of sons like Powhatan,
> And through her blood the lightning ran.
> Love-cries with the birds she sung,
> Birdlike
> In the grapevine swung.
> The Forest, arching low and wide
> Gloried in its Indian bride.
> Rolfe, that dim adventurer,
> Had not come a courtier.
> John Rolfe is not our ancestor.
> We rise from out the soul of her
> Held in native wonderland,
> While the sun's rays kissed her hand,
> In the springtime,
> In Virginia,
> Our Mother, Pocahontas.

Pocahontas is no longer merely the guardian angel of the Jamestown colony but the spirit of all America that animates her children in a great war.

> Because gray Europe's rags august
> She tramples in the dust;
> Because we are her fields of corn;
> Because our fires are all reborn
> From her bosom's deathless embers,
> Flaming
> As she remembers
> The springtime
> And Virginia,
> Our Mother, Pocahontas.

Hart Crane, who wrote *The Bridge* (1930), in which Pocahontas again appears as an American symbol, was an admirer of T. S. Eliot, whose *The Waste Land* had created a sensation among intellectuals on its publication in 1922. Crane, however, was irritated by Eliot's

Anglophile tendencies, and he thought it inappropriate for an American-born poet to draw his imagery from such esoteric sources as Frazer's *The Golden Bough* and the legend of the Holy Grail. In treating "the Myth of America" in *The Bridge*, Crane wanted to show, he said, "the continuous and living evidence of the past in the inmost vital substance of the present." In the poem, to which he once referred as "an American epic," the dominant symbol is of course the Brooklyn Bridge, but other notable symbols are Columbus, Rip Van Winkle, Walt Whitman, and Pocahontas. The five poems which make up Part II are entitled "Powhatan's Daughter." In interpreting this difficult poem critics have been forced to rely heavily upon the poet's own explanation. In a long letter of September 12, 1927, Crane wrote:

Powhatan's daughter, or Pocahontas, is the mythological nature-symbol chosen to represent the physical body of the continent, or the soil. She here takes on much the same role as the traditional Hertha of ancient Teutonic mythology. The five subsections of Part II are mainly concerned with a gradual exploration of this "body" whose first possessor was the Indian.

Although Crane does not mention "Our Mother Pocahontas," his indebtedness to Lindsay's poem seems obvious.

In the subsection entitled "The River" the poet names among the many who have trekked westward the pioneers, the hoboes, and the "Pullman breakfasters." These and many others, says the poet, "have touched her without [knowing] her name."

> From pole to pole across the hills, the states
> —They know a body under the wide rain;
> Youngsters with eyes like fjords, old reprobates
> With racetrack jargon,—dotting immensity
> They lurk across her, knowing her yonder breast
> Snow-silvered, sumac-stained or smoky blue—
> Is past the valley-sleepers, south or west.
> —As I have trod the rumorous midnights, too,
>
> And past the circuit of the lamp's thin flame
> (O Nights that brought me to her body bare!)
> Have dreamed beyond the print that bound her name.
> Trains sounding the long blizzards out—I heard
> Wail into distances I knew were hers.

More beautiful perhaps is the subsection entitled "The Dance," which begins:

> The swift red flesh, a winter king—
> Who squired the glacier woman down the sky?

She ran the neighing canyons all the spring;
She spouted arms; she rose with maize—to die.

But I have quoted enough to suggest both the beauty and the difficulty of the poem.

Paul Green's pageant, *The Founders* (1957), is, as I have said, the best-known literary production occasioned by the 350th anniversary of the planting of the Jamestown colony; but it is, in my opinion, a less notable drama than *The Lost Colony* or *The Common Glory*. In an essay in his *Dramatic Heritage* (1953)—"Jamestown—Thoughts for a Symphonic Drama"—Mr. Green had suggested that the hero of his play would not be John Smith but John Rolfe. "It is," he wrote, "in John Rolfe's philosophy of work that his greatness and true heroism lie. . . .In him was represented the essential character of the English race. . . . She has been a nation of men who worked."

Workers no doubt played a greater part in the making, not only of Virginia but of all our thirteen colonies, than did the gentlemen adventurers; and the farmer's importance in American history is far larger than his place in our literature. But it is difficult to see why Mr. Green should, after reducing Captain John Smith to a minor figure, give the lead to this unattractive Puritanic widower whose chief claim to fame rests upon his marriage to an Indian "princess." He was also, it is said, the first Virginia farmer to produce tobacco of a marketable quality. Mr. Green makes of him a defender of the rights of the settlers, and an advocate of friendship with the Indians who hopes that his marriage to Pocahontas will bring peace between the two races. The hope is vain. Pocahontas dies in England, and Rolfe himself is killed in the Indian Massacre of 1622. Mr. Green's Rolfe is a good American citizen, but in the words of Vachel Lindsay, "John Rolfe is not our ancestor." In the epic of Jamestown he played a far humbler role than that of Pocahontas or Captain John Smith; and I do not believe that our American writers can ever make of him an American symbol comparable to what the great Captain and the Indian princess have become.

The Pocahontas of *The Founders* is an attractive figure. She first appears as "a spirited, petted young girl about thirteen years old." From the very first Rolfe is "all eyes for her and she for him." She is frantic when the settlers temporarily abandon Jamestown, and she prays to the God of her white friends for their safe return. She saves the colony from destruction at the hands of her uncle, Opecan-canough; but though a Christian she dies in England as a result of the incantations of her uncle's witch doctor.

Although the author of *The Founders* obviously does not care much for Captain John Smith, he gives him credit for courage and resourcefulness. When he first comes to Jamestown, the Captain is "about 28 years old, a stiff stocky figure of a man, bareheaded, bearded and in armor," but as a disturber of the peace he is in irons. He warns the colonists of the danger of an Indian attack. No one heeds his warning, and a little later one of the colonists is killed by an Indian arrow. He warns them that the food in the ship will spoil if not properly cared for. It does spoil; and it is Smith who goes to the Indians for food that saves the colonists from starvation. When Smith is captured by the Indians, the villainous Opecancanough wants to kill him. It is Pocahontas who out of pity rescues him, "claiming him for herself," getting him adopted into the tribe, but it is not Smith but Rolfe that she really wants. Jonas, who is Mr. Green's spokesman in the play, sums up for us: "A right-hearted man was Captain Smith, but with a mouth too big and quick-speaking for his own good, no doubt, and always projecking and jumping ahead till he got blowed up by gunpowder in an accident one day and went away half-dead to England forevermore." Smith simply drops out of the play. Mr. Green omits altogether the historic meeting with Pocahontas in London.

The vitality of the Smith-Pocahontas legend is abundantly proved by the extraordinary number of poems, plays, novels, short stories, and biographical works that deal with it. It is unquestionably one of our most memorable national legends; and if no poet has yet celebrated it in a poem as familiar as *The Courtship of Miles Standish* or *The Song of Hiawatha*, still it has inspired two or three poems of as high a poetic quality. Unfortunately, "Our Mother Pocahontas" and *The Bridge*, especially the last, involve difficulties that baffle the ordinary reader; and only a minority of Americans have yet seen the Indian princess as a beautiful and appropriate American symbol. But the end is not yet; there will surely be many more poems, novels, and plays retelling the fascinating story of Captain John Smith and the Princess Pocahontas and the beginnings of the Jamestown colony.

"Primus ego in patriam mecum ... deducam Musas"; for I shall be the first, if I live, to bring the Muse into my country.

VERGIL, *Georgics* as quoted in Willa Cather,
My Antonia (1918), Book III, Chapter 2

John Cotton: The Poet-Historian of Bacon's Rebellion

[When I began work on my projected history of Southern literature, no one knew who had written "Bacon's Epitaph, Made by His Man" or the history of Bacon's Rebellion known as "The Burwell Papers," in which it appears. I could not be content without full investigation merely to endorse the conclusion reached by my old teacher and friend, Professor W. P. Trent, who had written in his *History of American Literature* (1903): "It is the irony of fate that this devoted follower, who in a more favorable environment might have added another name to the galaxy of Restoration poets, should have left behind not only no other traceable verses, but not even an ascertainable name."

I found my first clue to the authorship of "The Burwell Papers" in a footnote in Moses Coit Tyler's history of our Colonial literature, published as long ago as 1878. It was not until later that I discovered that both Lyon G. Tyler and Lawrence Wroth had anticipated me in suggesting that the author of this notable history of Bacon's Rebellion was John Cotton of Queen's Creek, Virginia. Those scholars who have discussed "The Burwell Papers" since my article appeared in *American Literature* in May, 1938, seem to have accepted Cotton's authorship as an established fact.

Until my article appeared, no one had suggested that John Cotton was the author of the two poems on Bacon as well as the prose account of the Rebellion. I have pointed out those stylistic resemblances between the prose and the verse which led me to conclude that Cotton wrote the poems as well as the prose. My Duke University colleague, Allan H. Gilbert, whose knowledge of seventeenth-century English literature is unexcelled, confirmed my judgment that the poet and the historian were one and the same person. I am indebted to the late Morgan P. Robinson of the Virginia State Library for pointing out to me the various indications which convinced him that the manuscript of "The Burwell Papers" is in an eighteenth-century hand and so could not be Cotton's original manuscript. I wish I could have found materials with which I might have painted a clearer picture of our first important American poet, but such materials are in all probability no longer in existence.

The best and most recent account of Bacon's Rebellion is found in Volume I of Richard L. Morton's *Colonial Virginia* (1960). For two excellent discussions of the literature dealing with Bacon's Rebellion, see Howard Mumford Jones, *The Literature of Virginia in the Seventeenth Century* (1946) and Bertha-Monica Stearns, "The Literary Treatment of Bacon's Rebellion in Virginia," *Virginia Magazine of History and Biography*, LII, 163-179 (July, 1944). In my essay on the Virginia Cavaliers I have briefly discussed two of the more interesting items: Mrs. Aphra Behn's *The Widow Ranter* and William Alexander Caruthers' *The Cavaliers of Virginia*.]

Critics and literary historians have given high praise to the anonymous seventeenth-century poem, "Bacon's Epitaph, Made by His Man." Professor W. P. Trent, for example, has said of this memorable elegy, for it is an elegy rather than an epitaph:

. . . in this epitaph we have what is in all probability the single poem in any true sense—the single product of sustained poetic art—that was written in America for a hundred and fifty years after the settlement of

Jamestown. The twenty-two couplets would not have made Andrew Marvell blush could he have been taxed with writing them.

The poem appears in a manuscript account of Bacon's Rebellion generally known as "The Burwell Papers." The manuscript, now in the library of the Virginia Historical Society in Richmond, is in an eighteenth-century hand, and it lacks title page, signature, and the opening and closing pages. Congressman William A. Burwell, of Virginia, who sent the manuscript to his fellow-congressman, Josiah Quincy, of Massachusetts, wrote to the latter on December 20, 1812, that the manuscript "was found among the papers of the late Capt. Nathaniel Burwell, of King William County." Captain Burwell had procured it from "an old and respectable family of the Northern Neck of Virginia." Quincy sent the manuscript to the Massachusetts Historical Society, which printed it in its *Collections* for 1814 and again more fully and accurately in its *Proceedings* in 1866 under the title "The History of Bacon's and Ingram's Rebellion." After the second printing, the manuscript was placed in the keeping of the Virginia Historical Society.

1

The findings reported in this essay were reached by following up a clue contained in a footnote in Moses Coit Tyler's *A History of American Literature, 1607-1765*, published as long ago as 1878. After quoting "this noble dirge," Tyler asked: "Who was there in Virginia two hundred years ago with the genius and the literary practice to write these masterly verses? They alone shed splendor upon the intellectual annals of Virginia in the seventeenth century." Only in his footnote did Tyler suggest a clue to the authorship of "The Burwell Papers." Apparently it did not occur to him that the author of the prose narrative might also be the author of the poem. The footnote reads in part:

The authorship of these interesting manuscripts is still a matter of conjecture. My own opinion is that they were written by one Cotton, of Acquia Creek, husband of Ann Cotton, and author of a letter written from Jamestown, June 9, 1676, printed in Force, Hist. Tracts, I, No. 9. For this opinion, which I suppose to be new, the reasons cannot be given here.[1]

[1] For an illuminating study of how Tyler reached this conclusion, see C. E. Schorer, " 'One Cotton, of Acquia Creek, Husband of Ann Cotton,' " *American Literature*, XXII, 342-345 (Nov., 1950).

The first volume of Peter Force's *Tracts and Other Papers, Relating Principally to the Origin, Settlement, and Progress of the Colonies of North America* . . . (Washington, D. C., 1836) contains four items relating to Bacon's Rebellion, "The Burwell Papers" being No. 11. M. C. Tyler's footnote refers to Cotton's letter "To his Wife A. C. at Q. Creek," which is appended to another narrative of Bacon's Rebellion in Force's *Tracts*. This narrative—to which Tyler made no reference—is "An Account of Our Late Troubles in Virginia. Written in 1676, by Mrs. An. Cotton, of Q. Creeke," which Force had reprinted from Thomas Ritchie's Richmond *Enquirer* of September 12, 1804. John and Ann Cotton lived on Queen's Creek in York County not far from Williamsburg and not, as Moses Coit Tyler had supposed, on Acquia Creek in Stafford County over a hundred miles away.

Tyler must have observed certain stylistic resemblances between Cotton's fragmentary letter and "The Burwell Papers." In fact, Tyler's quotations leave the reader in no doubt on this point. If he carefully compared "The Burwell Papers" with Mrs. Cotton's narrative, he must have perceived that her account is little more than a condensation of his or else his narrative is an expansion of hers. Whole phrases are borrowed by one or the other. One often—if we may trust the *Enquirer* text—follows the other's erratic spelling. The sequence of events in both narratives is the same, and her dates and estimates of numbers seldom vary from his. Two examples must suffice here:

"The Burwell Papers"	Ann Cotton
Haueing [made] this resalution, and destroyed all things in the fort, that might be servisable to the English, they [the Indians] bouldly, undiscovered, slip through the Leagure, (leaveing the English to prossecute the seige, as Schogin's wife brooded the eggs that the Fox had suck'd) in the passing of which they knock'd ten men o' th head, who lay carelessly asleep in there way.	For the Indians haveing in the darke, slipt through the Legure, and in there passage knock'd 10 of the beseigers on the head, which they found fast a-sleep, leaveing the rest to prosecute the Seige (as Scoging's Wife brooding the Eggs which the Fox had suck'd) they resolved to imploy there liberty in avenging there Commissioners blood. . . .
This strange and unexpected news put him [Bacon], and som with him, shrodely to there trumps,	This strange newes put him, and those with him, shrodly to there Trumps, believeing that a few such

| beleveing that a few such deales, or shuffles (call them which you please) might quickly ring the cards and game too, out of his hand. | Deales or shufles (call them which you will) might quickly ring both cards and game out of his hands. |

A strong argument for John Cotton's authorship of "The Burwell Papers" is found in the manner in which a certain Henry Page, one of the leaders of the Rebellion, is mentioned in the two narratives. Mrs. Cotton refers to him as "one Leift. Collonell Page, (one that my Husband bought of Mr. Lee, when he [Cotton?] kep store at your howse)." In "The Burwell Papers" Page is called "Major Page, (once My Sarvant, at his [fir]st coming [into] the Countrey)."

My chief reason for regarding "The Burwell Papers" as the earlier account is that Ann Cotton's style in general is simpler and more direct than her husband's. I can explain her two incongruous modes of expression only by supposing that she was condensing and paraphrasing his narrative. While she was condensing his account—from forty-four pages in its fragmentary form to eight of her own—she could not resist the temptation to throw in some of her husband's "conceits," many of which seem to a modern reader far-fetched and out of keeping with his professed historical aims. At the end of her account Mrs. Cotton tells her friend C. H. that she has performed her task "too wordishly; but I did not know how to help it. . . ."

Ann Cotton's account of the Rebellion takes the form of a personal letter addressed "To Mr. C. H. at Yardly in Northamptonshire." C. H. (Christopher Harris?), who had lived in Virginia but was now back in England, had apparently asked for a copy of John Cotton's history of the Rebellion. In the Richmond *Enquirer* Mrs. Cotton's narrative—from which something is clearly missing at the very outset—begins:

Sr.

    I haveing seene yours directed to ——— [John Cotton?] and considering that you cannot have your desires satisfied that way, for the forementioned reasons, I have by his permition; adventured to send you this breife acount, of those afaires, so far as I have bin informed.

One can only speculate as to the "forementioned reasons." Cotton perhaps was unwell or unable to write and had no copy of his longer narrative to send to C. H. Not improbably also the Cottons may have felt that although he had tried hard to write an accurate and objective history of the Rebellion, his history contained passages that would give offense to the Royal Governor, who had hanged many of Bacon's followers. Cotton had some admiration for Bacon, but his history contains no defense of the Governor's conduct and he has praise for few of the Governor's lieutenants except Major Robert Beverley. In her account Ann Cotton makes no mention of the two poems included in her husband's narrative. If the vengeful Governor was still in Virginia and could have read "Bacon's Epitaph, Made by His Man," he would have wanted to hang the poet who had written it.

Moses Coit Tyler was the first to note a remarkable parallel between a passage in "The Burwell Papers" and Cotton's fragmentary letter appended to his wife's narrative. Here is the letter as it appeared in the Richmond *Enquirer* for September 12, 1804:

To his Wife, A. C. at Q. Creek.

My deare

Allthough those who have depicted that fickle Godes, Fortune, have represented her under various shapes, there by to denote her inconstancys; yet do I thinke there is not any thing sublunary, subjected to the vicissetudes of her temper so much as is the condition and estate of mankinde: All things ells partakes som thing of a stedfast and perminent decree excepting Man in the state of his affaires. The sun is constant in his Anuall progress through the Zodiack, the Moone in her changes, the other Planits in ther Asspects: The productions of the Earth have a fixed constant season for there groath and increase, when that man (in his creation litle inferiour to the Angles) cannot promise unto himself a fix'd condition, on this side Heaven.

How many hath thou and I read off, that the sun hath shined upon in the East, with honours and Dignityes, which his western beames hath seene clouded with poverty, reproaches and contumelles. The same moment that saw Ceaser cheife Man in the senate, beheld him in a worse condition then the meanest slave in Rome; and in less than 6 howers Phoebus ey'd the Marquis of Ancrey, in the midst of his Rustling traine of servitures, not onely streameing out his blood, but spurn'd and drag'd up and down the dirtie streets of Paris, by the worst of mecanicks. It is but the other day that I did see N.B.[1] in the condition of a Tratour, to be tryed for his life; who but a few days before was judged the most accomplish'd Gen:man, in Verginia to serve his King and countrey, at the councell Table, or to put a stop to the insolencies of the Heathen [Indians], and the next day rais'd to his dignities againe; Thus doth fortune sport her self with poore mortells, som times mount them up in to ye aire (as Byes [boys] do Tennis balls) that they may com with

[1] Nathaniel Bacon. (This note appears in the *Enquirer*.)

the grater violence downe, and then a gane strike them a gainst the earth that they may with ye grater speed mount up into the Aire, &c, &c.

From Towne, June 9, '76.

The same figure of fickle Fortune appears in "The Burwell Papers" four times and—what makes it the more remarkable—one of them appears in a passage dated on the margin of the manuscript "June 10. [Bacon] promised a Commission." At this point in the writing of his narrative Cotton must have remembered, if not his letter to his wife, at least the figure of speech which he had used in his letter from Jamestown.

And here who can do less than wonder at the muteable and impermanent deportments of that blinde Godes Fortune; who, in the morning loades Man with disgraces, and ere night crownes him with honours: Somtimes depressing, and againe ellivating, as her fickle humer is to smile or frowne, of which this Gen^t:mans fate was a kinde of Epittemey, in the several vicissetudes and changes he was subjected to in a very few dayes. For in the morning, before his triall, he was, in his Enimies hopes, and his Friends feares, judged for to receue the Gurdian [guerdon] due to a Rebell (and such hee was proclamed to be) and ere night, crowned the Darling of the Peoples hopes and desires, as the onely man fitt in Virginia, to put a stop unto the bloody ressalutions of the Heathen: And yet againe, as a fuller manifestation of Fortune's inconstancye, with in two or three days, the peoples hopes, and his desires, were both frusterated by the Governours refuseing to signe the promised Commission.

2

The evidence already given warrants, I think, the conclusion that John Cotton, the husband of Ann (or Hannah) Cotton, was the author of "The Burwell Papers." I believe he was also the author of the two poems which he gives: "Bacon's Epitaph, Made by His Man" and the reply to it entitled "Upon the Death of G.B. [General Bacon]." There is no conclusive evidence that he wrote either poem, and I shall merely present the considerations which led me to ascribe them to him.

My first reason is that among the known writers of seventeenth-century Virginia, Cotton is the only one who could conceivably have written either poem. There may have been, as Cotton states, many poems written on the death of Bacon, but I doubt it since I have been able to find only one other, this bit of doggerel ascribed to "an honest minister":

      Bacon's dead. I am sorry at my heart
      That lice and flux should act the hangman's part.

Cotton's prose style is a kind of belated Euphuism; it has little in common with the styles of his Virginia contemporaries, who seldom aim at elaborate literary effects. Cotton's excessive fondness for alliteration, balance, antithesis, "conceits," and classical allusions frequently—for the modern reader—spoils what is otherwise a good narrative style. The following passage illustrates the devices which he commonly employs:

But he [Major Lawrence Smith] perceueing that the Gloster Man did not weare (in there faces) the Countinances of Conquerors, nor there Cloathes the marks of any late ingagement (being free from the honourable Staines of Wounds and Gun shott) he began to hope the best, and the Gloster men to feare the worst; and what the properties of feare is, let Feltham tell you, who saith, That if curage be a good Oriter, feare is a bad Counceller, and a worse Ingineare. For insteade of erecting, it beates and batters downe all Bullworks of defence: perswadeing the feeble hart that there is no safety in armed Troops, Iron gates, nor stone walls. In opposition of which Passion I will appose the Properties of it's Antithesis, and say That as som men are never vallent but in the midst of discourse, so others never manifest there Courage but in the midst of danger: Never more alive then when in the jawes of Death, crowded up in the midst of fire, smoke, Swords and gunns; and then not so much laying about them through despareation, or to saue there lives, as through a Generosety of Spirit, to trample upon the lives of there enimies.

It seems to me that the two poems included in "The Burwell Papers" show the same general stylistic characteristics as Cotton's prose. I give both poems and the few lines of prose with which Cotton introduces them—after telling us that Bacon had "surrendered up that Fort he was no longer able to keepe, into the hands of that grim and all conquering Captaine, Death":

After he was dead he was bemoned in these following lines (drawne by the Man that waited upon his person, as it is said) and who attended his Corps to there Buriall place; But where depossited till the Generall day, not knowne, onely to those who are ressalutly silent in that particuler. There was many coppes of Verc̃es made after his departure, calculated to the Lattitude of there affections who composed them; as a rellish taken from both appetites I haue here sent you a cuple.

Bacons Epitaph, made by his Man

    Death why so crewill! what no other way
  To manifest thy spleene, but thus to slay

                                                      John Cotton

Our hopes of safety; liberty, our all
Which, through thy tyrany, with him must fall
To its late Caoss? Had thy riged force
Bin delt by retale, and not thus in gross
Griefe had bin silent: Now wee must complaine
Since thou, in him, hast more then thousand slane
Whose lives and safetys did so much depend
On him there lif, with him there lives must end.
    If't be a sin to thinke Death brib'd can bee
Wee must be guilty: say twas bribery
Guided the fatall shaft. Verginias foes
To whom for secrit crimes, just vengance owes
Disarved plagues, dreding their just disart
Corrupted Death by Parasscellcian art
Him to destroy; whose well tride curage such,
There heartless harts, nor arms, nor strength could touch.
    Who now must heale those wounds, or stop that blood
The Heathen made, and drew into a flood?
Who i'st must pleade our Cause? nor Trump nor Drum
Nor Deputations; these alass are dumb,
And Cannot speake. Our Arms (though nere so strong)
Will want the aide of his Commanding tongue,
Which Conquer'd more than Ceaser: He orethrew
Onely the outward frame; this Could subdue
The ruged workes of nature. Soules repleate
With dull Child could [dull chill cold], he'd annemate with heate
Drawne forth of reasons Lymbick. In a word
Marss and *Minerva*, both in him Concurd
For arts, for arms, whose pen and sword alike
As *Catos* did, may admireation [wonder] strike
In to his foes; while they confess with all
It was there guilt stil'd him a Criminall.
Onely this differance doth from truth proceed
They in the guilt, he in the name must bleed
While none shall dare his *Obseques* to sing
In disarv'd measures; untill time shall bring
Truth Crown'd wth. freedom, and from danger free
To sound his praises to posterity.
    Here let him rest; while wee this truth report
Hee's gon from hence unto a higher Court
To pleade his Cause: where he by this doth know
WHETHER TO CEASER HEE WAS FRIEND, OR FOE.

Upon the Death of G: B.

Whether to Ceaser he was Friend or Foe?
Pox take such Ignorance, do you not know?
Can he be Friend to Ceaser, that shall bring
The Arms of Hell, to fight against the King?

(Treason, Rebellion) then what reason haue
Wee for to waite upon him to his Grave,
There to express our passions? Wilt not bee
Worss then his Crimes, to sing his Ellegie
In well tun'd numbers; where each Ella beares
(To his Flagitious name) a flood of teares?
A name that hath more soules with sorow fed,
Then reched Niobe, single teares ere shed;
A name that fil'd all hearts, all eares, with paine,
Untill blest fate proclamed, Death had him slane.
Then how can it be counted for a sin
Though Death (nay though my selfe) had bribed bin,
To guide the fatall shaft? we honour all
That lends a hand unto a T[r]ators fall,
What though the well paide Rocht² soundly ply
And box the Pulpit, in to flatterey;
Urging his Rethorick, and straind elloquence,
T' adorne incoffin'd filth and excrements;
Though the Defunct (like ours) nere tride
A well intended deed untill he dide?
'Twill be nor sin, nor shame, for us, to say
A two fould Passion checker-workes this day
Of Ioy and Sorrow; yet the last doth move
On feete impotent, wanting strength to prove
(Nor can the art of Logick yeild releife)
How Ioy should be surmounted, by our greife,
Yet that wee Gĩve it cannot be denide,
But 'tis because he was, not cause he dide,
So wep the poore destressed Ilyum Dames
Hereing those nam'd, there Citty put in flames,
And Country ruing'd; If wee thus lament
It is against our present Ioyes consent.
For if the rule, in Phisick, trew doth prove,
Remove the cause, th'effects will after move,
We haue outliv'd our sorows; since we see
The Causes shifting, of our miserey.
    Nor is't a single cause, that's slipt away,
That made us warble out, a [ah] well-a-day,
The Braines to plot, the hands to execute
Projected ills, Death Ioyntly did nonsute
At his black Bar. And what no Baile could save
He hath commited Prissoner to the Grave;
From whence there's no repreive. Death keep him close
We haue too many Divells still goe loose.

I have not thought it advisable by the use of italics to indicate
the devices common to the prose and to both poems: the balancing

² A vestment of linen resembling a surplice often worn by bishops and abbots.

214   *John Cotton*

of word or phrase against word or phrase and the employment of alliteration partly for its own sake and partly to heighten the contrast. The following examples are drawn respectively from Cotton's prose, from "Bacon's Epitaph," and from "Upon the Death of G.B." All three have the same striking stylistic characteristics:

. . . Bacon knit more knotts by his owne head in one day, then all the hands in Towne was able to untye in a wholl weeke: While these Ladyes white Aprons became of grater force to keepe the beseiged from salleing out then his works (a pittifull trench) had strength to repell the weakest shot, that should haue bin sent into his Legūre, had he not made use of this invention.

> Our Arms (though nere so strong)
> Will want the aide of his Commanding tongue,
> Which Conquer'd more then Ceaser: He orethrew
> Onely the outward frame; this Could subdue
> The ruged workes of nature.

> A name that hath more soules with sorow fed,
> Then reched Niobe, single teares ere shed. . . .

The same type of figurative language appears in the prose and in both poems. Classical allusions are common in them all and are rare in the work of other historians of the Rebellion. The warlike subject would seem enough to suggest the allusions to Mars, but the other historians ignore Mars. The poems are too short for us to expect many parallels in word or phrase, and I have noted only two that are striking. In his prose Cotton refers to Bacon's burning of Jamestown as a "Flagitious, and sacralidgious action." In "Upon the Death of G.B." he has the phrase "To his Flagitious name." Cotton is fond of the legal term "non-suit" quite apart from legal matters. In "Upon the Death of G.B." we find:

> . . . Death Ioyntly did nonsute
> At his black Bar.

In his narrative Cotton writes of Governor Berkeley's misfortune in the selection of his "chiefe-commanders":

. . . that when his cause should com to a day of heareing, they should want Curage to put in there pleay of defence, against there Adverssarys arguments; and pittifully to stand still and see themselves nonsuted, in every sneakeing adventure, or Action. . . .

The language in which Cotton introduces the poems makes it seem probable that he was trying to divert from himself any suspicion of authorship. His suggestion that "Bacon's Epitaph" was composed by "his Man" seems almost incredible in spite of the fact that the Virginia planters occasionally employed educated indentured servants as tutors for their children. The poem is obviously the work of a very well-read man and of a practiced poet; so also is "Upon the Death of G.B.," of the authorship of which Cotton says nothing. Not much praise has been bestowed upon this poem, but some of the lines—and especially the concluding paragraph—are not unworthy of the author of the "Epitaph."

"Upon the Death of G.B." is obviously a reply to "Bacon's Epitaph, Made by His Man," and the language and the versification strongly suggest that both poems were the work of a single author. The two poems belong together, whether we take them as radically divergent expressions of Cotton's changing conception of Bacon or as a poetic debate—a well-known literary type—as to Bacon's character. The "Epitaph" is clearly the better poem of the two. It has the wit, the learning, and the technical skill which one might expect of one of the better minor English poets of the seventeenth century. It also has real feeling. It is entirely worthy of its place as our first notable poetic tribute to an American patriot who gave his life for his country.

"Upon the Death of G.B.," which is a point-by-point attempt at refuting the claims made for Bacon in the "Epitaph," expresses the disillusionment which many planters—and probably Cotton among them—felt after Bacon burned Jamestown and even more when, after Bacon's death and the collapse of the Rebellion, Virginians counted the cost of their disastrous civil war. Since "Upon the Death of G.B." was obviously composed after the "Epitaph" had been written, one may infer that the poet had changed his mind about Bacon. In his prose account—which I think was also written after the "Epitaph"—Cotton treats Bacon's death as due to "an admireable, and ever to be cellibrated providence."

The contrasting estimates of Bacon's character found in the two poems anticipated later American estimates. These tend to fall into two classes. Eighteenth-century Virginia writers painted Bacon as an ambitious demagogue, if not indeed as an actual traitor to King and country. It was not until after the Revolution that John Daly Burk and other American historians played up Bacon as a patriotic soldier-statesman who led an unsuccessful rebellion against a tyrannical

Royal Governor just a century before the signing of the Declaration of Independence. The earlier view of Bacon has recently been revived and forcefully presented in Wilcomb E. Washburn's *The Governor and the Rebel* (1957). But Richard L. Morton, whose *Colonial Virginia* (1960) gives our best account of the Rebellion rightly regards Washburn's book as not the history of the Rebellion implied in its subtitle but "a brief for the defendant, Berkeley." In spite of his shortcomings, it would seem that Nathaniel Bacon will continue to hold a place of honor among American soldiers who gave their lives in defense of their country's rights.

Cotton was a Virginia planter or merchant-planter. A number of the men in his social class and section for a time supported Bacon against the governor. After the burning of Jamestown, however, if not before, most of the planters deserted him. Thenceforth, says Cotton, the rebel soldiers were "sum'd up in freemen, [indentured] searvents and slaues; these three ingredience being the Composition of Bacons Army, ever since that the Governour left Towne."

Cotton's admiration for Bacon appears not only in the lines:

> In a word
> *Marss* and *Minerva*, both in him Concurd
> For arts, for arms, whose pen and sword alike
> As *Catos*, did admireation strike
> In to his foes. . . .

But also in his prose:

For though he was but a yong man, yet they found that he was master and owner of those induments which constitutes a Compleate Man, (as to intrinsecalls) wisdom to apprehend and descretion to chuse

and again in his fragmentary letter from Jamestown to his wife:

It is but the other day that I did see N. B. in the condition of a Tratour, to be tryed for his life, who but a few days before was judged the most accomplish'd Gen:man in Verginia to serve his King and countrey, at the councell Table, or to put a stop to the insolencies of the Heathen, and the next day rais'd to his dignities againe. . . .

For Ingram, who succeeded Bacon as commander of the rebel army, Cotton had nothing but contempt. It was probably Ingram and others of his kind that prompted the poet to write: *"We have too many Divells still goe loose."* Cotton shows no sympathy with Berkeley's cruelty in punishing the captured rebel leaders which (it is said) led King Charles II to exclaim: "As I live, the old fool has put to death more people in that naked country than I did here for the murder of my father." Near the very end of Mrs. Cotton's narrative appears a passage which would seem to have been based upon Cotton's lost conclusion:

[Those whom Berkeley executed were] enough (they say in all) to out number those slane in the wholl war; on both sides: it being observable that the sword was more favourable then the Halter, as there was a grater liberty taken to run from the sharpness of the one, then would be alowed to shun the dull imbraces of the other: the Hangman being more dredfull to the Baconians, then there Generall was to the Indians; as it is counted more honourable, and less terable, to dye like a soulder, then to be hang'd like a dogg.

3

In a passage quoted above, Cotton, without directly quoting, refers to Owen Felltham's essay "Of Fear and Cowardice" in the latter's *Resolves: Divine, Moral, and Political*, the second and third editions of which appeared in 1628 (the eighth appeared in 1661). Cotton's sentence: "I haue eather heard, or haue read, That a Compleate Generall ought to be owner of these 3 induments: Wisdom to foresee, Experience to chuse, and Curage to execute" is clearly derived from a similar passage in Felltham's "Of War and Soldiers": "The commanders in war ought to be built upon these three virtues: they should be wise, valiant, experienced."

In Felltham's *Resolves* Cotton could have found passages dealing with the acts of fickle Fortune in a Euphuistic style somewhat similar to his own. Felltham's first essay is entitled "Of Sudden Prosperity," and among the others one notes "Of the Uncertainty of Life," "Of Man's Inconstancy," "That All Things Have a Like Progression and Fall," "Of Misery after Joy," and "Of Fate." A figure in Cotton's letter, already quoted, resembles the following from Felltham's "That All Things Are Restrained": "We are all here like birds that boys let fly in strings: when we mount too high, we have that which pulls us down again."

Cotton's language suggests a familiarity with the medieval conception of tragedy as the fall of great men from high to low estate. The chief lesson which as historian he drew from the momentous events which took place around him is the uncertainty, the instability of human life. Perhaps he had read that passage in *The Faerie*

Queene in which Edmund Spenser stressed the mutability of the
human lot;

> What man that sees the ever-whirling wheel
> Of Change, the which all mortal things doth sway,
> But that thereby doth find, and plainly feel,
> How Mutability in them doth play
> Her cruel sports, to many men's decay?

And if Cotton had read Herodotus, he may have remembered that
on the eve of Cyrus's last battle and death his captive, the ill-fated
Croesus, had warned him that "there is a wheel on which the affairs
of men revolve, and that its movement forbids the same man to be
always fortunate."

Felltham was fond of such devices as balance, antithesis, and
alliteration. The following sentences in his "Against Compulsion"
might have been written by Cotton:

No doubt, nature meant Ceaser for a conqueror, when she gave him
both such courage and such courtesy; both which put Marius in a muse.
They who durst speak to him, he said; were ignorant of his greatness;
and they who durst not, were so of his goodness.

Felltham always renders into English the poetical passages from the
Latin which he quotes. In these one often finds the same devices that
we have noted in Cotton's poems. In the essay "That All Things
Have a Like Progression and Fall" appears this couplet:

> All that man holds, hangs but by slender twine,
> By sudden chance the strongest things decline.

More striking still are the lines from Horace's First Epistle—and the
antithesis in Felltham's English version is much more striking than
in the Latin original.

> Sad men hate mirth; the pleasant sadness shun;
> Swift men the slow; the slothful those that run.
> Who drinks, at midnight, old Falernian wine,
> Scorns him that will not take his cups.

I would not go so far as to suggest that Owen Felltham is Cotton's
original. If, as seems probable, Ann Cotton's parents and her friend
C. H. came from Northamptonshire, she and they may have had
some personal knowledge of Felltham, who lived in that shire with
his patron, the Earl of Thomond.

It is evident that John Cotton had read widely and was not

averse to making some display of his learning. Howard Mumford Jones comments on Cotton's reading:

He has read *Scoggan's Jests* and the *Resolves* of Owen Feltham, Thomas Fuller and the *Iliad*; he refers to the Koran, *Reynard the Fox*, Scanderbeg, *Euphues*, "Bellonies Bagpipe" and "Marsses whisle," the Copernican theory, "the hoggs the devill sheard," the fables of Aesop; the astrolabe, three essential properties of a general, and the titmouse which became an elephant.

The echo of the Eighth Psalm in "Man (in his creation litle inferiour to the Angles)" and references to Jacob, Esau, and Noah suggest a familiarity with the King James Bible which one might expect in the son of the Reverend William Cotton.

4

The published Virginia records indexed in Earl Gregg Swem's indispensable *Virginia Historical Index* tell us comparatively little about either John or Ann Cotton. He was a Virginia planter—very likely also a merchant—but not one of the great landholders although associated with them. From 1653 to 1681 extant court records suggest the friendly relations with other planters which are implied in his and his wife's accounts of the Rebellion. In a will dated April 30, 1660, the widow Eleanor Wheeler bequeathed "to John Cotton a gold seal ring," presumably because he was one of the witnesses to her will. The Widow Wheeler lived in York County, west of the Chesapeake Bay, but Cotton was at that time apparently still living in Hungars Parish in Northampton County on the Eastern Shore of Virginia. The church records of Hungars Parish show that to John and Hannah Cotton were born two children: Mary, who was baptized on October 21, 1660, and John, who was baptized on December 8 of the following year. On January 28, 1662, 350 acres of land in Northampton County, formerly granted to Nicholas Waddilow, were assigned to John Cotton. Cotton's name is not mentioned in "A List of Tithables in Northampton County, Anno Dom., 1666," probably because he had moved across the Bay to York County. At any rate, on December 31, 1666, he bought from Francis Wheeler all of the latter's land situated between Queen's Creek and Townsend Creek (later known as Yorktown Creek). Queen's Creek was the entry to the port of Williamsburg from the York River, and lighters came up Queen's Creek from the larger vessels in the York River to Capitol Landing, which is only a mile away. At some unspecified time Cotton conveyed the property he had bought from Francis Wheeler to Colonel Nathaniel Bacon, the wealthy and conservative cousin of the rebel General. Since the Colonel's house—"Ringfield," on King's Creek—was near his own, it seems not improbable that Cotton may have met the younger Bacon there. In 1678, two years after the Rebellion, Cotton was still living in York County. The incomplete records of the county on August 26 of that year mention one "Martin Palmer, Juryman in case of John Cotton, Pltf. vs John Harris & Philip Cocke." During the last quarter of the seventeenth century the larger planters were absorbing many of the smaller plantations and the smaller planters were moving westward or southward to take up new land. In Swem's *Virginia Historical Index* there are references to a John Cotton who in 1711 and 1712 lived at South Key (or South Quay) in Nansemond County in southeastern Virginia near the North Carolina line. If this was not our John Cotton— who by this time would have been nearly seventy years old—it was probably his son and namesake.

John Cotton was probably the second son of a man better known to Virginia antiquarians, William Cotton, the minister of Hungars Parish in Northampton County, the parish in which are found two of the earliest records of John and Ann Cotton. The Reverend William Cotton, who is supposed to have received a university education, was the son of Andrew Cotton, Gent., of Bunbury in Cheshire, and the grandson of Richard Cotton, Esquire, of "Combermere," Cheshire. Andrew Cotton's mother, Mary Mainwaring Cotton, was the daughter of Sir Arthur Mainwaring, Knight, of Ightfield, High Sheriff of Cheshire in 1563. Some time in the early 1630's William Cotton patented in his own name and that of his wife, Ann Graves Cotton, 350 acres on Hungars Creek. He named his Virginia estate "Bunbury" after his English home. It has been suggested that William Cotton may have accompanied John Winthrop to New England in the great Puritan migration of 1630. Be that as it may, we find him in the early 1630's on the Eastern Shore of Virginia, where it is known that a number of New Englanders settled. Whether or not William Cotton had leanings toward Puritanism, it is certain that his neighbor and brother-in-law, William Stone, later governor of Maryland, was a Puritan. Incidentally, there is a spirited letter from Cotton's aunt, Verlinda Stone, to Lord Baltimore, April 13, 1655, written while Governor Stone was in prison, which reveals some education and the ability to write excellent English prose.

After the death of her husband, Ann Graves Cotton married the notorious Nathaniel Eaton (*circa* 1609-1674), one-time head of Harvard College but without the title of President. Cotton Mather refers to him as "one fitter to be master of a Bridewel than a colledge." Eaton, who had studied at Trinity College, Cambridge, came to Massachusetts in 1637. He was charged with avarice, cruelty, and other offenses and was finally excommunicated. Leaving behind him his family and debts aggregating a thousand pounds, he came to the Eastern Shore of Virginia as an assistant rector. (Perhaps he was William Cotton's assistant.) After the death of his own wife, Eaton married Cotton's widow, whom James Truslow Adams describes as "the only surviving child of Thomas Graves of Dorchester, Mass." Eaton apparently soon deserted her. He returned to England and died in a debtors' prison in Southwark.

William Cotton's will—dated August 20, 1640—was proved on November 11, 1646. In the will, as Lyon G. Tyler describes it, the minister desires to be buried by his two little children; to his child yet unborn he gives his plantation at "Bunbury" and his Negro slaves; in default of issue to his mother, Joane Cotton, and the other one-third to his wife Ann [Graves] Cotton; brother-in-law Captain William Stone and Captain William Roper to be overseers of his will. Both of Cotton's surviving sons, John and William, Jr., must have been born after the minister made his will on August 20, 1640. John Cotton could hardly have been more than thirty-four or -five at the time of Bacon's Rebellion.

Cotton shows his greatest familiarity with those events of the Rebellion which occurred in or near York County, where he lived. He must have known three of the executed rebels from that county —Hansford, Farlow, and Chisman (or Cheesman)—and he was obviously disgusted with the governor's treatment of Mrs. Chisman (he called her a "whore" when she begged Berkeley to punish her instead of her husband). In his narrative Cotton has little to say about Bacon's projected reforms; but as the nephew by marriage of William Stone, who had led an insurrection in Maryland eleven years earlier, he may have had more sympathy with the Virginian rebel than most men in his class.

Cotton gives in some detail the events which took place at "Ringfield," the home of his neighbor, Colonel Bacon. It was at "Ringfield," where the governor landed after General Bacon's death, that the rebel leader Drummond was captured. Mrs. Cotton states that the governor came ashore "at coll, Bacons, where he was presented with Drumond; taken the day before in Cheekanonimy [Chickahominy] swomp, half famished, as him self related to my Husband." Cotton is more impersonal than his wife, and he never specifically mentions any part which he had in either aiding or suppressing the Rebellion. Nevertheless the imperfect lines at the end of "The Burwell Papers" and the passage just quoted from his wife's account strongly suggest a first-hand knowledge of Drummond's last hours. Cotton himself was in all probability the person referred to in the very last fragmentary sentence of his narrative: "He [Drummond] discoursed very much, with that person who comm[anded] his gard, concerning the late troubles, affirming that he was wholly innocent of those. . . ." Cotton was one of "a party of Horse" that conveyed Drummond from the elder Bacon's home at "Ringfield" to Colonel Bray's for trial; and it was probably Cotton who offered Drummond a horse to ride (which he refused), permitted him to rest on the road and smoke his pipe, and listened to what Drummond had to say shortly before his execution. If Cotton was to write a history of the Rebellion, it was essential that he hear what one of Bacon's ablest advisors had to say in defense of the general and himself.

Cotton's account of the meeting at Middle Plantation—it runs to nearly five pages—is so detailed that I believe he was present when Bacon forced the reluctant planters to take an oath to defend him not only against the governor but against any soldiers who might be sent over from England until an appeal could be made to the King. This "Illegal Oath" to Cotton's mind marked the real beginning of "rebellion." In describing the meeting Cotton's style becomes more vivid and direct; there are few Euphuisms in these pages. He refers to Bacon's "specious and subtill pretences," but his presentation of Bacon's eloquent indictment of Governor Berkeley suggests that it made a profound impression upon the historian. He concludes his summary of one of Bacon's impassioned speeches by turning from indirect to direct discourse and giving us in half a page the General's moving peroration. It was probably with this speech in mind that the poet wrote:

> Our Arms (though nere so strong)
> Will want the aide of his Commanding tongue,
> Which Conquer'd more then Ceaser: He orethrew
> Onely the outward frame; this Could subdue
> The ruged workes of nature.

Cotton's professed attitude is that of the objective historian, and he is careful to distinguish between what he believes to be true and what may be only hearsay. After mentioning one incident, he adds: ". . . but this I have only upon report, and must not aver it upon my historicall reputation." In another instance he writes: ". . . (and further I cannot go for want of a guide)." On the other hand, when he tells us that at Colonel Bacon's place the rebels had made away with property valued at not less than £2000, he inserts the phrase " (to my certaine knowledge)."

What we know or can legitimately infer in regard to John Cotton is very little. He apparently held no important office such as would have given him a larger place in Colonial records. He tells us that he talked with Captain Grantham, who induced Ingram to surrender to Berkeley, but Grantham in his own narrative makes no mention of Cotton. The one record which seems to give us a glimpse of the man suggests only that, like many of his contemporaries, he sometimes drank to excess. In the York County Court on June 21, 1681, one John Heyward testified that two and a half years earlier he had met John Cotton at the home of James Pardoe, where Cotton had gone to demand payment in tobacco of a bill which Pardoe owed to Thomas Bevins. Heyward testified that "by the request of the said Pardoe" he and Cotton "did continue drinking all day till at night we went to cards" and that he and Cotton quarreled over cards. Cotton then went to bed, but Heyward and Pardoe "did fall to drinking again." Pardoe later asked Heyward "to look over Tho. Bevins' papers and to see if his bill was not there." Heyward concluded his testimony by saying: "Your Deponent in looking over the papers did find the said Bevins' his bill uncanceled and did give it to the said Pardoe and your Deponent will swear and further saith not." Presumably this is our John Cotton, but since there were others of the same name in Virginia, one cannot be sure. It could have been Cotton's son and namesake.

Ann Cotton is said to have been "a descendant of the Harrisons of Gobion's Manor, Northamptonshire, and a cousin of Sir John Bernard of Abington." The Harrisons, like Francis Wheeler, from whom John Cotton bought his Queen's Creek property, were Cavaliers. Cotton himself had some sympathy for their cause, for he refers to "Verginia (the Onely Citty of Refuge left in his Majesties dominians, in those times, for destressed Cavallers)." John and Ann Cotton and their friend C. H., whom the late Francis Burton Harrison tentatively identified as Christopher Harris, were associated with the more prominent Virginia planters of the Tidewater. They were near neighbors of the elder Bacon of "Ringfield," one of the great landholders, a member of the Council of State, and at a later period Acting Governor of Virginia. Christopher Harris's wife was a stepdaughter of this conservative planter. Harris was in Virginia as early as 1641 but returned to England before the younger Bacon arrived in 1674. In 1661 Harris took his seat for the last time on the bench of the York County Court. In the same year the elder Bacon was buying property from Mrs. Harris. It would seem that the Harrises were about to return to Northamptonshire. In her account of the Rebellion Ann Cotton twice refers to a "former letter" in which she had said something about the Indian troubles which occasioned the Rebellion and had mentioned the meeting of planters at Middle Plantation where Bacon forced them to take an oath to support him against the governor. Christopher Harris would naturally ask for further information about the insurrection. He had known a number of persons, on both sides, who were actively involved in the Rebellion. John Cotton in his narrative gives us few of the names mentioned below, but Ann Cotton mentions by name the "cheife men" who subscribed to the oath which Bacon forced on them at Middle Plantation: "coll. Swan, coll. Beale, coll. Ballard, Esq. Bray, (all foure of the councell) coll. Jordan, coll. Smith, of Purton, coll. scarsbrook, coll. Miller, coll. Lawren[c]e, and mr. Dromond, late Governour of [North] Carolina; all persons, with whom you have bin formerly acquainted." Mrs. Cotton, unlike her husband, gives us the names of prominent planters' wives whom Bacon seized and paraded on the breastworks he had erected at Jamestown to prevent an attack by Berkeley's superior forces: "coll. Bacons Lady, Madm. Bray, Madm. Page, Madm. Ballard, and others." Mrs. Cotton also mentions George

Washington's first American ancestor, Colonel John Washington "(him whom you have sometimes seene at your howse)." He also had come to Virginia from Northamptonshire. Ann Cotton names among the rebels who were hanged some persons that C. H. had known: "James Wilson (once your servant) and one Leift. Collonell [Henry] Page, (one that my Husband bought of Mr. Lee, when he kep store at your howse) . . . and Anthony Arnell (the same that did live at your howse)."

5

It is evident that John Cotton was a man of some education and a practiced writer of considerable talent. The care with which his narrative was composed indicates that he intended it either for publication or, much more probably, for circulation in manuscript. It is apparently, like William Byrd's *History of the Dividing Line*, describes the Eastern Shore peninsula in considerable detail. No Cotton assumes no detailed knowledge of Virginia geography. He describes the Eastern Shore peninsula in considerable detail. No Virginian reader would have needed to be told that Middle Plantation, or Williamsburg, is situated in the "very heart of the Countrey." Few Virginian readers would have needed to be told that West Point is "an Isthmos which gives the Denomination to the two Rivers, Pomunkey and Mattapony (Indian names) that branch forth of York River, Som 30 Miles above Tindells point." Ann Cotton omits her husband's detailed description of the "island" on which Jamestown was situated and adds: ". . . it [the isthmus connecting the "island" with the mainland] being the onely place (as you do know well enough) for those in towne to make a salley at." Only twice does Cotton seem to have an individual reader in mind. In introducing the two poems about Bacon he writes: "I have here sent you a cuple." And again, in introducing his description of Jamestown he writes:

. . . this being the onely place, by land, for him [Bacon] to make his entrey, into the Towne: But for your better satisfaction, or rather those who you may show this Naritive to, who have never bin upon the place, take this short description.

Perhaps Cotton wrote his history of the Rebellion for Christopher Harris with the expectation that it would find other readers in

England but finally decided that there were passages in his narrative—including the "Epitaph"—which would be difficult to explain to the Royal Governor or his partisans or Englishmen having any official connection with the Virginia colony.

We are fortunate in that both John and Ann Cotton kept copies of their accounts of the Rebellion. One copy of Cotton's narrative became the chief source of Ebenezer Cooke's Hudibrastic satire, "The History of Colonel Nathaniel Bacon's Rebellion in Virginia."

Cotton's prose style is somewhat pedantic and old-fashioned. Neither in his prose nor in the two poems does he show the influence of Neoclassical writers. His couplets are not those of Waller or Dryden, and his prose is not that of the new school. Indeed, we should hardly expect a writer, born in Virginia, who apparently never was in England, to keep up with the latest literary fashions. As a prose writer, Cotton belongs with the later English Euphuists; as a poet, with the so-called Metaphysical school. In reading Cotton's two poems I have been reminded of some of the poems of Ben Jonson, John Donne, Andrew Marvell, and Bishop Henry King. Cotton was an amateur writer; but like that better-known Virginian, William Byrd II, he exhibits the draftsmanship of a professional. We have only two of Cotton's poems, but even so he deserves to rank with that other American Metaphysical poet, Edward Taylor of Massachusetts, whose poems were still unpublished when this essay first appeared in 1938.

Since Nathaniel Bacon's death in 1676 many men and women have written about the Rebellion that bears his name; but nothing thus far published rises to a higher level of literary excellence than "Bacon's Epitaph, Made by His Man." When the student of our Colonial literature comes upon this poem after struggling through the crabbed verses of *The Bay Psalm Book* and the feeble and fulsome elegies that bemourn the deaths of Puritan and Anglican divines, his reaction is like that of an editor of the *North American Review* who when he first read Bryant's "Thanatopsis" in manuscript exclaimed: "That was never written on this side of the water!" The "Epitaph" is, in the words of Louis Untermeyer, "our first indubitable poem."

. . .it is my solemn conviction that being a Virginian has a significance not attached to nativity in any other State. . . . A recent study has given me a fresh impression of the reality of the Virginian tradition. The stuff is there. Virginians have no need to inflate their State pride with myths and legends. . . .

GERALD W. JOHNSON, "A Tarheel Looks at Virginia," *North American Review*, CCXXVIII, 238 (August, 1929).

Cavaliers and Indentured Servants in Virginia

[This essay, first published in the *South Atlantic Quarterly* in January, 1927, was a part of my Columbia University dissertation, "Virginia Life in Fiction." The dissertation, never published in its entirety, was completed five years before the publication of F. P. Gaines's *The Southern Plantation* (1924).

In 1919, so far as I could ascertain, only an Englishman, Arthur Granville Bradley, was fully aware of the extent of the Virginian idealization of the past. As a young man Bradley had spent ten years as a farmer in Virginia. He afterwards edited the works of Captain John Smith and wrote many articles on Virginia topics for British magazines. Most of these were reprinted in his *Sketches from Old Virginia* (1897) and *Other Days* (1913). In an article published in *Blackwood's Magazine* in April, 1913, he wrote: "In all current literature there is nothing more remarkable than the way in which writers have unconsciously conspired to over-idealise Virginia."]

1

Whatever the actual number of Cavaliers who settled in Virginia, nothing is clearer than that both their number and their social status came to be greatly exaggerated. In England the term implied, not a social distinction but a political affiliation: the Cavaliers supported Charles I against the Parliament. Englishmen of all classes were divided by the Civil War, but the Parliamentary party drew more heavily from the middle classes and the townsmen while the King's adherents came more often from the higher and the lower classes and from the country.

There is no way of ascertaining how many Cavaliers came to Virginia or what proportion of those who came belonged to the gentry, but undoubtedly more Cavaliers came to that colony than to any other. The Virginia historians who have most thoroughly studied the subject have failed to agree in their interpretation of the rather meager evidence. Philip Alexander Bruce thought their numbers considerable and their influence very great. Thomas J. Wertenbaker in his *Patrician and Plebeian in Virginia* contended that the number of Cavalier gentlemen who came to Virginia was negligible and their influence not very important. In an unpublished University of Virginia dissertation John E. Manahan questioned the accuracy of Wertenbaker's conclusion. In a recent study, "Social Origins of Some Early Americans,"[1] Mildred Campbell concluded that the great majority of the immigrants to Virginia were not gentlemen or political prisoners or convicts or "laborers at the bottom of the economic scale. . . both those who came under indenture and those who paid their own fare, were drawn from the middling classes: farmers and skilled workers, the productive groups in England's working population."

All authorities seem to agree that the most important section of the large-scale Virginia planters belonged to families of merchant stock. In England many merchant families were sprung from or allied with the gentry, and younger sons of country gentlemen often went into "trade." In Virginia, as Governor William Berkeley noted, "a small summe of money [would] enable a younger brother to erect a flourishing family in a new world, and add . . . strength,

[1] *Seventeenth-Century America*, ed. James Morton Smith (Chapel Hill, N. C., 1959), pp. 63-89.

wealth, and honour, to his native country." Bruce estimated that in the three eastern counties of Essex, Lancaster, and Middlesex there were forty-seven families entitled to the use of a coat-of-arms. Lyon G. Tyler estimated a total of at least one hundred and seventy-five for the whole colony. No doubt the majority of these families were Cavaliers or of Cavalier ancestry.

In his edition of the *Writings* of William Byrd II, John Spencer Bassett wrote:

The aristocratic form of Virginia society was fixed soon after the Restoration of the Stuarts. It proceeded from economic, social, and political causes. On its economic side it was supported by land and servitude; on its social side it was sustained by the ideals, and somewhat by the blood of the English country gentlemen; on its political side it was fostered by a system of appointments to office which left the least room for a democracy.

Of the influence of the Cavalier planters, Bassett said:

They were not numerous, as compared with the older population, but they had an influence out of proportion to their numbers. They gave manners a warmer tone; they emphasized the ideal of country life; they gave Virginians their passion for handsome houses and fast horses; and they gave public life something more than it had before of the English notion that offices should be held for the benefit of the gentry.

To illustrate the growth of the Cavalier legend, I give in chronological order a number of estimates, taken chiefly from historical works. Sir Josiah Child, writing before 1670, said: "Many of them [the Cavalier soldiers] betook themselves to the aforesaid *Plantations* [Virginia and the Barbadoes]." The Earl of Clarendon in his history of the English Civil War wrote about the same time: "Many persons of condition and good officers in the war had transported themselves [to Virginia] with all the estates they had been able to preserve." John Cotton, the historian of Bacon's Rebellion, writing soon after 1676, referred to Virginia as "the Onely Citty of Refuge left in his Majesties Dominians, in those times, for destressed Cavallers." In 1701 Governor Nicholson wrote: "In the Civil War several gentlemen of quality fled hither." In 1708 the English historian Oldmixon wrote: "Several Royalists remov'd thither." He added: "Many Gentlemen of *Virginia* may boast as good Descents as those in *England*: But there's no need as yet of an Herauld-Office to be set up at *James-Town*." Robert Beverley wrote in his *History of Virginia* (1705): "Several good Cavalier families went thither with their effects." Hugh Jones wrote in *The Present State of Virginia* (1724): "This safe receptacle enticed over several *Cavalier* Families." The word "several," which appears in four of the passages just quoted, does not suggest the wholesale migration of the gentlemen who followed Charles I.

The *Virginia Gazette* for March 11, 1737, stated that Sir John Randolph's father "resolved (as many other *Cavaliers* did) to take his Fortune in this Part of the World." Lord Adam Gordon, who visited Virginia in 1764, wrote: "The first Settlers were many of them younger Brothers of good Families, in England." Writing about the time of the American Revolution, William Robertson, the British historian, said: "Many adherents to the royal party, and among these some gentlemen of good families . . . resorted thither."

After the American Revolution the numbers of the Cavaliers supposed to have come to Virginia increased rapidly, and the fact that the majority of the immigrants did not belong to the gentry was quickly forgotten. In 1804 John Marshall in his *Life of Washington* referred to "the great number of cavaliers, who, after the total defeat of their party in England, fled for refuge and safety to Virginia." John Daly Burk was too good a democrat to wish to magnify their numbers, yet even he said in his *History of Virginia*: "The vigilant and severe government of the Protector, had compelled the cavaliers to resort in crouds to Virginia."

The increase in the number of the Cavaliers supposed to have come to Virginia is particularly noticeable in the 1830's. The phrase "Southern chivalry," apparently unknown in the Colonial period, now came into use. Dr. William Alexander Caruthers' *The Cavaliers of Virginia* (1835) marks the first important literary treatment of the Virginia Cavaliers. Caruthers saw in them "the first founders of the aristocracy . . . the immediate ancestors of that generous, fox-hunting, wine-drinking, duelling and reckless race of men, which gives so distinct a character to Virginians wherever they may be found." Caruthers even turned into Cavaliers the numerous men of the lower classes who followed Nathaniel Bacon at the time of the Rebellion. In his *History of the United States* George Bancroft, stretching the language of Clarendon, wrote: "Many of the recent emigrants had been royalists in England, good officers in the war, men of education, of property, and of condition." Dr. Francis L. Hawks wrote in his *Ecclesiastical History of the United States*

(1836): "Hundreds of the cavaliers sought and found refuge within her [Virginia's] borders." In 1849 a New York writer, James Kirke Paulding, wrote in *The Puritan and His Daughter*: "It [Virginia] was, as everybody knows, originally settled by Cavaliers." In 1859 W. C. Rives wrote in his life of James Madison: "Down to the period of the Restoration . . . the great mass of the emigration from England to Virginia must have been, as unquestionable historical proofs show that it was, of the Cavalier strain."

The later Virginia writers we need not notice in detail. It should be stated, however, that John Esten Cooke's *Virginia: A History of the People* (1883), much used by later novelists, continued the tradition undiminished. Even John Fiske, who in his *Old Virginia and Her Neighbors* (1897) refuted the popular notion that the term "Cavalier" implied gentle birth, said: "There can be little doubt that these Cavaliers were the men who made the greatness of Virginia."

In the final stage of the legend Southerners in all the Southern states became descendants of the Cavaliers. In 1860 Senator Robert Toombs of Georgia is reported to have said: "We [of the South] are a race of gentlemen." An English writer, Arthur Granville Bradley, who came to live in Virginia after the Civil War, wrote: "A legend exists among the more uninformed circles of modern Virginia, that quite a considerable portion of the population are, in some mysterious fashion, sprung from the loins of the 'British Nobility.' "

Against this tendency to exaggeration there were, even in antebellum Virginia, occasional protests. Bishop William Meade, who knew something of Virginia genealogy, thought the number of Cavaliers not large enough "to make an impression on the Virginian character." In 1855 Hugh Blair Grigsby, in the midst of an oration upon the Virginia statesman of the Revolution, indignantly spurned the "outrageous calumny" of a Cavalier ancestry. He denounced the Cavalier as "essentially a slave—a compound slave—a slave to the king and a slave to the church." "Sir, I look with contempt," he said, "on that miserable figment, which has so long held a place in our histories, which seeks to trace the distinguishing and salient points of the Virginia character to the influence of those butterflies of the British aristocracy."

The Civil War inevitably suggested the traditional contrast of Puritan and Cavalier, and in Southern war poems "knightly" and

"Cavalier" are epithets of frequent occurrence. Northerners quite naturally resented such epithets as "low-born shop-keepers" which Southerners freely bestowed upon them, and retorted in no kindly manner that the Virginians were the descendants of criminals. "Not one-tenth certainly, probably not one-thousandth, of the fathers of Virginia were of gentle blood," wrote Frederick Law Olmsted. "The majority of them," he added, "were sold and bought as laborers." Even as late as 1864 so widespread in the North was the belief in the Cavalier tradition that Charles Sumner felt it necessary to devote over one-fourth of a long political speech in the U. S. Senate to a learned attempt to prove that the Virginians were in reality the descendants of convict servants of a most disreputable character.

The most amazing proof of the power of the tradition is found in the manner in which it impressed itself upon British visitors. G. P. R. James wrote in 1858: "The Virginians, sprung for the most part from the old Cavaliers, retain the more frank and profuse spirit of their race." Thackeray embodied the tradition in *The Virginians* (1857-1859). As late as 1883 Matthew Arnold wrote from Richmond: "Virginia . . . was colonised not by the Puritans, but by English gentry." In fact, it was probably the Cavalier tradition as much as anything else that gave the English their sympathy for the Confederate cause. In 1884 Bradley wrote: "Every one will remember the vulgar notion with which a certain portion of the English public, during the American civil war, became impregnated, namely, that the South was a nation of gentlemen in the social sense, fighting against hordes of *canaille*."

The greatest increase in the number of Cavalier families supposed to have settled in Virginia came about in the 1830's, and it coincided with a change in the Virginian attitude toward slavery. Slavery, which had seemed a moribund institution that no one defended on principle, again became profitable (or so it seemed) because of the great demand for slaves on the new cotton plantations in the Southwest. Thomas R. Dew, Beverley Tucker, George Fitzhugh, and other representatives of "Young Virginia" began defending slavery as a beneficent institution and attacking the "free society" of the industrial North. About this time there was, one recalls, a reaction against democracy in Europe, too, and there was a conservative "Young England."

In this period Virginia was slowly rebuilding its planter aristocracy, much of it out of new materials. The *nouveaux riches* there and elsewhere have been known to lay claim to ancestors not certainly their own. The years that followed the Revolution saw hard times in the Old Dominion. Few of the great planter families managed to hold on to their ancestral estates, many of which were weighed down by old inherited debts to British merchants. Jefferson had managed to have repealed the laws of primogeniture and entail which had enabled planters to keep their large estates intact from generation to generation. Unscientific agricultural practices had in many places exhausted the once rich soil of the Tidewater. The slaves had become too numerous to be profitable. John Randolph of Roanoke is said to have predicted that eventually the masters would run away to avoid having to feed and care for their slaves. The fine Colonial houses of the old First Families by 1830 had almost all passed into alien hands. In 1833 Henry Clay, who had grown to manhood in Virginia, said in one of his most eloquent passages:

In whose hands now are the once proud seats of Westover, Cerles, Maycocks, Shirley, and others on the James and in lower Virginia? They have passed into other and stranger hands. Some of the descendants of illustrious parentage have gone to the far West, while others, lingering behind have contrasted their present condition with that of their venerated ancestors. They behold themselves excluded from their fathers' houses, now in the hands of those who were once their fathers' overseers, or sinking into decay.

Is it any wonder that descendants of the First Families looked back to the years before the Revolution as a golden age and magnified their ancestors? They knew that the Colonial farmers had modeled their way of life upon that of English country gentlemen, and by now they had come to imagine that all of King Charles's Cavaliers had belonged to the gentry if not indeed to the nobility. The historical romances of Sir Walter Scott, Harrison Ainsworth, Bulwer-Lytton, and G. P. R. James may have had some influence upon the tendency to magnify the Cavaliers; but one must not imagine that Virginian farmers really thought that their way of life was that of the Norman nobles who overran England in 1066 or their descendants in the time of Richard Coeur-de-Lion.

While the Virginians were boasting of their Cavalier ancestors, Americans in other states were idealizing their own forefathers. New Yorkers of Dutch descent were pointing with pride to the old

Knickerbocker families, and Pennsylvanians and Marylanders were magnifying the virtues of the early Quaker and Catholic settlers. New Englanders were idealizing both the Pilgrims who settled in Plymouth and the sterner Puritans who founded Salem and Boston. With not a few persons in all sections interest in the past too often took the form of what John Fiske called "ancestor worship." Some New Englanders convinced themselves that American democracy had originated in the Mayflower Compact and that the American national character was of New England manufacture. Likewise in later years Californians, Oregonians, and Texans would idealize the pioneers who fought the Indians and planted the flag beyond the Mississippi.

In the nineteenth century the Virginian, even more than other Southerners, was a deteriorationist. He believed in the inevitable superiority of former times. The typically Virginian view was well expressed in George W. Bagby's once popular lecture, "The Old Virginia Gentleman": "I can but think that, since the Colonial and Revolutionary days, each generation has shown a slight falling away from those grand models of men and women who really existed in Virginia, but whom we have come to look upon almost as myths." In my boyhood there were Virginia farmers who would tell you that since the Civil War everything had deteriorated—crops, farmhands, climate, manners, morals—everything. One farmer I knew insisted in all seriousness that the sap in the sugar maple was not so sweet as it had been when he was a boy.

In *Swallow Barn* (1832), John Pendleton Kennedy described an elderly free Negro named Scipio, who had once been a servant in one of the great houses on the lower James:

He had a great deal to say of the "palmy days" of Virginia, and the generations which in his time had been broken up, or, what in his conception was equivalent, had gone "over the mountain." He expatiated with a wonderful relish upon the splendors of the old-fashioned style in that part of the country; and told me very pathetically, how the estates were cut up, and what old people had died off, and how much he felt himself alone in the present times,—which particulars he interlarded with sundry sage remarks, importing an affectionate attachment to the old school, of which he considered himself no unworthy survivor.

Scipio resembles Uncle Ish in Ellen Glasgow's *The Voice of the People* (1900), who says: "Der ain' no manners dese days, nohow.

Dey ain' no manners en dey ain' no nuttin'. De niggers, dey is gwine plum outer dey heads, en de po' white trash dey's gwine plum outer dey places." Civil War and Reconstruction, like the American Revolution, made it difficult for the older generation, whether white or black, to adjust themselves to a radically new social and economic order. "Evil-minded men . . . ," says Thomas Nelson Page, "laid snares and trapfalls for 'Colonel Theodoric Johnston's Robin, of Bullfield, suh', as he loved to style himself, to trip him and inveigle him into admissions that something was as good now as before the war; but they had never succeeded." Page's contemporary, Mark Twain, tells the story of an old Negro woman who, after hearing a New Yorker's ecstatic praise of the beautiful Southern moon, shook her head and said: "Ah, bless yo' heart, honey, you jes' ought to seen dat moon befo' de waw!"

The tendency to magnify one's real or imaginary ancestors is ordinarily only a harmless species of vanity; but in a time of increasing sectional controversy rapidly developing into open hostility between North and South, such perversions of historical fact as one finds too often—in Massachusetts as well as in Virginia—undoubtedly contributed their share to sectional misunderstanding and hatred. The "Cavalier" image of the South as seen in Boston and New York was a very different thing from what Southerners in Richmond and Charleston saw in themselves. And the Southern image of the "low-born shopkeepers" who boasted of their Puritan ancestors doubtless encouraged Southerners to imagine that the Confederate armies would encounter only feeble opposition on the battlefield. On November 2, 1860, Francis Lieber wrote from New York to his son Oscar, who to his father's grief was to lose his life fighting for the Confederate cause: "It sometimes has occurred to me that what Thucydides said of the Greeks at the time of the Peloponnesian war applies to us. The Greeks, he said, did not understand each other any longer, though they spoke Greek. Words received a different meaning in different parts."

And yet we would do well to remember sometimes that heredity is quite as potent a factor in human beings as in horses and dogs. If it is permitted to boast of one's ancestors, where in the whole range of the American past could one find worthier than in the Virginians of the Revolutionary period? It was at that time and not in the seventeenth century or the nineteenth that Virginia reached the high-water mark of her greatness.

One final word. The planter's Cavalier blood—if he inherited any—was of less importance than his belief in it. That belief helped to give him an ideal to live up to in peace and in war. And the exploits of the dashing captain of King Charles's cavalry, Prince Rupert, are no more remarkable than those performed in Virginia by Turner Ashby and "Jeb" Stuart. In "The Virginians of the Valley" Dr. Francis Orray Ticknor, whose wife was a Virginian, paid his tribute to the Confederate soldiers from that state:

> The knightliest of the knightly race,
>   Who, since the days of old,
> Have kept the lamp of chivalry
>   Alight in hearts of gold. . . .
>
> We thought they slept! the sons who kept
>   The names of noble sires,
> And slumbered while the darkness crept
>   Around their vigil fires.
> But still the Golden Horse-shoe Knights
>   Their Old Dominion keep,
> Whose foes have found enchanted ground,
>   But not a knight asleep.

2

The Cavalier legend makes little account of the yeomen farmers, the poor whites, or the indentured servants. In the legend the farmers of Colonial Virginia are gentlemen planters. Yet, as Governor Nicholson's Rent Roll of 1704 makes abundantly clear, at that time the small farmers greatly outnumbered the planters, as they were to do again in the 1850's.

In the histories, as the numbers of the Cavaliers increase, the numbers of the indentured servants decline. Until some time after the Civil War few nineteenth-century historians even mentioned them. In 1786 Jefferson had estimated that not over two thousand in all came to Virginia. He did not know that soon after the Restoration Governor William Berkeley had estimated that there were already six thousand in the colony and stated that they were coming to Virginia at the rate of fifteen hundred a year. No one knows how many came to Virginia or to the other twelve colonies and the

British possessions in the West Indies. In the eighteenth century, however, as the numbers of Negro slaves imported increased, the number of incoming indentured servants declined. Few came in the years immediately preceding the Revolution.

Of the various types of indentured servants the so-called "redemptioners" were the best. These were men and women who, not having the money needed (about £5) to pay for their passage to the New World, bound themselves by indentures to serve for a period, usually four years. The redemptioners often came as a family group, and when their terms of service were up, became small farmers or mechanics.

A number of indentured servants were convicts, some of them condemned to serve for life. By present-day standards, however, few of them were hardened criminals. In seventeenth-century England some three hundred legal offenses were punishable by death or transportation. During the English Civil War both the Royalists and the Puritans sent captured soldiers to the colonies as indentured servants.

The lot of the indentured servant varied from one colony to another. He was better off in Virginia than in Maryland, where the laws were exceptionally severe. In Virginia the planter or shipowner who bought his indentures was allowed a head-right entitling him to fifty acres of free land, but the indentured servant could expect to take up land only after his term of service had expired. Abbot Emerson Smith, whose *Colonists in Bondage* (1947) is the latest detailed study of the subject, estimates that from 50 to 75 per cent of the indentured servants died without ever having a decent chance of survival. In 1671 Governor Berkeley reported that in recent years four out of every five had died before their terms expired.

Mildred Campbell suggests that while Abbot Smith's account of the lot of the convict servants may be definitive, he has rather neglected the ordinary men and women who came under indentures. She estimates that half of the immigrants who came to the colonies came as indentured servants, but she finds no great difference between those who came in that manner and those who paid their own way. The chief difference between them, she pointed out, was economic, "the poorer farmers and 'decayed' tradesmen coming under indenture." The great majority of the indentured servants were young, and the chief attraction was the opportunity to own land.

Richard Beale Davis, whose *William Fitzhugh and His Chesapeake World* (1963) throws light upon the master's treatment of redemptioners, believes that most of them worked no harder than those who came as freemen. Daniel Defoe is probably right in suggesting that whatever the legal rights of the master, his relations with his indentured servants were often friendly, like the relations which prevailed between master and slave on farms and plantations in ante-bellum Virginia.

Malaria took a heavy toll of the unseasoned immigrants. Of those who survived the severe sifting of Colonial life many must have settled on the frontier. The poor whites whom William Byrd found on the North Carolina border in 1728 were probably most of them of this class. Edward Eggleston thought that the backwoods Hoosiers of Indiana described in *The Hoosier Schoolmaster* were the descendants of indentured servants in Virginia and the Carolinas.

The most unfortunate among the indentured servants were the victims of kidnapers. Few of these were as lucky as David Balfour in Stevenson's *Kidnapped*, who escaped from his captors. The methods used to induce persons to go to the colonies were often so unscrupulous that on the London stage—even before the founding of the Jamestown colony—Virginia had come to be regarded as the last refuge of the destitute and the dishonest. In *Eastward Hoe*, the brilliant comedy written by George Chapman, John Marston, and Ben Jonson, there is a memorable scene in the Blue Anchor Tavern in which a ship's captain drums up emigrants by tall tales of the New World. The play was produced in London two years before the founding of Jamestown.

In fiction the role of the indentured servant is a peculiar one. In early English novels and plays he appears as the typical Virginian. In American fiction he was ignored until Mary Johnston in *Prisoners of Hope* (1898) showed that he might be a hero and a gentleman, even though he was a convict and a "white slave."

In Philip Massinger's *The City Madam*, acted in 1632, three men disguise themselves as Indians and pretend that they have been brought to England to be Christianized. They do this because they wish to spy upon the brother of one of the three, a rich merchant.

The villainous brother, to whom the merchant has entrusted his property, plans to sell his own nieces and sister-in-law to the Indians to be sacrificed to the devil. When he proposes to the three women a voyage to Virginia, they protest:

> *Lady Frugal.* How! Virginia!
> High Heaven forbid- Remember, sir, I beseech you
> What creatures are shipped thither.

> *Anne.* Condemned wretches,
> Forfeited to the law.

> *Mary.* Strumpets and bawds,
> For the abomination of their life,
> Spewed out of their own country.

Doubtless the London audience applauded when the villain's wicked schemes were exposed and his brother bade him:

> Hide thyself in some desert,
> Where good men ne'er may find thee; or in justice
> Pack to Virginia, and repent.

In 1625 Francis Bacon, who knew something about colonization, wrote in his essay "Of Plantations": "It is a shameful and unblessed thing to take the scum of people, and wicked condemned men, to be the people with whom you plant. . . ."

Mrs. Aphra Behn's *The Widow Ranter*, first acted in 1690, the year after her death, is a curious mixture of comedy, tragedy, and romance. It is primarily a satire on colonial self-government. The story of Nathaniel Bacon's love for the Indian queen Semernia supplies a romantic motive, and their deaths furnish a tragic conclusion. Few of the incidents or characters bear any resemblance to those of history. Bacon is the typical romantic hero, "generous, brave, resolv'd and daring." His only crime is "serving his Country without Authority." The tragic motive is found in Bacon's love for the Indian queen, in whose bosom duty and love contend for mastery. Failing to recognize her in disguise, Bacon kills her in battle and then takes poison. The Indians have nothing of the savage about them. They speak the language of English lords and ladies; they consult an oracle in a temple, like the ancient Greeks; and they fight their enemies with sword and battleaxe. They are ideal creations like Oroonoko and Imoinda.

The comic scenes of the play, some of them very coarse, are concerned chiefly with the members of the county court, who are as rascally, cowardly, and ignorant a set of men as ever breathed. "For want of a Governour," says Friendly, "we are ruled by a Council, some of whom have been perhaps transported Criminals, who having acquired great Estates, are now become your Honour and Right Worshipful, and possess all Places of Authority." One member of the county court has been a tinker, another a "broken Excise-Man," a third a pickpocket; Parson Dunce has been a farrier. The following is a fair example of their deliberations, which are held around a bowl of punch:

Whiff. Brothers, it hath often been mov'd at the the Bench, that a new Punch-Bowl shou'd be provided, and one of a larger Circumference; when the Bench sits late about weighty Affairs, oftentimes the Bowl is emptied before we end.

Whimsey. A good Motion; Clerk, set it down.

Clerk. Mr. Justice *Boozer,* the Council has order'd you a Writ of Ease, and dismiss your Worship from the Bench.

Boozer. Me from the Bench, for what?

Whimsey. The Compaint is, Brother *Boozer,* for drinking too much punch in time of hearing Tryals.

Whiff. And that you can neither write nor read, nor say the Lord's Prayer. . . .

Boozer. Why, Brother, though I can't read my self, I have had *Dalton's* Country-Justice read over to me two or three times, and understand the Law. This is your Malice, Brother *Whiff,* because my Wife does not come to your Warehouse to buy her Commodities,—but no matter, to show I have no Malice in my Heart, I drink your Health.

Nevertheless, Mrs. Behn does not think Virginia hopelessly bad. "This country wants nothing," says Friendly, "but to be peopled with a well-born Race, to make it one of the best Colonies in the World." We learn that Surelove, "a *Leicestershire* younger Brother, came over with a small Fortune, which his Industry has increas'd to a thousand Pounds a year; and he is now Colonel *John Surelove,* and one of the Council." Hazard, another younger brother, after squandering his fortune, comes to Virginia, saying, "I had rather starve abroad, than live pity'd and despis'd at home." In Virginia he manages to win a fortune by marrying Surelove's widow. The Virginia women have nothing in common with Mary Johnston's

241

heroines. The Widow herself, a wealthy, buxom virago, who smokes and drinks, is

a Woman bought from the ship by old Colonel *Ranter*; she served him half a Year, and then he marry'd her, and dying in a Year more, left her worth fifty thousand Pounds Sterling, besides Plate and Jewels: She's a great Gallant, but assuming the humour of the Country Gentry, her Extravagancy is very pleasant, she retains something of her primitive Quality still, but is good-natur'd and generous.

The indentured servant plays a notable part in Daniel Defoe's *Moll Flanders* and *Colonel Jacque,* both published in the year 1722. Defoe, who probably knew more about the American colonies than any other English writer before the time of Edmund Burke, had a keen interest in people of all kinds. He once said: "I am most entertained by those actions which give me a light into the nature of man." There may, however, have been a more personal reason for his interest in indentured servants who came to the Southern colonies. There is a tradition that one of his sons emigrated to the Carolinas.

There is also the somewhat dubious story told by Mrs. Mary E. Ireland in "The Defoe Family in America" (*Scribner's Monthly,* May, 1876) which if substantially true might explain why in a single year Defoe published two novels dealing with indentured servants in Virginia and Maryland. Mrs. Ireland, who claims to have got the story from descendants of Defoe's niece, Elizabeth Maxwell, states that at the age of eighteen this girl, angered because her mother had made her break off her engagement to a man whose name is unknown, arranged with a ship's captain for her passage to Philadelphia. She was sold to a planter from Cecil County, Maryland. Somewhat later she was freed and married the son of her master. She then wrote to her mother and her uncle. In reply Defoe wrote that her mother was dead but had left her a large property in case she were ever found alive. Professor W. P. Trent, who knew more about Defoe than any other scholar of his generation, told me that there were so many errors in Mrs. Ireland's story where he could check it that he was inclined to reject it altogether. Professor John Robert Moore, in what is probably the best life of Defoe, refers to Mrs. Ireland's article as "semi-fictional." He points out that Defoe's sister Elizabeth married Robert Davis and not a man named Maxwell, and he notes that her daughter had a different marriage from that in Mrs. Ireland's story. When I first read Mrs. Ireland's article years ago, I thought that her story supplied a partial explanation of why in a single year (1722) Defoe twice gave a leading role to an indentured servant who came to Virginia. But Mrs. Ireland says that Defoe knew nothing of the fate of his niece until 1725. In any event Defoe's niece was certainly not the original of Moll Flanders.

Defoe's reason for bringing his two notorious rogues to Virginia is perfectly plain. His favorite solution of the pauper and criminal problem was to send such people to the colonies, where they would have a second chance. "In a word," says Colonel Jacque,

every Newgate wretch, every desperate forlorn creature, the most despicable ruined man in the world, has here a fair opportunity put into his hands to begin the world again, and that upon a foot of certain gain and in a method exactly honest, with a reputation that nothing past will have any effect upon; and innumerable people have raised themselves from the worst circumstances in the world—namely, from the cells in Newgate.

Mrs. Behn had already pointed out that it was vastly easier for the unfortunate to rehabilitate themselves in Virginia than in England. "Many men," says Philip Alexander Bruce, "who began in this humble character accumulated, after the close of their terms, good estates, exercised wide influence and even filled important offices."

Moll's mother, a transported criminal, tells her how it is possible for the penniless jailbird to establish himself as a farmer in Virginia:

"When they come here," says she, "we make no difference; the planters buy them, and they work together in the field, till their time is out. When 'tis expired," said she, "they have encouragement given them to plant for themselves; for they have a certain number of acres allotted them by the country, and they go to work to clear and cure the land, and then to plant it with tobacco and corn for their own use; and as the merchants will trust them with tools and necessaries, upon the credit of their crop before it is grown, so they again plant every year a little more than the year before, and so buy whatever they want with the crop that is before them. Hence, child," says she, "many a Newgate-bird becomes a great man, and we have," continued she, "several justices of the peace, officers of the trained bands, and magistrates of the towns they live in, that have been burnt in the hand."

The story of Moll Flanders, however, gives only a poor illustration of the feasibility of Defoe's scheme. After a disreputable early life, Moll captures a third husband in the person of a Virginia merchant-planter, who, by the way, is nothing of the traditional Cavalier; and she comes to Virginia to live with him. On discovering that he is her half-brother, she returns to England. There she becomes a thief; but after twelve years of good luck, she is caught and sent back to Virginia as an indentured servant. With the help of her fourth husband, she obtains her freedom the very day she lands in Virginia; and they buy an estate on the Chesapeake Bay and live in ease and plenty until they decide to return to England. It should be noted, however, that Moll's prosperity in Virginia is due solely to a bequest from her mother and to the profits of her years of thieving. Defoe seems to have perceived the weakness of his plot; and accordingly he undertook in another story—this time with a man as leading character—to show what a social outcast might make of himself in Virginia. Professor Moore notes an important difference between the leading characters in the two novels: "Moll's forlorn hope of living as a gentlewoman was the primary cause of her shame; for Jack, the dream of becoming a gentleman was the source of his ultimate salvation."

In *Colonel Jacque*, published eleven months after the earlier story, we have as hero a sort of male counterpart of Moll Flanders. Jack, the illegitimate son of an English gentleman, has become a pickpocket before he is old enough to know the wrong of stealing. When he grows up, he resolves to reform and live honestly, as a gentleman should. He goes to Scotland and enlists as a soldier, but deserts when he finds that the army is actually going into a campaign. At Newcastle, while seeking passage to London, he is kidnaped, carried to Virginia, and sold to a planter. Here he again resolves to reform. In a short time he is made an overseer. At the end of three years his master gives him his liberty and assists him to start a plantation of his own in that part of Maryland which is now included in the District of Columbia. In a few years Jack has acquired three plantations and a hundred servants and slaves. His various military and marital adventures in Europe and his trading experiences in Spanish America need not detain us here. It is sufficient to note that Jack's success in Virginia enables him to return to England and pass as a prosperous merchant. Unlike Moll Flanders, Jack owes his success solely to his own honesty, intelligence, and industry, for the money which he laid up while a pickpocket is lost at sea.

Defoe, who is astonishingly modern in many of his ideas, had a second motive in shifting the scene of *Colonel Jacque* to Virginia. He wished to institute a reform in the treatment of slaves in the colonies. As an overseer, Jack discovers that even the worst of the Negro slaves may be "brought to a compliance without the lash." "It is certainly wrong, sir," he tells his master; "it is not only wrong as it is barbarous and cruel; but it is wrong, too, as it is the worst way of managing and of having your business done." Defoe devotes over twenty pages to the explanation of his own system of management, which turns upon arousing the slave's feeling of gratitude for mercy shown him when he knows that he ought to be punished.

The Virginia scenes of both novels lack many of the realistic details which we find in the English background. Defoe describes his American setting only in the most general terms, but his Virginia scenes are surprisingly free from error. Once, however, he makes the curious blunder of placing the Rappahannock east of the Potomac. His knowledge of the legal status of the indentured servant is correct, apparently, even in minute details. Defoe's chief error lies in his failure to make any social distinction whatever between freedmen and other classes.

3

The first American novelist to introduce the Virginia Cavalier into fiction was Dr. William Alexander Caruthers. In his first novel, *The Kentuckian in New York* (1834), he had written: "Poor, exhausted eastern Virginia! She is in her dotage." A realistic treatment of the rundown Tidewater region of his native state did not appeal to Dr. Caruthers. Why not a historical romance picturing that region in its heyday with all the glamour and local coloring of the Waverley novels? That would be something worth doing. Cooper had shown how Scott's methods could be successfully adapted to American materials, and in Captain Jack Lawton of *The Spy* he had created a dashing Virginia cavalryman. In Colonial Virginia there were Cavaliers and backwoodsmen, faithful servants, Indians, and even a few Puritans; and there, too, were those picturesque neglected figures, Nathaniel Bacon and Alexander Spotswood. Virginia had begun to look backward and glorify the past. The Cavalier legend had developed to the point where many men imagined that the Colonial population was made up of English gentlemen and nobles—the indentured servants had been all but forgotten. Even Bacon's ragamuffin army was in the novelist's imagination made up largely of Cavaliers and not of small farmers, frontiersmen, and indentured servants.

In *The Cavaliers of Virginia* (1835) the Cavalier gentlemen and ladies serve well enough in place of their British prototypes. Caruthers' conception of the Cavaliers is that expressed in John Daly Burk's *History of Virginia*, his chief historical source.

The cavaliers, or, as they stiled themselves, the gentlemen of that day . . . piqued themselves on their lineage and descent; and modelled their manners on those gallant and adventurous knights, who freed Europe from dwarfs and giants, the ruthless proprietors of enchanted castles, and who rescued distressed beauty from the dungeons of enchanters and magicians.

Burk and Caruthers—not to mention some American historians of a later time—confused the age of chivalry with the age of Cromwell and the Stuart kings.

Caruthers' romance, however, is not primarily about the Virginia Cavaliers. His subject is Bacon's Rebellion, and he plays it up as a premature war for independence. "Exactly one hundred years before the American revolution," he writes, "there was a Virginian revolution based upon precisely similar principles." With a mystery over his birth Nathaniel Bacon enters the story as an unmarried Cavalier of twenty-one. In reality Bacon had a wife and two children. The story ends not with his death but with the burning of Jamestown, a complete triumph over his enemies, and his marriage to the fictitious Virginia Fairfax. Shakespeare and his contemporaries could take such liberties with historical fact, and few were the wiser; but Caruthers was severely reprimanded by James E. Heath in the *Southern Literary Messenger* for making of Bacon "a kind of half frantic, inconsiderate stripling—something of a dandy— but more of a wild and reckless lover, whose thoughts were principally occupied by his 'Ladye love'; and but lightly, if at all, by the wrongs of his suffering country." Caruthers was no doubt chagrined to find that the most unfavorable review of his book was written by a Virginian and published in a Virginia literary magazine. *The Cavaliers of Virginia* is a better book than Heath was willing to admit. A just estimate is that found in Curtis Carroll Davis's life of Caruthers, one of the best biographies of Southern writers:

. . . Caruthers was a story teller first and foremost. As such he has, in *The Cavaliers*, produced an early example of the slap-dash, swords-and-cloaks historical romance of the "old school" before that school was old. The work is a catch-all of melodrama laced with the elements of improbability and coincidence, gallantry *vs.* knavery, lovely women and bold men.

There is less emphasis upon the Cavaliers in Caruthers' last and best novel, *The Knights of the Horse-Shoe* (1845), which has for its historical hero Governor Alexander Spotswood and its chief theme his journey of discovery and adventure over the Blue Ridge. *The Knights* is by much Caruthers' best novel, but he unwisely permitted it to be brought out in Wetumpka, Alabama, by a publisher who did not have the facilities for distribution held by Harper & Brothers, who had published Caruthers' earlier novels.

With the revival of historical romance in the 1880's and 1890's Colonial Virginia again became a favorite background. Three of Mary Johnston's earliest romances deal with it and are quite as full of mysteries and melodramatic incidents as *The Cavaliers of Virginia*.[2] Her Virginia is "the land of good eating, good drinking, good fighting, stout men and pretty women." "Virginia is God's country." " 'Tis the garden of the world." These quotations are from her first novel, *Prisoners of Hope*, published in 1898. Its hero is an indentured servant.

The historical incident about which *Prisoners of Hope* is built is the little-known Oliverian Plot, the attempt of some four hundred of Cromwell's old soldiers, sent to Virginia as indentured servants, to free the slaves and seize the government. The incident offered Miss Johnston an opportunity to use the traditional contrast of Puritan and Cavalier in a new setting. The most conspicuous of the Virginia Cavaliers is Colonel Verney, of "Verney Manor." He is "trader, planter, magistrate, member of the council of state, soldier, author on occasion, and fine gentlemen all rolled into one, after the fashion of the times." His kinsman, Sir Charles Carew, a Cavalier from the court of Charles II, is in love with Colonel Verney's daughter, who bears the apt name of Patricia. This beauty is the incarna-

[2] In some of her later novels—especially *The Long Roll* and *Cease Firing*—Miss Johnston took great pains to make her historical scenes and characters accurate and lifelike.

tion of aristocratic loveliness and pride. She has no pity for the unfortunate servants, whose hard lot Miss Johnston, unlike Defoe, pictures as that of the most cruel slavery. Most of the servants she represents as hopelessly ignorant and degraded. A striking exception is Godfrey Landless, her hero. Landless is a Roundhead soldier and gentleman who has been condemned to lifelong servitude in Virginia. When Landless falls in love with Patricia, she has only contempt for him as a social inferior. Her scorn and his hard lot finally drive him into the conspiracy of the Oliverians. On learning, however, that a mulatto leader of the conspirators is plotting to call in the Indians and murder the whites, Landless deserts them and fights to defend his mistress against the savages. When she is carried off by the Indians, Landless and an Indian friend, whose life he has saved, pursue them and rescue her, after the fashion of Hawkeye and Uncas. But a price has been set upon his head, and he dares not return to the settlements. After a dramatic farewell, Patricia, vowing she will never love another, goes home with her father, while Landless, with a broken ankle, is left alone in the mountains, choosing to take his chances there rather than trust himself in the hands of Governor Berkeley.

Miss Johnston's popular romances of Colonial Virginia had a considerable influence upon later writers. At the suggestion of a publisher Mary Wilkins Freeman temporarily left off writing her realistic stories of decadent New England to write *The Heart's Highway*, a romance of Colonial Virginia. It was a dismal failure. John Masefield, who had edited a book of selections from Defoe, published two novels in which Englishmen stop off in Virginia on their way to Spanish America in quest of treasure and adventure: *Lost Endeavour* (1910) and *Captain Margaret* (1916). The hero of the earlier is kidnaped and sold to a planter in Accomac County, Virginia. Two years later he is rescued by a fellow-servant who has taken to smuggling. After a stirring fight with the Indians (reminiscent of Cooper) and a chase in the Chesapeake by a government frigate, in Cooper's best manner, the story leaves Virginia. The background in both novels is extremely hazy and, wherever definitely described, likely to be inaccurate. For instance, the Virginians, Masefield tells us, "had no wines. . . . They did not play cards. They would often ride forty miles to a prayer meeting in a wood." All of which sounds more like Massachusetts than Virginia.

One of the best stories of Colonial Virginia is *Salute to Adventurers* (1917), by John Buchan, later to become Lord Tweedsmuir and Governor-General of Canada. The background is the Virginia of about 1690, the period described by Defoe and Masefield; but Buchan's model was probably Mary Johnston. The net effect, however, is rather original, for though all the old elements of Colonial romance are here—pirates, Indians, duels, haughty aristocrats, proud and beautiful heroines—the novelist handles them all with a fresh and skilful touch. The most original and effective figure is Muckle John Gib, a religious fanatic, who, when sent to Virginia as an indentured servant, breaks away, flees to the mountains, and heads a tremendous Indian confederation whose object is the utter destruction of the colony. The hero is a fighting Scotch merchant who thwarts Gib's designs. The historical setting is more accurate than that of most other Colonial novels. There are good satiric descriptions of the indolent, conservative Virginia planters, who despise the merchant as a "shopkeeper" until he has shown them that he can fight as well as he can trade.

July 4. Statistics show that we lose more fools on this day than in all the other days of the year put together. This proves, by the number left in stock, that one Fourth of July per year is now inadequate, the country has grown so.

MARK TWAIN, "Pudd'nhead Wilson's Calendar."

Jesse Holmes the Fool-Killer

[In 1930 my friend Ernest E. Leisy contributed to the *Publications* of the Texas Folk-Lore Society a brief article on Jesse Holmes the Fool-Killer. He referred to O. Henry's story, "The Fool-Killer," reprinted a brief passage from the *Southern Literary Messenger,* and concluded with a portion of a letter which he had received from Mr. R. R. Clark, formerly editor of the Statesville, N. C., *Landmark.* Clark's reference to the Milton, N. C., *Chronicle* as the source of the Jesse Holmes stories prompted me to try to learn something more of the Fool-Killer.

There are, as I soon discovered, few extant numbers of the Milton *Chronicle.* I found scattered numbers in the Duke University Library, in the library of the University of North Carolina, in the North Carolina State Library, and in the collection of the North Carolina Department of Archives and History in Raleigh. I could not find a single copy in Milton when David Jackson and I visited that picturesque and charming town, but I found two copies in Yanceyville, the county seat of Caswell County. I saw one other copy in Danville, Virginia, which is only a few miles from Milton.

In a Greensboro paper I found certain passages which had been copied from numbers of the *Chronicle* no longer extant. Of approximately fifty copies of the *Chronicle* that I have examined only four contain letters from Jesse Holmes.

The details of my brief sketch of the life of Charles Napoleon Bonaparte Evans, the creator of Jesse Holmes, are drawn partly from the scattered numbers of the newspapers which he edited and partly from data sent me by his two grandchildren: Mrs. Louis Voss, of Tallahassee, Florida, and Mr. Charles N. B. Evans, a retired banker from Cincinnati. Without their assistance my sketch would be much slighter than it is.

After this essay was read before the North Carolina Folklore Society, of which I am the only surviving charter member, it was published in the *South Atlantic Quarterly* for October, 1937, under the title "Charles Napoleon Bonaparte Evans, Creator of Jesse Holmes the Fool-Killer." In this revised version of the essay I have added at the end some account of the Fool-Killer's literary role in a poem by Ambrose Bierce and in two short stories, or rather fables, by George Ade and Stephen Vincent Benét.]

1

When O. Henry wrote "The Fool-Killer," he doubtless recalled the legendary figure of whom he had heard during his boyhood in Greensboro, North Carolina. This short story, which appeared in *The Voice of the City* (1908), begins:

> Down South whenever any one perpetrates some particularly monumental piece of foolishness everybody says: "Send for Jesse Holmes."
> Jesse Holmes is the Fool-Killer. Of course he is a myth, like Santa Claus and Jack Frost and General Prosperity and all those concrete conceptions that are supposed to represent an idea that Nature has failed to embody. The wisest of the Southrons cannot tell you whence comes the Fool-Killer's name; but few and happy are the households from Roanoke to the Rio Grande in which the name of Jesse Holmes has not been pronounced or invoked. Always with a smile, and often with a tear, is he summoned to his official duty. A busy man is Jesse Holmes.
> I remember the clear picture of him that hung on the walls of my fancy during my barefoot days when I was dodging his oft-repeated devoirs. To me he was a terrible old man, in gray clothes, with a long, ragged, gray beard, and reddish fierce eyes. I looked to see him come

stumping up the road in a cloud of dust, with a white oak staff in his hand and his shoes tied with leather thongs. I may yet—

The creator of Jesse Holmes the Fool-Killer was Charles Napoleon Bonaparte Evans (1812-1883). He was a first cousin of O. Henry's mother, and he once lived in Greensboro, where O. Henry spent his boyhood. He was born in Norfolk County, Virginia, in or near the town of Suffolk (which figures in one of the Jesse Holmes letters) on October 18, 1812. Presumably his father, James S. Evans, was an admirer of the French Emperor, who was on the point of beginning his disastrous retreat from Moscow. The father died in 1823. When the mother remarried, the eleven- or twelve-year-old boy ran away from home. At that time or soon afterwards he probably apprenticed himself to the owner of a newspaper in Greensboro or Hillsboro; he had relatives in both towns.

The record is blank until 1836. In that year the journalist, now twenty-four years old, married on May 24 Elizabeth Clancy of Hillsboro. The young man whom Elizabeth Clancy married had less than two months earlier become one of the proprietors of the Greensborough *Patriot*. This newspaper had belonged to O. Henry's maternal grandfather, William Swaim, who had recently died. Swaim's wife née Abia Shirley, was Evans's aunt; and Evans was a first cousin once removed of William Sydney Porter, who is better known by his pen name "O. Henry." Evans may have learned the newspaper business under his uncle in Greensboro. At any rate, the *Patriot* for April 5, 1836, announced A. E. Hanner and C. N. B. Evans as the new owners of the paper. In their Prospectus it was stated that one of the copartners was "a practical printer and intending to devote great attention to that department." Beyond question Evans was the "practical printer." Hanner, who was "Clerk of the Court of Pleas and Quarter Sessions," died within a few months. By September 14, 1836, Evans was named as sole "proprietor and publisher." Something over a year later, on December 19, 1837, we learn that the paper now belongs to Evans and John D. Clancy, whose name indicates that he was a relative of Evans's wife. A year later Clancy was editor and proprietor, and Evans was gone. Three years later, in 1841, Evans founded the Milton *Chronicle*. Evans very likely had had some connection with the Milton *Spectator*, of which the *Chronicle* was a continuation. In the *Chronicle* for July 14, 1853,

Evans wrote: ". . . although we have been printing (for bread, not *fame*) for the last thirteen years, in this town, we are still no million-a[i]re!"

In John H. Wheeler's *Historical Sketches of North Carolina*, Second Series (1851) Evans, whose name is wrongly set down as "C. N. B. Webb," is described as "a native of Virginia, aged 37 [he was actually 39] . . . 'profession is printer, publisher, and post master.' " (The post office will be referred to again.) In 1861 the editors and proprietors of the *Chronicle* were C. N. B. Evans and T. C. Evans. In that year Thomas Clancy Evans, an only son, left the University of North Carolina to join the Milton Blues, of which he became captain in the course of the Civil War.

In January, 1870, we find "Father Evans," as the newspapermen of the state now called him, discontinuing the Milton *Chronicle* and removing to Hillsboro to join his son on the Hillsborough *Recorder*. The issue of the *Recorder* for January 26, 1870, conveys the elder Evans's "Greeting" to the subscribers:

It may be expected, by those readers of the *Recorder* to whom I am a stranger, that I should indicate or define my political position. The political elements are so mixed up—Governments have been so changed —that I really feel "at sea, without rudder or compass." Banned as I am by the 14th Article, perhaps I have no right to cherish or express political sentiments. I am thoroughly reconstructed, but not exactly harmonized! The fault is not mine, however, but the Government's! I am deemed too great a sinner to be pardoned! I killed no one during the war! Never fired a gun at Gen. Grant or any of his men! I did visit our "boys" in Gen. Lee's army occasionally, but when they commenced shooting I commenced "getting away!" Tho' if I had once gotten mad all over—like some of the fellows did *after* the war, (who played-out the army behind fifteen "niggers,") when ordered to eat an acre or two of dirt—there's no telling what I *might* have done! No, I burnt not a grain of gunpowder, and did my best to prevent secession and avert the unnatural war—but it came! and right or wrong I stood by my birth and "hurrah'd" for our side!—But what is the offence for which I am today *outlawed*? I once held a three-cent Post Office!

. . . I propose to leave the political status of the paper mainly to the junior Editor, as I am "sick of Politics" and considerably disgusted with parties and jack-snap politicians.

While living in Hillsboro, Evans was hanged in effigy, apparently by members of the Ku Klux Klan who had disobeyed General Forrest's order to disband. When the Hillsboro Klansmen kept up their meetings for purposes of their own of which he disapproved,

Evans condemned their actions. So angry were they that, it is said, only the pleadings of Judge Emeritus Boyd saved Evans from personal injury. Mr. Charles N. B. Evans vividly recalls the hanging in effigy:

. . . I spent one night at my grandfather's home, and next morning there was consternation when the front door was opened, for lying on the little railed front porch that overhung the pavement was a little black coffin. On the coffin, painted in white, were a skull and cross-bones and a scribbled note stating that twenty-four hours were given my grandfather to leave town. I think it was the cook or the housemaid who opened the door and made the discovery, in the midst of which my grandfather came to the front door, took in the scene, and proceeded to kick the contraption onto the pavement.

He returned to breakfast, entirely unruffled, and after breakfast I walked with him to the office, a distance of several blocks. . . .

Upon our arrival there were people congregated and staring into the basement, for in plain sight there hung from one of the sleepers a natural-size figure of a man, noose around his neck, and a placard bearing my grandfather's name. The suit worn by the figure was stuffed with straw; and aside from ordering that it be taken down and consigned to the office stove, my grandfather seemed undisturbed. He certainly did not obey the mandate to leave town.

In 1873 the son went to Richmond to work on the *Enquirer*, while the father returned to Milton and resurrected the *Chronicle*. The records of the North Carolina Press Association show that he attended, as a representative of the *Chronicle*, the first meeting of that body in 1873. The *American Newspaper Directory* for 1873, issued by George P. Rowell and Company, contains the following:

Milton Chronicle; Thursdays; four pages; size 22 x 32; subscription $2.50; established 1873; C. N. B. Evans, editor; Evans & Smith, publishers; circulation 500.

Later newspaper directories give much the same figures. In 1880, according to the *American Newspaper Annual*, issued by N. W. Ayer and Son, the circulation of the *Chronicle* reached 879, the maximum figure given in the available newspaper directories. In 1883, the year of his death, his son was again with him on the *Chronicle*, which did not long survive him. In that year he was a member of the State Senate as the representative of Caswell, Orange, and Person counties. The published records of the Senate show that he was a member of the committees on education and corporations and that he faithfully performed his duties until March 2, when he was given an indefinite leave of absence. He died of pneumonia in Milton on March 10 and was buried there soon afterwards. Both branches of the General Assembly voted resolutions on the occasion of his death and made an appropriation to pay his funeral expenses.

Evans's grandson recalls one occasion when a letter from the Fool-Killer brought to the newspaper office in Milton an angry victim seeking revenge:

I sat near the stove one summer's day, idly whittling into the sand box surrounding the stove, while my grandfather, over near a window, was seated on a high stool fronting a case of type from which he was "setting" directly into his printer's "stick" matter as he composed it for publication. Hearing a slight noise, I turned to behold a stranger who had quietly entered from the open street door. Top-booted, shaggy-haired, and wearing a corduroy cap, he strolled slowly to the center of the office, glanced about him, and finally glared over at my grandfather.

"Be you the editor?" he asked.

"I am," came the answer.

"Named Evans, or Holmes—or somethin'?"

"My name is Evans, my friend—and I am the editor," replied my grandfather, pushing his spectacles high upon his forehead and half moving from his high stool. "What can I do for you?"

"You cain't do nothin' for me;—you've already did it," came the quick response. "An' I've come to town to beat h——l out o' you for that thing you writ about me in the paper."

Silently grasping the stove poker and slipping to a convenient stance behind the scene, I waited with bated breath. Possibly seasoned to such situations, the editor did not appear to be perturbed, but moved toward the stranger with a half-smile on his lips.

"Well, now, my friend, let's first get at this thing in a quiet way. Suppose you just calm down for a moment or so and give me the facts. We can then discuss them and if you still feel like chastising me, why," with an appraising glance, "you appear to be strong enough, big enough, and brave enough to make a good job of it."

"Of course," continued the editor, "a little bloodsplashing around and a general rumpus here in the office would only cause the whole matter to be brought into court; witnesses to swear into the records, wide publicity, and proof established of things which might prove both embarrassing—and in any case would be expensive. Let's first get at the facts—and then do our fighting—if any has to be done.—Just what was printed about you that gave offense?"

"Oh, you know well enough," exclaimed the exasperated caller. "One of them dern Fool-Killer pieces, where you writ about a farmer over in the Holly Hill section (that's where I live) payin' a dollar for some Love Powders an' scatterin' 'em in a note writ to a widder 'bout sellin' her some shoats.—Every danged man I meet, in the neighborhood, hails me to know if Love Powders is helpin' me to sell pigs—or askin' how I'm gittin' along courtin' that widder. It's been gittin' on my nerves so that I jest made up my mind to come here and either beat h——l out o' you—or sue for damages!"

"Ah, I see, I see," mildly commiserated the editor; "but now let's get down to the real facts. Did the paper, in the article, print your name?"

"No."

"The widow's name?"

"No."

"Well, I hardly understand. How could it have happened, then, that the people connected you with the matter? Did the widow tell?"

"She didn't have to tell!" blurted out the stranger, "—or mean to tell. She just happened to be at the post office at mail-openin' time, when all o' them good-for-nothin' loafers was hangin' round, and when she opened the letter, some o' that sweet-smellin' stuff flew out—an' the crowd commenced laughin' an' accused her of gettin' a love letter. Womanlike, this het her up, and to prove that 'twan't no love letter but a letter from me 'bout some pigs, she showed it to 'em."

"Ah, now, I see it all," exclaimed the editor. "What a hot case there is for Jesse Holmes to work up! You weren't there, but the crowd recognized Love Powders—and evidently there are other buyers besides yourself—also some unprincipled merchant to sell them, whose hide should be made to smoke. Now, you just sit down at the table and give me a few confidential pointers and I think the Fool-Killer's next letter will make *you* laugh—and some others squirm. That will be far better than either fighting or suing."

Evidently the stranger saw the logic of this course. Certainly a belligerent attitude softened quickly, and was followed by whisperings, elbow-nudging, and an evident spirit of congeniality, at the conclusion of which I witnessed the exchange of two silver dollars from the stranger's pocket to the *Chronicle's* subscription fund. It may be added that the next issue carried the "mauling" of a drug clerk for retailing in small pill boxes powdered and highly scented chalk as "Love Powders"—also there were sundry raps given swains of the Holly Hill section—whose identity was but thinly veiled through occupational reference only.

The older inhabitants of Milton who remembered "Father Evans" described him to me as tall, rather slender, "rawboned," not handsome but with a face kindly in expression, a broad forehead, and a jaw indicating determination. He was evidently, in Mr. R. R. Clark's words, "quite original." He was independent and outspoken, and he was something of a sage as well as a wit. "His stuff," writes Mr. Clark, "was much copied, and when he wrote something that went the rounds he would say that 'it had legs.'" Just why a man of his undoubted ability should have spent nearly all of his life in a village I do not know. Perhaps he was unambitious. Certainly he loved Milton; and no one who has been there will deny the charm of the place and its people.

Jesse Holmes the Fool-Killer made his appearance in the pages of the *Chronicle* some time before 1851. Letters from the Fool-Killer were headed by a woodcut showing Jesse Holmes in action with his club drawn back, grasping the victim by the lapel of his coat. The victim's hair is on end, his hat falling to the ground, and his hands trembling with fear. The cut reminds one of the lines of another Holmes, the author of "Dorothy Q":

> Who the painter was none may tell,—
> One whose best was not over well. . . .

The character of Jesse Holmes was regarded by other newspaper editors as Evans's creation, and I see no reason for doubting that it was his. There may have been before his time other fool-killers, but I have yet to learn of them. I have been unable to trace the word *fool-killer* or the conception of a killer of fools further back than the Milton *Chronicle*. I know of no folklore stories of a fool-killer, and the word does not appear in the *Oxford Dictionary*. It does appear in the *Dictionary of American English*, but the earliest entry is in 1853. The late Charles A. Fenton, the biographer of Stephen Vincent Benét, told me that Washington Irving somewhere mentioned a fool-killer, but I have not found the passage. Three leading authorities on American folklore—Louise Pound, George Lyman Kittredge, and Stith Thompson—wrote me that they could throw no light upon the origin or the history of the word *fool-killer*. Jesse Holmes as we know him is as much Evans's creation as Rip Van Winkle is Irving's. He is worthy of a place among American folk legends along with Paul Bunyan, Pecos Bill, Mike Fink, and John Henry. On the literary side Evans belongs with those newspaper writers whom Jennette Tandy called "crackerbox philosophers." Their heyday came between 1830 and 1870, but something of the humorous tradition survived in Mark Twain, George Ade, Ring Lardner, and Will Rogers.

That Evans knew the newspaper humorists of his time is shown by numerous allusions and extracts. Among the comic characters of the type there are a number of rascals and fools. Did Evans, I wonder, reading of such characters as Simon Suggs and his victims, see an opportunity to create his two leading figures, the Fool-Killer

257

and the Rascal-Whaler? Or did the folly and rascality of which a journalist sees so much in human nature suggest to his mind the Fool-Killer as a concrete conception "that Nature has failed to embody?" Many of the men to whom I mentioned the Fool-Killer said or wrote to me to this effect: "If you find him, please let me know, for I have work for him." Every sensible man would often like to maul a fool or a rascal, but he seldom yields to the impulse. Jesse Holmes had no such inhibitions, and we take a vicarious pleasure in seeing him give a fool what he so well deserves.

2

It is time to give some illustrative extracts from the wit and wisdom of Jesse Holmes. The earliest letter of whichan y portion survives was copied in part in the Greensborough *Patriot* for August 2, 1851. That Jesse's racy comments were no novelty in 1851 is shown by the way in which the editor of the *Patriot* introduced the extract from the *Chronicle*:

We have always read with interest the alas! too truthful, letters from Jesse Holmes, the fool killer, which always appear original[ly] in that gem of [a] newspaper, the Milton Chronicle.—Let others boast of their Downing and Doesticks, they will do when nothing better is at hand, but give us the epistles of the good, kind-hearted, though ever-dreaded Jesse, and we are satisfied.

The extract from Jesse's letter is chiefly a complaint in regard to the younger generation, who, says Jesse, "are not raised to work, but rather retained as 'parlor ornaments.' "

The chap jumps into calf skin up to his knees as soon as he is born and with cigar in mouth wonders why he isn't married. The Miss comes forth with snuff-brush in mouth, thumping the keys of an old piano, and chanting "I wish I were a girl again." The old man [Jesse Holmes] has seen these things. Boys are raised to look upon work as degrading—the girls are taught to shun the man of labor, particularly the mechanic: And I have seen mechanics' daughters turning up their noses like gourd-handles at mechanics simply because they worked for their bread and meat, in compliance with scriptural injunction. And when these mechanics have married and raised up daughters I have seen them treat young men just as their daddies had been treated.

The earliest letter which survives in full may be found in the Duke University Library. It is dated February, 1857, and it chronicles Jesse's activities in the neighborhood of Durham's Station (now Durham) and Red Mountain (Rougemont). After telling how he has mauled several persons who are foolishly excited by fear of a slave insurrection, Jesse continues:

On the 29th of Dec. I slayed a party at Durham's which had been "sold" by the report that "professor" H., of Salisbury, would then and there ascend in a balloon—carrying up with him a six-horse wagon and team.

Again:

The gal who thinks more of herself than any one thinks of her, has been slayed.—And divers youngsters and old frisky widowers have bit the dust in these diggins.

Two years later—March 10, 1859—comes the second letter, which is in the University of North Carolina Library. Jesse has just returned from Raleigh, where he had gone to "adjourn one of the most worthless Legislatures that ever disgraced the State." On his way to Raleigh Jesse had mauled a young man who wanted to marry a certain girl *if* it was true that she would inherit her rich aunt's property. "I pitched into him," says Jesse, "with the savageness of skinning skunks, and mauled him about right." On his arrival in Raleigh, Jesse goes to the office of the *Standard*, edited by W. W. Holden, one of Evans's aversions, who had not yet become the Reconstruction Governor of unsavory memory. Holden, however, rascal though he may be, is no fool. As Jesse enters the *Standard* office, the editor, thinking the Rascal-Whaler had come for him, "jumped out at a back window and ran like a quarter horse, but I made his [printer's] devil chase him down and bring him in." Jesse gets the foolish House adjourned and starts toward Petersburg to find the Rascal-Whaler, whom he sends to Raleigh to work on the unadjourned Senate.

I next exercised my club on the head of the man who had a certificate written for the widow to sign before she promised to marry him—this happened near Riceville, and you better believe that I made the lark sing that good old religious tune "farewell, vain world." Going out on the R[ichmond]. & D[anville]. Road, to peep about a little, I met with a beautiful and highly accomplished young lady who thought it would be no harm for me to pry into the love affairs of a Station agent on the road, as he was known to have a heap of business in *court* in a county below. I resolved to do so, but he treated me so politely and kindly that I concluded to let it pass, and you may tell the girls, Editor, that that young man will do to "tie to."

In the newspaper collection of the North Carolina Department of Archives and History there is an interesting letter from "Down about Norfolk, Va.," dated June, 1861. It begins:

Editors:

Can the old man's voice once more be heard? or is it to be drowned by the roar of cannon and musketry and the clashing of steel? Alas! poor country of Washington, thou art gone—forever and a day after. If the old man's counsels had been heeded, things would not be as they now are . . . , Editor, when the historian comes to record the course of the downfall of this once proud and mighty Republic, tell him, for me, to put it in these words, to wit: "It fell by the hands of Fools!" I tried my best to avert the dire calamity—I wielded my club by day and by night—I bathed it in the blood of demagogues, designing politicians, fanatics, rapscallions and scoundrels—I cried loudly for help to demolish the fools that seemed to be everywhere springing up like the green grass of this mother earth on which you and I tread, but alas, alas! too few heard my warning and came to the rescue. What was the result? Why, a prince of fools was elevated to the Presidential chair, and sensible men swore in their wrath that he should not rule over them. The old man, however, thinks that he could have prevented the election of this king fool, but for the unwise counsels of ranting demagogues and little upstart Editors, politicians whose presumption outstripped their brains and who mistook ambition for Office (there's the curse of Government!) for patriotism. And but for your scheming politicians and hireling Editors, your old uncle thinks he could have secured an honorable Compromise. The scheming politicians, however, swore that they didn't want any compromise and would not have any. Editor, can you tell me where the gentlemen that held this language are now to be found? I have had a peep into the tented field, and I do not find many there that I had a right to look for.

. . . .

Down in Suffolk (Va.) I noticed entirely too many young bucks displaying their *gallantry* in the wrong way: Instead of arming themselves with the musket and entering the tented field to defend Virginia's booty and beauty, too many of these "nice young men" preferred to remain at home and *arm* the girls about in evening promenades. Nice chaps! to see troops [come] hundreds of miles to protect them and their mothers and sisters, as well as also their property, and they too *nice* or cowardly to protect themselves! One of these nice young upstarts made some disparaging remarks about the North Carolina troops, and I put G. D. Bradsher, Lt. E. B. Holden and a few other man-eaters, on the lark's track, with instructions to wear him out if they caught him, and I guess they did it. Some of the Suffolk people treated the troops kindly and some again didn't hurt themselves by their kindness. They know how to charge poor soldiers two or three prices for every thing they buy in and about Suffolk. And I want you to inform the young man who keeps the Post Office there, that I think he would make a good-looking soldier: An old gent, or a trundle-bed boy could attend to the Post Office.

. . . .

In the vicinity of Buncome Hill I overheard a customer begging a member of the Legislature to have him appointed a magistrate so as to escape fighting in the war. One jodarter from the old Man's club knocked the cowardice out of him—he received an extra blow because he had been a strong immediate secessionist.

But I have not time to give you a detailed statement of my maulings, so excuse my shortcomings, and believe me

Yours foolishly,

JESSE HOLMES, The Fool Killer.

In November, 1861, appeared the following note:

Uncle "Jesse Holmes" wants to know if the people are not tired reading war news such as the papers have been filled up with for a few months—publishing substantially the same news over a dozen times. And he wishes it to be borne in mind that he, too, is prosecuting a war, of not less importance than the war between the North and South —his being a war of extermination against Fools and Rascals in general, and the old man claims to be heard from once in a while. If no sane man objects, he will report soon.

A paragraph of a lost letter of Jesse's was copied in the *Southern Literary Messenger* in 1862 by the editor, George W. Bagby, himself one of the best-known Southern humorists:

JESSE HOLMES is the name of the "Fool Killer," employed by the Milton (N. C.) Chronicle. He is supposed to carry a great club, with which he beats out the brains of fools. Since the war broke out, all the fools he has killed have been knaves. As for example:

In Pittsylvania I nabbed a "patriotic" lark who charged soldiers five dollars a piece for taking them packages of clothing. You see he was going to Winchester any how . . . arriving there he made each soldier shell out five dollars on the bundle. My indignation was so great, that on collaring him, I walked into him with my club without pausing for an explanation or to learn his name, and made him "walk-talk ginger-blue, get over on 'tother side of Jordan," where the road is a hard one to travel.

When Jesse is out of employment [continues the *Messenger*], let him come to Richmond. What would he do with a man who would carry on Sunday a barrel of snacks—each snack composed of a slice of meat, between two slices of bread—and sell them to Gen. Lee's soldiers at a dollar a piece? What would he do with a man who would boast that he had made $65 on a barrel of apples, sold to the soldiers? Such a man is said to live in Richmond.

The latest letter from the Fool-Killer that I have found appeared in the *Chronicle* for February 13, 1879, a copy of which may be found in the North Carolina State Library. It is dated from "Mountain Cave, Jan. 30th, 1879." It begins:

Editor—Again the wheel of time has rolled another year into the vortex of oblivion, and the old man seats himself in his cave among the rocks and cliffs of the wild woods to drop a tear over the rapid flight of time and send you a report for the new year up to date. Editor, it is sad to contemplate the past, and he who stops to do it and brood over his adversities will be in danger of going crazy. "So let's be gay," &c., but at the same time keep "right side up, with care," always seeing to it that the children do not depart the paternal roof without their mammas knowing they are out; for, as a child is brought up will it toddle all through life, and if the indulgent parent gives a boy that stands in calf-skin up to his knees an inch, he'll take an ell—certain. Editor, parents have much to answer for in this world and the world to come, for the training up of their children. You may search the world and where you find one man honest and just from innate principle —from a spontaneous love of right and justice—I'll show you two who are honest and just only from the force of circumstances. That is to say, they would cheat, lie and steal at the drop of a hat but for the fear of it being found out, and the dread of punishment by the laws of government and society. Now, Editor, when the children are raised up to love honesty, justice and virtue, and to spurn vice, because it is right and proper to do so, even if there were no laws of government or society to punish them, then the glorious Millenium will come! when chickens may "roost lower," and bolts and bars to doors may be thrown away, and men's simple words will be far better than many of their bonds are now.

This letter deals with some members of the younger generation. One is a young man whom Jesse finds swimming the Hyco River in midwinter to see a girl who cares nothing for him. Another young fellow who has been so foolish as to allow an old bachelor to see his young lady home from a party, has just learned that the bachelor took her straight to a magistrate and married her. Other fools are some fiddlers who have stolen the Christmas candy which an old Negro woman bought for her children. In the following paragraph he describes some more foolish people:

Not far from North Hyco I took the starch out of the sails of a young man who was sleigh-riding some ladies in more mud than snow— he upset the ladies; and the mud pulling off a lady's overshoe, he displayed great gallantry in putting it on her foot. It was not discovered until she got home that the shoe had been put on the wrong foot and over another overshoe. I hated to do it but it was my duty to shake my club at the lady, and I did so with an admonition.

I caught the same ladies out rabbit hunting in the cold snow, and warming their hands by holding them in a rabbit's bed out of which they had just flushed a Molly cotton-tail. I could but laugh at them.

Although I have found no more letters from Jesse Holmes, there is a communication, with the picture of the Fool-Killer in action, published in the Hillsborough *Recorder* for June 1, 1870. Jesse has caught a delegate to a political convention who cast six votes instead of the permitted two. The *Recorder* prints a letter from the conscience-stricken delegate. Here is the last bit I have found: "A hotel clerk in Dallas, Texas, has undertaken to fast 365 days. What a fool! Kill him." That was in 1880. In the same year the Wilmington *Star* had said: "Uncle Jesse Holmes has a great deal of work to do yet."

3

In 1892, when he published *Black Beetles in Amber*, Ambrose Bierce included a poem entitled "To the Fool-Killer." Bierce's fool-killer, who has no name, is only a distant relative of Jesse Holmes. It is not a club but a dirk that he uses to liquidate his victims. The three pests at whom Bierce's wrath is directed apparently all had San Francisco originals. One of these pests is the inveterate hand-shaker. Another is

> the "title" man
> Who saddles one on every back he can,
> Then rides it from Beersheba to Dan!

Becoming personal, the poet adds:

> I trust when next we meet you'll slay the chap
> Who calls old Tyler "Judge" and Merry "Cap"—
> Calls John P. Irish "Colonel" and John P.
> Whose surname Jack-son speaks his pedigree. . . .

But the pest that the poet most dislikes he reserves to the last:

> But chief of all the addle-witted crew
> Conceded by the Hangman's League to you,
> The fool (his dam's acquainted with a knave)
> Whose fluent pen, of his no-brain the slave,
> Strews notes of introduction o'er the land
> And calls it hospitality.

Bierce is of course primarily a prose writer, but some of his other poems are far superior to "To the Fool-Killer." He might well have recommended to the Fool-Killer the man whom the old Union soldier bitterly denounced in "To E. S. Salomon, Who in a Memorial Day Oration Protested Bitterly against Decorating the Graves of Confederate Dead."

Much closer to Jesse Holmes is the leading figure in George Ade's "The Fable of How the Fool-Killer Backed out of a Contract," published in *Fables in Slang* (1900). Ade does not describe his Fool-Killer, but the figure in Clyde J. Newman's illustration carries a club. In the wild beast's skin which is his only garment, the Fool-Killer looks more like Tarzan than Evans's Jesse Holmes. Ade's Fool-Killer is looking over a high fence at a crowd of people milling around in the dust and heat of the smoky oven that is a county fair. "The whimper or the faltering Wail of Children, the quavering Sigh of overlaced Women, and the long-drawn Profanity of Men.—These were what the Fool-Killer heard as he looked upon the Suffering Throng."

> "Why [he asked the Marshal] do the People congregate in the Weeds and allow the Sun to warp them?"
> "Because Everybody does it."
> "Do they Pay to get in?"
> "You know it."
> "Can they Escape?"
> "They can, but they prefer to Stick."
> The Fool-Killer hefted his Club and then looked at the Crowd and shook his Head doubtfully.
> "I can't tackle that Outfit to-day," he said. "It's too big a Job."
> So he went on into Town, and singled out a Main Street Merchant who refused to Advertise.
> MORAL: *People who expect to be Luny will find it safer to travel in a Bunch.*

A fable with a more serious moral than Ade's is Stephen Vincent Benét's "Johnny Pye and the Fool-Killer," which first appeared in the *Saturday Evening Post* on September 18, 1937—just a month before my essay was published in the *South Atlantic Quarterly*. In 1938 Farrar & Rinehart republished it in book form. The story comes from the same rich mine of literary materials as Benét's "The Devil and Daniel Webster," which, he said in 1942, was the kind of story he "had wanted to write for a good many years. We

Jesse Holmes the Fool-Killer

have," he continued, "our own folk-gods and figures of earth in this country—I wanted to write something about them."

Benét's Fool-Killer, like O. Henry's, is a terrifying figure, especially in Charles Child's illustrations. "He was a big man, too, in a checked shirt and corduroy trousers, and he went walking the ways of the world, with a hickory club that had a lump of lead in the end of it." Benét's Fool-Killer sometimes talks like the Button-Moulder in Ibsen's *Peer Gynt*, but in reality he is a blend of Death and Father Time.

Johnny Pye, the central figure of the fable, represents mankind. An orphan, he is adopted by a miller who treats him as a fool. Whenever the miller hears that a man has died, he smacks his lips and exclaims: "Well, the Fool-Killer's come for so-and-so." Johnny runs away from the miller. His next employer is an herb doctor who admits that he is a little in the Fool-Killer's line of business himself. He is kind enough to Johnny, but in other respects he resembles those prize rascals of *Huckleberry Finn*, the Duke and the King. Johnny leaves him when the doctor is ridden out of town on a rail by angry townsmen who had been swindled by the quack doctor. Johnny next works for a merchant but quits when he realizes that he does not really want the kind of success the merchant has achieved. He leaves his next employer, an inventor, who cannot tell what good his perpetual-motion machine will be when he has perfected it. Johnny leaves a minister when he discovers that the good man would never admit into Heaven those who do not believe in his particular brand of religion. Johnny spends some time traveling with a drunken fiddler, who dies drunk in a ditch one night, and for a while he is with a company of soldiers who are fighting Indians. But always he leaves when he hears the footsteps of the Fool-Killer far off in the sky. He tries book learning with no great enthusiasm. He goes to Washington to see the President, who he thinks surely has nothing to fear from the Fool-Killer. He declines the President's suggestion that he go into politics, but he accepts an appointment as a small-town postmaster so that he can marry Susie Marsh. He has found that when he is in love with Susie he can forget the Fool-Killer.

When he is sixty-one, Johnny Pye meets an old scissors grinder who has "a lank, old white horse . . . with every rib showing." The old man, who is sharpening a scythe, says that he is the Fool-Killer and asks if Johnny is ready. Johnny of course is not ready. The Fool-Killer remarks: "Here you spend your youth running away from being a fool. And yet, what's the first thing you do when you're man grown? Why, you marry a girl, settle down in your home town, and start raising children when you don't know how they'll turn out. You might have known I'd catch up with you then. . . ." The Fool-Killer finally lets Johnny go for a while. He even offers to let him off permanently if he will answer one question: "How can a man be a human being and not be a fool?" When he is approaching ninety-two, Johnny Pye meets the Fool-Killer once more. His wife is dead and he is tired of living. He now has an answer to the Fool-Killer's question: "For you asked me how a man could be a human being and yet not be a fool. And the answer is—when he's dead and gone and buried. Any fool would know that." And yet, he adds: "I wouldn't give much for a man that some folks hadn't thought was a fool in his time." Since Johnny has answered his question, the scissors grinder offers to let him off again. Johnny hesitates and wants to know if after death he will see his friends again. "I can't tell you that," says the Fool-Killer. "I only go so far."

I cannot help thinking that there will be more and better stories of the Fool-Killer. Think, for instance, what Rabelais or Cervantes or Swift or Mark Twain might have made of the idea! I am still hoping that some gifted American writer will revive Jesse Holmes and his friend the Rascal-Whaler and make them leading figures in a memorable novel, play, or narrative poem. And Charles Napoleon Bonaparte Evans surely deserves to be remembered on his own account as one of the finest specimens of the small-town newspaper editors of the Old South.

III. The West

Ministrels latent on the prairies!
(Shrouded bards of other lands you may rest, you have done your work,)
Soon I hear you coming warbling, soon you rise and tramp amid us,
  Pioneers! O pioneers!

WALT WHITMAN, "Pioneers! O Pioneers!"

Though Turner's interpretation has been challenged, it has con-
tinued to grow, and its influence has spread to literature, political
science, philosophy, and even to psychiatry. It is today imbedded in the
fabric of American thought, and is slowly invading other frontier so-
cieties.

WALTER PRESCOTT WEBB, The Great Fron-
tier (1952), p. 6n.

The Frontier in American Literature

[It was in 1893 that Frederick Jackson Turner read before the American Historical Association in Chicago his epoch-making paper, "The Significance of the Frontier in American History." By 1924 so much work had been done by historians on the subject that in that year Frederic L. Paxson was able to publish *A History of the American Frontier*. Yet not until the 1920's did scholars in the field of American literature seem aware that Turner's hypothesis might lead to a new interpretation of that literature. Miss Dorothy Dondore and Mrs. Lucy L. Hazard were the first to publish books revealing clearly an indebtedness to Turner.

I think it was in Turner's book *The Frontier in American History*, published in 1920, that I discovered his memorable essay. I began soon afterwards tentatively applying his hypothesis in my teaching of Western writers. The first version of "The Frontier in American Literature" was published in the *Southwest Review* in January, 1925. In December, 1924, I had read it before the American Literature Group of the Modern Language Association in New York. The essay underwent considerable revision and expansion before it appeared in *The Reinterpretation of American Literature* (1928), which Norman Foerster edited for the American Literature Group. The concluding section was added after my removal to Duke University in 1927, and it owes something to critical comments made by two of my Duke University colleagues, Richard H. Shryock and Paull F. Baum. The present version embodies only a few slight changes and additions.

Most of the attacks upon Turner's theory came after 1928. Two of the most important are Benjamin F. Wright's "American Democracy and the Frontier," published in the *Yale Review*, XX, 349-365 (Winter, 1930), and Thomas P. Abernethy, *From Frontier to Plantation in Tennessee* (1932). A decade later George W. Pierson in two articles reported the mixed results of an investigation he had undertaken for the American Historical Association: "The Frontier and American Institutions," *New England Quarterly*, XV, 224-255 (June, 1942) and "American Historians and the Frontier Hypothesis in 1941," *Wisconsin Magazine of History*, XXVI, 35-60, 170-185 (Sept. and Dec., 1942). See also Pierson's "Recent Studies of Turner: The Frontier Doctrine," *Mississippi Valley Historical Review*, XXXIV, 453-458 (December, 1947). Other scholars, like Ray Billington and Walter Prescott Webb, have expressed a somewhat more favorable view. In *British Essays in American History* (1957) Professor H. C. Allen of the University of London maintained that a reconsideration of Turner's hypothesis "leaves a remarkable proportion of his thesis standing." He added: "Broad generalizations about whole societies are always difficult and seldom absolutely true, but it is not really possible to doubt the deep and lasting influence of the frontier upon the history of the United States, nor to question that it directly contributed to the formation of many of the most pronounced characteristics of the American people."

The Reinterpretation of American Literature was an important book in its field. Before it was reprinted in 1959, it had become a collector's item. The symposium was in effect a co-operative challenge to all students of American literature—a subject which in many quarters was in 1928 not considered quite a respectable study. The contributors to *The Reinterpretation* hoped, as Foerster stated in his Introduction, "to encourage and in some measure direct a fresher, more thoughtful, more purposeful approach to the understanding of our literature." In 1955 one of the ablest of a still younger generation of scholars, C. Hugh Holman, could say that *The Reinterpretation* "was, in a way, a turning point, and [that] its objective, organized scholarship devoted to American literature, has since been realized."

The idea of such a book came to me while I was reading Arthur M. Schlesinger's *New Viewpoints in American History* (1922); and when I suggested the project to the American Literature Group, they agreed to sponsor it.

Something like a renaissance in American literary studies followed the publication of *The Reinterpretation* in 1928 and the launching in March, 1929, of the quarterly *American Literature*, published by the Duke University Press as the semi-official organ of the American Literature Group. In these two ventures those pioneer scholars—Fred Lewis Pattee, Arthur Hobson Quinn, Killis Campbell, and William B. Cairns—were joined by a number of younger scholars whose ability and enthusiasm gave a new impetus to the study of American writers.]

1

The frontier as a factor in American literature furnishes a striking example of the protracted neglect, by students of our literature, of methods and points of view that had been found revolutionary in the field of American history. In a memorable paper on "The Significance of the Frontier in American History," read in 1893 before the American Historical Association, Frederick J. Turner emphasized the importance of the frontier and outlined a program for the study of the field. Since that time the historians have worked the entire field so thoroughly that in 1924 Frederic L. Paxson could publish a *History of the American Frontier*. Yet it was thirty years after the publication of Turner's paper before anyone made a real application of his point of view to American literature. As one looks back now, one wonders why it was necessary to wait for Turner to show us the historical or the literary importance of the frontier. It is implicit in Whitman's "Pioneers! O Pioneers!" and in Emerson's famous remark, "Europe extends to the Alleghanies; America lies beyond." Surely, in the field of American literature, we need not only a more exact but also a more imaginative scholarship.

Every discussion of the frontier must inevitably begin with

Turner's paper of 1893. The following extract makes clear his point of view:

The wilderness masters the colonist. It finds him a European in dress, industries, tools, modes of travel, and thought. It takes him from the railroad car and puts him in the birch canoe. It strips off the garments of civilization and arrays him in the hunting shirt and the moccasin. It puts him in the log cabin of the Cherokee and Iroquois and runs an Indian palisade around him. Before long he has gone to planting Indian corn and plowing with a sharp stick; he shouts the war cry and takes the scalp in orthodox Indian fashion. In short, at the frontier the environment is at first too strong for the man. He must accept the conditions which it furnishes, or perish, and so he fits himself into the Indian clearings and follows the Indian trails. Little by little he transforms the wilderness, but the outcome is not the old Europe, not simply the development of Germanic germs. . . . The fact is, that here is a new product that is American. . . . Thus the advance of the frontier has meant a steady movement away from the influence of Europe, a steady growth of independence on American lines. And to study this advance, the men who grew up under these conditions, and the political, economic, and social results of it, is to study the really American part of our history.

By the term *frontier* the historians do not, of course, mean anything resembling the sharply defined and strongly fortified Franco-German border. The American frontier is (or was) the no man's land which separates civilization from savagery. In its widest sense the word has come to be used as almost identical with the geographic environment. It includes such factors as the immense and isolating distance which separated America from Europe—and, in turn, the Atlantic seaboard from the region west of the Appalachians; the absence of many European customs and institutions; the abundance of free land, which gave America an unparalleled economic opportunity; and the presence of many nationalities and many shades of opinion on the border. The frontier was a rapidly shifting, ever-changing thing; as it gradually receded westward, it continually took on new colors from the changing environment. It was less a definite area than a form of society or a complex of habits of thought, feeling, and action.

Among the historians there has been as yet [in 1928] singularly little adverse criticism of Turner's point of view. A skeptic, distrustful of formulas, might ask whether the historians, in their interpretation of American history, have not leaned too heavily upon the economic and geographic factors. Is it not possible that the frontier influence has, in the main, merely accentuated tendencies already in operation in the Old World? For example, the worldwide growth of democracy during the past century would suggest that other influences have played an important part in that growth in this country as well as in Europe. England, always remote from the frontier, has perhaps a better working democracy than our own. One might ask further whether the frontier in Latin America, Australia, and South Africa has exerted such an influence as it is supposed to have exerted in the United States. Such questions must of course be answered by the historians themselves. They are mentioned here merely to suggest that, if we push the frontier influence in American literature too far, we shall ultimately have to revise our interpretation in the light of later developments in American historical study. We cannot assume that the continued study of our history will lead to no new approaches or interpretations.

In applying Turner's point of view to American literature, we should also remember that history and literature are not interchangeable terms. If, as Turner believes, "The true point of view in the history of this nation is not the Atlantic coast; it is the Great West," does it necessarily follow that the true point of view in our literary history is the same? Perhaps it does, but one should remember that our literature has always been less American than our history; possibly it is not even yet a national literature in the full sense of the word. Our intellectual dependence upon Europe continued long after the political separation from the mother country —and it still continues. In our cultural history foreign influences have been stronger than in our political and economic life. Although much of our political history was made on or near the frontier, our books have, as a rule, been written by authors, and for readers, quite remote from it. American literature is, necessarily, a paler, less distinct reflection of the frontier than is our history. In *The Cambridge History of American Literature* in 1917 Carl Van Doren noted an "analogy between the geographic and the imaginative frontier of the United States" and added: "As the first advanced, thin, straggling, from the Atlantic to the Pacific, widening from Canada to Mexico, and reaching out in ships, the other followed, also thin and straggling but with an incessant purpose to find out new territories which the imagination could play over and claim for its own."

There is yet another consideration to be borne in mind. Even those of our writers who have been most determined to employ only native materials have been dependent upon Europe for all that we call form or technique. Without Scott's novels, we should never have had the Leather-Stocking Tales, nor perhaps *The Scarlet Letter*. For *The Song of Hiawatha*, Longfellow borrowed the metrical form of the Finnish *Kalevala*. In Taine's *Art of the Netherlands* Edward Eggleston found a suggestion for the method which he employed in *The Hoosier Schoolmaster*. Owen Wister's first Western story was, by his own admission, modeled on a story by Prosper Mérimée. And, if we may believe Conrad Aiken, our contemporary poets are as deeply indebted to Europe as any of their predecessors. Amy Lowell, for example, probably owed as much to Europe as did her kinsman, James Russell Lowell.

2

The frontier, as I see it, has made two distinct and important contributions to our literature: it has given our writers a vast field of new materials, and it has given them a new point of view, which we may call American.

Our early nineteenth-century authors fell heir to a new and varied natural background, which appealed strongly to the Romantic imagination. Here they found the primeval forest, practically gone from Europe, and the great plains, not to be paralleled in Europe outside of Russia; they found rivers which made the Thames and the Tweed seem like pigmies, and mountains loftier than the Alps. Here was a new country, practically as large as the whole of Europe and rivaling Europe in its natural wonders and in its variety of climate and topography. To the imagination of Romantic poets, America was almost Utopia come true; it was Nature (with a capital) comparatively uncorrupted by the defiling hand of man.

The American scene, too, was filled with new and striking character types. There was that romantic and mysterious child of Nature, the Indian, who enjoyed a vogue in the literatures of Europe before America had a literature. There was a whole tribe of frontier and semifrontier types: the half-breed, the trader, the hunter, the trapper, the bush-ranger *(coureur de bois)*, the scout, the missionary, the frontier soldier, the cowboy, the sheepherder, the miner, the ranger, the gambler, the Pike, the "bad man," the "greaser," the squatter, the Mormon, the circuit rider, the lumberjack, the Hoosier, the poor white, the Southern mountaineer, who lives in a curiously retarded frontier region; and we may perhaps include the varied types found in the Western oil fields of today. To these we must add the frontier women, less numerous but not less interesting than the men. All these frontier types were racy, individual, and quite distinct from European types. And their variety was greatly increased by the presence on the border of contrasting racial strains: Indian, English, Scotch-Irish, German, Scandinavian, French, and Spanish.

It was in many respects a sordid and futile life which the pioneers led, but it abounded in adventure, change, and freedom; and it was close to nature. On the border, truth was often stranger than the wildest of fiction. It is no wonder that our novelists have found in frontier life a wealth of incidents or that a few writers like Frank Norris have seen in the westward movement the last great epic event in our history.

One must not forget that the conquest of a great continent has not found expression adequate to its magnitude or importance. Cooper's Leather-Stocking Tales have a certain epic quality, but for too many of our writers the frontier has been a legend rather than a reality. Most of the novels that deal with the frontier were written by men who had no first-hand experience of pioneer life. Consequently our frontier fiction is, as a rule, no "document" for the social historian; it represents a literary convention. Most of our major writers, living in metropolitan centers, had little opportunity to know frontier life; and the pioneers themselves were seldom writers, or even readers, of books. Socially, the frontier represents a primitive stage, an unliterary stage. Many other stages—not necessarily many years—had to follow before the descendants of the pioneers had any vital interest in describing the frontier and before the West had reached the economic and cultural level at which literature begins to be produced. Indeed, some parts of the West cannot be said even yet to have reached that level. It is not surprising, then, that many aspects of frontier life vanished before being accurately described; and now that the frontier is gone never to return, much of that life will probably never be adequately recorded. Few, except an occasional Hamlin Garland, care what the reality was. The popular novel, the cheap magazine, and the motion picture theater have commercialized the legend of the frontier; Zane Grey flourishes and Andy Adams is practically forgotten.[1]

3

The study of the frontier as literary subject matter is much less difficult than the accurate appraisal of the frontier influence in other directions. For here we deal with an influence which is indirect, protean, incessantly changing, interplaying with other factors almost equally elusive. The frontier influence in *The Last of the Mohicans* and "The Outcasts of Poker Flat" is easy to see, but what of the indirect frontier influence in Emerson's "The American Scholar" and Whitman's "Song of the Open Road"? Here we need to walk warily and to remember that this particular field has not yet been systematically studied. I merely suggest tentatively certain conclusions which I believe further investigation will warrant, and I do this primarily to suggest what lines our study should follow.

The frontier had an influence upon many of our writers who never saw it. The appeal of this vast Western hinterland to the imagination of those tho lived upon the Atlantic seaboard is difficult to estimate, but it undoubtedly existed. If Henry James could explain the difference between Turgenev and the typical French novelist by saying that the back door of the Russian's imagination was always open upon the endless Russian steppes, surely the existence of the American frontier helps to explain some of the differences between Emerson and Whitman and their British contemporaries, Carlyle and Tennyson. Hawthorne told Howells that he "would like to see some part of the country on which the . . . shadow of Europe had not fallen"; and even the domestic Longfellow longed to share Frémont's exhilarating experiences in the Far West, although he sighed, "Ah, the discomforts!"

If our literature is a reflection of the national character, it should be strongly colored by our experience with the frontier. For it was chiefly the frontier influence which, as Norman Foerster has said, "transformed the European type into such men as Jefferson, Jackson, Lincoln, and Theodore Roosevelt, or, among the writers, Emerson, Whitman, and Mark Twain." Turner believed that the

[1] I note in 1965 that the "Westerns" are the most popular of stories seen on television. For all their realism in external details, they present a conventionalized and very incomplete picture of life on the American frontier.

frontier supplied the key to the American character. "To the frontier," said he, "the American intellect owes its striking characteristics. That coarseness and strength combined with acuteness and inquisitiveness; that practical, inventive turn of mind, quick to find expedients; that masterful grasp of material things, lacking in the artistic but powerful to effect great ends; that restless, nervous energy; that dominant individualism, working for good and for evil, and withal that buoyancy and exuberance which comes with freedom—these are traits of the frontier, or traits called out elsewhere because of the existence of the frontier."

To what extent are these frontier traits to be seen in our literature? Mr. Turner himself, in a letter to the writer, said, "I thoroughly agree that what is distinctive in American, in contrast to general English literature, comes out of our experience with the frontier, broadly considered." It is natural, I think, to conclude that there is, in the writings of such men as Whitman, Mark Twain, and William James, something distinctively American which comes indirectly from the frontier; but it is no easy matter to put one's finger upon it and say, here it is. A good case can be made out for much of our political writing, which is closer to our life than most of what is known as belles-lettres. Indeed, Bliss Perry finds that the dominant note in American literature is the civic note, which surely owes much to frontier democracy. Henry Seidel Canby has argued, too, that the "nature book," perhaps the only new literary type which America has given the world, grew out of our fathers' experience with the frontier and our own longing for the vanished frontier environment.

Much of what we are accustomed to call American literature, however, has no discernible connection with the frontier; the work of Edgar Allan Poe is a conspicuous example. Much of our literature is un-American, imitative of Europe. Too often, as John Macy has pointed out, it is distinguished by just those qualities which the American intellect is supposed to lack: it is dainty, polished, fanciful, sentimental, feminine, and "literary." The contemporary revolt against our cis-Atlantic Victorians, however, would indicate that many of our older writers were out of harmony with what now seems to be the genuine American tradition.

American literature has become a national literature—if we may now call it national—largely through what Van Wyck Brooks, in a letter to the writer, called "the sublimation of the frontier spirit." American literature has become increasingly American. It may be well here to try to indicate the part which the frontier has played in the nationalization of our literature.

The American Revolution, the historians tell us, was in large measure due to the political and economic influence of the frontier. In the new environment had grown up a people to whom the English were comparative strangers. Under the stress of the common struggle, first against France and later against England, a new national consciousness had developed in the thirteen colonies, which finally declared themselves a new nation. The frontier conception of democracy, modified of course by European political theory and experience, was written into the Declaration of Independence. Eventually it brought about something akin to a social and economic revolution in American life.

With the achievement of political independence and with the natural reaction against all things English, it was inevitable that there should arise a demand for a national literature which would express the new national culture. It was felt that a nation whose political and social life was based on democratic principles should have a literature quite unlike that of undemocratic Britain. A good deal of ignorance of literary history and a certain lack of logic are seen in the reasoning of the advocates of a national literature; and the literature which they prophesied was not born full-grown like Minerva from the brain of Jove. Nevertheless from the early nineteenth century down to the present there has been a succession of declarations of cultural and intellectual independence from England. These include Emerson's "The American Scholar," Whitman's Preface to *Leaves of Grass*, Mark Twain's *Innocents Abroad*, and Van Wyck Brooks's *America's Coming of Age*. The new national literature, however, did not come in response to the immediate demand. It was the Romantic movement, and not the outmoded neoclassical literary tradition, which gave American writers the technical methods of putting the national life into literature. Ultimately, however, as Carl Van Doren has pointed out, the Revolution became one of the "three matters of American romance," the other two being the settlement and the frontier.

Perhaps the influence of Jacksonian democracy had something to do with Whitman's attempt to create a native American literature. Whitman of course was not a frontiersman, but there is a certain analogy between what he and the Jacksonian democrats tried to accomplish. Emerson was too much the scholar and the gentleman to attempt all that Whitman tried to do, but he saw hope even in the Jacksonians for the future of American literature. Lamenting the cultural dependence of America upon England, he wrote in his *Journals* in 1834: "I suppose the evil may be cured by this rank rabble party, the Jacksonism of the country, heedless of English and all literature—a stone cut out of the ground without hands;—they may root out the hollow dilettantism of our cultivation in the coarsest way, and the newborn may begin again to frame their own world with greater advantage."

The Civil War gave a great impetus to national tendencies in all fields and did much to complete the work left incomplete by the Revolution. It brought about "the birth of a nation," and in literature it led to what Fred Lewis Pattee has called "the second discovery of America." By abolishing slavery and settling the question of secession, the war made the nation a political unit that it had never been before. Americans gradually ceased to say, "The United States *are*," and began to say, "The United States *is*." Political and military leadership passed from New England and the South to the more thoroughly American Middle West, which, in Lowell's phrase, gave us "the first American," Abraham Lincoln. The Civil War stimulated the progress of the economic or industrial revolution, which, more than any other influence besides the frontier, has made the whole country an economic and cultural unit. In ante-bellum days American literature was little more than an aggregation of sectional literatures; after the war it became national in a sense of the word not applicable before that time.

In the Americanization of our literature the West, especially the Middle West, played a leading part. The writings of New Englanders and New Yorkers did not satisfy the West. Edward Eggleston, jealous of the literary domination of New England, wrote *The Hoosier Schoolmaster* to show that Indiana furnished as rich materials for the novelist as Massachusetts. Bret Harte and other young men, so he tells us, were trying to create a California literature. A more important spokesman for the West was Mark Twain. What Ibsen and Tolstoy were to nineteenth-century Europe, that or something like it Mark Twain was to the United States: a new region had found a spokesman, and what he had to say did not resemble the work of Hawthorne and Longfellow. A new spirit also began to move the reconstructed and reviving South; and the more cosmopolitan spirit of the Middle Atlantic states blended with the influence of the South and the West to create something approximating a national point of view in our literature.

Meanwhile the best work of nearly all the great New Englanders had been done. The Romantic impulse had become conventional, and the influence of European realism was becoming apparent. Upon Howells, a Westerner by birth, had descended the editorial mantle of the *Atlantic Monthly*. But Howells was thoroughly de-Westernized, and New England assimilated him without great difficulty. It was to his friend Mark Twain that New England objected as representing the Western barbarians of literature. At the Whittier birthday dinner of the *Atlantic* in 1877, the custodians of the Brahmin tradition condemned in no uncertain manner the vulgarity of the literary West. Howells tells us that of the Boston-Cambridge group only Francis James Child and Charles Eliot Norton made anything of the man whom Howells regarded as "the Lincoln of our literature"; even Lowell did not warm to him. The current of events, however, was too strong for the Brahmins. Howells himself went to New York, thereby admitting that the literary scepter had passed from Boston. New York is now our publishing center, our literary capital, if we have one; but the productive center of American literature is perhaps nearer Chicago. Certainly the Middle West aspires to cultural as well as industrial leadership, and it is significant that the favorite background of contemporary fiction is the Middle West.

4

One must not, as I have said, push the frontier influence too far. Our literary history is the result of the interplay of complex and changing influences, political, economic, social, cultural, educational —sectional, national, foreign. Properly to understand and appraise the influence of the frontier, one must thoroughly understand other influences and their interrelations.

The frontier influence is not the only influence making for nationalism in American literature. At least two other historical factors have had a part in it. In the first place, many of the immigrants who came to this country from the very beginning did not represent the English type in race, in religious beliefs, or in social status. They were, to a large extent, nonconformists; nor were these by any means confined to New England, as we too often suppose. The nonconformists played a large part in the development of the American bourgeoisie, with its well-known attitude toward art and literature. Immigration, moreover, was itself a selective process. The more restless and the more aggressive came, whereas the conservative, as a rule, remained in Europe. The character of our immigrants accounts in part for the peculiar American blend of radicalism and conservatism which strikes our foreign critics as odd. Many of the immigrants, however, even in Colonial times, were not English or even British. Mr. Mencken and Professor Schlesinger have argued that the fine arts in America have been developed largely by men of mixed blood. At any rate, the typical American would not be a typical Englishman even had there been no influence from the frontier.

Another influence making for nationalism is the economic or industrial revolution. In the course of a century American life has become predominantly urban; and it is based very largely upon machinery. As a result, American life is to a great degree uniform throughout the country. The same tendency toward standardization is found in our books, our magazines, and our schools. Even those who rebel against the tyrannous uniformity of American life and thought seem to rebel *en masse,* as it were, and merely substitute the conventions of the *American Mercury* for those of the *Saturday Evening Post*—as if one could by any such change of front become individual and original.

In our eagerness to point out the national tendencies in our literature, one should not overlook the sectional. Most of those engaged in research in American literature have been prejudiced against the sectional approach by the poor quality of existing sectional studies. Even the political historians have neglected sectional tendencies, except as they concern the slavery issue, so much that Turner has felt it necessary in a recent article to urge a new study of sectionalism in American history. The frontier influence, in the main a national one, has at times made for sectionalism. In Colonial times it was the frontier which created the first sectionalism of West

281

against East. In recent years we have seen the semifrontier West, sometimes allied with the South, arrayed against the industrial belt of North and East.

To understand the literary influence of the frontier, one must study it in connection with the influences which came from Europe. Influences from abroad have increased rather than diminished, for the revolution in methods of transportation and communication has brought Europe closer to New York than Boston and Philadelphia were a century ago. European literary fashions have to a large extent determined the manner in which our writers have portrayed the pioneers.

5

Before bringing this essay to a conclusion, it seems necessary to insist that, if our literary historians are to continue to use the term *frontier*, it must be carefully defined. To a layman, it would seem that even the historians sometimes use the term loosely. "In the census reports," says Turner, "it is treated as the margin of that settlement which has a density of two or more to the square mile. The term is an elastic one, and for our purposes does not need sharp definition.[2] We shall consider the whole frontier belt, including the Indian country and the outer margin of the 'settled area' of the census reports." In justice to Turner, it should be stated that he was, in his own words, attempting only "to call attention to the frontier as a fertile field for investigation, and to suggest some of the problems which arise in connection with it." Professor Paxson notes that "The American frontier was a line, a region, or a process, according to the context in which the word is used," but even he attempts no exact definition of the term.

Careful historians like Paxson and Turner doubtless have a fairly definite meaning in mind even though they do not take the trouble of defining the word. Many persons without the scholar's

[2] "In the United States the word frontier has an entirely different meaning, and carries a different set of implications and connotations. It becomes a concept with such wide ramifications and so many shades of meaning that it cannot be wrapped up in a neat definition like a word whose growth has ceased and whose meaning has become frozen. It is something that lives, moves geographically, and eventually dies" (Walter Prescott Webb, *The Great Frontier*, 1952, p. 2). What Webb undertook to do in this notable study is explained in his own words: "It is the American frontier concept that needs to be lifted out of its present national setting and applied on a much larger scale to all of Western civilization in modern times" (p. 7).

The Frontier in American Literature

feeling for accuracy use the term very loosely. The word has acquired certain connotations which do not properly belong to it. It
has a poetic flavor; it suggests something native, something fine and
romantic which other countries conspicuously lack. But to one who
has read Hamsun's *Growth of the Soil*, the opening pages of Butler's
Erewhon, or the *Oxford Book of Australasian Verse*, it is permissible
to doubt whether the American frontier is quite unique. We are
in danger of forgetting the sordid side of the American frontier.
Among Westerners in particular the term has much the same
glamour that the *Old South* has in Virginia or the *Pilgrim Fathers*
in New England. There is a halo about the forehead of the pioneer.
Such provincial pride, amounting sometimes to ancestor worship,
inevitably interferes with the historian's seeing things as they are.
After all, are the economic and geographic influences implied in
the term *frontier* essentially different from those to be found in
sparsely settled regions the world over?

Our literary historians have used the word *frontier* more loosely
than the historians; the term has become increasingly vague and
ambiguous. Like the *Celtic spirit*, the *Greek influence*, *Romanticism*, *Classicism*, and *Realism*, the term *frontier* may be made to
mean whatever the user wishes it to mean. The frontier should not
be identified with all the national influences in our literature; it
should not be identified with the geographic environment. The
frontier passes; the natural background remains, often unchanged.
The Adirondacks and the Marshes of Glynn once belonged to the
frontier, but not today.

In literature there are two fairly definite uses of the word which
seem legitimate. We may properly refer to the frontier as a literary
background. There is no ambiguity here except when we include
semifrontier regions, as we often do. We may also use the word
when we refer to the beginnings of literary activity on the frontier,
as in Professor Rusk's *The Literature of the Middle Western Frontier*.

A third common use of the term, however, calls for closer definition. We have too often identified the frontier with *all* the national
influences in our literary history. The sources of the national spirit
are, as I have tried to indicate, more numerous; and the whole
problem is quite complex. If we do not use the term more carefully,

we shall soon find it as thoroughly discredited as Taine's famous formula: race, environment, and epoch. I do not think we can dispense with the term, but I do expect that we shall use it more accurately. If we do not, the results of our investigation may be no more creditable to American scholarship than are the works of certain of our predecessors whom we need not name here.

Man, especially the Nordic, cannot tear himself loose from the soil he has rooted in for centuries and move to a new land, where even the very air chills by its strangeness without paying a great price. There is intimate kinship between the soul and the soil in which it grows. Traditions are spun slowly; they can never be bought. To build a Fatherland is a long process.

> OLE RÖLVAAG, "The Vikings of the Western Prairies"

> *. . . we receive but what we give,*
> *And in our life alone does Nature live.*

> SAMUEL TAYLOR COLERIDGE, "Dejection: An Ode"

The Great Plains: A Study in Landscape

[This essay is based in part upon wide reading in the literature of the West but also to a great extent on my own reactions to the landscape of the Texas plains.

I had my first sight of a prairie in October, 1915, while I was on my way from New York to Dallas, where I was to teach in Southern Methodist University, which had opened its doors for the first time a month earlier. The prairie landscape in Oklahoma and Texas fascinated me, but I was not sure that I liked it. I remembered that Carl Van Doren had said to me just before his first visit to Europe: "I know that the Swiss Alps and the Italian lakes are supposed to be more beautiful than anything on the Western plains, but to me there is nothing on earth more beautiful than an Illinois prairie." The few buildings at S.M.U. seemed inappropriately set on the Johnson grass prairie, but there were many fine trees along the Trinity River and the creeks that ran into it. In 1923 I first saw the treeless plains as I drove across the Texas Panhandle on my way to the University of Colorado. The ranch country seemed to me in its own way beautiful, but it was a country for cattle and cowboys, not for men and women looking for a home. Seen in the distance, the small Texas towns were like piles of empty cardboard boxes which the wind would soon blow away. On my return to Dallas at the end of the summer, driving alone at night and tired, I could not bring myself to realize that I was on the plains and not on some familiar road in rural Virginia. I saw the high plains again in 1933, and in 1949 I saw the semidesert country of New Mexico, Arizona, and California. In the spring of 1960 I saw much of the South Plains during the four months when I was Visiting Professor at Texas Technological College in Lubbock. This region was once the home of the dreaded Comanches. Later it was cattle-land, but now, thanks to irrigation, it is given over largely to the cultivation of cotton. At this time I thought much about the immigrant's problem of learning to feel at home on the treeless plains. Except during a dust storm, it seemed to me a place where one might in time come to feel at home. My West Texas students, however, were hardly aware that the plains landscape presented any problem for the immigrant who came to the Staked Plains from the Eastern seaboard.

In Texas, Colorado, and California I have noted among my students varying reactions to the landscapes of the West. One of them, Henry Nash Smith, is the author of that fine study, *Virgin Land: The American West as Symbol and Myth*. Another student, a native of West Texas whose name I remember as Bowden, told me of his experiences in the wooded country of the Ozarks, where he had spent a summer. "Up there," he said to me, "you can never see more than a quarter of a mile in any direction. I had at times a feeling akin to suffocation. I felt hemmed in and I longed for the open spaces of the region where I grew up." Quite different was the reaction of an undergraduate named Dawson Powell, who had grown up in Massachusetts before coming to Texas. I remember the look of astonishment and incredulity on the faces of the other members of the S.M.U. poetry club ("The Makers") when they heard the opening line of a poem he had written: "Hell, I think, is like a prairie."

In the years 1924-1927 I was editing the *Southwest Review* and planning a book (never written) on the frontier in American literature. I was particularly struck by the differences between the reactions to the prairie landscape written by visitors from the outside and those who had grown up on the plains. Finally, after using the materials I had collected in lectures to my students overseas and at home, I decided to put them in their present form.]

1

When the American pioneers from Kentucky and Indiana came to the treeless prairies of Illinois, they were brought to a standstill. The land that wouldn't grow trees, they had been taught, was very poor land indeed. How was it possible to live in a treeless country? The whole technique of the pioneer farmer, which had been slowly and laboriously perfected in the wooded country east of the Appalachians, depended upon trees, the rifle, the ax, and the saw. Without timber the pioneer could not build his log cabin or find wood to keep it warm in winter. He could not build fences to keep his cattle from straying. Slowly the pioneers learned to their surprise that the prairie land was more fertile than almost all the land they had left behind in Virginia and the Carolinas. At first they followed the rivers and creeks, where there were some trees, but finally they moved out upon the treeless land, plowed up the tough prairie sod, and grew bumper crops far from Eastern markets. The New England farmers, after the opening of the Erie Canal in 1825, left their rocky hillsides in great numbers to migrate hundreds of miles to the prairie land where there were no rocks and the rich soil was many feet deep.

The resourceful pioneers soon learned to adapt their way of life to the prairie lands in those areas where the rainfall was sufficient to grow the crops they had always cultivated. But when the pioneer farmers or their sons and grandsons went still further westward and came to the land where the rainfall was insufficient to grow corn or even wheat and oats, they saw themselves stopped by a great natural barrier. Finally, learning that on the Pacific coast there was an abundance of well-watered land with magnificent forests, they began making the two-thousand mile journey in their covered wagons to that land of promise. With the discovery of gold in California in 1848 other men set out for the gold fields. Some of them, like Bret Harte, went by sea and across the Isthmus of Panama, but many went overland in their prairie schooners. It was a long and difficult journey across the high and dry plains through an unfriendly and unhomelike land, and many never lived to see the Pacific coast country. Among the perils that lay in wait for the unwary emigrants were sand storms, blizzards, long waterless stretches along the trail, quicksands in the rivers, and the added dangers that confronted the emigrants if they left the trail looking for an easier route or seeking food for themselves or their horses and cattle. Many died from disease, hunger, or thirst, and some were killed by the Indians. Many of those who reached Oregon or California had lost their horses, cattle, wagons, and precious articles they were carrying to a land that lacked modern conveniences. Is it any wonder that early explorers named the high and dry plains the Great American Desert and that map makers represented it graphically in the same way they represented the Sahara Desert? The Spaniards, who had first explored this inhospitable country and found no gold, had long since given most of it back to the Indians.

There were living creatures on the high and dry plains that had adapted their way of life to the difficult environment: buffaloes, antelopes, coyotes, jackrabbits, tarantulas, and prairie dogs. There were also those latecomers, the fleet wild horses of the plains known as mustangs. They were the offspring of domestic horses that in Mexico had escaped from their Spanish owners and run wild. The plains Indians, whose lives had been miserable before they acquired horses, were now superb horsemen and in battle more than a match for the United States Cavalry or the Texas Rangers. The Comanches, the Apaches, and the Sioux were a formidable obstacle to the settlement of the plains.

It was not until the Texas Rangers were supplied with revolvers invented and manufactured by a Connecticut Yankee, Samuel Colt, that they were a match for the Indians. Years after a disastrous fight with the Rangers a Comanche chief said that he never wanted to fight Jack Hays and his Texas Rangers again. They each had a shot for every finger on the hand, and he had lost half his warriors who died for a hundred miles along the trail that led to Devil's River. The story of the invention of the revolver and of other things which made it possible for men to settle the high and dry plains has been told in detail in Walter Prescott Webb's *The Great Plains*.

Close to the 98th meridian there is a line running from central

Texas to the Dakotas that Webb calls "an institutional fault," which he likens to a geological fault:

At this *fault* the ways of life and living changed. Practically every institution that was carried across it was either broken and remade or else greatly altered. The ways of travel, the weapons, the method of tilling the soil, the plows and other agricultural implements, and even the laws themselves were modified. . . . In the new region—level, timberless, and semi-arid—they [the pioneers] were thrown by Mother Necessity into the clutch of new circumstances.

Meanwhile as the buffaloes were being wantonly killed off for their hides or shot for sport, their places on the plains were taken by the half-wild longhorn cattle. The American cattlemen took over a way of life which had been developed in Mexico and skilfully adapted to the environment. In time much of the land became too valuable to be left as an open range for the cattlemen to roam. It was long, however, before the pioneer settlers were able to solve the problem of living in a treeless country with deficient rainfall. The sod house replaced the log cabin in many places; and windmills, deep wells or artesian wells, irrigation, and new methods of "dry farming" helped to solve the problem of insufficient water. New and improved varieties of grain, imported from Russia and the Orient, proved better than the grain the settlers had brought with them to the plains. The invention of barbed wire made it easier and far less expensive to fence the open prairie.

At best, however, a large portion of the high and dry plains, including much of the Rocky Mountain country, is suitable only for grass and cattle. If the sod is plowed up the farmer may, if the weather is favorable, be able to grow a crop of wheat or some other grain. That was the case at the time of the First World War when the need for grain was great and farm laborers were few, but soon there came a succession of dry years and millions of acres on the high plains became a dust bowl, and thousands of farmers left for California. The American pioneers were a brave and a resourceful people, but they had little respect for the natural resources of the land in either East or West and took no thought of the needs of future generations. Slowly their descendants have had to learn to care properly for the land. In 1878 Major John Wesley Powell, the explorer of the Grand Canyon, published a remarkable official report on *Lands of the Arid Region,* in which he warned of the dangers of overgrazing, erosion, and destruction of the timber on watersheds. He pointed out the need for new laws governing water rights in a land where water was scarce, and he noted that much of the land ought never to be plowed up. He understood that in many places the settler could not possibly make a living on the 160-acre tract which was the largest one could obtain under the Homestead Act. Western congressmen did not take kindly to Major Powell's recommendations.

2

In addition to the economic problem of learning to make a living on the high and dry plains, the rancher and the farmer had the human problem of learning to love the land and to feel themselves spiritually at home in it. D. H. Lawrence, who lived for a time in the American Southwest, wrote:

> The American landscape has never been at one with the white man. Never. And white men have probably never felt so bitter anywhere, as here in America, where the landscape, in its very beauty, seems a bit devilish and grinning, opposed to us.

The homesick cattlemen sang:

> O bury me not on the lone prairie
> Where the wild coyotes will howl o'er me.

It was long, I think, before the women who settled on the plains cared to sing:

> Oh, give me a home where the buffalo roam,
> Where the deer and the antelope play,
> Where seldom is heard a discouraging word
> And the skies are not cloudy all day.

There was much on the plains to interest the adventurous traveler who wished to hunt big game; but the visitor's first emotional reaction to the landscape was to find it dreary, monotonous, and inhospitable. There was nothing like that landscape in New England, Pennsylvania, Virginia, or the Carolinas. There was, indeed, nothing like it in the European background of the American pioneers. There was in English no name for such a country, and so the pioneers took over the word *prairie*, which the French explorers had adopted for want of a better.

The Great Plains: A Study in Landscape

The first notable writers to describe the plains were visitors from the outside world, and they found the country lacking in the elements of beauty. Charles Dickens, who went out of his way to see the Looking Glass Prairie in Illinois, recorded his disappointment in *American Notes* (1842):

Great as the picture was, its very flatness and extent, which left nothing to the imagination, tamed it down and cramped its interest. I felt little of that sense of freedom and exhiliration which a Scottish heath inspires, or even our English downs awaken. It was lonely and wild, but oppressive in its barren monotony.

Many years later Rudyard Kipling in his *American Notes* (1889) described a landscape in Montana as "a wilderness of sage brush" beside which the desert country of India seemed to him "joyous and homelike." The sage, he said, "wraps the rolling hills as a mildewed shroud wraps the body of a long-dead man. It makes you weep for sheer loneliness, and there is no getting away from it. When Childe Roland came to the dark Tower he traversed the sage brush."

In *Across the Plains* (1892) Robert Louis Stevenson described the plains of Nebraska as "a world almost without a feature; an empty sky; an empty earth; front and back, the line of railway stretched from horizon to horizon, like a cue across a billiard-board. . . ." Stevenson thought of the pioneers in their covered wagons, bound for Oregon or California "at the foot's pace of Oxen," "with no landmark but that unattainable evening sun for which they steered and which daily fled them by an equal stride." How, he wondered, could a human being reconcile himself to making his home in this inhospitable land?

What livelihood can repay a human creature for a life spent in this huge sameness? . . . A sky full of stars is the most varied spectacle that he can hope. He may walk five miles and see nothing; ten, and it is as though he had not moved; twenty, and still he is in the midst of the same great level, and has approached no nearer to the one object within view, the flat horizon which keeps pace with his advance. . . . [His eye] quails before so vast an outlook, it is tortured by distance; yet there is no rest or shelter, till the man runs into his cabin, and can repose his sight upon things near at hand.

Such was Stevenson's impression of the cattle country, of the Nebraska that was to be the background of some of Willa Cather's best novels. Stevenson had forgotten the concluding phrases of his delightful essay, "On the Enjoyment of Unpleasant Places": ". . . there is no country without some amenity—let him only look for it in the right spirit, and he will surely find."

Stevenson, homesick for the Scottish hill country, looked forward to seeing the Black Hills of Wyoming and the Rockies, but: "Alas!" he wrote, "it [Wyoming] was a worse country than the other." He found it an "unhomely and unkindly world . . . not a tree, not a patch of sward, not one shapely or commanding mountain form; sage-brush, eternal sage-brush. . . . Except for the air, which was light and stimulating, there was not one good circumstance in that God-forsaken land."

Yet this is the country of which Owen Wister was to write: "Wyoming burst upon the tenderfoot resplendently, like all the storybooks, like Cooper and Irving and Parkman come true. . . ." If the plains were to be celebrated in literature, it must be done by American writers and preferably by those who, like Willa Cather and Carl Sandburg, had grown up on the plains.

3

The first American writers to leave us notable descriptions of the plains country were natives of New York and New England: Cooper, Irving, Bryant, and Parkman. Although he apparently never actually saw a prairie, Fenimore Cooper in *The Prairie* (1826) made the plains the scene of the last years and death of Leather-Stocking. His descriptions of the oceanlike plains are vividly done, and the background adds much to the effectiveness of the story. Leather-Stocking, far from the New York forest lands in which he had lived, sees the plains as almost a desert; and the Bush family of squatters from Kentucky, land of meadows and forests, find the land strange and unhomelike. It is, however, an appropriate setting for the exploits of those rival Indian warriors, the Pawnees and the Sioux, all superb horsemen. In certain scenes and episodes, like the prairie fire and the buffalo stampede, Cooper anticipated many a later romantic novelist.

In *A Tour on the Prairies* (1832) Irving made a travel book out of the journal he had kept on a journey into the Arkansas and Oklahoma country. After his long sojourn in the Old World, Irving was in the mood to enjoy exploring his own country. In an unpublished letter in the Duke University Library Governor John Campbell of Virginia wrote to his sister after hearing Irving speak of his journey into the Western country:

He declar'd to me he never enjoy'd the *same time* as much in his life. The sublime beauties of nature untouch'd by human hands—the romantic scenes of the wilderness lying silent & undisturbed by the sound of industry—the lofty hills and solitary valleys where "tygers steal along *and buffaloe remote low'd far from human home"*—he described to us in the richest colouring of his brilliant fancy.

William Cullen Bryant loved best the Berkshire country of his native Massachusetts and he was not always sure that the prairies were beautiful; but he wrote our first fine poetic description of the plains landscape. In 1832, the year of Irving's book, he visited his two brothers at Jacksonville, Illinois. On horseback he explored the prairie land for a hundred miles to the northward. "The Prairies" begins:

> These are the gardens of the Desert, these
> The unshorn fields, boundless and beautiful,
> For which the speech of England has no name—
> The Prairies. I behold them for the first
> And my heart swells, while the dilated sight
> Takes in the encircling vastness. Lo! they stretch,
> In airy undulations, far away,
> As if the Ocean, in his gentlest swell,
> Stood still, with all his rounded billows fixed,
> And motionless forever.—Motionless?—
> No—they are all unchained again. The clouds
> Sweep over with their shadows, and, beneath,
> The surface rolls and fluctuates to the eye;
> Dark hollows seem to glide along and chase
> The sunny ridges. Breezes of the South!
> Who toss the golden and the flame-like flowers,
> And pass the prairie-hawk that, poised on high,
> Flaps his broad wings, yet moves not—ye have played
> Among the palms of Mexico and vines
> Of Texas, and have crisped the limpid brooks
> That from the fountains of Sonora glide
> Into the calm Pacific—have ye fanned
> A nobler or a lovelier scene than this?

Another native of Massachusetts, Francis Parkman, saw much more of the West than Bryant had seen. The poet knew only the humid prairies of Illinois; the historian was to see the high and dry plains beyond the Mississippi and describe them in *The Oregon*

Trail (1847). The landscape in the Platte River country struck Parkman as "dreary and monotonous"; it had "not one picturesque or beautiful feature." Only "the wild beasts and wild men" made the Platte River Valley "a scene of interest and excitement to the traveller."

Two lines of sand-hills, broken often into the wildest and most fantastic forms, flanked the valley at a distance of a mile or two on right and left; while beyond them lay a barren, trackless waste, extending for hundreds of miles into the Arkansas on the one side, and the Missouri on the other. Before and behind us, the level monotony of the plain was unbroken as far as the eye could reach. Sometimes it glared in the sun, an expanse of hot, bare sand; sometimes it was veiled by long coarse grass.

At the time of his Western journey Parkman was a sick man and in need of medical care not available on the plains. Like a Spartan, he was driving himself on to complete the task he had set for himself. It is no wonder that on the high and dry plains the homesick New Englander had such a daydream as that he described in his journal for May 26, 1846:

Nooned on Black Walnut Creek. . . . Afternoon, not well—sat slouching on horse, indulging in an epicurian reverie—intensely hot—dreamed of a cool mountain spring, in a *forest* country—two bottles of Champagne cooling in it, and cut-glass tumblers, full of the sparkling liquor. A wide expanse of perfectly flat prairie—rode over it hour after hour—saw wolves—and where they had dug up a recent grave. Turkey buzzards and frequent carcases of cattle. . . .

Parkman had a low opinion of the westward-bound pioneers whom he saw crossing the plains on their way to Oregon. His attitude, I fear, was too much like that which in 1853 Thoreau expressed in a letter to Harrison Blake:

The whole enterprise of this nation, which is not an upward, but a westward one, toward Oregon, California, Japan, etc., is totally devoid of interest to me, whether performed on foot, or by a Pacific railroad. It is not illustrated by a thought; it is not warmed by a sentiment; there is nothing in it which one should lay down his life for, nor even his gloves,—hardly which one should take up a newspaper for. It is perfectly heathenish,—a filibustering *toward* heaven by the great western route. No; they may go their way to their manifest destiny, which I trust is not mine.

For really sympathetic and understanding portraits of the Western emigrants we must turn to American writers who were either born in the West or lived there long. Joaquin Miller began his auto-biographical *Overland in a Covered Wagon* with the sentence: "My cradle was a covered wagon, pointed west."

Walt Whitman was the one writer on the Atlantic seaboard who felt the need for a literature celebrating the prairies and the plains. His journey to New Orleans in 1848 had made him aware of the Mississippi Valley. When he set out to write the great poem of America, he meant to celebrate the West as well as the East and the South as well as the North. As early as 1860 in "The Prairie-Grass Dividing" he was calling for "the spiritual corresponding" in men and women of the West, and in "Pioneers! O Pioneers!" he was looking forward to poets to come out of the West.

> Minstrels latent on the Prairies!
> (Shrouded bards of other lands, you may rest, you have done your work,)
> Soon I hear you coming warbling, soon you rise and tramp amid us,
> Pioneers! O Pioneers!

The railroad journey to Colorado which as an old man Whitman took in 1879 revived his interest in the West and its future literature. In a brief speech intended for delivery at Topeka, Kansas, he wrote that it was the prairies that had impressed him most on this, his "first real visit to the West." Here he saw a "vast something, stretching out on its own unbounded scale, unconfined, which there is in these prairies, combining the real and the ideal, and beautiful as dreams." He began to think that perhaps "the Prairies and Plains" constitute "North America's characteristic landscape," and "fill the esthetic sense fuller" than Niagara, Yosemite, and the Yellowstone. In "The Prairies and Great Plains in Poetry," he looked forward to the time when there would be a hundred million people living in the Mississippi Valley, and he expressed a keen desire to see "all those inimitable American areas fused in the alembic of a perfect poem, or other esthetic work, entirely western, fresh and limitless—altogether our own, without a trace or taste of Europe's soil, reminiscence, technical letter or spirit." Whitman, however, knew that the great poem must be written by a poet of the West as yet unknown or unborn; but in his old age he did write the beautiful Imagistic "A Prairie Sunset" and "The Prairie States," which begins: "A newer garden of creation, no primal solitude. . . ."

Literature and art are often able to make life more livable by revealing beauty in places which the eyes of those who live there are slow to perceive. As Fra Lippo Lippi phrased it in Browning's poem:

> We're made so that we love
> First when we see them painted, things we have passed
> Perhaps a hundred times nor cared to see;
> And so they're better, painted—better to us,
> Which is the same thing. Art was given for that.

Few persons were aware of the beauty of the flat and swampy coast country of Georgia until after Sidney Lanier had written his "Hymns of the Marshes."

In March, 1911, the *Atlantic Monthly* published "A Step-daughter of the Prairie," an essay in which Margaret Lynn described her childhood difficulties in finding any relation between the literature she loved and the plains country in which she lived. "The beauty of the prairie," as she notes, "is not of the sort that appeals directly to a child." All the stories and poems that she loved had their setting in forested lands, and the few thin groves of trees that she saw on the plains hardly sufficed. The muddy little "crick" on the prairie was a poor substitute for Tennyson's brook. "It had no trout, no ripples over stones, no grassy banks." The nameless flowers on the prairie would have seemed more beautiful to her if they had been celebrated in poems by Burns or Wordsworth. "What did it avail," she asked, "to read of forests and crags and waterfalls and castles and blue seas, when I could know only barbed-wire fences and frame buildings and prairie-grass?" "Who had ever read of Iowa in a novel or a poem?" she asked, and as a child she knew of none. So far as she could see, if life on the prairie was to be translated into terms of literature, she would have to do it herself. She longed for the assurance that the prairie was worthy of a place in a book. "If Lowell and Whittier and Tennyson—most of all Tennyson—had written of slough-grass and ground-squirrels and barbed-wire fences, those despised elements would have taken on new aspects." She was urged to read the American poets. Is the outcome surprising?

I found due pleasure in them, but it was always tempered by a sort of resentment that, though American, their country was not my country. For New England was farther away than Old England; and I always went back to Tennyson.

4

As a child Miss Lynn, who in later years was Professor of English in the University of Kansas, probably did not read Mark Twain's *Roughing It* (1871), and even if she did read it, found it not to the taste of a bookish and romantic child. Yet Mark Twain was the first important American writer born west of the Mississippi River, and he knew the West as his Eastern contemporaries did not. In *Roughing It* there is a vivid description of his overland journey by stage to Nevada with his brother Orion in 1861. Ten years after going to Nevada he still remembered vividly "the gladness and the wild sense of freedom that used to make the blood dance in my veins on those fine overland mornings." In one of the memorable passages in the book he gives us a glimpse of the pony express mail carrier:

Presently the driver exclaims:
"HERE HE COMES!"
Every neck is stretched further, and every eye strained wider. Away across the endless dead level of the prairie a black speck appears against the sky, and it is plain that it moves. Well, I should think so! In a second or two it becomes a horse and rider, rising and falling, rising and falling—sweeping toward us nearer and nearer—growing more and more distinct, more and more sharply defined—nearer and still nearer, and the flutter of the hoofs comes faintly to the ear—another instant a whoop and a hurrah from our upper deck, a wave of the rider's hand, but no reply, and man and horse burst past our excited faces, and go swinging away like a belated fragment of a storm!
So sudden is it all, and so like a flash of unreal fancy, that but for the flake of white foam left quivering and perishing on a mail-sack after the vision had flashed by and disappeared, we might have doubted whether we had seen any actual horse and man at all, maybe.

Eastern poets like Whitman might look upon the plains as the garden of America, but the writers who lived there found it difficult to see the plains in that fashion. In the writings of E. W. Howe and Hamlin Garland one finds the sad overtones of disillusionment felt by immigrants who had failed to discover on the plains an agrarian utopia. In *The Story of a Country Town* (1883) Howe thus discribed the Fairview neighborhood in Kansas:

On the highest and bleakest point in the county, where the winds were plenty in winter because they were not needed, and scarce in summer for an opposite reason, the meetinghouse was built, in a corner of my father's field. . . . There was a graveyard around it, and cornfields next to that, but not a tree or shrub. . . .

Hamlin Garland, so Joseph Kirkland told him, was the first real dirt farmer in literature. In the 1890's Garland felt that he had the West almost to himself. The Wisconsin-Iowa region, which he called the Middle Border, however, is not a treeless land and is in general not deficient in rainfall. Garland, however, as a young man had gone with his father to the Dakota country to stake a claim on the virgin prairie land. There is a brief description of the Dakota country in "Across the Corn Rows," but a fuller account is found in *A Son of the Middle Border*. In South Dakota Garland first set foot on a land where there were no trees.

The endless stretches of short, dry grass, the gorgeous colors of the dawn, the marvellous, shifting phantom lakes and headlands, the violet sunset afterglow,—all were widely different from our old home, and the far, bare hills were delightfully suggestive of the horseman, the Indian and the buffalo.

In the spring the land was very beautiful. "The days of May and June succeeded one another in perfect harmony like the notes in a song, broken only once or twice by thunderstorms." Summer brought "an ominous change":

The winds were hot and dry and the grass, baked on the stem, had become as inflammable as hay. The birds were silent. The sky, absolutely cloudless, began to scare us with its light. The sun rose through the dusty air, sinister with flare of horizontal heat. The little gardens on the breaking withered, and many of the women began to complain bitterly of the loneliness, and lack of shade. The tiny cabins were like ovens at midday.

Winter was even worse. "No one," he said, "knows what winter means until he has lived through one in a pine-board shanty on a Dakota plain with only buffalo bones for fuel." "One blizzard followed another with ever-increasing fury. . . . Nothing lived on these desolate uplands but the white owl and the wolf." Garland's experience prompted him "to plan for other work in other airs" "to escape the terror and the loneliness of the treeless sod."

The tragic plight of women on the high and dry plains is well described in Dorothy Scarborough's *The Wind* (1925) and Ole Rölvaag's *Giants in the Earth* (1927). Miss Scarborough chose for her locale the drought-stricken cattle country in the neighborhood of Sweetwater in West Texas. There the winds were "the enemies of women . . . icy blasts in winter, burning them with hot breath in summer, parching their skins and toughening their hair, and trying to wear down their nerves by attrition, and drive them away." To this semidesert comes Letitia Mason, a penniless and rather helpless Virginia girl, to live with a cousin whom she had not seen for years.

Letty Mason lived a divided life, her spirit in rural Virginia, her body in the Texas wilderness. In Virginia she remembered "Old gardens, wide piazzas, treasured heirlooms of furniture and silver and books, traditions of gentility and family pride." "In Virginia there were rivers, calm and life-giving, in their unhurried flow to the sea; and lakes with water lilies, and alder-fringed banks; and little, talkative brooks that gossiped of the winds that blew over them. . . ." In West Texas there were "No friendly woods, nothing but vast, desolate stretches of sand and dead grass . . . and a demoniac wind lying in wait for its victims. . . . There were "no song birds left, only the buzzards." "Here there were no trees! Was hell just a place where no trees grew, no birds sang?"

Cousin Beverley's wife Cora is a coarse and jealous egotist who has only contempt for the gentle, well-bred Letty. It is Cora, aided by the sand and the wind, who drives Letty into marrying a cattleman whom she does not love. In the final scene Letty kills Wirt Roddy, who has taken advantage of a blizzard that terrifies her in order to seduce her. The story ends:

With a laugh that strangled on a scream, the woman sped to the door, flung it open and rushed out. She fled across the prairies like a leaf blown in a gale, borne along in the force of the wind that was at last to have its way with her.

Willa Cather was only eight years old when she left the Valley of Virginia to live in Nebraska. Her first impressions of the Nebraska plains are suggested in the opening pages of *My Ántonia*. Her narrator, Jim Burden, also born in Virginia, recalls his boyish impressions of the Nebraska plains as he was being driven at night from the railroad station to his grandfather's farm.

There seemed to be nothing to see; no fences, no creeks or trees, no hills or fields. . . . I had the feeling that the world was left behind, that we had got over the edge of it, and were outside man's jurisdiction.

I had never before looked up at the sky when there was not a familiar mountain ridge against it. . . . Between that earth and that sky I felt erased, blotted out.

What would Willa Cather's writings be like, I wonder, if she had grown up in Virginia? Very likely she would have felt as Ellen Glasgow did when she referred to "what would seem to Virginians to be the rootless life of the prairies." Willa Cather was fortunate in going to Nebraska at her most impressionable age.

It's a queer thing about the flat country [she once wrote]—it takes hold of you, or it leaves you perfectly cold. . . . I go everywhere, I admire all kinds of country. . . . But when I strike the open plains, something happens, I'm home. I breathe differently. That love of great spaces, or rolling open country like the sea—it's the grand passion of my life.

As a young writer, however, Willa Cather was in a rebellious mood. She detested the small Western towns, and in "The Sculptor's Funeral," the most powerful of her early stories, she denounced one of them for its failure to appreciate the one great man who had grown up there. Like Hamlin Garland, she had to go East to get a proper perspective upon the region she knew best. In her first novel, *Alexander's Bridge,* she was writing of an unfamiliar locality under the influence of Ibsen, Henry James, and Flaubert. It was her friend Sarah Orne Jewett who put her on the right track. "Of course," she said, "one day you will write about your own country. In the meantime, get all you can. One must know the world so well before one can know the parish."

In *O Pioneers* (1913) Willa Cather wrote of the kind of people she had known as a girl. Most of the Cathers' neighbors were Bohemian and Scandinavian immigrants, and as a child she had loved to listen to the older women who talked of their home country. "I used to think them underrated, and wanted to explain them to their neighbors. . . . Their stories used to go round and round in my head at night." Here was a rich mine of material for the novelist which she had long neglected.

O Pioneers [she writes] interested me tremendously, because it had to do with a kind of country I loved, because it was about old neighbours, once very dear, whom I had almost forgotten in the hurry and excitement of growing up and finding out what the world was like and trying to get on in it.

She wrote the novel to please herself, and she did not expect other people to care for a slow-moving story, without a hero, without humor, and with little action. Worse still, she thought, it was

a story concerned entirely with heavy farming people, with cornfields and pasture lands and pig yards,—set in Nebraska, of all places! As everyone knows, Nebraska is distinctly déclassé as a literary background; its very name throws the delicately attuned critic into a clammy shiver of embarrassment. Colorado, on the contrary, is considered quite possible. Wyoming really has some class, of its own kind, like well-cut riding breeches. But a New York critic voiced a very general opinion when he said: "I simply don't care a damn what happens in Nebraska, no matter who writes about it."

The story of *O Pioneers* begins:

The homesteads were few and far apart; here and there a windmill gaunt against the sky, a sod house crouching in a hollow. But the great fact was the land itself, which seemed to overwhelm the little beginnings of human society that struggled in its sombre waves.

The Bergson family endures years of drought and failure. Many farmers give up and go elsewhere. They discourage the Bergson boys, but their sister, Alexandra, stands up for the land, which "seemed beautiful to her, rich and strong and glorious." She will not give up. Instead she buys more land, and eventually her purchases pay off. The "wild land" is now like a garden. In the last chapter we have Alexandra's philosophy of life: "We come and go, but the land is always here. And the people who love it and understand it are the people who own it—for a little while."

My Ántonia (1918), which has much the same background and a heroine of the same type as Alexandra, is a better novel. It is in a sense a paean in praise of country life in the "garden of the West." Nebraska is also the locale of what is probably Willa Cather's finest short story, "Neighbour Rosicky," the leading figure in which is an immigrant from Czechoslovakia whose family in the Old World had never owned land. In Nebraska he finds the kind of life he has always craved.

The great discovery of Willa Cather's later life came on her first visit to New Mexico. She loved the semidesert country, like Mary Austin, who wrote in *The Land of Little Rain*: "For all the toil the desert takes of a man it gives compensations, deep breaths, deep sleep, and the communion of the stars." In the Southwest, moreover, Willa Cather found a rich historical past such as Nebraska lacked. She first treated the Southwest in a contrasting episode in *The Professor's House*. Eventually she wrote what is one of her two best novels, *Death Comes for the Archbishop*.

In the novels of Willa Cather there are some memorable portraits of immigrants from Czechoslovakia and the Scandinavian countries, but she did not know their European background like Ole Rölvaag, who came to this country from Norway as a young man. The problem of transplantation was peculiarly difficult for immigrants who knew no English. They found it hardest to feel at home in the alien wilderness. Rölvaag dealt with the Norwegian immigrants in several books, most notably in *Giants in the Earth* (1927). The novel was written in Norwegian, but with the help of several others—particularly Lincoln Colcord—he translated it into an English version which is said to be superior to the Norwegian original.

Rölvaag put his own ambivalent feelings into the two leading characters: Per Hansa and his wife Beret. The husband is an extrovert, a pioneer of the old Viking strain who loves the new land. Beret is an introvert of the Puritan type who from childhood had been brought up to believe in a doleful, morbid theology. Homesick for the Norwegian mountains and the sea, the sensitive, civilized woman sees the Dakota plains as a bleak, desolate, God-forsaken land. How, she asks, "could folk establish homes in an endless wilderness? . . . here she sat thousands of miles from home and kindred, lost in a limitless void." Beret, who believes that she will die in childbirth, begs Per Hansa to take the other children back to civilization lest "They grow into beasts!" It is the husband, however, not the wife, who perishes in the wilderness. Per Hansa, the fearless pioneer, goes out into a blinding snowstorm to find a doctor for a sick neighbor and does not return. And so, as Rölvaag phrases it, "the great plain drank the blood of Christian men."

5

The early travelers who ventured into the Far West were greatly impressed by the scenery of the Rocky Mountains and the Pacific coast, but they saw little to admire in the high and dry plains. John Muir dedicated his life to the exploration and celebration of California. There he had found the wonders of the Yosemite Valley and the giant sequoias. Joaquin Miller, who wrote the *Songs of the Sierras*, had crossed the plains on the way to Oregon at the age of thirteen, and what lingered in his mind was the vivid recollection of the hardships, especially as they befell the women and children. In "Exodus for Oregon" he emphasized the dust storms and the difficulty of finding water that men and animals could drink.

> They sat in desolation and in dust
> By dried-up desert streams. . . .

It was not until about the turn of the century that men began to see the desert country as a thing of beauty and not of horror. In the early 1890's in a poem entitled "A Nevada Desert" Charlotte Perkins described what she had seen from the window of a railroad car as "an aching, blinding, barren, endless plain," "corpse-red with white mounds of alkali." The editor of the *Atlantic Monthly* rejected the poem because it contained "no spot of color." In 1901, however, an art critic, John Van Dyke, published a book entitled *The Desert*, in which he pointed out that: "The desert had gone a-begging for a word of praise these many years." In 1903 Mary Austin published *The Land of Little Rain*, the first of her semi-mystical studies of the desert and the desert people. In 1912 a far more popular writer, Zane Grey, brought out his *Riders of the Purple Sage*. In 1955 Joseph Wood Krutch published *The Voice of the Desert*, in which he wrote:

And nothing, not even the sea, has seemed to affect men more profoundly than the desert, or seemed to incline them so powerfully toward great thoughts, perhaps because the desert itself seems to brood and to encourage brooding. To the Hebrews the desert spoke of God, and one of the most powerful of all religions was born. To the Arabs it spoke of the stars, and astronomy came into being.

Gradually also visitors came to appreciate the beauty and the grandeur of the high plains. The paintings of Charles Russell and Frederic Remington were no doubt an important influence, and so in later times was the work of many photographers, especially in our time of the cameramen of Walt Disney. The dime novelists, who emphasized American characters and backgrounds, were quick to see the cattleman as a romantic figure. By and by the cattle country attracted writers of literary importance, notably Owen

Wister, whose *The Virginian* (1902) is still one of the best romances of the cattle country. If Wister was never quite able to picture the cattleman's life from the inside, he understood better than other writers the historical significance of an important phase of American life that was quickly passing away. A more accurate picture of the cattle industry is found in *The Log of a Cowboy* (1903), written by Andy Adams, who knew the cowboy from first-hand experience better than any other novelist.

6

For the poet the Great Plains were an even less attractive background than the novelist had found them. Here there was little or nothing to distinguish one locality from another two hundred miles away in any direction. In this huge sameness there would develop few such local associations as had grown up in Massachusetts and Virginia. California had its beautiful valleys and seacoast, its mountains and its giant sequoias, but what was there to attract the poet to the Texas Panhandle or the plains of Kansas? Except in times of flood there were only sluggish rivers and dry arroyos. There was nothing remotely resembling Burns's bonnie Doon or the little Yarrow celebrated in three notable poems by Wordsworth. In Scotland every valley and mountain peak had its legend, and tales of strange adventures were handed down from one generation to the next. If these were not already incorporated in stirring folk songs and ballads, they were at least lying there ready-made for the writer who could use them. On the plains there were no Trossachs, no Loch Katrine, no Cheviot Hills. There were no picturesque ruined castles like Kenilworth, where Queen Elizabeth I had visited, no desolate churchyards like that at Kirk Alloway with its legend of dancing warlocks and witches who dared not cross a running stream. The plains were no place for the elves and fairies of European folklore. It was a featureless land almost without a history.

There were still other difficulties. Literature, and especially poetry, is in some ways a very conservative art. Life in its primitive state is seldom ready for the poet or the writer of fiction. In the American West one phase of life followed another so rapidly that none was adequately recorded. On the plains nothing seemed perma-

The Great Plains: A Study in Landscape

nent. The Indian and the buffalo quickly gave way to the cowboy and the Texas longhorn and these in turn to the farmer. But in a generation the farmer's way of life had altered radically; and soon there were more people in the Western towns and cities than there were on the ranches and the farms. Remembrance of the past lingered on only in the minds of old men and women, and many of these had long since left the plains. The traveler on railroad or highway found it difficult to distinguish one Western town from another. The city-dwellers of today spend most of their lives within doors, and most of them have no feeling of belonging to the land; and the land an earlier generation had learned to love is being rapidly covered over with asphalt or concrete in parking lots and highways. The population is in a state of flux. A native who left his home town in a trailer ten years ago would if he returned find little that he could recognize.

The Western historians have not found it easy to recover the past. The cattle country, which quickly captured the imagination of the young all over the world, underwent such rapid changes that it never got itself adequately recorded by writers who knew the life at first hand. The cowboy survives in the melodramatic and romantic Westerns of the pulp magazines, movies, and especially television. Based upon conventions and formulas, they do not give a faithful picture of the Old West. Even when they play up actual persons, like Wyatt Earp and Billy the Kid, they create an image of the Old West which except in external details has little resemblance to the original. Under such circumstances how can the epic of the West ever be written?

The difficulties that I have emphasized were real enough, but they differed only in degree, not in kind, from those that Irving and Cooper had to contend with when they wrote fiction dealing with life in their own state of New York. In that region Irving found so little to go on that he imported an old legend from Germany and made it the basis of "Rip Van Winkle." Yet on the plains there was—and is—the same endless variety of human nature that is embodied in the history, legends, and literatures of the Old World. ". . . in our life alone does Nature live," as Coleridge found it necessary to remind that worshiper of Nature, Wordsworth. Life on the plains had its heroes and its heroines, its villains and its victims. The history of that region abounds in examples of courage, loyalty, and sacrifice. Henry James, who complained of the barrenness of life in Hawthorne's New England, would have been appalled if he had had to write of the Great Plains; and yet the best Western writers must have felt that, in the words of William Dean Howells, in spite of the lack of those "items of high civilization" that James could not find in America, they had "simply the whole of human life left."

In 1910 John A. Lomax published that notable collection *Cowboy Songs and Other Frontier Ballads*. Many years later in *The Adventures of a Ballad Collector* he told how as a boy he had made a collection of cowboy songs in the Texas ranch country in which he grew up. As a student at the University of Texas he showed his manuscript anthology to Morgan Calloway, the head of the English department there. Professor Calloway no doubt was aware of the importance of the English and Scottish popular ballads; and yet he thought so little of the poems in Lomax's collection that he told him to burn them. Some years afterward when Lomax was a graduate student at Harvard, where I came to know him, Professors Barrett Wendell and George Lyman Kittredge were so impressed by the songs they heard Lomax sing that they induced the Harvard authorities to provide a fellowship which enabled Lomax to return to the cattle country and collect once again the songs which at Calloway's insistence he had destroyed. Theodore Roosevelt, who knew and loved the West, wrote an enthusiastic letter which in facsimile served as foreword to Lomax's book.

On the whole, these Western ballads are inferior to the British ballads, and they have not had on American poetry an influence comparable to that which the British ballads have had upon some English and Scottish poets and novelists. Nevertheless, there are a few fine ballads in Lomax's collection, and they have had an influence on a few Western poets, notably Badger Clark, author of *Sun and Saddle Leather*, and Walter Stanley Campbell, who under the pen name of "Stanley Vestal" published *Fandango: Ballads of the Old West*. One of Clark's best ballads, "The Glory Trail," was written in Western dialect, and the cowboys liked it so much that they sang this story of how High-Chin Bob roped a mountain lion and tried in vain to drag him to death. The poem closes:

"Oh, stranger, tell my pards below
I took a rampin' dream in tow,
And if I never lay him low,
   I'll never turn him loose!"

Time was on the side of the Western poets. The grandchildren
of the immigrants were at home on the plains, and they were proud
of their pioneer ancestors who had fought the Indians and outlaws,
lived in sodhouses, and driven cattle hundreds of miles to market.
All the Western states idealized the pioneers just as the original
thirteen had done long before. Karle Wilson Baker wrote in her
"Song of the Forerunners":

> The men who made Texas
> Laughed at fate and doom—
> Dreamers on horseback,
> Men who needed room;
>
> And the women in young Texas,
> Hanging homespun clothes to dry,
> Loved a prairie for a dooryard,
> For meeting-house, the sky—

Wide visions and wide spaces, man and land were large of lung:
Texas knew not cheap and easy, slack and small, when she was
   young.

It was a Westerner from Illinois, Abraham Lincoln, whom Lowell
praised as "New birth of our new soil, the first American." The
Westerner felt that his pride in his section was justified when
Frederick J. Turner pointed out that the West was the most American part of America.

Two of the best of the Western poets, Vachel Lindsay and Carl
Sandburg, were natives of Lincoln's own state, and they treated him
with distinction in prose and verse. These two poets, however, knew
not only the well-watered prairies of Illinois but also the plains
west of the Mississippi. Lindsay celebrated the Santa Fé Trail and
the Kansas wheat fields. In "Prairie," a poem that reminds one of
Walt Whitman, Sandburg wrote:

> I was born on the prairie and the milk
>   of its wheat, the red of its clover,
>   the eyes of its women, gave me a
>   song and a slogan.

Some Eastern poets learned to love the plains. Katherine Lee
Bates in 1893 was moved to write "America the Beautiful" while

on the summit of Pike's Peak. "It was then and there," she wrote, "as I was looking out over the sealike expanse of fertile country spreading away so far under those ample skies, that the opening lines of the hymn floated into my mind."—An Arkansas poet, John Gould Fletcher, after many years in Europe, returned to rediscover the South and the West. Among his Western poems are "The Seven Cities of Cibola" and a notable group of "Arizona Poems."

The favorite background of Robert Frost was northern New England, but he was born in San Francisco and he loved every part of the United States. "Desert Places" has its setting in Utah. In "Of the Stones of the Place" he remembered the descendants of those immigrants who left the rocky hillsides of New England to settle on the rich Western plains. In the poem a New England farmer is speaking to a Western friend whose grandfather was a native of New England:

> I farm a pasture where the boulders lie
> As touching as a basket full of eggs.

Since there are no rocks where his friend lives on

> wind-soil to a depth of thirty feet,
> And every acre good enough to eat,
> And fine as flour put through the baker's sieve,

he offers to send his Western friend a stone to serve as a symbol.

> I'd ship a smooth one you could slap and chafe
> And set up like a statue in your yard,
> An eolith palladium to guard
> The West and keep the old tradition safe.

IV. "And Gladly Teche"

A university should be a place of light, of liberty, and of learning.

BENJAMIN DISRAELI, Speech in House of
Commons, March 11, 1873.

Springtime in Vienna

[In the last twenty years professors who teach American literature and American history have had unprecedented opportunities to serve as visiting professors in Europe and elsewhere. I have had my share of such appointments. Under the auspices of the U. S. Army I was Visiting Professor of American Literature at the University of Vienna in the spring of 1949 and again in the spring of 1950. In the spring of 1953 I was Fulbright Professor of American Literature and Civilization in the University of Athens. I had majored in the ancient classics in college, and it was a great pleasure at long last to see Delphi, Olympia, Corinth, and the many historic sites in and around Athens. My last appointment, under the Smith-Mundt Act, was to the Hebrew University in Jerusalem. Unhappily my stay in Israel was cut short by the outbreak of the Suez War. Only eight days after our arrival my wife and I were ordered out of Israel by the American Embassy. We left Haifa on the U. S. Destroyer *Burdo* along with 120 other refugees. In Crete we were transferred to the transport *General Patch*, which took us and about two thousand

311

other refugees to Naples. We flew to London and two weeks later came home on the *Liberté*.

The man primarily responsible for my going to Vienna was Dr. Samuel H. Williams, a distinguished biologist who after a fine record in the U. S. Army became Chief of the Education Division of the U. S. Commission for Austria and Advisor to General Keyes. Dr. Williams and his staff selected me because they had made some use of my *American Life in Literature* in an edition published for the U. S. Armed Forces Institute.

Much of the following essay was written in 1949 after my return from Vienna. It is based in considerable measure on my official reports to General Geoffrey Keyes and on letters to my wife in the spring of 1949.]

1

In late April in 1949 the horse-chestnut trees on the wide Ring Street which encircles the heart of the city were in full leaf, and in all the parks lilacs were blooming, and red and yellow tulips, grown from bulbs given by the people of Holland, glowed in their enormous beds. Before noon on sunny days every seat in the parks was occupied by mothers, nurses, and old men taking the sun and reading newspapers or watching the children at play. On one April Sunday, so the papers said the next day, a million and a half men, women, and children went to the Vienna Woods. If the estimate was correct, not more than one Viennese in seven remained in the city. They crowded the busses and trams, and on foot or on bicycles they made the road difficult for the few passing cars. After the long cold winter the Viennese were eager to spend the day in the warm sunshine. It was on such a day that I saw from the Kahlenberg the Danube River, blue as the sky, curving around the city at the foot of the little mountain which marks the summit of the Vienna Woods.

On Monday morning they were back at work. There was no unemployment problem in Austria that spring. Good-humored if not gay, the people poured off the crowded trams, little streetcars linked two or three together, and hurried busily to their work. At that time there were few automobiles in Vienna, but their drivers liked to speed, and I often wondered why a thousand pedestrians were not killed every day. They would cross a street in the middle of a block without looking to right or left, and when a motorist blew his horn, they would act like startled rabbits and look as though they had never seen an automobile in the Ringstrasse before. Nearly every man on the sidewalk carried a briefcase, no matter how shabby. The briefcase is a symbol of gentility which serves to distinguish the professional man and the white-collar worker from those who earn their living with their hands. On the streets one heard a continuous patter in the soft and musical German of Vienna. When spoken by a woman, it often sounds like a snatch of song. The pedestrians were neatly but not fashionably dressed. Old clothes had to be kept presentable, for money was scarce in Vienna, and the Austrian schilling was not so stable as the Swiss franc or the American dollar. In the shop windows in the Kärtnerstrasse there were beautiful displays of luxury goods, jewelry, lace, furs, hand-bags, and leather goods of many kinds, a Viennese specialty. Many passersby stopped to gaze in the windows, but I saw few go in to buy. Tourists were few in Vienna, for Austria was still an occupied country. Women and children would look hungrily in bakeries and food stores and then hurry home to dine on what they could afford to buy. My Viennese friends always said to me: "Oh, we have plenty to eat now that the Marshall Plan has gone into operation." Nevertheless, I knew, they had vivid memories of recent years in which no one in Vienna had had enough to eat.

I had not seen Vienna before February, 1949, but when I remarked on its beauty to my Austrian acquaintances, they always replied: "Vienna is not the beautiful city it was." Beautiful still Vienna seemed to me, but its beauty was tinged with sadness. Coming to the city direct from the United States with the speed of a four-motored plane, I was shocked and dismayed when I saw with my own eyes the damage done by shells, bombs, and fire. Why, I wondered, was it necessary for Allied airmen to bomb the Art History Museum, the Imperial Theater, and the University of Vienna, where I was to lecture, and the State Opera House, which met my eye every time I looked from my window in the Bristol Hotel? Much of the damage, I was told, could be charged to the German General Dietrich, who even when Nazi defeat was imminent, refused to declare Vienna an open city. Much of the destruction, I was to discover later, was the work of the Russian and German armies fighting within the city. It was the Germans, I heard, who set fire to the roof of the great cathedral of St. Stephen's while shelling the Russians on the other side of the Danube Canal. When the Germans were finally driven out, so I was told, they took the fire engines with them, leaving much of the city in flames. When the war came to an end, the first step toward rebuilding the city was to take up a collection in order to repair St. Stephen's, that ancient symbol of which the Viennese are so justly proud.

The war had been over almost four years when I arrived in Vienna, but no peace treaty had been signed. Austria was still occupied by the armies of the four great powers and, like Germany, divided into zones among England, France, Russia, and the United States. Vienna, the capital, lay within the Russian Zone. Each of the four great powers, however, controlled a large section of the city; but the Inner City, the oldest of Vienna's twenty-one districts, was the joint responsibility of the four occupying powers. On the surface the situation was very like that in troubled Berlin, where the air lift was still on; but whatever the reason, in Vienna there was far less friction between Russia and the Western powers. Austria, unlike Germany, was treated not as a conquered country but a liberated one. The ingenious Austrians revived their republican constitution, which the Russians had considered unworkable, and governed themselves with only a general supervision by the occupying powers. They heartily disliked being an occupied country, and yet they feared the day when the Western powers would leave, for Austria is a little country half surrounded by Communist nations—Czechoslovakia, Hungary, and Yugoslavia. Vienna is the easternmost city of Western Europe. The Viennese, living a hundred miles behind the Iron Curtain, had no love for the Russians. Their memories were still strong of workers' houses and apartments looted by Russian soldiers who, never having seen anything so well equipped and comfortable, were sure that capitalists must live in them. One retired small businessman who lived just outside Vienna—so his son told me—saved his house from the looters by showing them the calluses which gardening had developed in his hands. After the war the Austrian Communists were not able to get more than 5 per cent of the votes. An Austrian lady in commenting on the much higher percentage of Communist votes in France remarked to me: "The French don't know the Russians as we do." In 1949 everything on

314   *Springtime in Vienna*

the surface was quiet in Vienna, but the Viennese were troubled now and then by the sudden and complete disappearance behind the Iron Curtain of some Austrian engineer or doctor who, it often developed, had declined to accept a position in Russia or one of the satellite countries.

2

My business in Austria was to give courses in American literature at the University of Vienna, which had nearly twelve thousand students. It was a cold February day when I landed in Vienna, but I felt that I was on the verge of a strange and memorable experience. The University of Vienna is one of three state universities, and the Viennese are intensely proud of it, especially its world-famous Medical School. After the University of Prague it is the oldest of the German-language universities and in 1965 it is celebrating the six hundredth anniversary of its founding. Duke University, which had given me leave of absence to come to Vienna, had celebrated its centennial as recently as 1938. It was not until 1924 that Trinity College became Duke University.

In memory I often retrace my steps as I walked along the Ringstrasse from the Bristol Hotel, where I was living, to the university past the State Opera House, the Art History Museum, the Natural History Museum, the Imperial Palace and adjacent to it the National Library, the Palace of Justice, the Volksgarten, the Burg Theater, and the Town Hall flanked on its right by the Parliament House and on the left by the University of Vienna's main building. That massive structure impresses one by its dignity and its spaciousness. Over the entrance there is the Latin inscription: UNIVERSITAS LITTERARUM VINDOBONENSIS. Just inside the door stands the porter's lodge. In the vestibule there is a marble tablet inscribed with the names of past rectors of the university. Near by is the noble monument to the university's war dead of 1914-1918. The halls and the corridors are beautiful, but in February and March they were dark and gloomy, and they were cold. I detected a faint and not very pleasant odor—common to unventilated public buildings—an odor compounded of stale tobacco smoke and other ingredients that defied identification. The classrooms and offices, however, I found warm and comfortable. The American Army had provided the coal that the university was not able to buy.

Soon after my arrival I was taken to the university library, which was on the top floor; it is still one of the best libraries of its kind in central Europe. I saw the library under the guidance of its distinguished chief, Hofrat Professor Dr. Johann Gans, who was, as he said to me, married to his library. The Nazis had kicked him out, but when they left Vienna, he came back to supervise its restoration. Of the bombs that fell on the building no less than twenty-seven struck the library. The rain and the snow that fell through holes in the roof had damaged many books, and in some instances the books which had been stored underground had suffered from mold. Volumes were missing from important sets, and everything was in confusion. Dr. Gans, however, was a hopeful person. Repairs were being made, and new books were coming from the United States, including some missing wartime volumes of the *Publications* of the Modern Language Association supplied by my Duke University colleagues.

On my way to the English Seminar, which was on the first floor, I walked along an open corridor in a courtyard which contained a plot of grass and Hellmer's marble fountain of Castalia, which an American visitor was likely to mistake for a statue of Alma Mater. In the corridor I saw busts and plaques of distinguished professors. I noted the names of the composer Anton Bruckner; Krafft-Ebing, the famous neurologist and psychiatrist; and Jacob Schipper, an authority on English versification. I did not find, though I looked for it, any memorial of Sigmund Freud. Several years after I left Vienna the university finally honored his memory with a suitable monument.

At the end of the long corridor we come to a large door marked SEMINAR FÜR DIE ENGLISCHE PHILOLOGIE. We push a button which rings a bell. Immediately we hear a rattling sound and the door swings open an inch or two. We pull it open, walk in, close the door behind us and find ourselves in an anteroom which contains not bookcases but wardrobes full of books, two chairs, and a table with an ashtray on it, for this is the only room in the English Seminar in which a student may smoke. We pass through another door into a study room with thirty or forty chairs placed crosswise in the room. At one side on tables we note the card catalogue of the seminar library. It contains a good collection of the English classics, but it is woefully weak in American literature, the subject I am to teach. Among the twenty-five or thirty students whom one sees reading and taking notes invariably one or more is munching a roll or eating an orange. The continental breakfast is not substantial enough to carry one comfortably through to the midday meal. Then, too, the Austrian students, though they had plenty to eat in 1949, had vivid memories of the lean years in which no one in Vienna had enough to eat.

Leaving the study hall, we come to yet another door, usually closed but seldom locked, which leads to a little anteroom, where we see a sign which suggests that this is no loafing place. The doors on right and left open into the professors' offices. Before we knock on a professor's door, we are expected to ask his assistant if the professor can see us. If in response to the assistant's knock, he says "Ja" or "Come in," we enter his *sanctum sanctorum*. The walls are lined with bookshelves and filled with books. We note also a divan with a table in front of it, a few chairs, and another chair beside the desk at which the professor is seated. The divan, as we shall learn later, is Seat No. 1 and is reserved for the most distinguished guests. The professor is my friend Leo Hibler, about whom I shall have more to say later. He is eminently courteous, but he might strike an American student as a little distant in his manner. The American would probably not realize how overworked this particular professor is with a staff not nearly large enough to care for the seven hundred students registered in the English Seminar. The former head of the English Seminar was a Nazi, now begging to be taken back. Until last fall, the English Seminar had no professor. Before Professor Hibler managed to get away from the University of Leipzig, which is in the Russian Zone, the acting head was Dr. Louis H. Paulovsky, the head of the Institute for Training Interpreters and Translators.

In a German or Austrian university a professorship carries with it such honor and prestige as are unknown in this country, even at Harvard or Columbia. The professor's wife shares in his various titles, and the "Frau Prof. Dr." sometimes gains admittance to places where ordinary women are turned away. In Europe most professors keep their students at a greater distance than is customary in the United States. Manners are more formal. Always in meeting or parting from a colleague the professor raises his hat and shakes hands. But one must not make the mistake of concluding that the Austrian professor's feeling for his friends and his students is less strong than an American's.

If all this seems somewhat undemocratic, one must not conclude that an Austrian university is thoroughly undemocratic. American universities have their undemocratic features, too. In our country the president and the deans are elected by a board of trustees which knows very little about them. In Austria the rector and the deans are elected by their colleagues, who know them best and have to work and live with them.

Before I met my first class, Dr. Paulovsky was kind enough to brief me on some Austrian notions of America. They are interested in America, he said, but this interest is mainly of recent origin; and they have inherited many curious misconceptions based upon ignorance or inherited prejudices or notions derived from Nazi and Communist propaganda. And I may say, he added, that what they have read from your American writers has only confirmed them in their mistaken notions. They know little about Emerson and Whitman or Robert Frost and Willa Cather, but they have read Theodore Dreiser, Upton Sinclair, John Dos Passos, Sinclair Lewis, and Ernest Hemingway. They think they know the real America, and they do not admire it. The heterogeneous elements that enter into an Austrian student's notions of America, he went on, hang together with a strange consistency. Their conception I shall sum up for you as follows: "You Americans are rich, but you are crass and materialistic, and you are here to advance your own interests and not those of the Europeans. The only culture you have is a veneer, and it is all borrowed from Europe. You have no manners; you are vulgar; and you spit. Your democracy is a sham. Your capitalists shamelessly exploit the workers, and the Negroes are as badly treated as when they were slaves. Your country is full of gangsters and political bosses. You know about mass production and you can build skyscrapers, but you cannot create anything beautiful. Over here," he continued, "your GI's took advantage of the want and demoralization which followed the end of the war. They bought what they wanted on the black market when two cigarettes or a bar of chocolate was the equivalent of a laborer's weekly wages. They took advantage of Austrian girls in such desperate straits that they would

Springtime in Vienna

give their bodies for food and clothing. In fact," he said, "some of the Austrians think you are little better than the Russians. You do not stand so well here," he added, "as the British, who are tops among foreigners in Austria at the present time."

You may imagine my feeling of trepidation as with Dr. Paulovsky's briefing in mind I went the next day to the little theater-like hall in which I was to deliver the first of my lectures on "American Literature and Its Historical Backgrounds." My responsibility weighed heavily upon me. Here was I, the only American scholar that in all likelihood most of my Austrian students would ever see and hear. I must do my best to appear as the fit representative of American universities which, or so it seemed to me, were the best in the world.

The Dean of the Philosophical Faculty, in the midst of last-minute preparations for a flying visit to the United States, took the time to come to the lecture room to introduce me. He spoke of course in German, and I understood just enough to know that it was a gracious introduction. I remembered thankfully that I was expected to lecture in English. The Dean finished his little speech and bowed to me. I bowed in return and climbed to the platform, which was covered with a wooden canopy. We shook hands. I said: "Thank you, Mr. Dean" and found myself confronting an audience of sixty or seventy students who held the absurd notions of my country about which I had learned the day before. But these young men and women had all risen to their feet as though I were the University Rector or the President of the Austrian Republic. With "Ladies and Gentlemen, please be seated," I plunged into the first of my eighteen lectures—the only one yet written, I remembered. This lecture had been written and several times rewritten before I left the States. Now I was wondering whether, even with the changes I had made in it last night, it would serve my purpose. I had hoped that it would suggest to these strangers that there are American writers who had something to say and said it in an individual manner not borrowed from any European. Would my first lecture make them willing to listen to the as-yet-unwritten seventeen lectures which were to follow? I spoke slowly and as distinctly as I could, for it was British rather than American English that was taught in Austrian schools.

I began by mentioning the great debt which all American uni-

versities owe to the universities of Germany and Austria and expressing my pleasure in having a very small part in repaying that debt.
"When you mention Vienna to an American," I went on, "he thinks
of the city where Gluck, Haydn, Mozart, Beethoven, Schubert, the
Strausses, and Brahms composed the finest music ever played or
sung anywhere in the world. Their music transcends international
boundary lines, and it speaks to all men a message of beauty, nobility, and good will. . . . The music which comes to us from Austria
helps to explain why Americans have rarely thought of Austrians
as their enemies." I noted that literature, like music, often transcends international boundary lines; and I quoted from a recent
article in *Foreign Affairs* by Dr. Karl Renner, then President of the
Austrian Republic: "Literature today is world literature."

Knowing that many Austrians had read *Gone with the Wind*, I
pointed to parallels between Austrian history since 1914 and the
period of Civil War and Reconstruction in the Southern states. My
mother was a child at that time, and I recalled hearing her tell of
the hardships caused by the war and the blockade. "When the
soldiers came home from the war—and not all of them came home,"
I said, "many of them found their houses burned, their horses and
cattle gone, their farm implements stolen or rusted away, and their
slaves scattered to the four winds." I mentioned difficulties of Reconstruction for those who had fought on the losing side. I went on:

But few Southern men or women were repentant, as Northern editors
and politicians thought they ought to be. They had fought for the
right to govern themselves in their own way. Why should they be
ashamed of what they had done? . . . In a famous speech in Parliament
in which he protested against taxing the Americans without their consent, Edmund Burke said: "I do not know the method of drawing up
an indictment against an whole people." There are too many men
living in our country who, I regret to say, have found no difficulty in
condemning indiscriminately the entire population of more than one
nation.

Borrowing a hint from Van Wyck Brooks, I suggested that the
dominant mood of American literature had been one of hopefulness,
courage, good will, faith in human nature and the Christian religion,
and a belief in the rights of man. I said that in the twenty years
that followed the First World War many of our younger writers
were primarily social critics and satirists, often cynical and disillusioned. I told them that *Babbitt* and *Main Street* are not photo-

graphic realism but satires. The American reader, I said, knows that the picture is incomplete—that Lewis left out many things which it did not suit his purpose to include in his satiric portraits of the American city and small town. I pointed out that during the Great Depression of the thirties many of our writers swung far to the political left. They were prematurely convinced of the failure of American democracy, and some of them saw salvation in Russian Communism. Most of these writers were disillusioned by the Stalin-Hitler pact of 1939 or by what happened in Munich or by the rape of Czechoslovakia; and if not, Pearl Harbor taught them that American democracy was something one must be willing to fight to preserve. I pointed to a change in mood in the later books of Hemingway, Dos Passos, and Steinbeck and suggested that American writers were returning to the traditional attitude which for nearly three centuries had characterized our literature. In *For Whom the Bell Tolls,* I said, Hemingway had abandoned the rather cynical attitude toward all warfare which he had taken in *A Farewell to Arms*; and in *The Ground We Stand On* Dos Passos had forgotten Russia and returned to Thomas Jefferson and the American Bill of Rights.

My lecture came at last to an end. Having been told by Dr. Paulovsky what the Austrian students do when they dislike the lecture or the lecturer, I wondered how they would take what I had said to them. What I did hear rather startled me until I realized that it was only the applause customary at the conclusion of every lecture, and the noise came from the tapping of pencils on the wooden desks and the stamping of feet on the wooden floor.

My other class was a seminar, or research course, designed for the more advanced students. I had not been told that I was expected to offer such a course until I was briefed on my mission in the Pentagon. I felt sure the Seminar library would have Poe's writings in both English and German though I knew that it was weak in American literature. So I offered a course entitled "Studies in Edgar Allan Poe." Poe is in some respects not a representative American writer, but his writings provide admirable materials for students to work on because his literary aims are so clearly defined and he had such a complete command of the technical means of carrying them out. (In 1950 I offered a seminar course in Emerson and Whitman.) The students were, I found, rather inclined to smile at "The

Raven," and I wondered why until I observed many of the great awkward birds strutting about the parks on the Ringstrasse. The croaking raven is not an exotic or romantic bird to the Viennese.

In an American university a professor is rarely willing to permit more than twelve or fifteen students to register for a seminar course. Before I had any idea how many were registering for mine, the number ran to the unheard-of total of forty-nine. That was of course far too many, but I soon discovered that an Austrian student who wishes to teach must have completed a seminar course before he can get a license. With more than seven hundred students to care for, the overworked English staff could not find places for my forty-nine. So I took them and did what I could for them. I lectured to all forty-nine for an hour and a half once a week, and I met them again in sections for another hour to give each student an opportunity to report on his research problem. I found it difficult, however, to get them to take part in such a general give-and-take discussion as often occurs in an American classroom. In this country such a discussion sometimes gets to the point where the professor finds it necessary to stop some voluble student who loves to talk and has nothing of importance to say. Not so in Vienna. The discussion was always between the individual student whom I called upon and me. Perhaps my tactics were wrong. When I visited one of Dr. Paulovsky's classes, I saw some of his students criticizing one another's translations almost ruthlessly. In European universities in 1949 if not in 1965 there was a greater barrier between student and professor than is found in the United States. The professor is the authority, and the student rarely questions it. My own attitude in class was quite informal, and I think most of my students liked it for its novelty if for nothing else.

My students interested me greatly, and I found myself immediately attracted to most of those with whom I talked. In numbers they were about equally divided between the sexes. My best seminar paper was written by a woman. The Austrian student is not so large as an American, who of course is taller than all his predecessors; but any one of them in American clothes and with an American haircut or hairdo would pass without difficulty for an American on the campus of an American university. They were always neat in appearance even though some of them, I felt sure, were wearing an

Springtime in Vienna

only presentable suit or dress. Many of them had the good looks and the personal charm which one associates with Vienna.

Since German is the language of Austria, they have long looked to Germany for leadership in education and in literature, much more than in music and the other arts. The noble monuments to Goethe and Schiller which stand near the Ringstrasse testify to a strong intellectual bond with Germany, but the Austrian does not like to have you confuse his country with the larger nation to the north. Sometimes he talks about Germany as unreconstructed Southerners once talked about the people who lived above the Mason-Dixon Line. Few of my students looked like typical Germans, and racially they seemed as cosmopolitan as the students at Columbia University or the University of California. Their names were German, Czech, Polish, Italian, and Yugoslavian. On my seminar classroll there were such names as Beranek, Borufka, Granadia, Francesconi, Janša, Matiasek, Petrasch, Templ, Turcu, and Weigert. Whatever the student's racial origin, he was first of all an Austrian and not a Czech, a German, a Hungarian, or an Italian. Most of them were natives of Vienna, and it may be said of the inhabitants of that city that they are first of all Viennese and only secondarily Austrians. The Viennese are a race apart, and to Austrians of the Tyrol or Carinthia or Styria they sometimes seem as foreign as New Yorkers seem to visitors from Oregon, Texas, or South Carolina. For centuries Vienna was the cultural and political capital of a great empire; but in 1949 the city with a population of a million and three quarters was the capital of a little country no larger than Maine with a population of about seven million. The rest of Franz Joseph's great empire lies on the other side of the Iron Curtain. Economically, the situation of Vienna is all wrong. The city lies on the natural highways of traffic between north and south, east and west. It is about as far from the center of modern Austria as it could be. With the dissolution of the Austro-Hungarian Empire after the First World War, there took place inevitably a great reduction in the number of state employees, court officials, bankers, and businessmen of all kinds. The Viennese had to exercise their wits to find new ways of earning a living. All of my students with the exception of one who might be called Old Perpetuity were born after the dissolution of the empire; and yet somehow their fathers and mothers had managed to educate their sons and daughters and to instil into them an appreciation of the fine arts, music, literature, and the art of living. In some respects this was easier in a city of great museums, palaces, libraries, and theaters where you could hear one of the world's best symphony orchestras for fifty cents or see a Mozart opera superbly performed for a maximum of a dollar and a quarter.

And yet students and professors complained that even these prices were so high that they could rarely afford to go. The university professors, I was told, were not paid much more than a first-class bricklayer could earn. In Austria as in America it seemed to me that the economic prospects of organized labor were brighter than those of men and women who spend years in preparing themselves to teach. I may add here that the sons and daughters of those who worked with their hands rarely went to the University of Vienna. Only one Austrian child in ten would attend high school, and very early comes the division between those who are to earn their living with their hands and those who hope to earn it by their brains. In Austria, as in other European nations, political democracy is generally better understood than its social counterpart. In this country it matters much less who your grandparents were or on which side of the railroad tracks you happen to have been born.

Wishing to become better acquainted with my students, I invited many of them in groups of four or five to have lunch or dinner with me in the Bristol Hotel, then occupied by senior U.S. Army officers and civilian experts employed by the army. The Bristol, where incidentally George Gershwin is said to have composed "An American in Paris," is one of Vienna's finest hotels. I found my students at first rather shy and in some instances suspicious, as if they were wondering what sort of propaganda I had come to Vienna to put over on them. In one of my last lectures I said that no one in the Pentagon had even remotely suggested that I was going to Austria as a propagandist or hinted that I would be less free to teach American literature in my own way than I was at Duke University.

Some of my students had been in the German army. One had been a fighter pilot, and he and several others had been prisoners of war in the United States. One of them had discovered Emerson's *Essays* in a camp in Tennessee. One of these men never tired of talking about Texas when he learned that I had lived there for twelve years. Not all, however, had fought with the Germans, for I remember one who had left Austria after the *Anschluss* to join the British army. After ten or fifteen minutes I found the students willing and often eager to talk, and they talked with apparent freedom about whatever subject came up. They could wisecrack in English as cleverly as American undergraduates. A group of my students liked the experience so well that they invited me to tea with them and entertained me with true Viennese hospitality.

I found my Austrian students on the whole quite as intelligent as American upperclassmen or graduate students. In some research techniques they were not nearly so well trained as our graduate students in English; but in literary appreciation, in a feeling for logic and order, and in the ability to analyze a poem or an essay I found them frequently superior to most of my graduate students. This surprised me because my Austrian students had to speak and write in what to them was a foreign language. The Austrian student's attitude toward his studies struck me as somewhat different from that of the practical American, who is preparing himself for the best position he can get. Most of my Austrian students seemed to me primarily interested in developing their own capabilities and in becoming genuinely cultivated persons. Most of my students were preparing themselves to become teachers, interpreters, or translators; and they were not very hopeful of finding the positions they wanted. There was no shortage of teachers in the Vienna public schools, and my students were preparing to wait for a year or two before finding the kind of position they wanted.

3

The two of my Austrian colleagues whom I came to know best were Professor Leo Hibler and Dr. Louis H. Paulovsky. They were gentlemen and scholars who would have been quickly recognized as such on any American university campus. They were modest and hard-working, and they were deeply interested in their students. Both are dead now and in each case as the result of a heart attack due, I suspect, in part at least to wartime hardships.

Dr. Paulovsky was the head of the Institute of Translation, which was training interpreters, translators, and teachers. I found that those of my students who had worked with him wrote and spoke better

English than the others. The Institute was Dr. Paulovsky's own idea; and, like many another professor with a new idea, he had found it difficult to convince the conservative academic authorities that it was a sound one. While I was in Vienna in the spring of 1949, he finally managed to get not only academic recognition but offices and classrooms in which to carry on his work. At that time, however, they were almost completely unfurnished. When David H. Stevens and Edward D'Arms of the Rockefeller Foundation came to Vienna, I pointed out to them Paulovsky's difficulties. Some months later the Foundation sent a check for two thousand dollars to buy equipment for the Institute.

Dr. Paulovsky was a native of Vienna, a graduate of the university, and an official interpreter for the Austrian government. He spoke English with no lapses in syntax, pronunciation, or idiom. I once said to his English wife: "Amy, I think you must be partly responsible for Louis' wonderful command of the English language." "No," she said, "he spoke quite as well when I first met him." When I knew him, he had never been in this country—he was to come later—yet he was an expert on the varieties of American speech. When the American Army came to Vienna, he had for the first time a chance to hear all the varieties of American speech. He was a Viennese and immensely proud of his beautiful city, and he knew intimately its history and traditions. With him as guide I saw many of the historic sites and buildings. He managed to make me almost see the great composers whose symphonies I was hearing played by the Vienna Philharmonic Orchestra at the time: Mozart, Beethoven, Schubert, and Brahms.

Professor Leo Hibler, the head of the English Seminar, was a native of the Austrian Tyrol, and he held the doctor's degree from the University of Innsbruck. Like many another native of the Tyrol, he was fond of skiing and he was an expert skier. He was at one time a lecturer in the University of London, and his English speech would have done credit to a don at Oxford or Cambridge. Not long after Hitler came to power, he sent to England his wife, a native of Scotland, and his daughter and son, now British citizens. When they parted, they reassured one another by saying that Hitler would soon be ousted from the Chancellory and they would all be together again. When I came to Vienna in February, 1949, he had not seen his family for many years. The long spring vacation of that year gave him his first opportunity to go to the British Isles to see his wife and children. Not long before he left Vienna for England he said to me: "It has been so long since I saw my family I am afraid I won't know how to behave." "That," I said, "should be the least of your worries."

At the end of the Second World War the Nazi head of the English Seminar was fired, and for three years Dr. Paulovsky was the acting head. Professor Hibler, who was teaching at the University of Leipzig, was offered the headship of the English Seminar at both the University of Vienna and the University of Munich. Leipzig is in East Germany, and it was not easy even then for one to cross the border into West Germany. In the summer of 1948 Hibler managed to get out by showing a letter from a publisher in West Germany who wanted him to write a textbook on American literature. He had put into a rucksack a few necessities and walked the long way to Vienna. It took him two weeks. I remember that once when I happened to mention the badly bombed railway station in Munich, he said: "I remember it well. I slept there one night on my way down here." I might add that his successor at the University of Leipzig soon fled to West Germany.

Professor Hibler and I soon found a common interest in our students, in English and American literature, and in music. We attended some magnificent concerts in the Music Hall of the Vienna Philharmonic Orchestra, and we saw and heard Beethoven's *Fidelio* and other operas in the Theater an der Wien. Especially memorable for both of us was a concert given by the one-armed pianist, Paul Wittgenstein. One evening after a concert Hibler took me to a coffee house, which had few customers. After a few minutes we were told that the coffee house would close at nine o'clock. Hibler was surprised. "This," he said, "is certainly not the Vienna I remember. Evidently the coffee house is not making money."

Hibler was greatly interested in American literature. He had been in the United States more than once, and he was as well prepared to write a history of American literature as any professor in the German or Austrian universities. "But," he said to me, "with seven hundred students in the English Seminar to look after when can I ever find time to write a book? Besides," he added, "we don't have all the basic materials in the Vienna libraries." The U. S. Commission for Austria, however, did help to supply these basic materials. I remember my surprise in the spring of 1949 when Dr. Williams said to me: "I've got three thousand dollars with which to buy books in American literature for the Seminar library. Will you bring me a list of the books you want with names of the publishers and the prices?" When I told Hibler of this windfall, he said: "When ever before did a victorious army in a conquered country ever do anything like that?" The books were very slow in coming. When Hibler in the fall of 1949 wrote me that the books had not come, I wrote to Dr. Williams, who discovered that some army official had taken it upon himself to hold up the order. Eventually the Seminar got the books. Professor Hibler somewhat later had the official name of the English Seminar changed to the Institute for English and American Literature and Language.

When Professor Hibler reached the retirement age of seventy, the university published on his birthday a well-deserved *Festschrift* symposium entitled *Anglo-Americana*. It was edited by his friend of many years, Karl Brunner of the University of Innsbruck. I contributed an essay, and so did Ernest E. Leisy, who lectured at the University of Vienna in 1951. But the university was slow in selecting Hibler's successor, and he continued to teach until his death on November 20, 1956. I have known many university professors who were both good teachers and fine scholars but Leo Hibler was not only a good teacher and a fine scholar; he was a man for whom I had the greatest respect, admiration, and affection.

We have not been in Vienna since June, 1950, but my wife and I often talk of our stay in that lovely city, especially when spring comes round again and we remember how lovely were the Vienna Woods and the parks bordering on the Ringstrasse. My friends at the university, Professor Hibler, Dean Leitmeier, and the Rector, Richard Meister, wanted me to return in 1951, but I felt that I had been away from my Duke students too long. Austria is not an occupied country now, and the Russians are not there any longer. It would be a great pleasure to see the university and the great public buildings on the Ringstrasse now fully restored. It would be thrilling once again to hear the Vienna Philharmonic Orchestra play a

Beethoven symphony and to visit the rebuilt State Opera House opposite the Bristol Hotel and see and hear a Mozart or Wagner opera performed by some of the best musicians in Europe. But a return to Vienna would inevitably bring many sad memories. Dr. and Mrs. Samuel Williams are gone and so are Harold Howland and the rest of the staff of the Education Division. Gone, too, are those fine army officers, Colonel Brotherton, Colonel Storke, and Major Dunlap. Gone, too, are those friendly and cultivated Viennese ladies: Frau Katetsky, who headed a fine language school, and Frau Hofbauer, whose husband was one of the great Viennese physicians. At the university there are professors and students whom we do not know. Hibler and Paulovsky are dead but I trust are not forgotten in the English Seminar. Our lives are the richer for having known such men and women as I have named, and the university, which this year (1965) is celebrating the six hundredth anniversary of its founding, will, I trust, place suitable memorials to Leo Hibler and Louis Paulovsky in the corridor leading to the English Seminar.

*Let it be remembered, then, that [when Lowell was a student at Har-
vard] the whole drift of fashion, occupation, and habit among the undergraduates ran in lines suggested by literature.*

EDWARD EVERETT HALE, *James Russell
Lowell and His Friends* (1899), p. 22

*. . . if, at my death, my executors, or more properly my creditors, find
any precious Mss. in my desk, then here I prospectively ascribe all the
honor and the glory to whaling; for a whale-ship was my Yale College
and my Harvard.*

HERMAN MELVILLE, *Moby-Dick* (1851),
chap. xxiv

The Creative Writer and the University, with Special Reference to the 1920's

[In this essay I have much to say about the complaints which the youthful poets and novelists brought against their English professors. There was a substantial basis in fact for some of their grievances, but there were notable exceptions, as I shall point out. I consider myself singularly fortunate in the professors under whom I studied and likewise in those who were colleagues of mine. Dean Briggs at Harvard, Carl Van Doren at Columbia, and Benjamin Sledd at Wake Forest College were always willing to give their time and thought to students who wanted to write.

In October, 1915, I became a member of the English staff at Southern Methodist University, which had opened its doors only a month earlier. My English colleagues there for the next twelve years were young men and women, most of whom wanted to write

330

poetry or fiction. There was none of the traditional hostility between elderly philologists and young creative writers. John H. McGinnis was the literary editor of the Dallas *News,* and George Bond and I were editors of the *Southwest Review.* During my years in Dallas eight or nine other literary magazines were published there. Dallas was headquarters for the Poetry Society of Texas, and Dallas had in its Little Theater one of the best in the whole country. Among the poets who gave lectures or readings to enthusiastic undergraduates were Vachel Lindsay, Carl Sandburg, Robert Frost, and Karle Wilson Baker. In 1922 a group of my ablest students organized a poetry club, "The Makers," whose remarkable story I hope to tell in another book. My work with these eager undergraduates convinced me that English departments should do much more for their kind than to offer a course or two in creative writing. At Duke University, to which I removed in 1927, there have always been capable and sympathetic professors willing to give their time to students who wanted to write. Successful writers or not, many Duke students remember gratefully William Blackburn and the late Newman I. White.]

1

"You know who the critics are?" asks a character in Disraeli's *Lothair,* and he answers his own question: "The men who have failed in literature and art." "Kill the dog," said the young Goethe; "he is a reviewer." These are but two examples of the traditional antipathy that the poet, the dramatist, and the novelist have felt toward those who presume to criticize what they have written. Their feeling about critics is much the same as that which the farmer has for the too numerous middlemen that stand between him and the ultimate consumer who pays for the farmer's corn, cotton, or tobacco a much higher price than the farmer receives. Why, indeed, say the novelist and the dramatist, should not those who read a novel or see a play on the stage form their own estimates without benefit of the reviewer or critic? At most, they hold, the critic should confine his function to explaining the author's intention and his means of carrying it out. (And yet when have poets, novelists, and dramatists ever hesitated to criticize the aims and methods of other writers?) If we must have critics, so the creative writers argue, let them be men who have earned reputations by their own creative work. And indeed it is easy to point to many distinguished critics who as first-rate creative writers have qualified for the role of critic. Off-hand one thinks of Lessing, Goethe, Anatole France, Coleridge, Arnold, Lowell, Henry James, Poe, and among our contemporaries, T. S. Eliot, Allen Tate, Donald Davidson, and John Crowe Ransom.

The traditional antipathy between creative writers and critics was especially acute in the 1920's, and there were reasons for it. Never before did the gulf which separates the attitudes of the old and the young seem so wide as in the years that followed the First World War. There was a deep misunderstanding on the one side and a profound distrust on the other. The elderly gentlemen in the National Institute of Arts and Letters disapproved strongly of the aims and methods of many of the younger writers; and many of the younger writers had broken with the traditions and conventions held up before them by the conservative older generation of critics and professors of English.

The literary rebels of the 1920's were inclined to look upon professors of English with either resentment or contempt. If those who taught literature were not literary critics, they appeared to the undergraduate as at least the semiofficial custodians and interpreters of the literary tradition. And many of the Young Intellectuals, as they were called, with unpleasant memories of college classrooms, had found the literary tradition held up for their emulation not to their taste and had pronounced it unusable.

There was in the 1920's too little mutual understanding on the part of creative writers, young or old, and the professors who were teaching English and other modern literatures. There is, for example, the story told of Ernest Brennecke, who wrote a doctor's dissertation on the Wessex novels of Thomas Hardy. After passing his final examination he sent a copy of the dissertation to Hardy, whom he was to see in England a little later. The manuscript carried on the margin some penciled notations by a distinguished Columbia University professor of English who shall be nameless here. Not long afterwards Brennecke, who himself recently retired from a Columbia University professorship, called upon Hardy at Max Gate. The novelist gave him a cordial welcome and praised his manuscript. "But," he asked, "who was the silly ass who wrote

The Creative Writer and the University

the comments on the margin?" This story was going the rounds in Cambridge, Massachusetts, in December, 1926, while the distinguished Columbia professor was being elected President of the Modern Language Association.

2

Not untypical was the attitude of Sinclair Lewis. In 1922 he declined to accept election to the National Institute of Arts and Letters. "Too many professors," he wrote to his first wife, Grace Hegger Lewis. Four years later he astonished the American public by declining to accept the Pulitzer Prize for fiction. He wrote:

> Between the Pulitzer Prizes, the American Academy of Arts and Letters and its training-school, the National Institute of Arts and Letters, amateur boards of censorship, and the inquisition of earnest literary ladies, every compulsion is put upon writers to become safe, polite, obedient, and sterile.

Lewis was no doubt shrewd enough to see that in declining the Pulitzer Prize he would attract more attention to himself and sell more copies of *Arrowsmith* than he would if he accepted the prize. The Nobel Prize was another matter, however, and Lewis did not fail to accept that when it was offered to him—even though Nobel, like Pulitzer, had stipulated that the prize should go to authors of books of an idealistic nature. Lewis was in 1930 the first American writer to win the Nobel Prize. Not so generally known is it that for several years he had been urging his publisher to do all he could to see that he got it.

When it was announced that Lewis would be awarded the Nobel Prize, Henry van Dyke, poet, Professor of English at Princeton, and Presbyterian minister, said publicly that Lewis was unworthy of it.[1] Lewis chose for his Stockholm address a topic that would have seemed to most men inappropriate and in bad taste, "The American Fear of Literature." Lewis lamented "the divorce in America of intellectual life from all authentic standards of importance and reality." He named twenty American writers who were not members

1. "It is the fashion of young men now to minimize the ability and influence of both [Hamilton Wright] Mabie and his close friend Henry van Dyke, but no two men in New York, in the nineties, showed more helpfulness to unknown writers, and it saddens me today to see such indubitable Christians thrown to the lions by young aliens who do not take the trouble to read their books" (Bliss Perry, *And Gladly Teach*, 1935, p. 141).

of the American Academy of Arts and Letters, of which he said: "It does not represent literary America of today—it represents only Henry Wadsworth Longfellow." No doubt he remembered the Princeton professor when he said:

To a true-blue professor of literature in an American university, literature is not something that a plain human being, living today, painfully sits down to produce. No; it is something dead; it is something magically produced by super-human beings who must, if they are to be regarded as artists at all, have died at least one hundred years before the diabolical invention of the typewriter. . . . Our American professors like their literature clear and pure and very dead.

Lewis could think of only four American colleges and universities— Middlebury, Rollins, Michigan, and Chicago—which had shown "an authentic interest in contemporary creative literature." Why, one wonders, had Lewis overlooked those professors—William Lyon Phelps and Chauncey B. Tinker—who had recognized his talent and given him encouragement while he was an unhappy undergraduate at Yale?

3

In 1930 there were in fact many professors of English who cared very little for contemporary literature, especially that being written in their own country. I shall have more to say about them later, but in 1930 there were not nearly so many of them as there had been in the first decade of the century when Lewis was in college. Long before 1930 there were many professors of English who had displayed "an authentic interest in contemporary literature," and some of them had done their best to help such of their students as were trying to write. Some of the professors were themselves writers and were publishing their work in the better literary magazines.

At Harvard, Yale, Princeton, and Vanderbilt—to name only four of the universities that Lewis failed to mention—there were enrolled a number of young writers who were to make memorable a great period in American literature. In these and other institutions most of those students who had talent and really wanted to become writers were able to find professors willing to give them advice and encouragement. Lewis might perhaps be excused for not knowing what was going on in the colleges and universities in California and Texas; but in 1930 he could hardly have been ignorant of what was going on at Vanderbilt and Harvard. He must have been aware also of the literary activity which had gone on at Yale after his graduation. At Columbia University Brander Matthews had given helpful advice to Stewart Edward White, as John Erskine and Mark Van Doren were to do later for many undergraduates.

Harvard had a long and impressive literary tradition, and even though few of the Harvard English professors displayed any keen interest in American literature, an extraordinary number of our twentieth-century writers were students there. Lewis Gates had helped Frank Norris to find himself as a writer. It was in Gates's class that he wrote *Vandover and the Brute* and parts of *McTeague*. Before 1900 Dean Le Baron Russell Briggs and Professor Charles Townsend Copeland were giving expert criticism to students in their classes in advanced composition. In Dean Briggs's English 5, which I took in 1906-1907, there were Edward Sheldon, John A. Lomax, and Van Wyck Brooks. By that time Professor George P. Baker had begun his 47 Workshop. Among his students were Edward Sheldon, Thomas Wolfe, and Eugene O'Neill. If Wolfe never wrote a successful play, he at least learned something about action, dialogue, and character portrayal that he was able to use when he wrote *Look Homeward, Angel* and *Of Time and the River*. Earlier at the University of North Carolina Wolfe had been fortunate enough to find two helpful advisers in Edwin Greenlaw and Frederick H. Koch, who was one of Baker's former students.

While an undergraduate at the University of Chicago in the late 1920's James T. Farrell wrote for a class in advanced composition a story which he called "Studs." Two of his English professors who read it encouraged him to expand the story into a novel. So, as Farrell wrote later: "In a sense Professor [James Weber] Linn and Professor [Robert Morss] Lovett are the spiritual godfathers of *Studs Lonigan*." Carl Sandburg, who was a student at Lombard College at the turn of the century, had a friend and adviser in Professor Philip Green Wright, who managed to get the poet's first book published. The professor paid the printer's bill out of his own pocket. Edmund Wilson, John Peale Bishop, and Scott Fitzgerald, who were undergraduates at Princeton, learned most from Christian Gauss, whose favorite authors were Dante and Flaubert.

Gauss "made us all," says Wilson, "want to write something in which every word, every sentence, every detail, should perform a definite function in producing an intense effect." Bishop, he notes, "came to Princeton intoxicated with Swinburne and Shelley," but by the time he graduated, he "was concentrating . . . on hard images and pregnant phrases."

4

After all, however, such professors of English as Copeland, Baker, Tinker, and Wright represented a comparatively small minority. There were, alas, more who had no "authentic interest in contemporary creative literature." Many young writers looked upon professors of English as the enemies of everything new. H. L. Mencken, trying to win recognition for Theodore Dreiser, wrote: "Alas! professors never learn anything." Edmund Wilson recalls that in 1912, when he entered college, "Ernest Dowson and Oscar Wilde were the latest sensational writers who had got in past the stained-glass windows of the Princeton University Library."

Van Wyck Brooks, a graduate of Harvard who had been for two years instructor in English at Stanford University, wrote in *America's Coming of Age* (1915): "It is a peculiar twist in the academic mind to suppose that a writer belongs to literature only when he is dead; living he is, vaguely, something else; and a habitual remoteness from the creative mood has made American professors peculiarly academic." There was, as he saw, a widespread feeling among professors of English that contemporary literature was not sufficiently remote to be the subject of objective scholarly investigation. Brander Matthews, who taught at Columbia University but regarded himself as primarily a man of letters, was fond of quoting Jules Lemaître's remark: "Criticism of our contemporaries is not criticism; it is only conversation." The general feeling among English professors was that anybody could write criticism, by which they meant appreciative criticism. There was also in some academic circles a strong feeling that it was professionally infra dig to write for even the quality magazines. As late as 1930 John Crowe Ransom had cause to lament that the professors who taught literature were "learned but not critical men." Nevertheless he hoped that eventually they would erect intelligent standards of criticism. "It is their business," he insisted. Ten years later Allen Tate spoke for many creative writers in "Miss Emily and the Bibliographer" when he attacked "the historical method." "The great historical scholars of our time," he said, "are notoriously deficient critics." When was it, he wondered, that the professors of English had "lost confidence in literature?"

Many of the ablest professors of English had been trained in German universities or in American universities by professors who had studied in Germany. The German scholars were at that time more concerned with philological problems than with the critical study of literary masterpieces, and they directed their chief efforts toward the language and the literature of the Old and Middle English periods. They were well aware of the circumstance that for a German it is easier to master Anglo-Saxon than it is for an Englishman or an American. They also knew that for one whose native language is not English it is difficult to appreciate the subtle shades of meaning and connotation in modern English poetry and prose.

When the American scholars who had studied in Germany returned to their own country, they naturally wished to teach the subjects they had studied in Heidelberg, Berlin, or Bonn. When they mapped out the requirements for the doctorate at Harvard, Yale, Chicago, and Johns Hopkins, they placed the emphasis upon the language and the literature of England before 1660. It was to be many years before pressure from students and intellectuals outside the universities would induce many departments of English to offer courses in contemporary English literature or in American literature in any period.

In defense of the "Germanic" system the professors told their graduate students that the important thing was not the period one specialized in but the mastery of the approved methods of scholarship. What one learned in the Chaucer seminar, they suggested, could easily be applied to the study of Carlyle or Emerson or even Kipling or Henry James. In later life many of those students who were to teach American literature or English literature written after 1660 came to feel that they had wasted much time in studying subject matter that they were never to teach. They also learned that successful research and teaching in the later literature often called for other methods than those they had learned in courses in Anglo-

337

Saxon, Gothic, Old French, and Middle English. The young instructor who wished to concentrate on Poe, for example, found that his graduate training had given him no inkling of the problems he faced in his exploration of the many magazines and newspapers to which Poe contributed.

American creative writers sometimes expressed their dissatisfaction with the way in which English and other modern literatures were being taught. In 1889 James Russell Lowell, who had been a Harvard professor, issued a warning in his Presidential Address to the Modern Language Association of America. After noting "the wonderful advance made in comparative philology of the modern languages" in recent years, he said:

I think that the purely linguistic side in the teaching of them seems in the way to get more than its fitting share. I insist only that in our college courses this should be a separate study, and that, good as it is in itself, it should, in the scheme of general instruction, be restrained to its own function as the guide to something better. And that something better is Literature. Let us rescue ourselves from what Milton calls "these grammatic flats and shallows."

Lowell's warning had little if any effect. Seventeen years later Edmund Clarence Stedman, poet and critic, wrote: "If I had accepted any one of the Chairs of Literature which have been offered to me [his alma mater, Yale University, had offered him one of these], I certainly never should have taught poetry or other creative literature in the technical and pedantic fashion introduced from Germany by our multitudinous Ph.D.'s."

Most of our graduate students in English—then as nowadays—had tried their hands at writing poetry, drama, or fiction, and some of them went to Harvard or Yale or Chicago or Johns Hopkins hoping that they might find someone who could help them develop their talents. What they found often left them with a feeling of frustration. Stuart P. Sherman, who had taken his doctor's degree at Harvard two years earlier, published in the New York *Nation* for May 14, 1908, a sweeping indictment entitled "Graduate Schools and Literature." Departments of English, he said, were cutting off their own noses by discouraging their students' "hope of training for creative literary work." Nothing, he said, is "more pathetic in the world than the sight of the ardent and aspiring souls from Utah, Oregon, Texas, and the isles of the sea, who come up to the graduate school, and, in the faith and heart-ravishing impudence of little children calling for bread, receive a gold brick." What wonder, then, he said, that "The very best men do not enter upon graduate study at all; the next best drop out after a year's experiment; the mediocre men at the end of two years; the most unfit survive and become doctors of philosophy, who go forth and reproduce their kind." At Harvard Sherman's essay prompted one of my professors, the late William Henry Schofield, to lay aside our lesson in Old Norse and spend the entire hour in a defense of the doctor's program at Harvard. The English department, he said, had permitted Sherman, who wanted to work on a "modern" author, to write a dissertation on the late Elizabethan dramatist, John Ford. "Modern" indeed! At the end of the hour one student remarked as we left the classroom: "If that's the best defense that can be made of the requirements here, I think I shall transfer to Columbia next year."

After the death of Adelaide Crapsey in 1914, Professor Raymond Weeks of the French department at Columbia asked Amy Lowell to read Miss Crapsey's doctor's dissertation. After reading it, Miss Lowell wrote:

That a young woman of Miss Crapsey's originality and talent should have spent innumerable hours counting the words in "Paradise Lost" and other poems in order to write a thesis for a doctor's degree, almost makes me weep. When will the new school of critics realize that art cannot be adequately treated without recognizing that its fundamental importance is as art? The pseudo-scientific method in regard to literature fails exactly here.

Miss Lowell's brother was President of Harvard University, but she had a low opinion of the way literature was being taught there.

For the last two years of my school course [she wrote], I attended lectures on Shakespeare by an eminent Harvard professor. . . . We learnt everything about the plays we studied except the things that mattered. Not a historical allusion, not an antiquarian tit-bit, escaped us. . . . Not once in those two years were we bidden to notice the poetry, not once was there a single aesthetic analysis. The plays might have been written in the baldest prose for all the eminent professor seemed to care.

On the other side of the continent Jack London dropped out of the University of California because, as he wrote later:

I had to unlearn about everything that the teachers and professors of literature in the high school and university had taught me. . . . They

339

did not know the trick of successful writing in the years of 1895 and 1896. They knew all about "Snow-Bound" and "Sartor Resartus"; but the American editors of 1899 did not want such truck.

Fred Lewis Pattee, who wanted to be a writer, got no help from his Dartmouth professors.

As a writer, I was forced to educate myself, and I did a poor job. . . . The college helped me not at all at this critical moment. Its whole vision was directed toward the past. I was told to form myself on Addison and Macaulay and the purists of the eighteenth century.

And yet when young Pattee applied for a position at Pennsylvania State College in 1887, it was his little volume of poems, *The Wine of May*, which induced President Atherton to appoint him rather than any other candidate.

As a student at the University of Nebraska Willa Cather came to dislike intensely the head of the English department there, Professor Lucius A. Sherman (A.B. and Ph.D., Yale). The result of her exposure to his methods was that, in the words of E. K. Brown, "Forever after she was suspicious of complicated or systematic literary analysis." This was no doubt a main reason why she forbade—and for all time—the publication of any of her private letters. Willa Cather learned most from William Ducker, who taught her Latin and Greek. Those who have read *My Ántonia* will remember her account of Gaston Cleric and his memorable comments on a passage in Vergil's *Georgics*.

In the early 1920's a friend of Elizabeth Madox Roberts asked the senior members of the English department at the University of Kentucky to consider Miss Roberts' stories and give her some encouragement. I quote from *Elizabeth Madox Roberts* (1956) by two professors of English, Harry M. Campbell and Ruel E. Foster:

But not one of them would take the time and trouble. So ten years elapse, and Miss Roberts becomes a leading American novelist. All, all, all is changed. The faculty editor of *Letters* writes a fulsome letter asking for material. Other members desire interviews and, on receiving them, write their accounts in local newspapers in glowing terms, basking in the reflected light of glory. How easy, she must have reflected, to acquire the aid after the aid is no longer required.

Witter Bynner, who graduated from Harvard in 1902, took a composition course under Karl Young, who was to become a distinguished Professor of English at Wisconsin and later at Yale and was in 1940 to be elected President of the Modern Language Association. When Young learned that some of his freshmen were daring to write poetry, he gave them a stern lecture on their conceit in imagining that any one of them could possibly add anything important to the huge corpus of literature in English. "Why," he said, "there is more great poetry written in the English language than any one man can read in a lifetime." That night the discouraged young poet made his protest in a poem entitled "Dante":

> Perhaps they laughed at Dante in his youth,
> Told him that truth
> Had unappealably been said
> In the great masterpieces of the dead:—
> Perhaps he listened and but bowed his head
> In acquiescent honour, while his heart
> Held natal tidings,—that a new life is the part
> Of every man that's born,
> A new life never lived before,
> And a new expectant art.
> It is the variations of the morn
> That are forever, more and more,
> The single dawning of the single truth.
> So answers Dante to the heart of youth.

When I heard Witter Bynner tell this story, he had just come to Dallas from Madison, Wisconsin, where he had read his poems to a university audience. It was Professor Karl Young who had introduced him.

One valid complaint of the young writers in the 1920's was that our critics and literary historians had not provided them with a usable past. In an article entitled "On Creating a Usable Past," published in the *Dial* on April 11, 1918, Van Wyck Brooks wrote:

The European writer . . . has his racial past *made available* to him. The American writer, on the other hand, not only has the most meager of birthrights but is cheated out of that. For the professorial mind . . . puts a gloss upon the past that renders it sterile for the living mind.

With some reason Brooks complained that our literary histories too often ended about the year 1890 and disparaged "almost everything that comes out of the contemporary mind." Apparently the four stout volumes of *The Cambridge History of American Literature* (1917-1921)—a great boon to scholars—did not answer the need of the young creative writers. Brooks admitted that "the spiritual past,"

341

which "has no objective reality," "yields only what we are able to look for in it"; but, he added, if "we cannot use what our professors offer us, is there any reason why we should not create others of our own?"

After 1918 Parrington, Pattee, and Brooks himself were to do much toward putting the American literary past into a more usable form. In 1918, however, few American colleges or universities offered courses in the literature of the United States, and few of the older professors of English had any real interest in it. In the 1920's many of the younger poets and novelists felt that—apart from Poe, Whitman, and Mark Twain—they had nothing in common with our earlier writers. For Hemingway and Faulkner American literature began in 1884 with the publication of *The Adventures of Huckleberry Finn.*

Most of our youthful creative writers were not interested in the history of their own country. This, it now seems, was an astonishing attitude in men who had seen the United States depart from its traditional isolation and emerge as one of the great world powers. For this lack of interest in the American past some of our teachers of history must share the blame with the professors of English. Yet it was from two professors of history at Yale that Stephen Vincent Benét got his keen and intelligent interest in the American past.

After President Roosevelt devalued the dollar, many of our expatriates came trooping back to their native land. It was no longer cheaper to live in Paris or London. Some of them felt, like Malcolm Cowley, that since (as they thought) America had no literary tradition, it was up to them to create one. On the other hand, Ezra Pound and T. S. Eliot chose to remain in Europe and to create, each for himself, an eclectic and artificial literary tradition out of various European and Oriental literatures. Tradition, wrote Eliot in 1917, "cannot be inherited, and if you want it you must obtain it by great labour." Shakespeare and Scott in Britain and Hawthorne in New England had been more fortunate. Eliot and Pound did each manage to create for himself a usable "tradition"—if one may call it that—"by great labour." Unfortunately their readers had to share this "great labour" if they were to understand the allusions and quotations drawn from many writers outside the main currents of European literature. In Pound's mind Emerson, Whitman,

Chaucer, and Shakespeare were less important than Propertius, the troubadours from Provence, certain minor Elizabethan dramatists, and John Donne and other Metaphysical poets. For Eliot, George Herbert was a "major" poet; Pound and Eliot had no use for Milton. Few American authors aroused any enthusiasm in them or their disciples.

5

Many professors thought that it was not their business to give the young creative writer the training he needs. When Ezra Pound wrote to Felix E. Schelling urging that the University of Pennsylvania establish fellowships for young creative writers, Professor Schelling replied: "The University is not here for the unusual man." Schelling, who, as he told me, had contributed to the support of the aged Walt Whitman, no doubt agreed with the view expressed in Cardinal Newman's classic, *The Idea of a University*:

[A university] neither confines its views to particular professions on the one hand, nor creates heroes or inspires genius on the other. Works indeed of genius fall under no arts; heroic minds come under no rule; a University is not a birthplace of poets or of immortal authors, of founders of schools, leaders of colonies, or conquerors of nations. It does not promise a generation of Aristotles or Newtons, of Napoleons or Washingtons, of Raphaels or Shakespeares, though such miracles of nature it has before now contained within its precincts.

Emerson, who was Newman's contemporary, did not subscribe to that view. He wrote in his *Journals* in May, 1845:

There is not the slightest probability that the college will foster an eminent talent in any youth. If he refuse prayers and recitations, they will torment and traduce and expel him, though he were Newton or Dante.

In a book bearing the title *Let Me Lie* (1947) James Branch Cabell referred "with a sort of incredulous awe" to "the record of the College of William and Mary," from which he had graduated in 1898:

. . . this college has contrived, somehow, throughout the length of two and a half centuries, to produce, with but one exception, in the lank figure of Thomas Jefferson, no graduate who after leaving Williamsburg became distinguished in any branch of creative art.

The event seems not surprising but miraculous. It defies all granted laws of probability that the name of no fairly well known painter, or musician, or sculptor, or novelist, or poet, or playwright, or prose artist, should adorn the long list of the thousands of persons who have been educated, at William and Mary.

I once heard the late Charles W. Eliot, the great President of Harvard University, express his conviction that the university's first obligation was to its superior students. From among these men, he said, would come the future leaders of the nation. If we can expect the colleges and universities to do their best to prepare for their professions the lawyers, ministers, engineers, scientists, and journalists, I do not think we can escape our obligation to the young men and women who wish to become writers. The great majority of our twentieth-century writers have attended some college or university, and the proportion is steadily increasing. Those who teach must reckon with the fact that from among the millions of young men and women who will attend our colleges and universities in the next three decades will come those who are to write the best American poetry, fiction, and drama that will come out of the last quarter of the twentieth century. The Department of English cannot afford to shirk its obligation to these men and women.

Yet it is difficult for the Professor of English to imagine that in one of his classes there is a boy or girl who may one day win the Nobel Prize for Literature. John Livingston Lowes, who directed Thomas Wolfe's master's thesis at Harvard, told him that he had it in him to become a distinguished scholar but would never be able to write an important novel or play.

We who teach the literary masterpieces written in the English language need at times to be reminded how unimportant our function would be if we had nothing better to teach than the subliterary fiction of the pulp magazines and the sensational paperbacks. Imagine a college curriculum in which the student had no opportunity to study such writers as Shakespeare and Milton or Emerson, Whitman, and Henry James! It is so also with the other arts. Once at a rehearsal the National Broadcasting Company's Symphony Orchestra applauded its great conductor, Arturo Toscanini. The conductor shook his head rather sadly and said: "No, gentlemen, that is not I but Beethoven."

I believe that our English departments should do their best to help gifted young writers to master their craft; and yet a cursory

The Creative Writer and the University

review of either the English or the American literary past will bring to mind many eminent writers who never had a college education. First, there is the greatest of them all, Shakespeare, who, as Ben Jonson informs us, "had small Latin and less Greek." Indeed the fact that the great poet and dramatist was educated not at Oxford or Cambridge but only in the Stratford grammar school is, I think, a main reason why so many deluded persons have concluded that *Hamlet* and *The Tempest* must have been written by Francis Bacon or some other British nobleman who had studied at one of the universities.

Many an English and American writer might have complained, as did Charles Lamb on a visit to Oxford, that he had been "defrauded in his young years of the sweet food of academic institution. . . ." Winston Churchill did not attend Oxford or Cambridge, nor did Robert Burns study at one of the great universities in Scotland. He wrote in his "Epistle to John Lapraik, an Old Scottish Bard":

> A set o' dull conceited hashes
> Confuse their brains in college classes!
> They gang in stirks, and come out asses,
>   Plain truth to speak;
> An' syne they think to climb Parnassus
>   By dint o' Greek!
> Gie me ae spark o' Nature's fire,
> That's a' the learning I desire. . . .

Sir Walter Scott was not college-bred, nor Charles Dickens nor John Keats; and on our side of the Atlantic the list is a long one, and it includes Irving, Whittier, Melville, Whitman, Mark Twain, Howells, Cable, Harris, Garland, Emily Dickinson, Ellen Glasgow, Ernest Hemingway, and many more.

Ellen Glasgow, who was a voracious reader, wrote in *A Certain Measure*:

Since I have never approached literature by way of college courses in English, arranged neatly with dates of birth and death in a lank row of epitaphs, books have been, for me, one of the vital elements of experience; and a thing apart, not a collection of classified facts.

Perhaps it was fortunate for Hamlin Garland that he did not have money enough to study at Harvard. So he rented a hall bedroom and educated himself in the Boston libraries. "The true University of these days," wrote Thomas Carlyle, "is a collection of books."

Of those American writers who entered college not a few left without taking a degree. Fenimore Cooper was suspended at Yale. Poe had one year at the University of Virginia, and after a few months at the U. S. Military Academy he got himself dismissed. Brief and unsatisfactory were the college careers of Stephen Crane, Theodore Dreiser, William Faulkner, Edwin Arlington Robinson, and Robert Frost. At Harvard James Russell Lowell was rusticated for neglect of academic exercises, and so was a much greater poet, John Milton, at the English Cambridge. Shelley was expelled from Oxford.

Before the Civil War and again in the twentieth century many of our best writers were college-bred, but in the later nineteenth century many came into literature through the gateway of journalism. Some of the best of them, like Joel Chandler Harris, William Dean Howells, and Mark Twain, attended only what Lincoln called the poor man's college, the newspaper printing office. Some of our twentieth-century writers of fiction have profited from this experience in journalism, notably Dreiser, Lewis, Hemingway, and Willa Cather. The newspaper reporter learns much about life, but the journalistic experience does not encourage the endless rewriting which is generally essential to the production of a work of art.

Maxwell Perkins, who gave expert advice to Scott Fitzgerald, Ernest Hemingway, Thomas Wolfe, and other Scribner authors, wrote to an unnamed young writer that while there were other advantages in going to college, that was not the way to learn to write. ". . . the way they teach literature and writing in college is harmful," he said. "It results in one getting into the habit of seeing everything through a kind of film of past literature, and not seeing it directly with one's senses." Robert Frost once spoke to another poet, Robert P. Tristram Coffin, of his fear that "a boy who had it in him to write poetry might be hurt by college. It might blight his natural knowledge of people's nature and of nature itself, and substitute knowledge of too many books and too many ideas at second hand." Frost himself wrote a poem entitled "Boeotian":

> I love to play with the Platonic notion
> That wisdom need not be of Athens Attic
> But well may be Laconic, even Boeotian.
> At least I will not have it systematic.

Some poets but not all seem to have found their learning an asset rather than a handicap. Among British poets one remembers Ben Jonson, John Milton, Thomas Gray, Samuel Taylor Coleridge, and Matthew Arnold. James Russell Lowell once told William Dean Howells that "he himself had been hurt for literature by his scholarship," but Lowell did not have it in him to be a great poet. Among contemporary writers there are such learned poets as John Crowe Ransom, T. S. Eliot, and Ezra Pound. In 1914 Pound wrote to Harriet Monroe: "He [Eliot] is the only American I know of who has made what I can call adequate preparation for writing." Eliot himself had written in 1917 that the historical sense is "nearly indispensable to any one who would continue to be a poet beyond his twenty-fifth year." The historical sense, he continued, "compels a man to write not merely with his own generation in his bones, but with a feeling that the whole of the literature of Europe from Homer and within it the whole of the literature of his own country has a simultaneous existence and composes a simultaneous order." The preparation that Pound and Eliot desired is not easily acquired outside a university; but Pound had some reason to complain that among college professors he found "no man with a view of literature as a whole, or with any idea whatsoever of the relation of the part he himself taught to any other part." Eliot in 1921 in an essay on William Blake insisted that "the artist should be highly educated in his own art"; but he felt that the education planned for the ordinary man consisted too much in "the acquisition of impersonal ideas which obscure what we really are and feel, what we really want, and what really excites our interest." Tennyson, whom he contrasted with Blake, seemed to Eliot "a very fair example of a poet almost wholly encrusted with opinion, almost wholly merged into his environment." Blake, on the other hand, "approached everything with a mind unclouded by current opinions."

6

In the future we may be sure that nearly all our best writers will be among the many millions who will register at some American college or university. If we are to assist these young men and women to develop their talents, our first problem is how to identify them. It is easy enough to inspect transcripts of the student's academic record in high school or college, for what it may be worth. But just how much reliance can we place in a student's grades? Any one who inspected the record of Robert E. Lee at West Point might well have predicted for him an exceptional military career; but who with nothing better to go on than the record at the same institution of Thomas Jonathan Jackson would have seen in him a military genius of the first order? Thomas A. Edison's first teachers rated him as an unusually stupid child. Sir Winston Churchill's teachers and parents regarded him as stupid because he could not or would not learn Latin; and yet, if we judge him by his multifarious attainments in later life, Churchill came closer to being a universal genius than any man among his contemporaries. Franklin D. Roosevelt was anything but a superior student in either Harvard College or the Columbia University Law School. The genius of Mozart declared itself early, but Giuseppe Verdi was refused admittance to the Milan Conservatory on the ground that he lacked musical talent. Neither Wordsworth at Cambridge nor Emerson at Harvard proved to be a superior student, but each of them had a brother whose academic record was first-class. Literary genius often flowers late. John Crowe Ransom began writing poetry when he was twenty-eight years old. Not until middle age did either Dryden or Cowper succeed in writing a memorable poem; and who would have predicted that in his old age a pamphleteer named Daniel Defoe would in his very first novel produce such a classic as *Robinson Crusoe*?

Eventually perhaps our educational psychologists may be able to develop intelligence tests that will reveal not merely a high IQ but also the special and elusive qualities that reveal themselves in literary or artistic genius. At the present time, however, the teacher of English relies with more confidence on the way in which the ambitious student writes an essay on an assigned topic which he must complete in two or three hours. This may be a method useful in testing the young journalist, who must learn to write with facility on all sorts of subjects; but was ever a literary classic produced by such a method?

Those teachers of literature who place implicit confidence in such methods of testing should read in James Barrie's *Sentimental Tommy* (1897) the chapter entitled "Of Four Ministers Who Afterwards Boasted That They Had Known Tommy Sandys." Tommy was a penniless orphan youth with a gift for writing, but he was in rebellion against "book-learning." There were, to his mind, "two kinds of cleverness, the kind you learn from books and a kind that is inside yourself, which latter was Tommy's kind. . . ." After failing to win a scholarship which would have enabled him to attend the University of Aberdeen, Tommy tried to redeem himself by competing for the Hugh Blackadder Prize, which was "given for the best essay in the Scots tongue, the ministers of the town and glens to be the judges." The subject of the essay was "A Day in Church," and it had to be completed in two hours. Tommy had only one competitor, a mediocre student from a rival school; yet he was "ignominiously beaten" because he failed to finish his essay. In the eyes of his judges Tommy's explanation of why he was stuck in the middle of the second page seemed only to confirm his incapacity: "He wanted a Scotch word that would signify how many people were in church, and it was on the tip of his tongue but would come no further." "Puckle" was nearly the word, but it suggested too few. The teachers and examiners asked him why he did not use "manzy" or "mask"—"a fine Scotch word"—or "flow" or "curran." Tommy explained that he wanted a word that meant "middling full," but when asked why he had not written "middling full" or "fell mask," his answer was: "I wanted one word." Tommy left the room in disgrace but came back just as the judges and teachers were preparing to go home. His face was "tear-stained but excited. 'I ken the word now,' he cried, 'it is hantle!' " The judges were disgusted, and Tommy's teacher, Cathro, resolved to chase the boy out of his school so that he would be "sent to the herding." Meanwhile Mr. Ogilvy, the teacher whose pupil had won the prize, said to himself: "He *had* to think of it till he got it—and he got it. The laddie is a genius!" The dominie placed the unfinished essay in his pocket, and when Cathro exclaimed: "Well, I have one satisfaction, I ran him out of my school," Mr. Ogilvy, who himself had wanted to be a great writer, replied: "Who knows but what you may be proud to dust a chair for him when he comes back?"

7

What can the Department of English do for the gifted college student who wants to become a writer? Who is to look after him? Even if the teacher in charge of the freshman course in writing has managed to discover such a student in one of his classes, how can he, with a hundred other students to look after, find the time to give to any one student more than a few hours of his time in the course of the academic year? There are, to be sure, courses in advanced composition but in them the enrollment is limited to ten or twelve, and such courses are rarely open to sophomores and never to freshmen. Meanwhile our neglected superior student is not unlikely to decide to choose as his major subject journalism or physics or business administration—subjects from which he may expect a larger and more certain income than he can ever expect from creative writing.

In a course in advanced composition the student who wishes to become a successful journalist or lawyer or doctor presents no great problem to the instructor, who knows something about correct and clear expository writing. But the instructor is not often one who has any special qualification for training a young novelist or poet to make the best use of his talent.

Many of the students who register for such courses fancy that they want to become writers, but few of them possess the talent, the ambition, and the industry that make one willing to give his days and nights to the laborious task of writing and again rewriting, as for instance Stevenson did while he "played the sedulous ape" to one great writer after another. Once or twice in a lifetime the teacher may be so fortunate as to have in his class one or two students who possess not only great talent but also the passionate desire to make of themselves writers of permanent worth.

Stephen Vincent Benét, who entered Yale as a precocious poet some years after Sinclair Lewis had graduated, did not share the usual distrust of professors of English. He profited from his association with Henry Seidel Canby and other members of the English staff, who permitted him to submit a group of his own poems in lieu of the conventional master's thesis. Yet he said in 1915:

You cannot devise any course to teach people to write. If you have the right sort of man, however, he can teach something about writing to most people. Even he, in my mind, cannot teach an original creator of the first or second rank although he might help him to avoid certain mistakes.

The teacher can do much more for such a student by working with him in his office or in his study at home. That kind of student is only too likely to find it difficult to conform to academic regulations. He may perhaps, like Thomas Wolfe, call up his teacher—in this case the late Fred Koch—at three in the morning and demand to see him immediately. I remember also Conrad Aiken's unfortunate experience at Harvard, as Robert Frost described it to me many years ago. Aiken was so fascinated by Théophile Gautier's short story, "La Morte amoureuse," that he began writing a poem based upon it. So absorbed was he in his self-imposed task that he cut his classes for ten days. Inevitably he was called to the dean's office and placed on probation. Perhaps Aiken should have been given a gold medal for what he had done or at least allowed the privilege of attending classes only when he liked. And yet how was a dean at Harvard or any other university to know that he was dealing with a youth of marked literary talent who would one day win the Pulitzer Prize with a volume of his poems?

Emerson on May 23, 1839, outlined in his *Journals* his ideal of a college. For teachers he wanted the best living creative writers and artists of the age: Bryant, Irving, Carlyle, Allston, and Greenough. "Then," said he, "I should see the lecture-room, the college, filled with life and hope. . . . I should see living learning; the Muse once more in the eye and cheek of the youth."

To attend such a college would be a great privilege and a fascinating experience—for a time—but I do not think the experiment would prove to be a notable success. It does not follow that a successful painter or sculptor or writer will become an effective teacher any more than that he would make a good congressman, businessman, or soldier. And if he turned out to be a good teacher, one with a talent for inspiring in his students the passionate desire to become writers, he would probably make disciples of them. If he belonged to the older generation, he might teach them outmoded techniques and attitudes. And if the creative writer-teacher had his share of the impatience and irritability so often attributed to the artistic temperament, he would find it difficult to conform to academic regulations and to refrain from expressing his boredom or disgust at the compositions of some of his students.

Katherine Anne Porter, after some experience with courses in creative writing, concluded that "creative writing cannot be taught, but only learned, and learned by the individual in his own way, at his own pace and in his own time. . . ." She congratulated Endora Welty, because she had

escaped, by miracle, the whole corrupting and destructive influence of the contemporary, organized tampering with young and promising talents by professional teachers who are rather monotonously divided into two major sorts: those theorists who are incapable of producing one passable specimen of the art they profess to teach; or good, sometimes first-rate, artists who are humanly unable to resist forming disciples and imitators among their students.

There are creative writers who have made successful college teachers. I think of Robert Frost at Amherst, Donald Davidson at Vanderbilt, John Crowe Ransom at Kenyon College, Allen Tate at Minnesota, Paul Engle at Iowa, Hudson Strode at Alabama, and Wallace Stegner at Stanford. Harvard has had Robert Hillyer and Archibald MacLeish, and Yale has had Robert Penn Warren.

Yet, even if the college has a poet or novelist who is a good teacher, it will be well if the students who wish to write have an opportunity to learn from professors whose points of view are different. The poet, for example, as T. S. Eliot has pointed out in an essay entitled "The Music of Poetry," "is not so much a judge as an advocate." He is "always trying to defend the kind of poetry he is writing, or to formulate the kind that he wants to write." He values chiefly those poets from whom he has learned and is quite indifferent to others who may be intrinsically much greater. Hence, Eliot concludes, "We must return to the scholar for ascertainment of facts, and to the more detached critic for impartial judgment."

In his later years Eliot came to the conclusion that Milton, though a bad model for poets of the twentieth century to follow, was a very great poet and that George Herbert, whom he had found much more congenial, was not after all a "major" writer. Perhaps John O'Hara will eventually discover that Ernest Hemingway is probably not the greatest writer who has lived since Shakespeare died in 1616. Some knowledge of literary history might help the young poet or novelist to understand better the particular historical moment in which he must live and write. The young writer seeking to learn from such supreme artists as Dante and Shakespeare needs to know enough about the historical background to grasp the significance of passages which otherwise might mean nothing to him. There are linguistic difficulties which he encounters in reading the

The Creative Writer and the University

great Elizabethans, for many familiar words have since the seventeenth century acquired new meanings and connotations. The lack of an established text of *Henry VIII* in 1817 led William Hazlitt, one of the best English critics, to find in certain passages now believed to be the work of John Fletcher "a pathos which only the genius of Shakespear could lend to the distresses of a proud, bad man, like Wolsey."

8

Is it good for the poet or the novelist to teach? Edmund Wilson in 1944 noted what seemed to him the "curious phenomenon—which would have been quite inconceivable in my college days—of young men teaching English or French in the most venerable schools and universities at the same time that they hold radical political opinions and contribute to 'advanced' magazines." He added: "The good fortune of the college faculties in acquiring some of the ablest of them has, I fear, been offset by the curbs thus imposed on the writers themselves." In the mid-nineteenth century Longfellow and Lowell taught modern languages at Harvard, but neither thought that being a professor was good for the poet in him. Milton, who taught school for a few years and wrote a notable essay on education, did not complain that teaching injured his poetic faculty. Schiller lectured on history to enthusiastic classes at the University of Jena.

Santayana was of the opinion that it would be better for the philosopher not to teach but that if he must teach, he should teach only the writings of the great philosophers of antiquity. Similarly, W. H. Auden has expressed the opinion that if poets must teach, they "should at least demand that they give academic courses in the literature of the dead and refuse to have anything to do with modern literature or courses in writing." He adds that he does not think that as a rule the poets should either read or write "critical studies in contemporary poetry." A. E. Housman was a Professor of Latin, and I wonder if *A Shropshire Lad* might not have been a very different book if he had earned his living by teaching the poems of Wordsworth and Tennyson.

There is the further difficulty that if the writer spends many years on the college campus, he may discover that the academic life is the only life he knows well enough to write about. Dylan Thomas, when he found so many writers in American colleges and universities which he visited, once asked: "When do these writers learn about life?"

There are of course in our colleges some successful teachers of creative writing who are not themselves well-known poets, novelists, dramatists, or even practicing literary critics; but there are too few of them. In many colleges the course in advanced composition is taught by a professor who cannot himself write an article acceptable to the editor of a literary magazine. When can we find among our graduate students the kind of teacher we want, and what kind of training should we give him? The typical doctor's program is of questionable value to such a teacher, and yet if the instructor does not have the Ph.D. degree, he is likely to be passed over while an inferior man is promoted over his head. Charles Townsend Copeland (affectionately known to his students as "Copey") probably did more for Harvard students than any one of the well-known writers who have succeeded him; yet he was long held back because he did not have the doctor's degree.

To become a successful teacher of creative writing, one must in his youth have had a desire to write and must have learned enough about the craft to help younger writers to avoid certain pitfalls. Such a teacher was Mr. Ogilvy in Barrie's *Sentimental Tommy*. His great ambition had been to become a writer, but finally he realized that he simply did not have the talent. As Barrie puts it, "He knew that [for him] oblivion was at hand, ready to sweep away his pages almost as soon as they were filled . . . but he had done his best and he had a sense of humor, and perhaps some day would come a pupil of whom he could make what he had failed to make of himself."

9

Since the Second World War there have been more courses in creative writing offered than in all the years that elapsed between the time Harvard College was founded in 1636 and the end of the war. And yet I see little indication that our universities and colleges, with their four million students, have turned out anything even approximating the number of first-rate writers who enrolled in our colleges between 1900 and 1920. The two greatest periods in American literature came at times when there were few or no courses in creative writing. One of these was the period between the two world wars; the other was the period of the New England Renaissance, 1830-1870.

There were no courses in creative writing in Bowdoin College in the early 1820's when Longfellow and Hawthorne were students there; and there were none at Harvard in the 1820's and 1830's when Emerson, Holmes, Thoreau, and Lowell studied there. The college curriculum in those days consisted mainly of Latin, Greek, and mathematics. Harvard had as yet no Department of English, but it had in succession three great teachers of modern languages in George Ticknor, Longfellow, and Lowell. Students who wanted to write enrolled under the Boylston Professor of Rhetoric and Oratory, who taught composition. From 1819 to 1851 that post was held by Edward Tyrrell Channing, a younger brother of the great Unitarian divine. Edward Everett Hale, who studied under him, maintained that Ned Channing deserved "the credit of the English of Emerson, Holmes, Sumner, Clarke, Bellows, Lowell, Higginson, and other men whom he trained," including also Dana, Motley, and Parkman. Channing, who hated literary bombast, read his students' themes aloud with them. Dr. Holmes refers to the "pale student" who

> shivering in his shoes
> Sees from his theme the turgid rhetoric ooze.

Channing, as his published lectures suggest, emphasized forensic writing. He was no doubt an admirable teacher of students who would become lawyers and ministers, but was he the right teacher for Emerson or Thoreau? Channing's literary taste was old-fashioned. One of his students, Thomas Wentworth Higginson, in 1841 wrote in a preliminary draft of his Commencement oration: "Lay down your Spenser and Tennyson and look at life for yourselves." Channing was not impressed. "I regard Tennyson as a great calf," he said, "but you are entitled to your own opinion." Henry Seidel Canby, after examining the themes that Thoreau wrote for Channing, maintained that it was several years before Thoreau developed a style appropriate to the kind of writing he wanted to do. The worst passages in his first book, Canby thought, were chunks of writing of the sort Thoreau had learned to turn out in Channing's class. Emerson likewise had to work out for himself a style fitted to his thought. In his *Journals* he suggests his debt to Edward Everett, the Professor of Greek, who had studied in Germany. "Everett," he wrote, "has put more stories, sentences, verses, names in amber for me than any other person."

What was it that Harvard College had that other colleges did not have? Edward Everett Hale of the class of 1839 wrote in *James Russell Lowell and His Friends* (1899):

> Let it be remembered, then, that the whole drift of fashion, occupation, and habit among the undergraduates ran in lines suggested by literature. . . . The books which the fellows took out of the library, the books which they bought for their own subscription libraries, were not books of science, nor history, nor sociology, nor politics; they were books of literature.

Harvard College was fortunate in its location. William Dean Howells, who had grown up in the Middle West, wrote: "I arrived in Boston [in 1860] when all talents had more or less a literary coloring, and when the great talents were literary." After moving from New York to Boston, Thomas Bailey Aldrich wrote to Bayard Taylor on March 26, 1866: "The humblest man of letters here has a position which he doesn't have in New York. To be known as an able writer is to have the choicest society opened to you. A knight of the quill here is supposed necessarily a gentleman. In New York—he's a Bohemian! Outside of his personal friends he has no standing." A minor Virginia writer, David H. Strother ("Porte Crayon"), once said: "I went to Richmond, and no one took any notice of me. I went to Boston and every one wished to have me to dinner. So I always go to Boston." Is it any wonder that in a region where writers were honored, so many talented students became writers?

In *Scenes and Portraits* (1954) Van Wyck Brooks included a notable account of Harvard College as he knew it in the years 1904-1907. He went to Harvard because he thought that Harvard was "the college for writers," and he found there a keen interest in literature and in art, but not in American literature and art. Emerson Hall was there, but the spirit of Emerson was absent. Everybody seemed to be reading Walter Pater. In the faculty there was old Charles Eliot Norton, the friend of Lowell and Emerson, who never set foot in England, he said, without feeling that he was, at last, at home. There were no courses in contemporary literature and few courses that

The Creative Writer and the University

dealt with literature later than the eighteenth century. While Brooks was in Cambridge, George Santayana was heard to remark: "We poets at Harvard never read anything written in America except one's own compositions." John Gould Fletcher, who studied at Harvard, and Ezra Pound, who went to the University of Pennsylvania, both discovered Whitman's *Leaves of Grass* in, of all places, London. In the Harvard faculty was Barrett Wendell, sometimes called "the last of the Brahmins," "who deplored the American Revolution that had sundered us from England and the guidance of the British ruling class." Wendell, as Brooks remembered, once pronounced Crane's *The Red Badge of Courage* "sensational trash." It was many years before Brooks recovered from his Harvard experience and discovered that older American literature to which he devoted five volumes of literary history. The Harvard of those years reminds one of Matthew Arnold's Oxford, which espoused only Lost Causes. Brooks sums up his impressions of Harvard College with an eye upon the development of a famous Anglo-American poet:

When one added these tastes together, the royalism and the classicism, the Anglo-Catholicism, the cults of Donne and Dante, the Sanskrit, the Elizabethan dramatists and the French Symbolist poets, one arrived at T. S. Eliot, the quintessence of Harvard.

This is the earlier Eliot who was interested in the literature and the literary tradition of almost every country except that in which he was born and educated—the poet and critic who after he became a British subject described his position as that of "an Anglo-Catholic in religion, a classicist in literature, and a royalist in politics."[1]

Mr. Brooks is not quite fair to the Harvard of his day which, whatever its shortcomings, managed to turn out an astonishing number of important American writers besides Eliot. Harvard College at least gave its students the feeling that literature was a very precious thing—a feeling much less prevalent in most other American colleges. Harvard's greatest gift to its young writers was the conviction that great literature is the supreme achievement of the human mind. Most of these writers discovered for themselves by 1917 that their country had a system of government worth fighting for. They also eventually discovered that Emerson's *Essays*, Hawthorne's *The*

---

[1] Eliot was more American than Brooks thought. A distinguished English scholar, Geoffrey Bullough, remarked to me in Vienna in 1950: "Of course no British poet could possibly have written *The Waste Land*."

Scarlet Letter, Whitman's *Leaves of Grass*, Thoreau's *Walden*, and Mark Twain's *Huckleberry Finn* had already taken their rightful place among classics written in the English language.

In the long run the young writer, with the beginning he has made in college, will continue to learn about his craft from the books he reads, the writers he comes to know, from literary agents, the editors of magazines, and from those who read manuscripts for publishing houses. In the 1880's and 1890's Southern and Western writers, few of whom had been to college, learned much from sympathetic editors like Richard Watson Gilder of the *Century* and Henry Mills Alden of *Harper's*. Henry James and Mark Twain were exceptionally fortunate in having as a friend so fine a critic as William Dean Howells, who opened to them the pages of the *Atlantic Monthly*. In Paris James was to learn much from Turgenev and from some of the great French writers of fiction. Guy de Maupassant had the rare good fortune to serve his apprenticeship under the watchful eyes of a literary genius like Gustave Flaubert. Another admirer of Flaubert, Willa Cather, learned from Sarah Orne Jewett that her best material lay in her knowledge of life on the plains. T. S. Eliot and other poets learned from Ezra Pound. Hemingway was indebted to Sherwood Anderson, Pound, James Joyce, and Gertrude Stein. Katherine Anne Porter felt that she could speak for "a whole generation of writers" when she maintained that many of our best American writers "were educated, not at schools but by five writers: Henry James, James Joyce, W. B. Yeats, T. S. Eliot, and Ezra Pound." Other writers would have added to her list the names of Marcel Proust, Thomas Hardy, Bernard Shaw, and half a dozen others. Elizabeth Madox Roberts named her masters as "Hardy, Shakespeare, Synge, Beethoven—with symphonies—Dickinson, Hopkins." She disliked "the private symbolism in the poetry of T. S. Eliot." For both Amy Lowell and Sara Teasdale a great stimulus to the writing of poetry came from the acting of Eleonora Duse. Henry James, like Washington Irving before him, profited from his acquaintance with painters. Hemingway once said to a reporter: "I learned to write by looking at paintings in the Luxembourg Museum in Paris." Walt Whitman said to J. T. Trowbridge in 1860: "But for the opera I could never have written *Leaves of Grass*."

Writers learn most perhaps from their reading, and often it is from books by older writers who are not in the current fashion. It was Chaucer's *Parliament of Fowls* that brought John Masefield to the realization that he was a poet. Auden and MacNeice profited from their reading of medieval English and Icelandic poetry; Eliot from his study of the lesser Elizabethan dramatists and the French Symbolists; Edgar Lee Masters and Edwin Arlington Robinson were indebted to the minor poets in the *Greek Anthology*.

The young writer often learns much from the writers of his own generation. The classic example in English literature is that of Coleridge and Wordsworth, who were near neighbors at the time each poet was maturing his own great talents. Melville was greatly indebted to Hawthorne, who was his neighbor for a short time in the Berkshires. The most remarkable group of American writers in the twentieth century came from Vanderbilt University. The university had a very able English staff, but there was not very much teaching of creative writing. On the staff were those fine poets and critics, John Crowe Ransom and Donald Davidson. They and their students—Allen Tate, Robert Penn Warren, Merrill Moore, Cleanth Brooks, Jesse Stuart, Randall Jarrell, and others—educated one another with the result that from these men have come some of the best in contemporary poetry, fiction, and literary criticism. There was something in the air on the Vanderbilt campus that led students with marked literary talents to devote themselves to literature rather than to journalism, business, or one of the professions.

10

In 1944 Edmund Wilson, who had graduated from Princeton in 1916, commented on the great change which had come over the colleges and universities since 1922. The publication in that year of *The Waste Land* and *Ulysses* had brought from the professors "howls of denunciation"; but when in 1939 Joyce published *Finnegans Wake*, the book "went straight from the hands of Joyce into the hands of the college professors." *Finnegans Wake*, he noted, was not a "literary issue but the subject of academic research."

There are many writers now on college faculties, and yet one still finds misunderstanding and distrust between the English professors and some of the poets and novelists who teach. In "The Age of Criticism" Randall Jarrell has said: "New critic is but old scholar writ large, as a general thing: the same gifts which used to go into proving that the Wife of Bath was really an aunt of Chaucer's named Alys Persë now go into proving that all of Henry James's work is really a Swedenborgian allegory." In an essay entitled "The Poet Against the English Department" Karl Shapiro has complained that the English professors now have all the "answers," and the "answers," he notes, were borrowed from the literary rebels of half a century ago: Yeats, Joyce, Pound, and Eliot. In 1953 Shapiro wrote in *Beyond Criticism* that he was "quite convinced" that "the official doctrines of art and codes of literary behavior are death to the young talents, as codes and doctrines always are." The young writer must still, like his predecessors, work out his own aims and methods *as he writes.*

The late Irving Babbitt used to maintain that, in the words of James Russell Lowell, "before we have an American literature, we must have an American criticism." Literary history gives little support to that position. Aristotle's essay on tragedy was a formulation of the practice of Aeschylus, Sophocles, and Euripides; and it did not foreshadow or promote the production of any later Greek masterpieces. Those English and American poets and novelists who excelled as literary critics—Coleridge, Arnold, Poe, and Henry James—worked out their critical standards *as they wrote.* In the same way Pound and Eliot consciously and painstakingly developed critical standards and techniques for their own use and that of like-minded younger poets. Future English and American poets may or may not admire Eliot, but the best of them are unlikely to model their poems upon *The Waste Land.* It is too late in the century for that. Nor can we expect the really original writers of fiction now in college to model their work on that of Faulkner, Dos Passos, or Hemingway.

W. H. Auden, who was troubled by the large number of poets teaching in our colleges and universities, noted in 1957 what seemed to him "a new and disturbing symptom": "a certain literary conformity, of a proper and authoritative way to write poetry." Malcolm Cowley has more than once lamented that so many of our younger novelists have been misled by certain critics into writing a rather barren type of "new" fiction corresponding to the "New Criticism" and the "new" poetry. Professor R. W. B. Lewis of Yale has suggested that most of our younger writers of fiction fall into two groups. One of these consists of those who have never really left school but have stayed on "still studying Faulkner and emulating him, teaching literature to a generation younger yet. . . ." From their courses in creative writing, he maintains, comes little that is genuinely creative but only "ever more competent works, carefully made, knowingly written, but self-protective and generally lifeless." Lewis finds more promise in young writers of a different stamp, even though their novels appear to be loosely constructed and episodic. He finds in them "a good deal of ragged life" and "a fresh set of literary affinities. Within the genre, too," he notes; "we detect no Faulkner and no Hemingway." "Genius," said Emerson, "is always sufficiently the enemy of genius by over-influence." By way of illustration he added: "The English dramatic poets have Shakespearized now for two hundred years." Faulkner is reported to have said that William Styron would do very well indeed if he would only quit trying to write like Faulkner. Professors of English who urge their students to take Faulkner and Hemingway and Eliot as their models are likely to find themselves looked upon by some of their ablest students as the enemies of all that is new.

11

For one really gifted writer the university may have there are a thousand who have neither the talent nor the determination that it takes to become a writer. In the end most of those students who take courses in creative writing will become competent professional men and women—especially teachers and journalists—and they will also, one hopes, be more discriminating readers of contemporary literature than most of those who review books. What the university can do for the young creative writer is, as I have insisted, quite limited. That, however, is no reason for shrugging off a difficult problem.

After the English department has discovered those students who appear to have talent and a strong desire to write, the next step is to bring them together and provide for them an advisor who can at least help them to avoid certain common mistakes. He need not himself be a successful poet or writer of fiction, but he must be able to teach his students to criticize one another's work objectively and to endure severe criticism without having their feelings hurt. The advisor can as a rule accomplish more if these students are not registered for a course under him. And if he must meet them as a class, he will do well to meet them in his home rather than in a classroom. If he must meet them in a classroom, he should demand that the university make it an attractive place with portraits and busts of great writers, a model of the Globe Theatre, and a goodly supply of phonograph records of authors giving readings from their poems, plays, or novels. Such a classroom would be far less expensive than any scientist's laboratory.

The university should maintain a literary magazine to give its student writers a chance to see their own writings more objectively. In the 1920's there were many "little magazines" published both on and off college campuses, and nearly every important American poet and writer of fiction profited from being able to see his 'prentice work in one or more of them. The most notable was the *Fugitive*, in which an extraordinarily able group of professors and students at Vanderbilt University printed their verses. In the early 1920's few if any of the so-called quality magazines would have accepted any of their poems.

Ideally the university should have on its faculty or living in the community a writer who by his presence can demonstrate that literature is a living thing. If the university has no such writer in its community, it can at least afford once or twice a year to bring some well-known writer to the campus to lecture or read from his own work. Better still if the writer can be induced to spend a week on the campus and talk with those students who are seriously interested in learning to write.

The university should do what it can to make the superior students feel that writers are as important to society as, say, journalists or lawyers. It should also teach its students the wide difference that separates a merely popular novelist from a master of his craft. On Student Recognition Day the undergraduate writers should share honors with the athletes and the Phi Beta Kappa key-men. For the exceptionally able student writer the university should be able to provide a substantial fellowship so that after graduation he may have a year or two free from the necessity of earning a living.

In an article in the *Yale Review* in 1961 Alfred A. Knopf, one of the best of American publishers, warned of the dangers of too early financial success that beset the young writer: "Let a man or woman print a single good short story in any well-known magazine and he is likely, very soon, to have half a dozen offers from publishers for a novel, each promising a substantial cash advance." The result, he points out, is the encouragement of people who really ought not to write and cash advances for novels that never get written. Great short stories have often been written by men and women in their twenties, but the great novels of the world have almost invariably come from writers in middle or old age. Only they possess the wide experience, the knowledge of life, and the wisdom that should go into the writing of a novel.

The university of course cannot control the development of its writers, especially when they are no longer students. It should, however, do something to warn them of the perils and pitfalls that await them. The right kind of writing is, as Hemingway put it in *The Green Hills of Africa*, "too lonely, too hard to do, and is not fashionable." We destroy our writers in this country, he insisted, in many ways. Some "are ruined by the first money, the first praise, the first attack, the first time they find they cannot write, or the first time they find they cannot do anything else, or else they get frightened and join organizations that do their thinking for them. Or they do not know what they want."

A final word. The English department should warn the undergraduate writer of the danger of too early specialization. He needs to know not only the better writers of his own time but should have read some of the classics of world literature as well. He ought to be able to read in the original some of the classics written in French, German, Italian, Spanish, Latin, or Greek. And finally he should know more than a smattering of the methods and achievements of modern science. He will understand better the world he lives in and writes about if he has studied other economists than Marx and Lenin. The young writer when he leaves the university should remember that his education has only begun.

Publications of Jay B. Hubbell

This list omits numerous book reviews published in *American Literature*, the *South Atlantic Quarterly*, the *Archive*, the *Southwest Review*, the *Yale Review*, the *Nation*, the *Virginia Quarterly Review*, the *Dallas News*, and other magazines and newspapers.

I. Books

Lives of Franklin Plato Eller and John Carlton Eller. Privately printed in Durham, N. C., 1910.

Virginia Life in Fiction. Abstract of Columbia University dissertation. Privately printed in Dallas, Texas, 1922.

An Introduction to Poetry. With John O. Beaty. New York: The Macmillan Company, 1922. Revised and enlarged edition, 1936.

An Introduction to Drama. With John O. Beaty. New York: The Macmillan Company, 1927.

Robert Louis Stevenson's *Treasure Island*. Edited by Jay B. Hubbell. New York: The Macmillan Company, 1927. The Modern Readers' Series.

The Enjoyment of Literature. New York: The Macmillan Company, 1929.

John Pendleton Kennedy's *Swallow Barn*. Edited by Jay B. Hubbell. New York: Harcourt, Brace and Company, 1929. The American Authors Series.

American Life in Literature. Edited by Jay B. Hubbell. 2 vols. New York: Harper & Brothers, 1936. Revised and enlarged edition, 1949. Abridged edition, 1951. U. S. Armed Forces Institute editions, 1944, 1945, and 1947.

The Last Years of Henry Timrod, 1864-1867: Including Letters of Timrod to Paul Hamilton Hayne and Letters about Timrod by William Gilmore Simms, John R. Thompson, John Greenleaf Whittier, and Others. With Four Uncollected Poems and Seven Uncollected Prose Pieces. Drawn Chiefly from the Paul Hamilton Hayne Collection in the Duke University Library. Edited by Jay B. Hubbell. Durham, N. C.: Duke University Press, 1941.

Robert Munford's *The Candidates; or The Humours of a Virginia Election*. Edited by Jay B. Hubbell and Douglass Adair. Williamsburg, Va.: Institute of Early American History and Culture, 1948. Also in the *William and Mary Quarterly*, April, 1948.

The South in American Literature, 1607-1900. Durham, N. C.: Duke University Press, 1954 (September 10). This book won the Mayflower Award in 1955 for the best non-fiction book written by a resident of North Carolina. Second printing, 1959. Third printing, June, 1964.

Southern Life in Fiction. Athens: University of Georgia Press. [1960.] The Eugenia Dorothy Blount Lamar Lectures, 1959, Mercer University.

II. Chapters in Books, etc.

PRAIRIE PEGASUS. Edited by Marie D. Hemke, George D. Bond, Jay B. Hubbell. Foreword by Witter Bynner. "The Makers" [Introduction] by Jay B. Hubbell. Privately printed in Dallas, Texas, 1924. [Poems by Southern Methodist University students.]

The Archive Anthology: Verses by Little-Known and Well-Known Writers. Edited by R. P. Harriss. With an Introductory Essay by Professor Jay B. Hubbell. Durham, N. C.: Duke University Press, 1926.

"The Frontier," *The Reinterpretation of American Literature: Some Contributions toward the Understanding of Its Historical Development.* Edited by Norman Foerster for the American Literature Group of the Modern Language Association. New York: Harcourt, Brace and Company, 1928. Pp. 38-61. Reprinted by Russell & Russell, New York, 1959.

"Southern Magazines," *Culture in the South.* Edited by W. T. Couch. Chapel Hill: The University of North Carolina Press, 1934. Pp. 159-182.

William Stanley Hoole, *A Check-List and Finding-List of Charleston Periodicals, 1732-1864.* Durham, N. C.: Duke University Press, 1936. Foreword by Jay B. Hubbell.

"Literary Nationalism in the Old South," *American Studies in Honor of William Kenneth Boyd,* by Members of the Americana Club of Duke University. Edited by David Kelly Jackson. Durham, N. C.: Duke University Press, 1940. Pp. 175-220.

" 'O, Tempora! O, Mores!' A Juvenile Poem by Edgar Allan Poe," *Elizabethan and Other Essays in Honor of George F. Reynolds.* Boulder, Colorado, 1945. *University of Colorado Studies,* Series B, II, 314-321 (October, 1945) .

"Who Are the Best American Writers? A Study of Some Critical Polls Sponsored by American Magazines," *Anglo-Americana: Festschrift zum 70. Geburtstag von Professor Leo Hibler-Lebmannsport.* Edited by Karl Brunner. Vienna, 1955. Pp. 80-91.

"Contemporary Southern Literature," *Addresses Commemorating the One Hundred Twenty-fifth Anniversary [of] the University of Richmond.* Richmond, Va., 1955. Pp. 42-54.

"Edgar Allan Poe." *Eight American Authors: A Review of Research and Criticism.* Edited by Floyd Stovall. New York: The Modern Language Association of America, 1956. Pp. 1-46. New edition published by W. W. Norton & Company, Inc., 1963.

III. Articles

"The Teaching of English in Secondary Schools," *Bulletin* of Wake Forest College, N.S. VII, 207-220 (January, 1913).

"Ellen Glasgow as a Literary Pioneer," *Dallas Morning News,* November 23, 1919. Special Book Section.

"De Tocqueville and Whitman," *Nation* (New York), CIX, 655 (November 22, 1919). Published as an unsigned editorial; author's name given in Index to the volume.

"On 'Southern Literature,'" *Texas Review,* VII, 8-16 (October, 1921).

"Wordsworth, Imagist," *Literary Review* of the *New York Evening Post,* June 19, 1920.

"The New Southwest," *Southwest Review* (formerly the *Texas Review*), X, 91-99 (October, 1924).

"The Frontier in American Literature," *Southwest Review,* X, 84-92 (January, 1925).

"Handbook for Graduate Students," Southern Methodist University *Bulletin,* Vol. IX, No. 5, February, 1925. 8 pp.

"The Poetry of John Hall Wheelock," *Southwest Review,* XII, 60-67 (October, 1926).

"Thackeray and Virginia," *Virginia Quarterly Review,* III, 76-86 (January, 1927).

"Cavalier and Indentured Servant in Virginia Fiction," *South Atlantic Quarterly,* XXVI, 22-39 (January, 1927).

"The Frontier Factor," review of Lucy Lockwood Hazard, *The Frontier in American Literature, Saturday Review of Literature,* IV, 105 (September 10, 1927).

"The Decay of the Provinces: A Study of Nationalism and Sectionalism in American Literature," *Sewanee Review,* XXXV, 473-487 (October, 1927).

"Foreword," *American Literature,* I, 2 (March, 1929).

"The Writings of Owen Wister," *South Atlantic Quarterly,* XXIX, 440-443 (October, 1930).

"A Commencement Address by Sidney Lanier," *American Literature,* II, 385-404 (January, 1931).

"Lincoln's First Inaugural Address," *American Historical Review,* XXXVI, 550-552 (April, 1931).

"Doctoral Dissertations in American Literature" (with Ernest E. Leisy), *American Literature,* IV, 419-465 (January, 1933). Also published in pamphlet form by the Duke University Press in 1933.

"George Henry Boker, Paul Hamilton Hayne, and Charles Warren Stoddard: Some Unpublished Letters," *American Literature,* V, 146-165 (May, 1933).

"Charles Napoleon Bonaparte Evans: Creator of Jesse Holmes the Fool-Killer," *South Atlantic Quarterly,* XXXVI, 431-446 (October, 1937).

"Two Letters by Uncle Remus" [Joel Chandler Harris], *Southwest Review,* XXIII, 216-223 (January, 1938).

"John and Ann Cotton of 'Queen's Creek,' Virginia," *American Literature,* X, 179-201 (May, 1938).

"A Lanier Manuscript," *Library Notes* [Friends of the Duke University

Library], II, 2-3 (November, 1938). An early version of "Rose-Morals I."

"Five Letters from George Henry Boker to William Gilmore Simms," *Pennsylvania Magazine of History and Biography,* LXIII, 66-71 (January, 1939).

"Some Uncollected Poems of Joseph Addison," *Modern Philology,* XXXVI, 277-281 (February, 1939).

"'On Liberty-Tree': A Revolutionary Poem from South Carolina," *South Carolina Historical and Genealogical Magazine,* XLI, 117-122 (July, 1940).

"Poe's Mother: With a Note on John Allan," *William and Mary Quarterly,* Second Series, XXI, 250-254 (July, 1941).

"The War Diary of John Esten Cooke," *Journal of Southern History,* VII, 526-540 (November, 1941).

"Some New Letters of Constance Fenimore Woolson," *New England Quarterly,* XIV, 715-735 (December, 1941).

"A New Letter by William Cullen Bryant," *Georgia Historical Quarterly,* XXVI, 288-290 (September-December, 1942).

"William Wirt and the Familiar Essay in Virginia," *William and Mary Quarterly,* Second Series, XXIII, 136-152 (April, 1943).

"Some New Letters of Walter Savage Landor," *Virginia Magazine of History and Biography,* LI, 283-296 (July, 1943).

"A Persimmon Beer Dance in Ante-bellum Virginia," *Southern Literary Messenger,* New Series, V, 461-466 (November-December, 1943).

"Robert Munford's *The Candidates: or The Humours of a Virginia Election.*" Edited by Jay B. Hubbell and Douglass Adair, *William and Mary Quarterly,* Third Series, V, 217-257 (April, 1948). Also published in book form by The Institute of Early American History and Culture in Williamsburg in 1948.

"New History of American Literature," review of *Literary History of the United States,* ed. Robert E. Spiller *et al., Yale Review,* XXXVIII, 558-561 (Spring, 1949).

"The Old South in Literary Histories," *South Atlantic Quarterly,* XLVIII, 452-467 (July, 1949).

Review of Rollin G. Osterweis, *Romanticism and Nationalism in the Old South, South Atlantic Quarterly,* XLVIII, 472-475 (July, 1949).

"Charles Chauncey Burr: Friend of Poe," *PMLA,* LXIX, 833-840 (September, 1954).

"Negro Boatmen's Songs," *Southern Folklore Quarterly,* XVIII, 244-245 (December, 1954).

"James Kirke Paulding's Last Letter to John C. Calhoun," *North Carolina Historical Review,* XXXII, 410-414 (July, 1955).

"Old Books: *Innocents Abroad,* by Mark Twain," *Georgia Review,* XI, 99-102 (Spring, 1957).

"The Smith-Pocahontas Story in Literature," *Virginia Magazine of History and Biography,* LXV, 275-300 (July, 1957).

"Oliver Wendell Holmes, Rev. Joseph Cook, and the *University Quarterly,*" *New England Quarterly,* XXXI, 401-410 (September, 1958).

"Dr. James R. M'Conochie's *Leisure Hours:* A Rare Book by a Scottish-

American Doctor Who Knew Robert Burns," *Virginia Magazine of History and Biography,* LXVII, 172-179 (April, 1959).

"Edgar Allan Poe and the Southern Literary Tradition," *Texas Studies in Literature and Language,* II, 151-171 (Summer, 1960).

"Note on 'Old Virginia Never Tire,'" *North Carolina Folklore,* XII, 26 (December, 1964).

"*Southwest Review,* 1924-1927," *Southwest Review,* L, 1-18 (Winter, 1965).